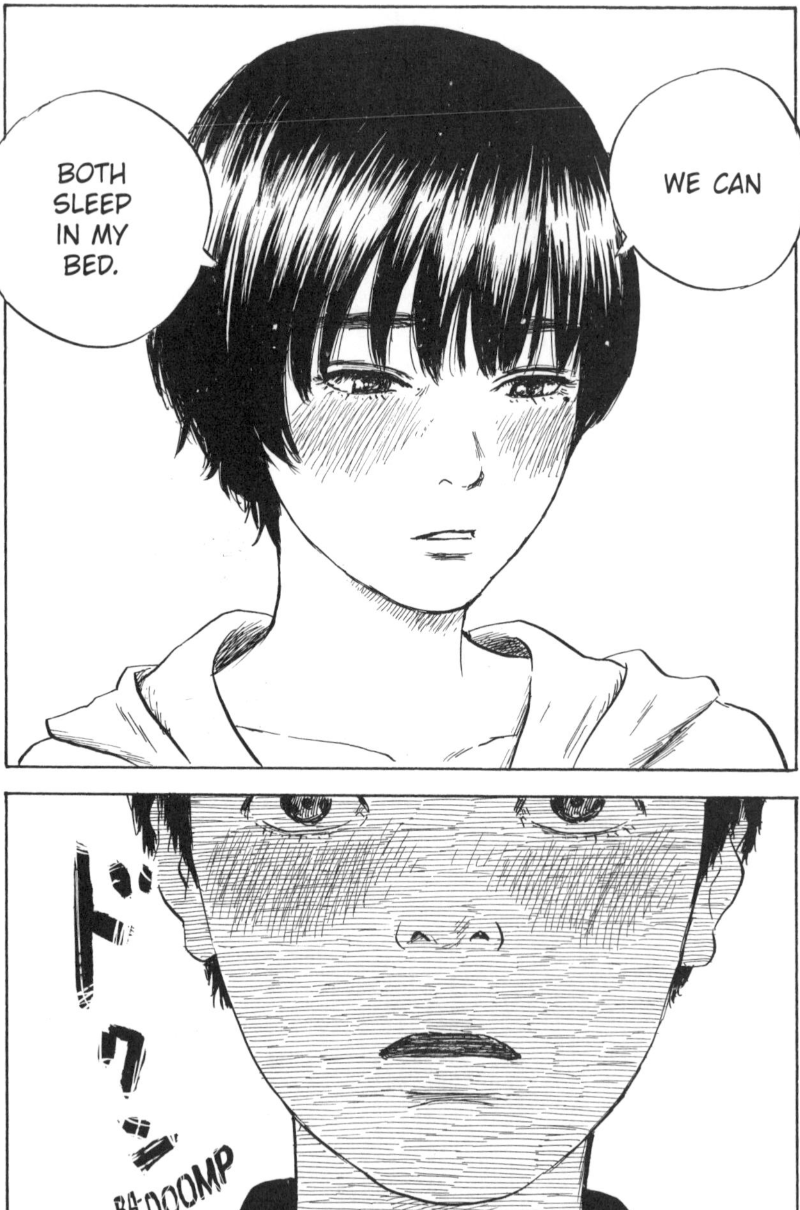
WE CAN
BOTH SLEEP IN MY BED.
ドクッ
BA-DOOMP

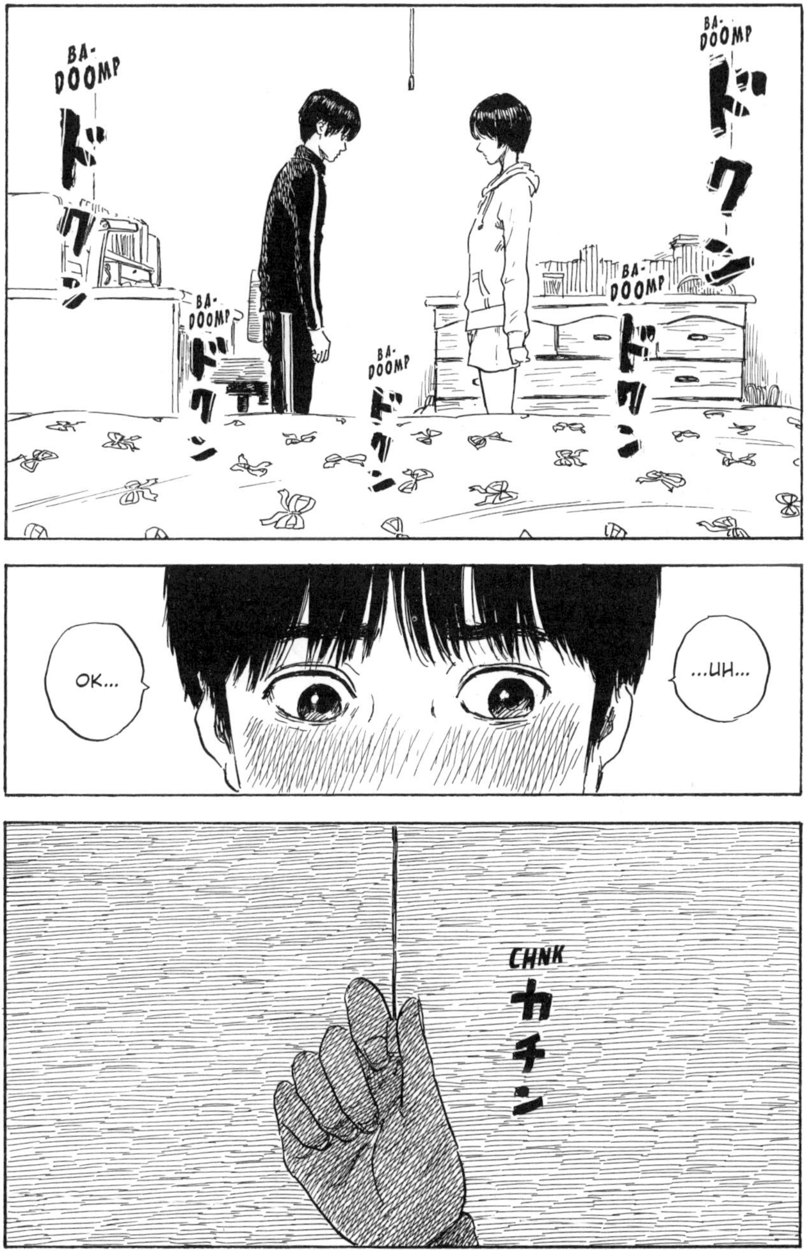
BA-DOOMP
ドクン
BA-DOOMP
ドクン
BA-DOOMP
ドクン
BA-DOOMP
ドクン
BA-DOOMP
ドクン
...UH...
OK...
CHNK
カチン

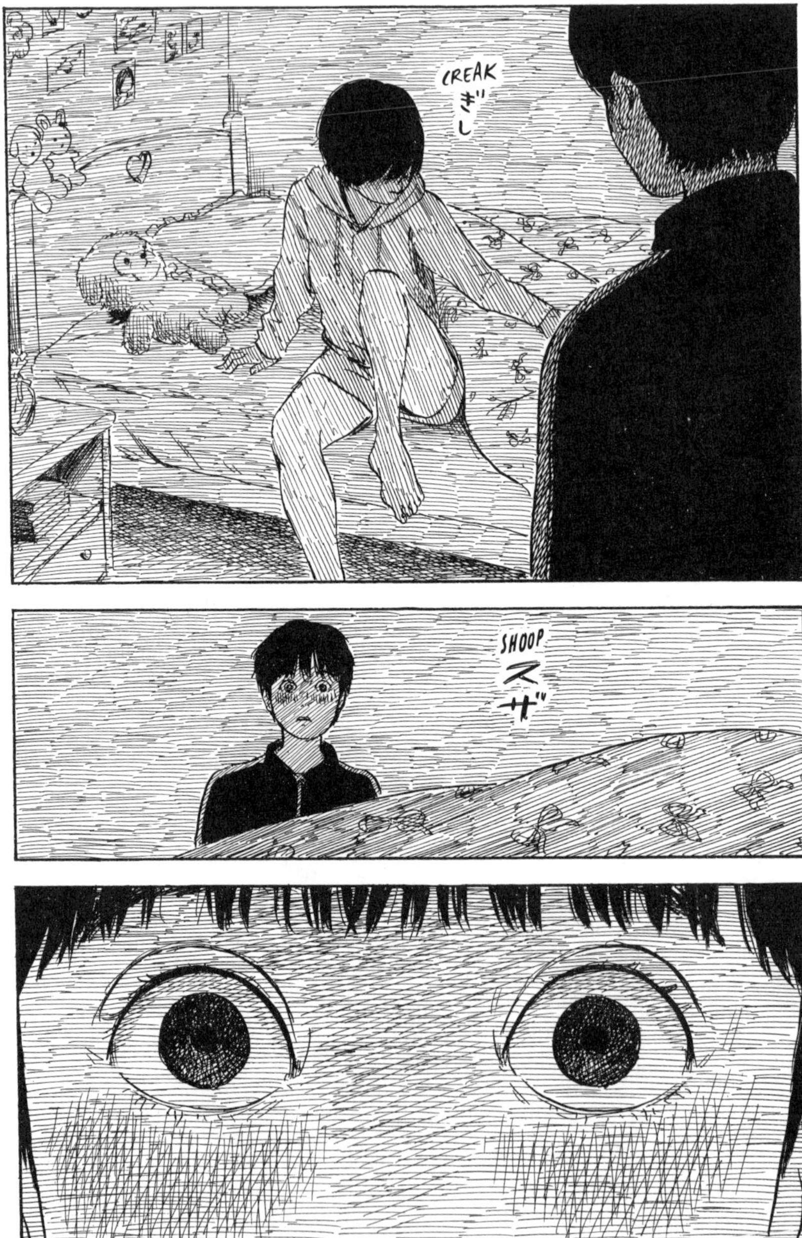
CREAK
ぎし
SHOOP
スザ

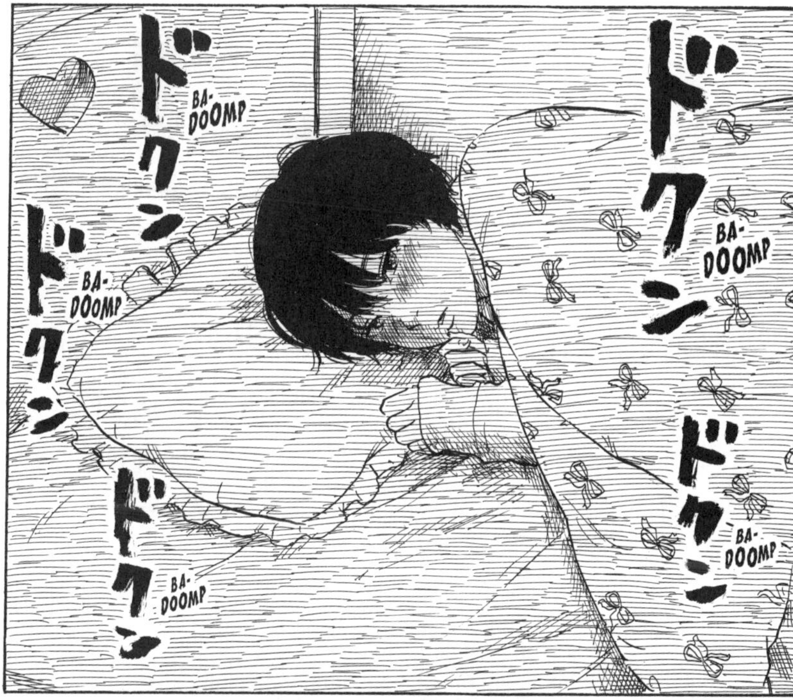
ドクン
BA-DOOMP
ドクン
BA-DOOMP
ドクン
BA-DOOMP
ドクン
BA-DOOMP
ドクン
BA-DOOMP

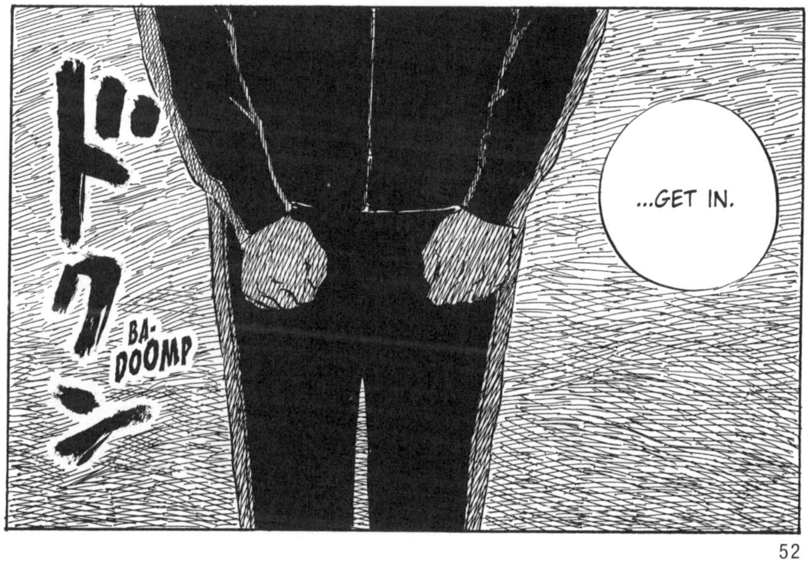
...GET IN.
ドクン
BA-DOOMP

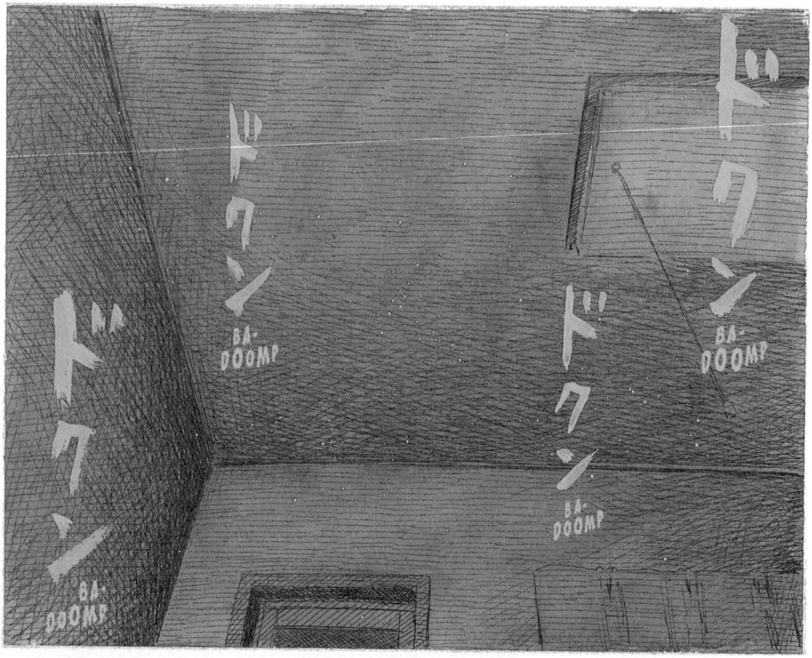
ドクン
BA-DOOMP
ドクン
BA-DOOMP
ドクン
BA-DOOMP
ドクン
BA-DOOMP

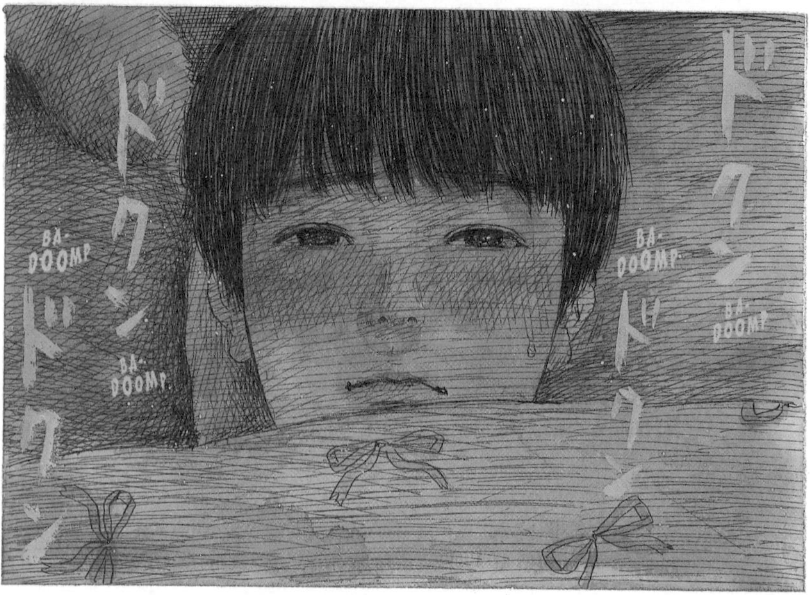
ドクン
BA-DOOMP
ドクン
BA-DOOMP
ドクン
BA-DOOMP
ドクン
BA-DOOMP

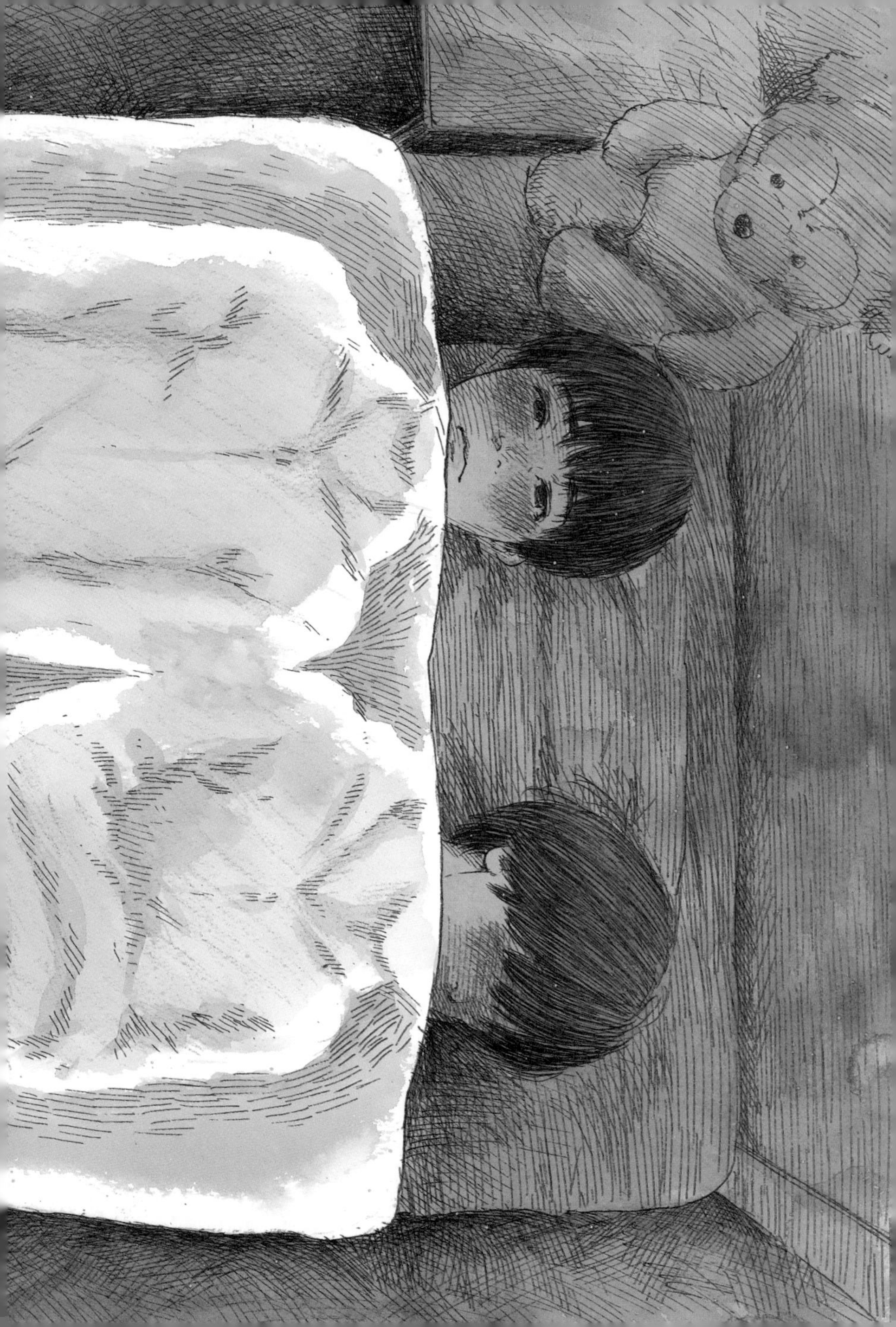

CHAPTER 36 Pledge

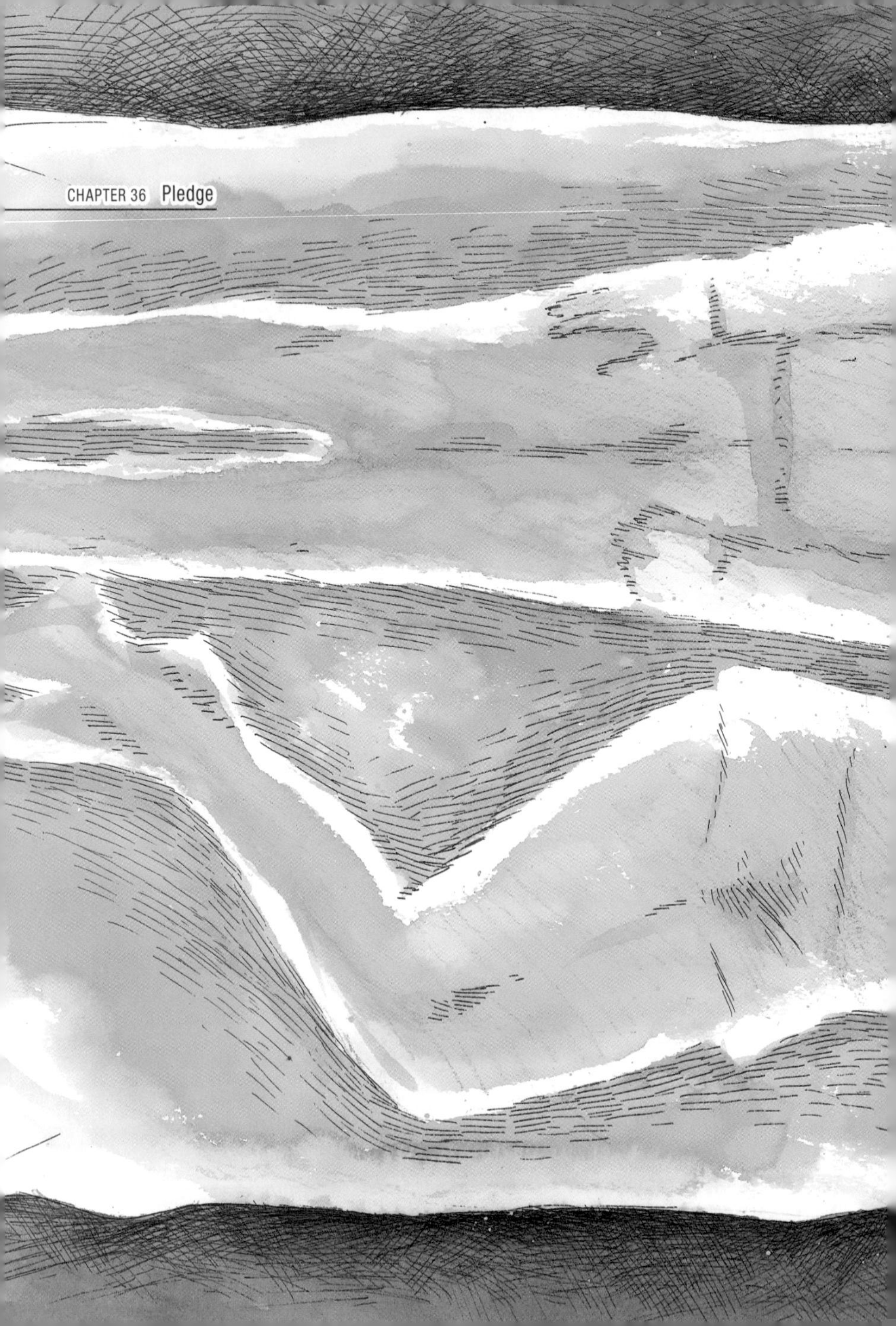

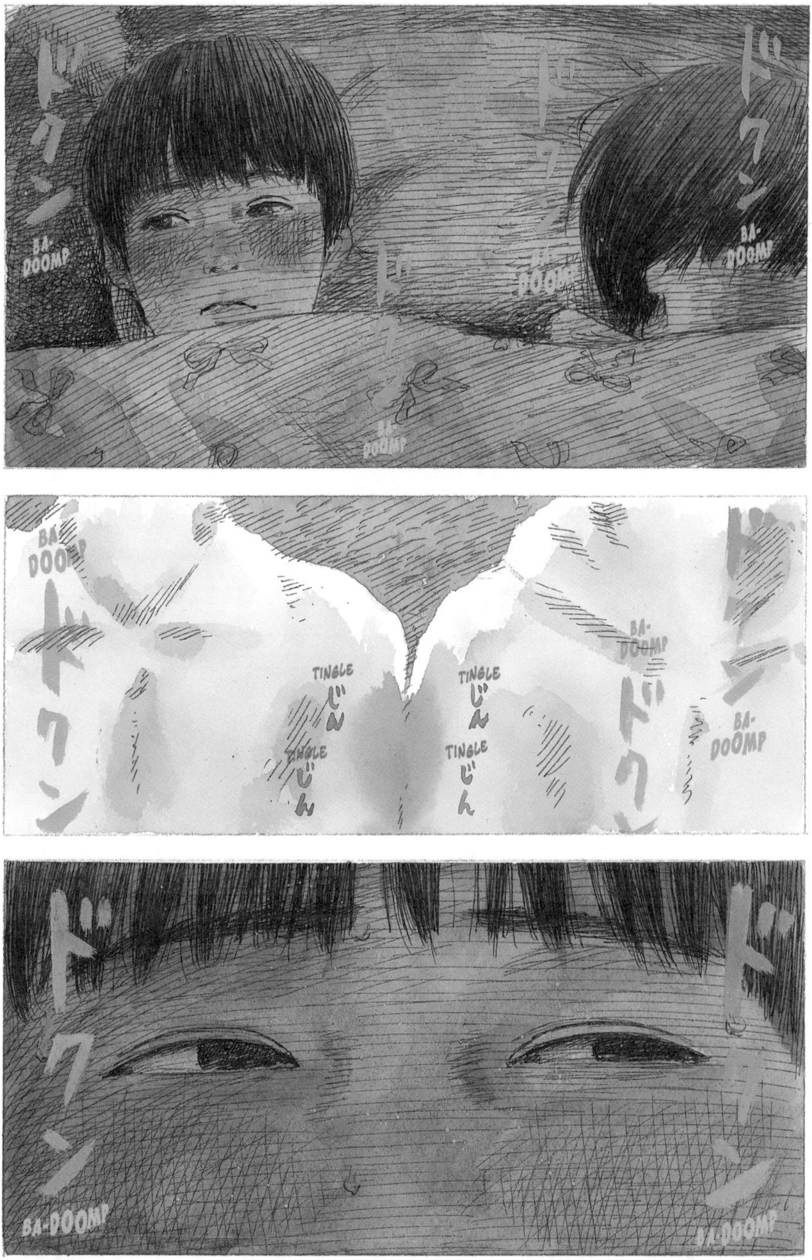
ドクン
BA-DOOMP
ドクン
BA-DOOMP
ドクン
BA-DOOMP
ドクン
BA-DOOMP
ドクン
BA-DOOMP
ドクン
BA-DOOMP
TINGLE
じん
TINGLE
じん
TINGLE
じん
TINGLE
じん
BA-DOOMP
ドクン
ドクン
BA-DOOMP
ドクン
BA-DOOMP

Blood
on
the
Tracks

volume
5

Shuzo
Oshimi

CHAPTER 34 Ditch

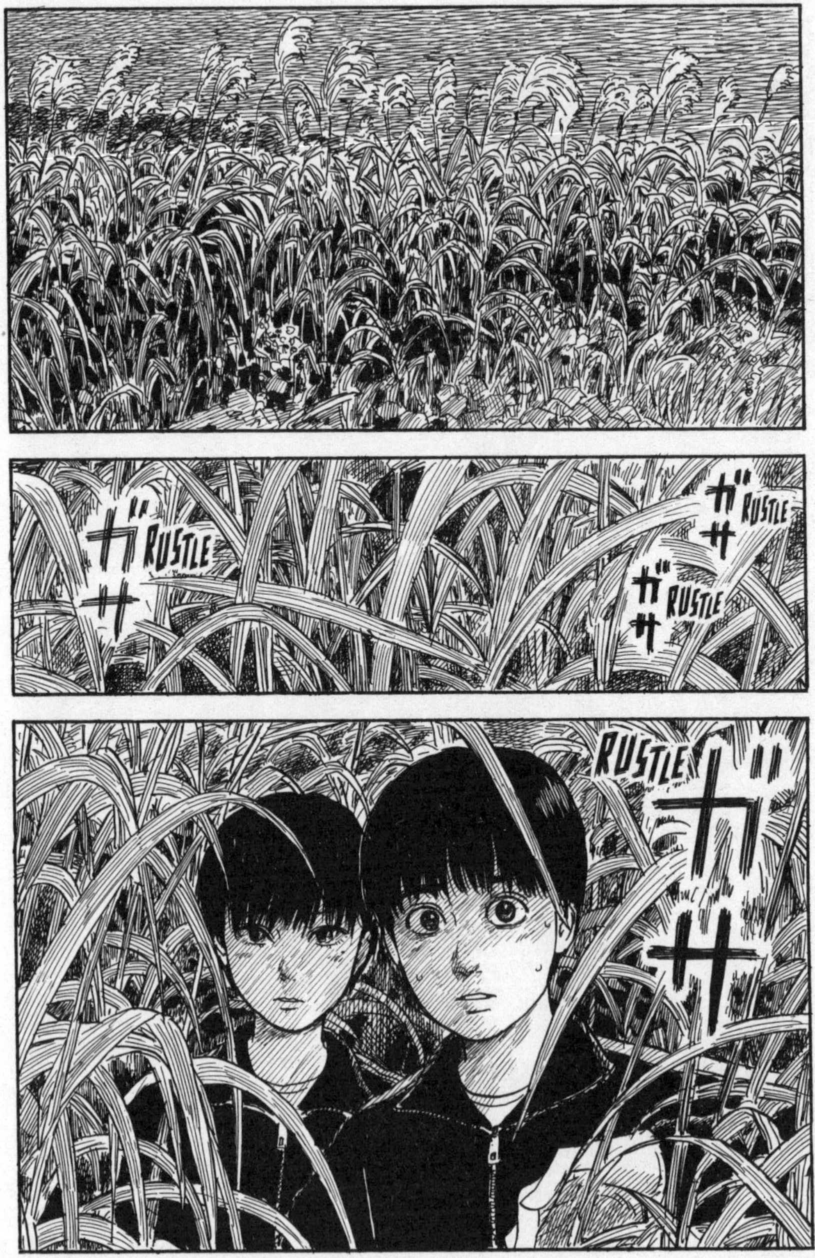

ガサ RUSTLE
ガサ RUSTLE
ガサ RUSTLE
RUSTLE ガサ

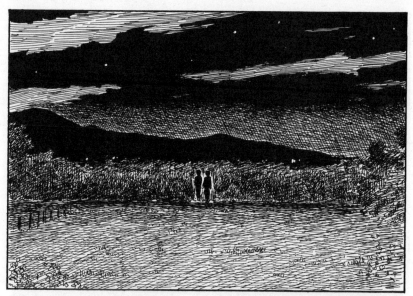

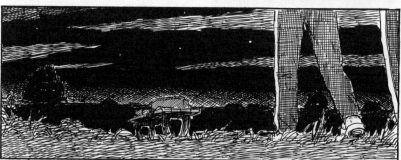

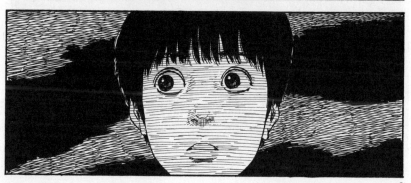

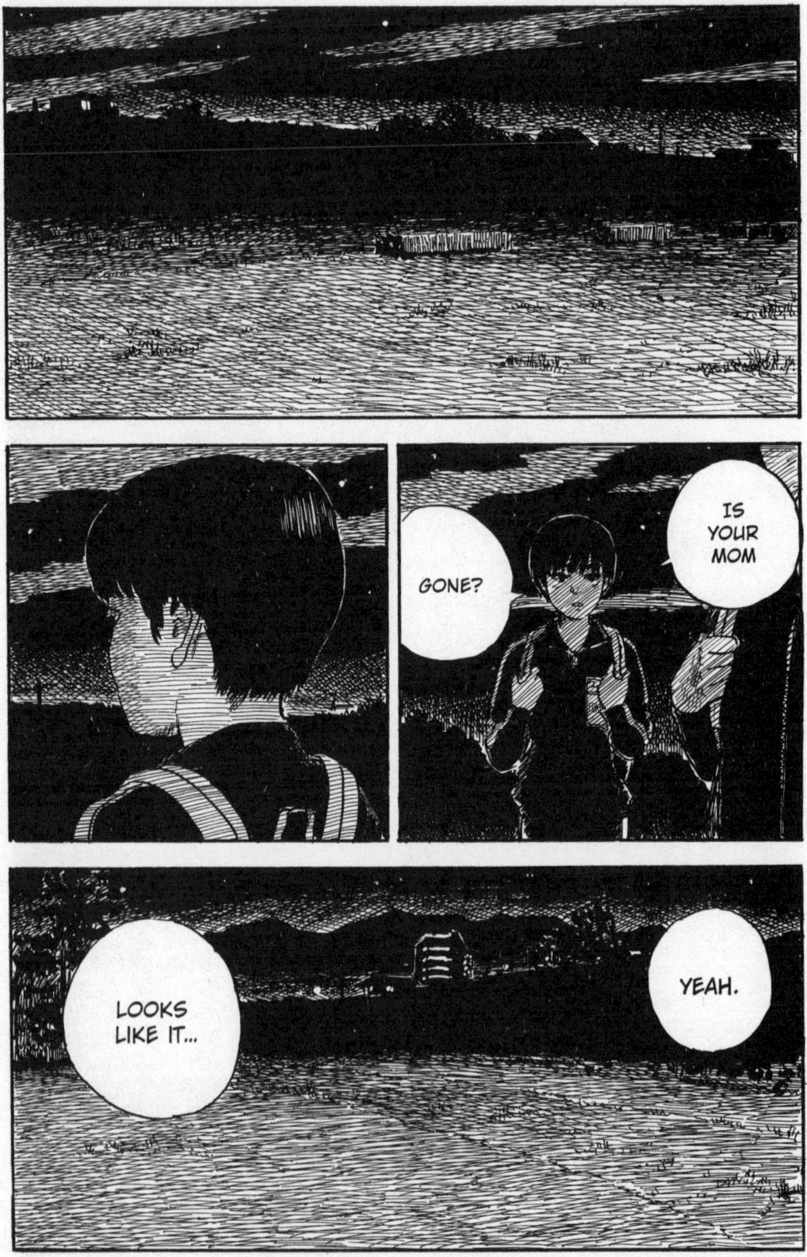
IS YOUR MOM
GONE?
YEAH.
LOOKS LIKE IT...

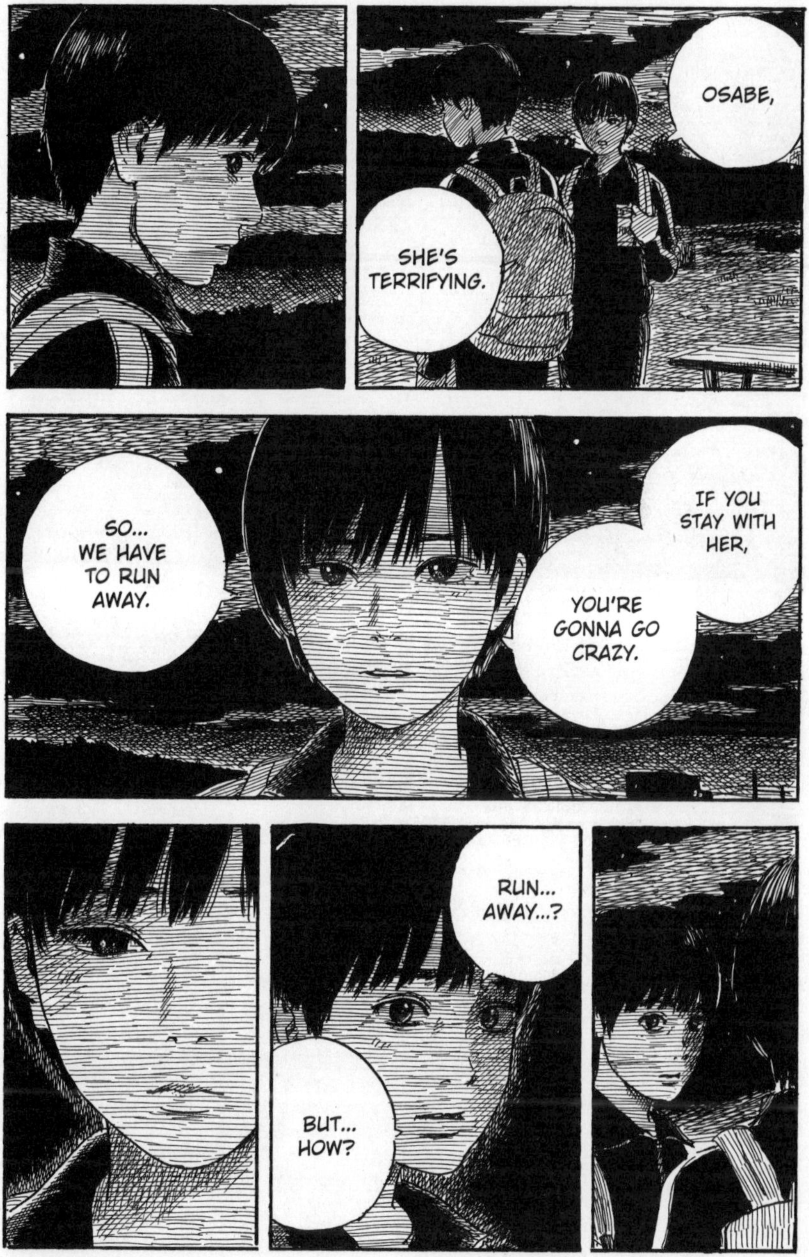
OSABE,
SHE'S TERRIFYING.
IF YOU STAY WITH HER,
YOU'RE GONNA GO CRAZY.
SO... WE HAVE TO RUN AWAY.
RUN... AWAY...?
BUT... HOW?

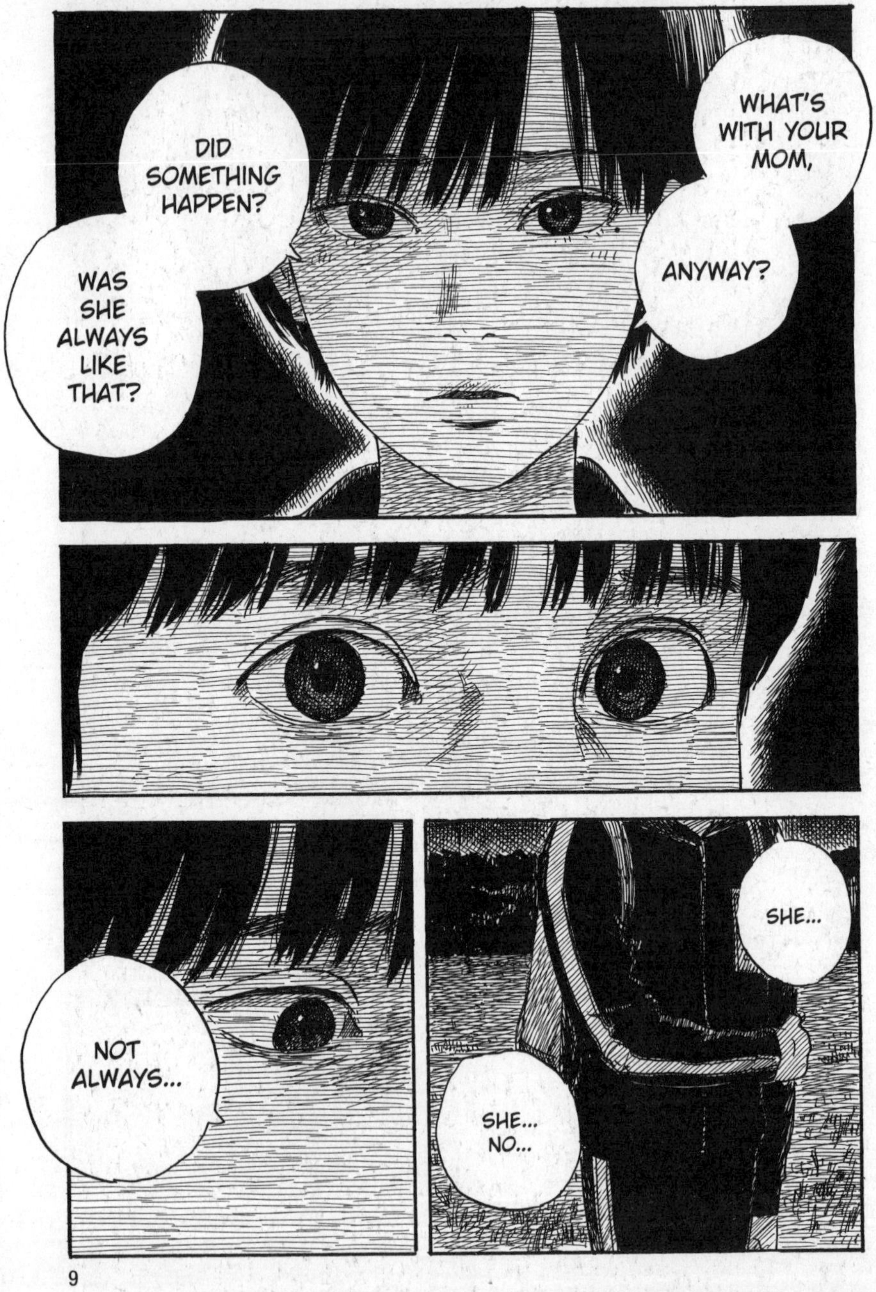
WHAT'S WITH YOUR MOM,
ANYWAY?
DID SOMETHING HAPPEN?
WAS SHE ALWAYS LIKE THAT?
SHE...
SHE... NO...
NOT ALWAYS...

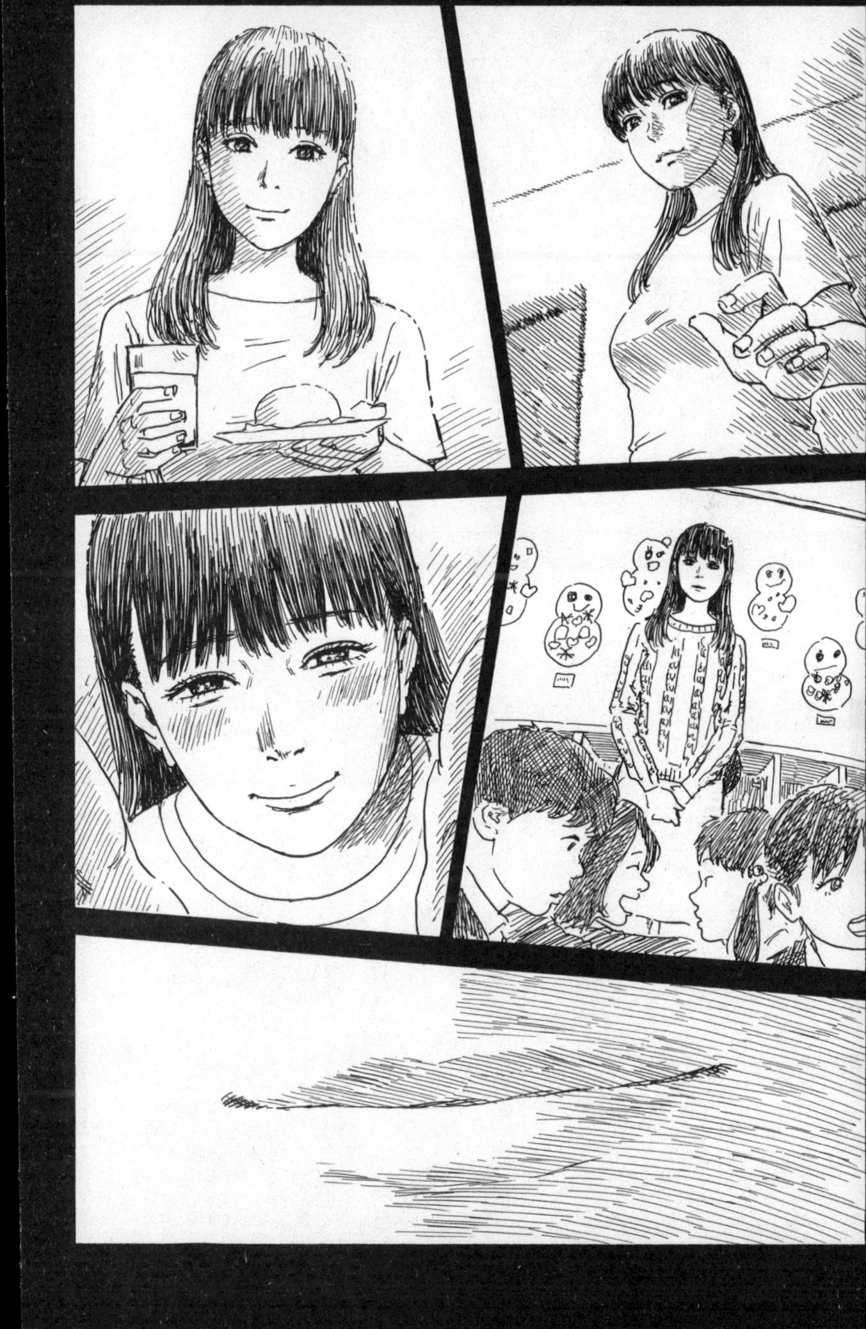

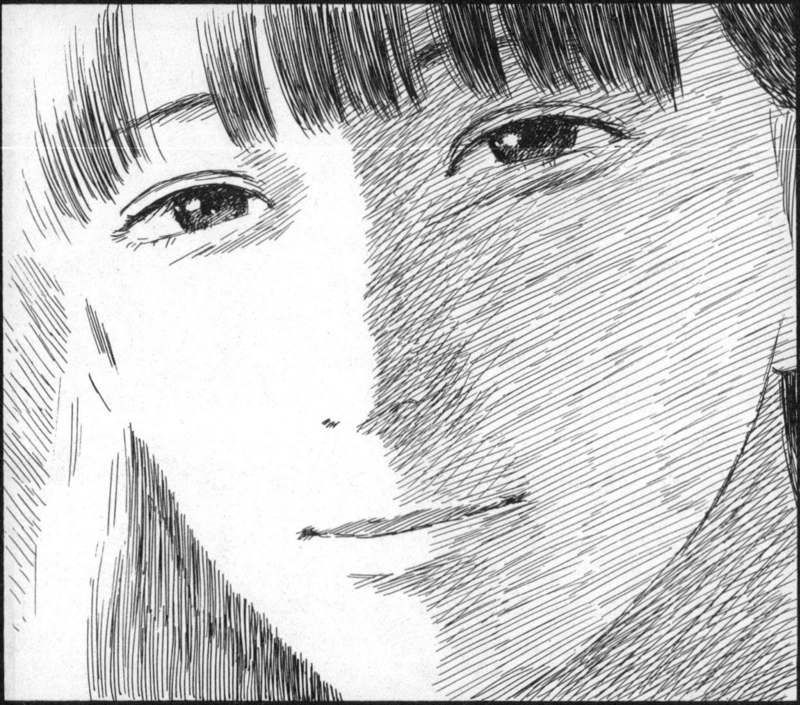
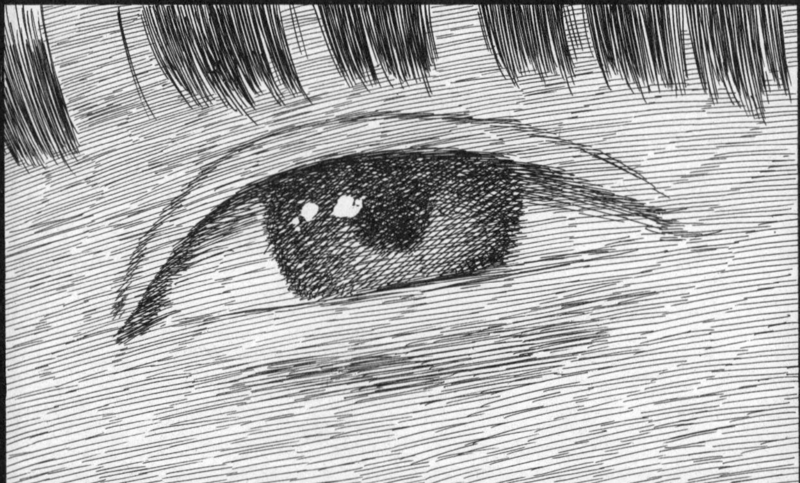

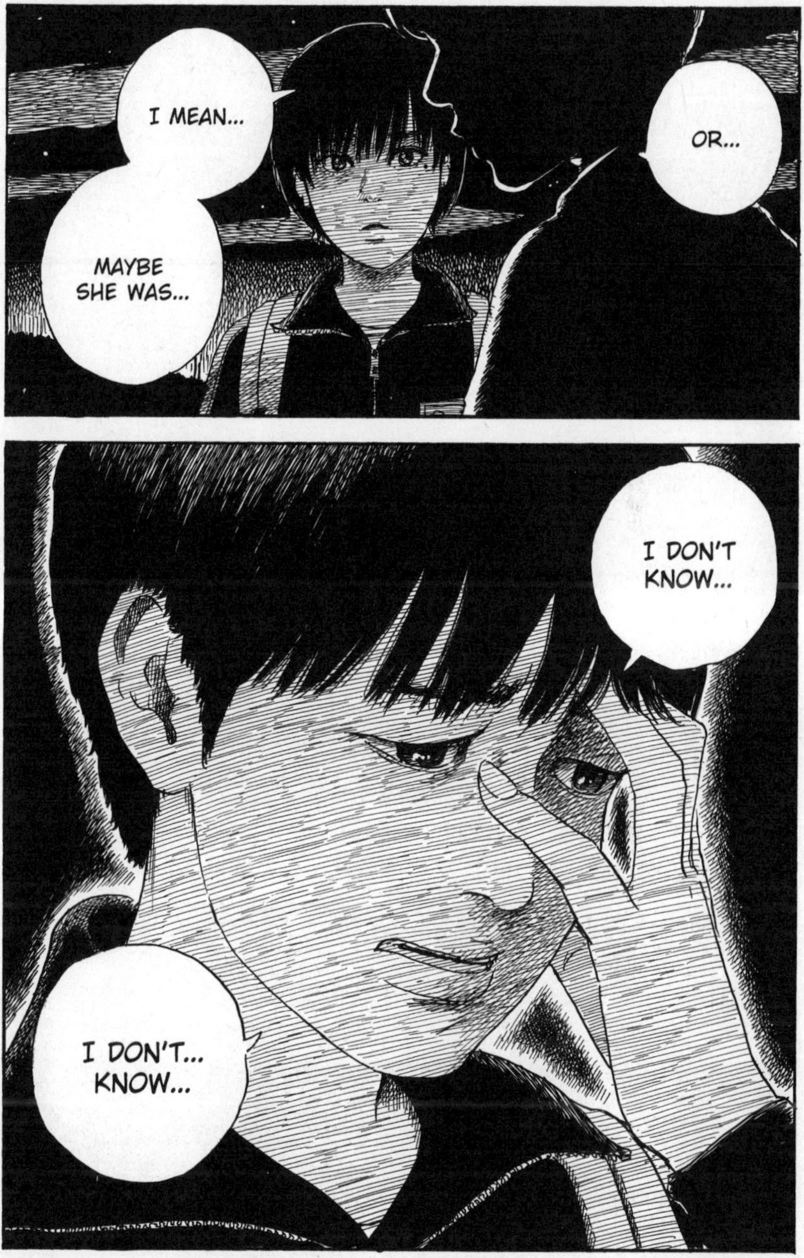
OR...
I MEAN...
MAYBE SHE WAS...
I DON'T KNOW...
I DON'T... KNOW...

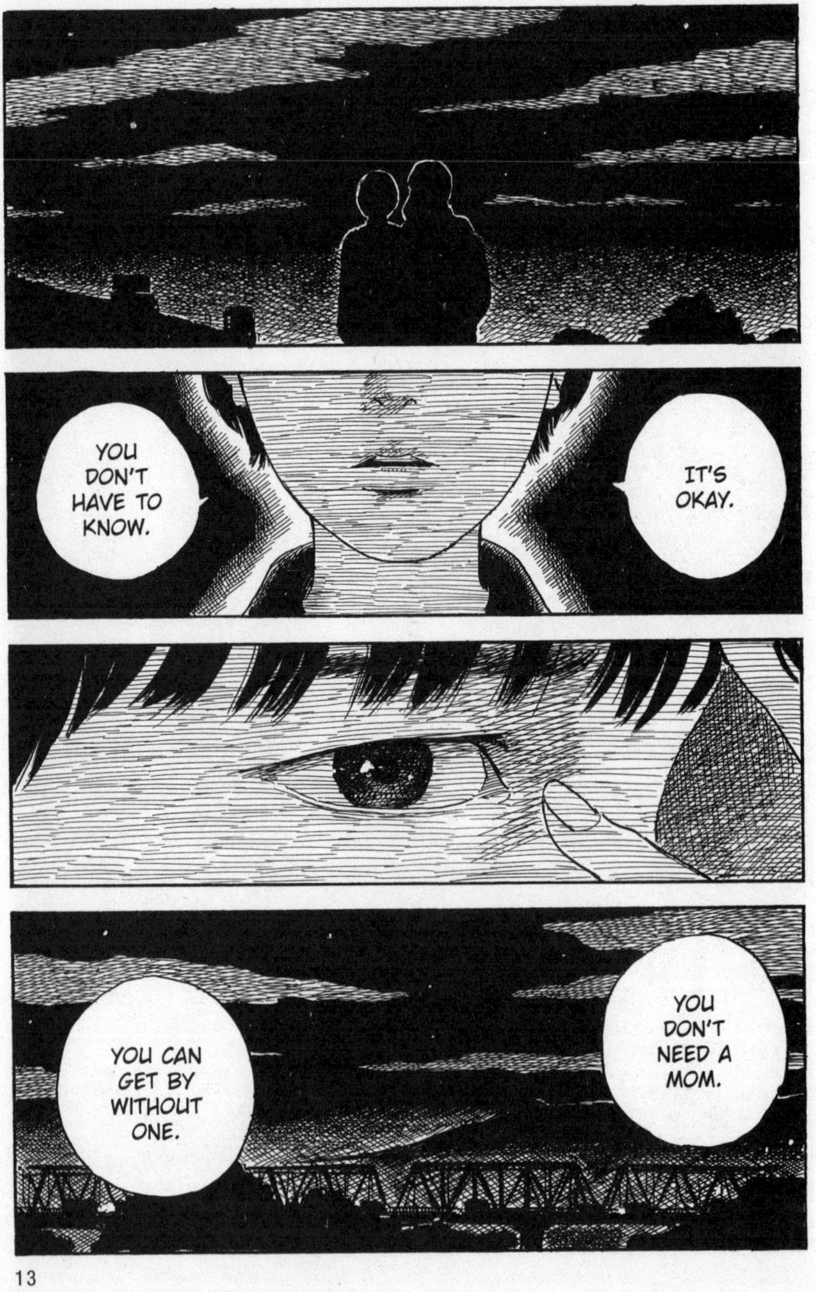
IT'S OKAY.
YOU DON'T HAVE TO KNOW.
YOU DON'T NEED A MOM.
YOU CAN GET BY WITHOUT ONE.

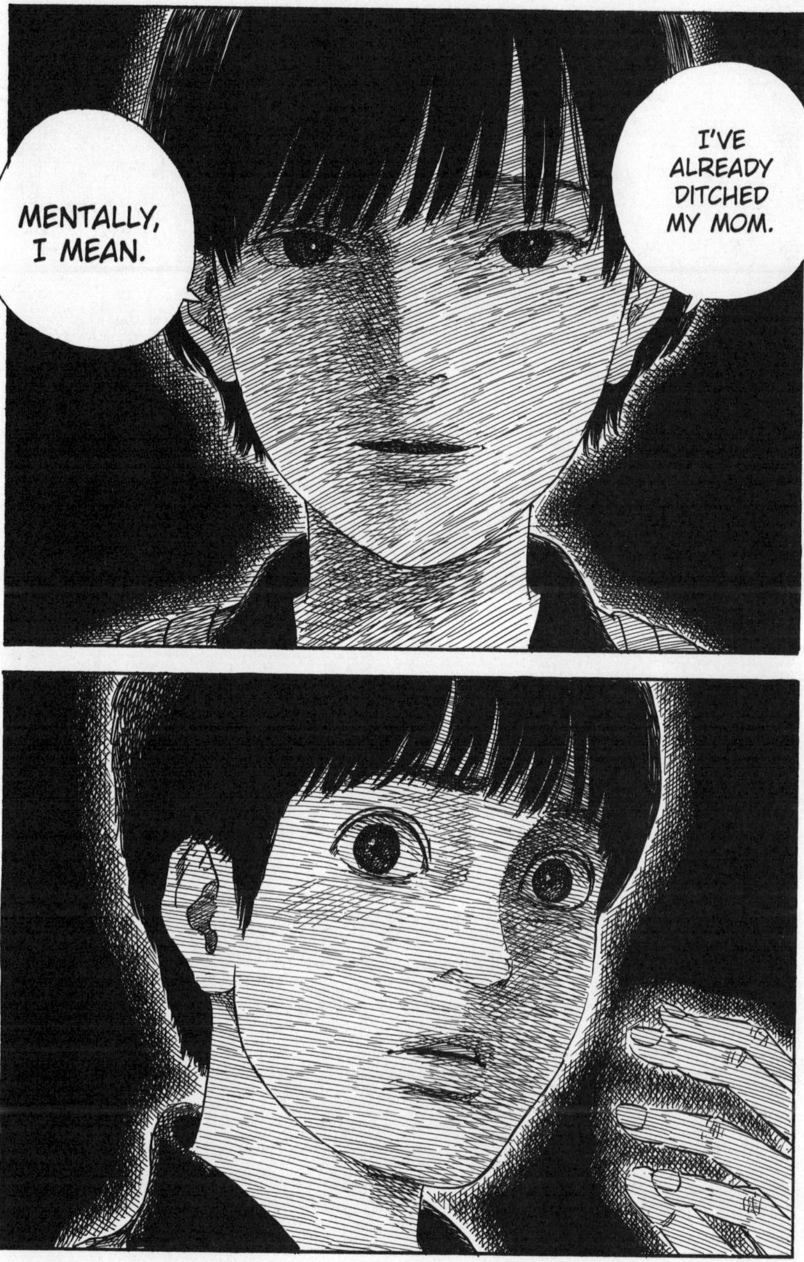
I'VE ALREADY DITCHED MY MOM.
MENTALLY, I MEAN.

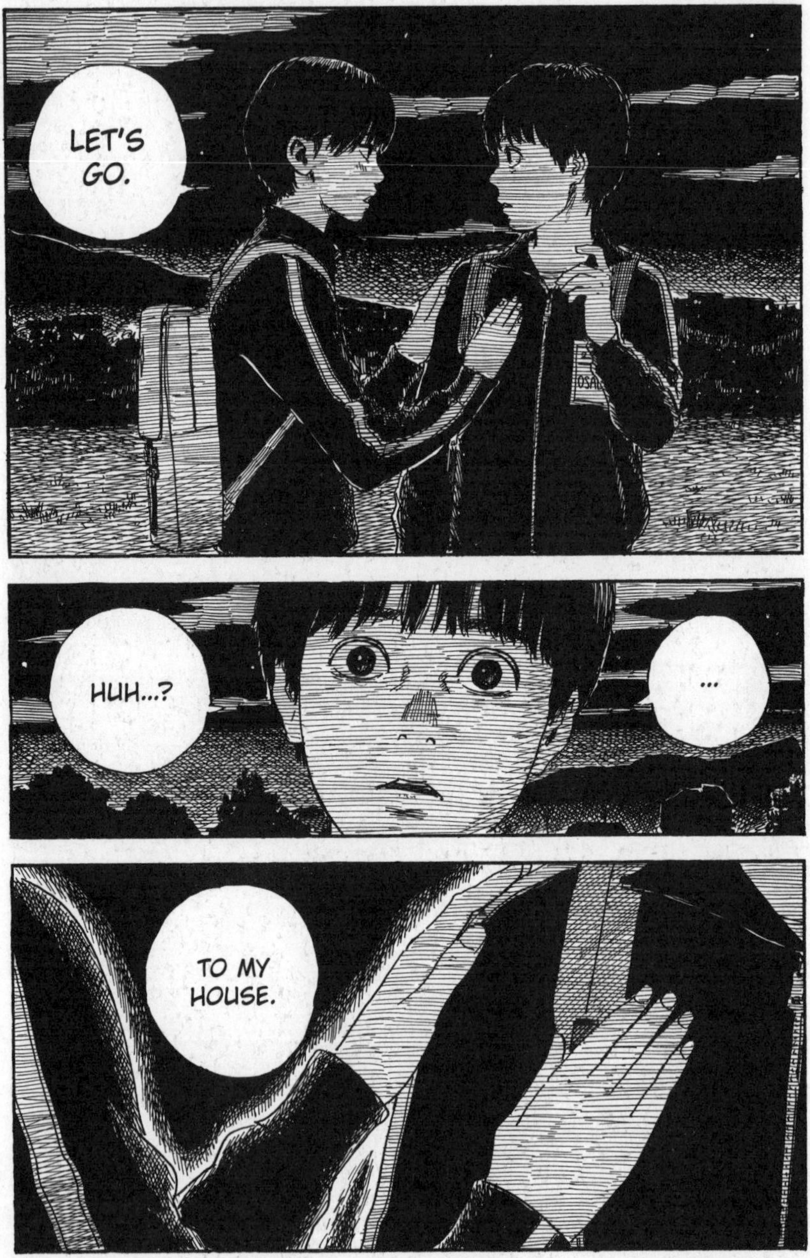
LET'S GO.
...
HUH...?
TO MY HOUSE.

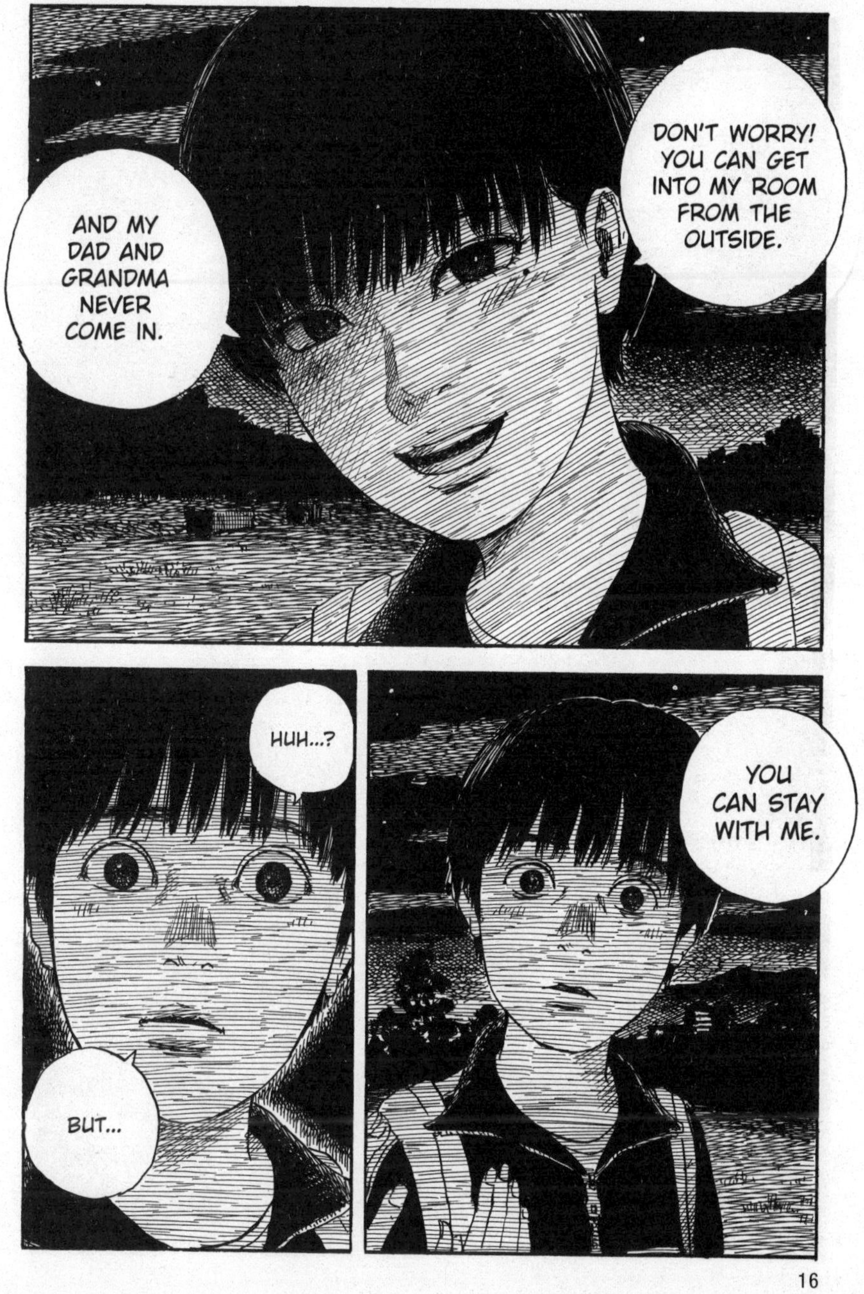
DON'T WORRY! YOU CAN GET INTO MY ROOM FROM THE OUTSIDE.
AND MY DAD AND GRANDMA NEVER COME IN.
YOU CAN STAY WITH ME.
HUH...?
BUT...

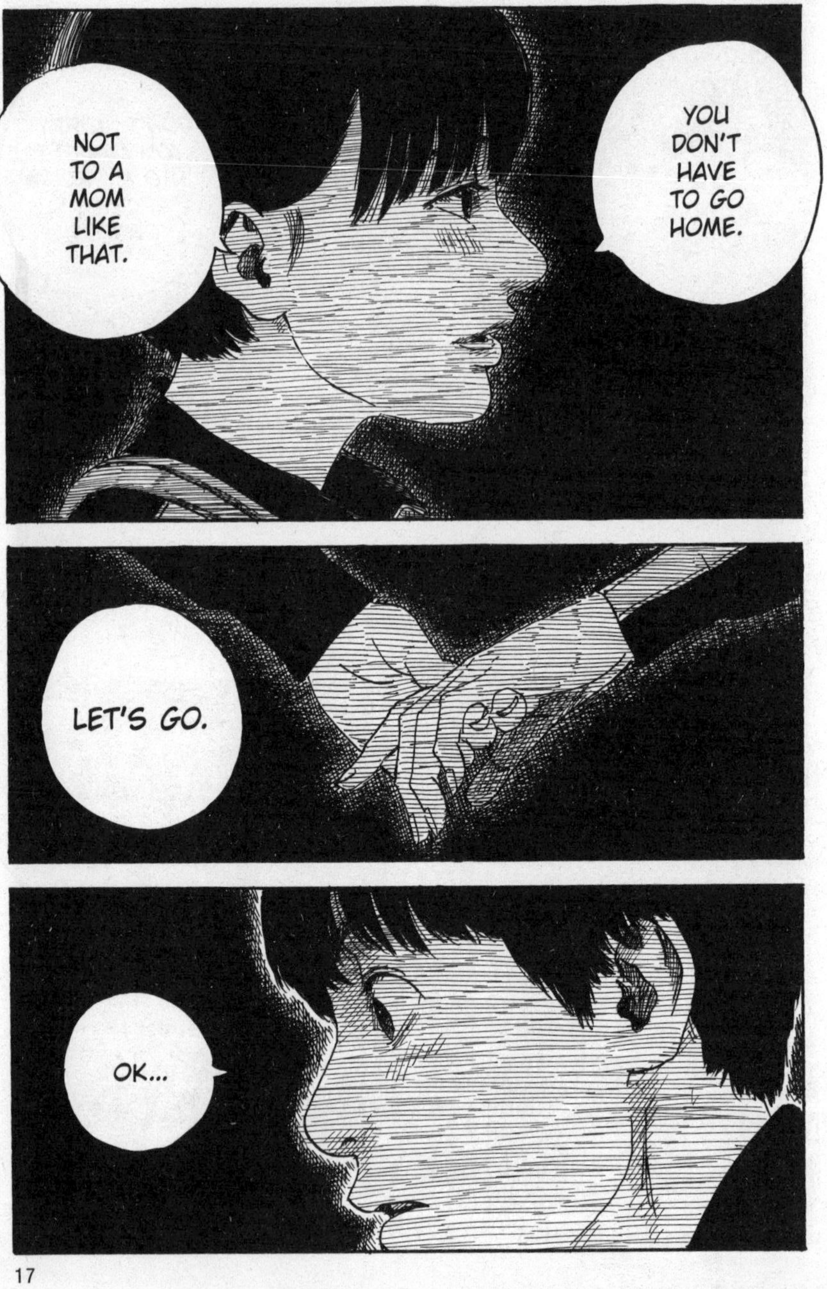
YOU DON'T HAVE TO GO HOME.
NOT TO A MOM LIKE THAT.
LET'S GO.
OK...

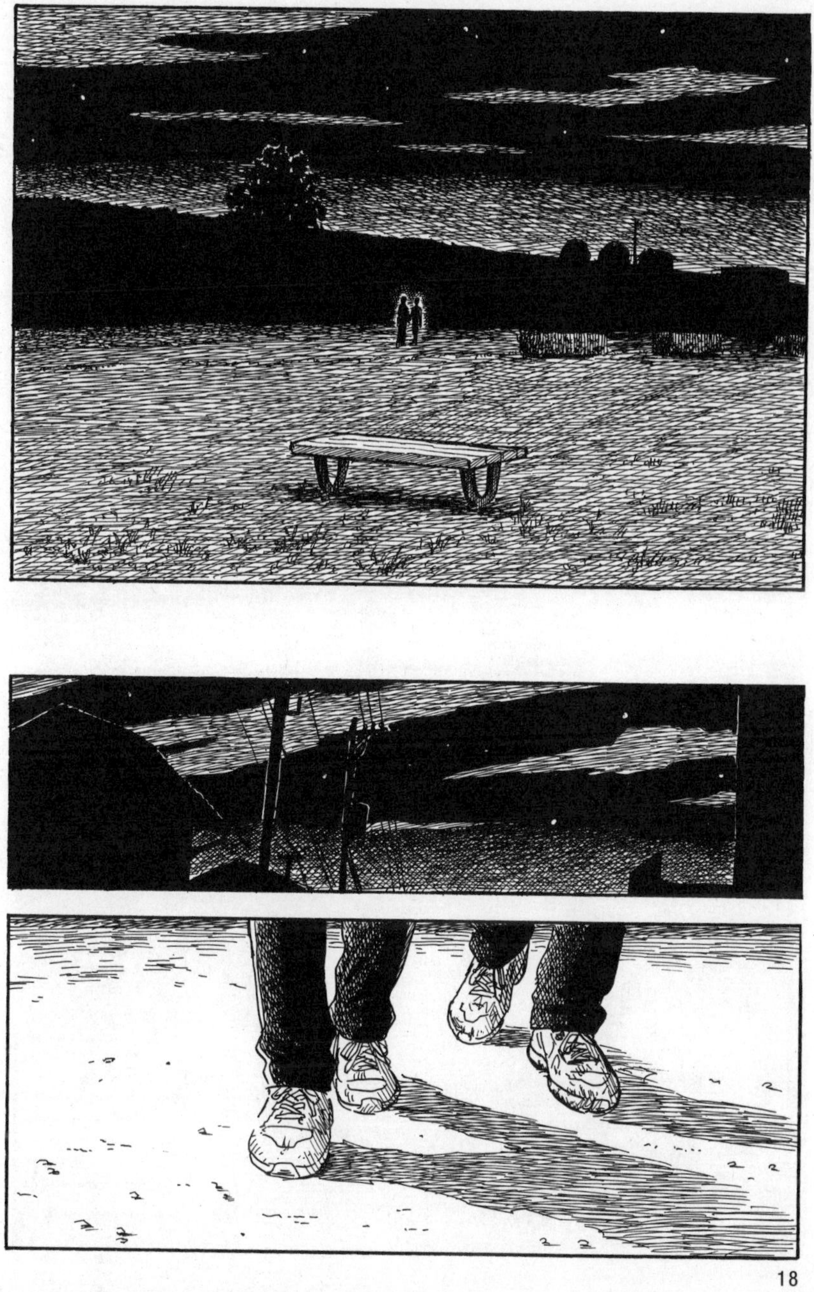

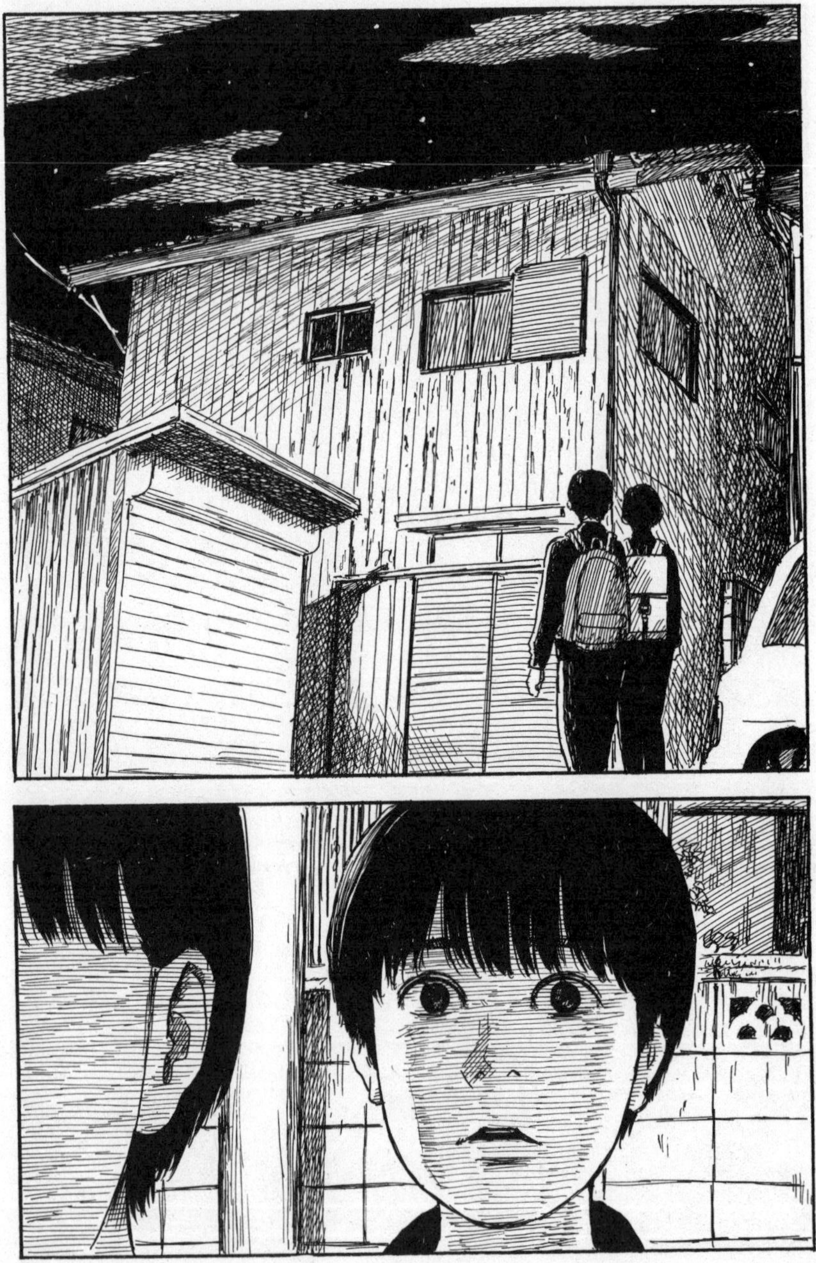

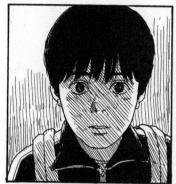
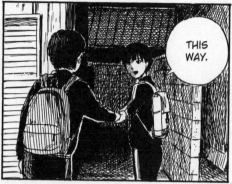

THIS WAY.

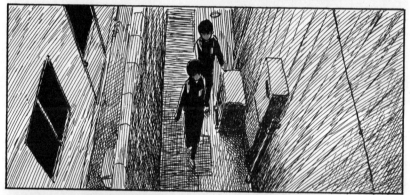

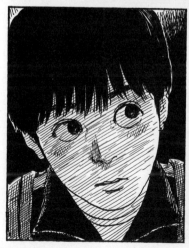
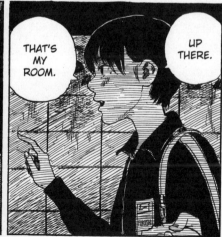

THAT'S MY ROOM.

UP THERE.

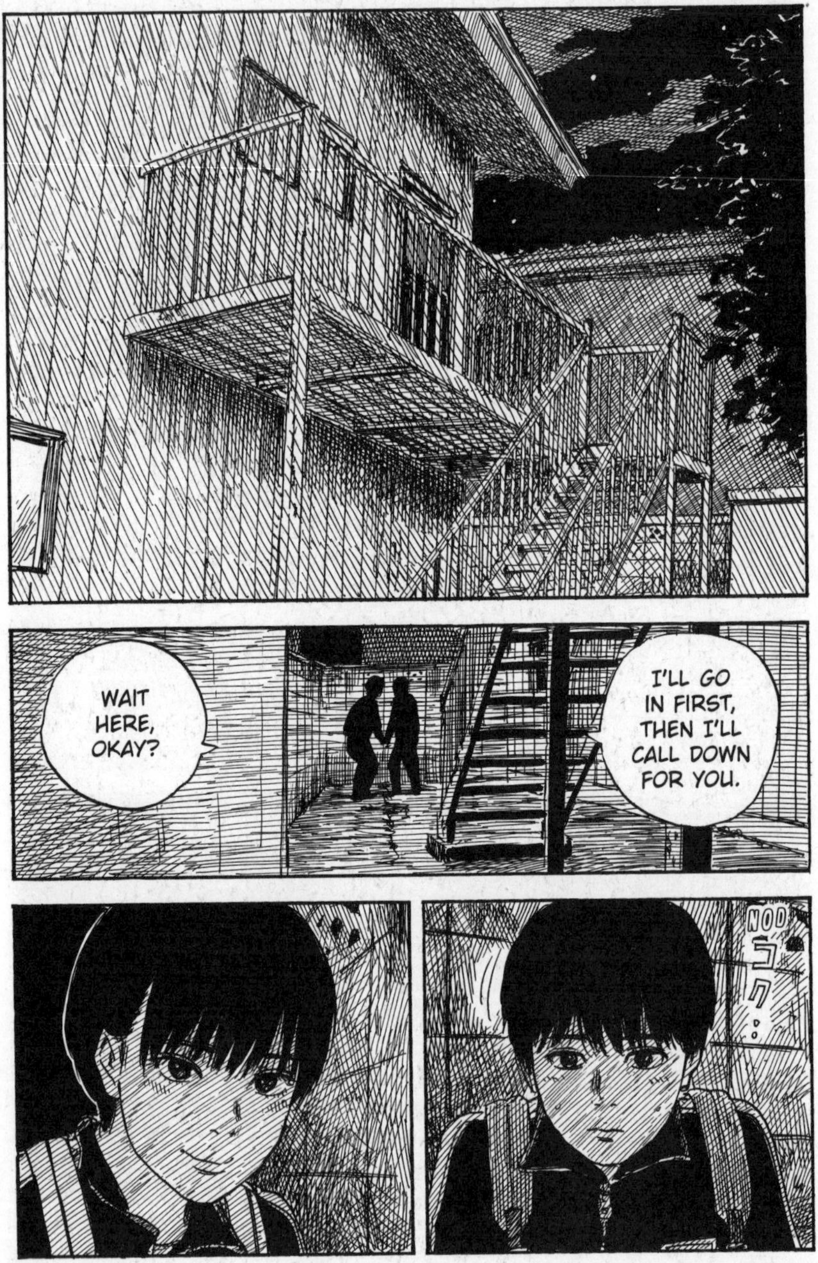
I'LL GO IN FIRST, THEN I'LL CALL DOWN FOR YOU.
WAIT HERE, OKAY?
NOD
コク‥

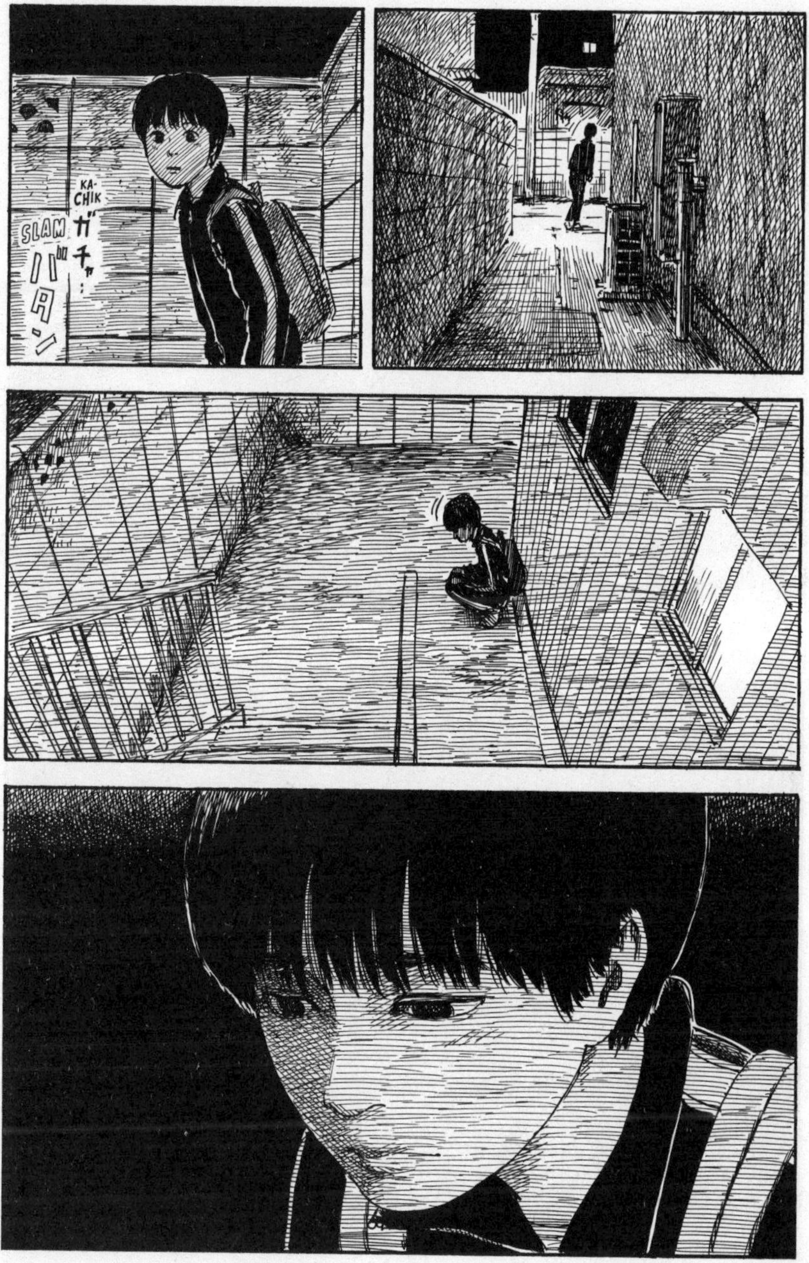
KA-CHIK
ガチャ…
SLAM
バタン

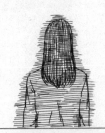

I DON'T NEED YOU!!

GO AWAY!

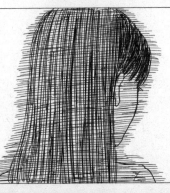

DITCHED MY MOM.

I'VE ALREADY

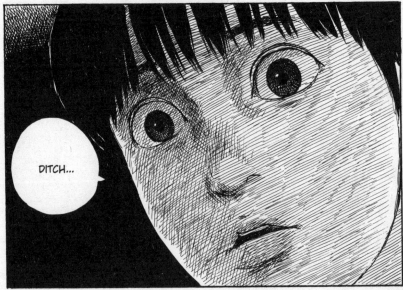

DITCH...

OSABE!
OSABE
TUNK
コン
TUNK
コン

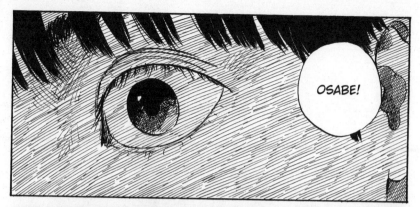

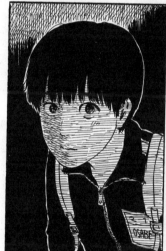

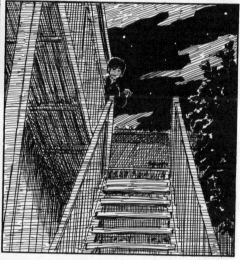

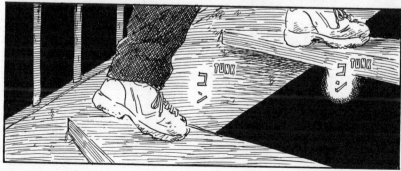

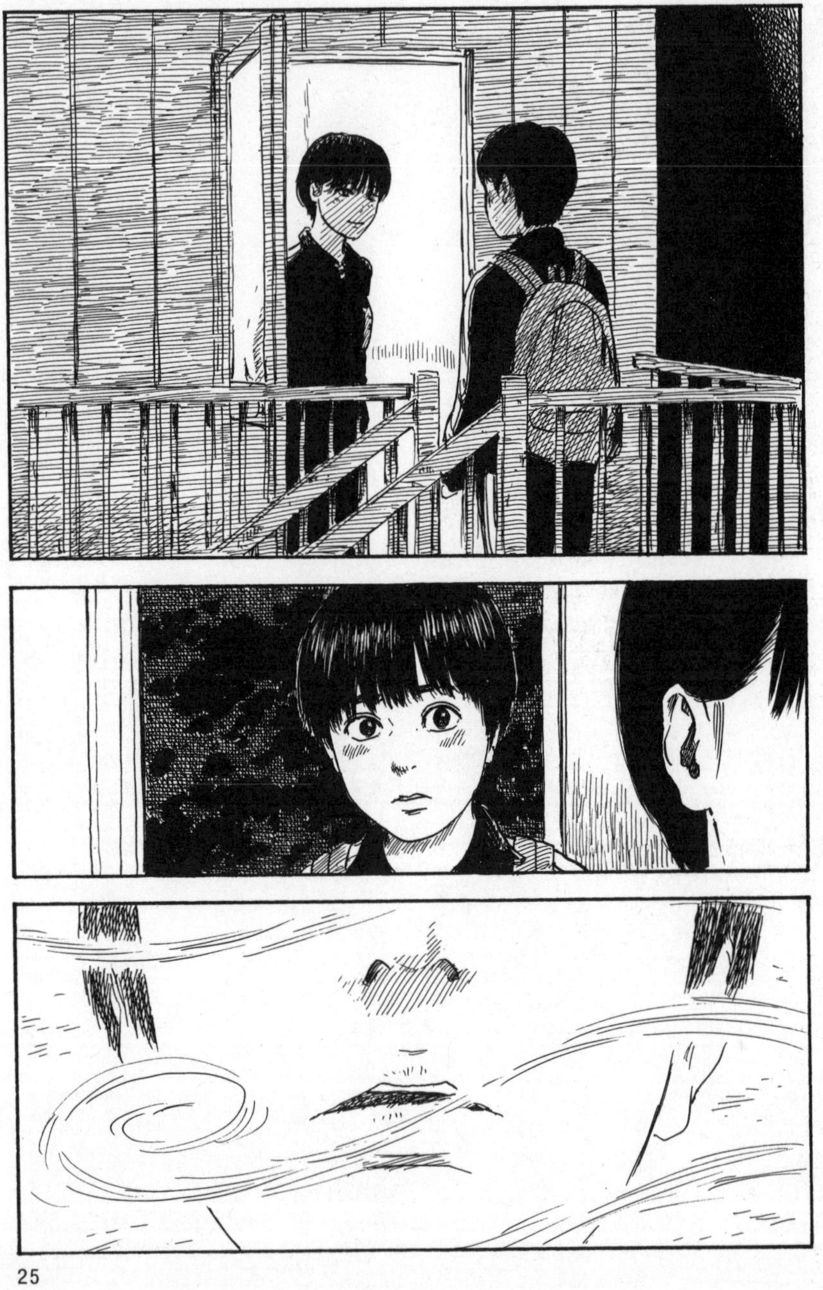

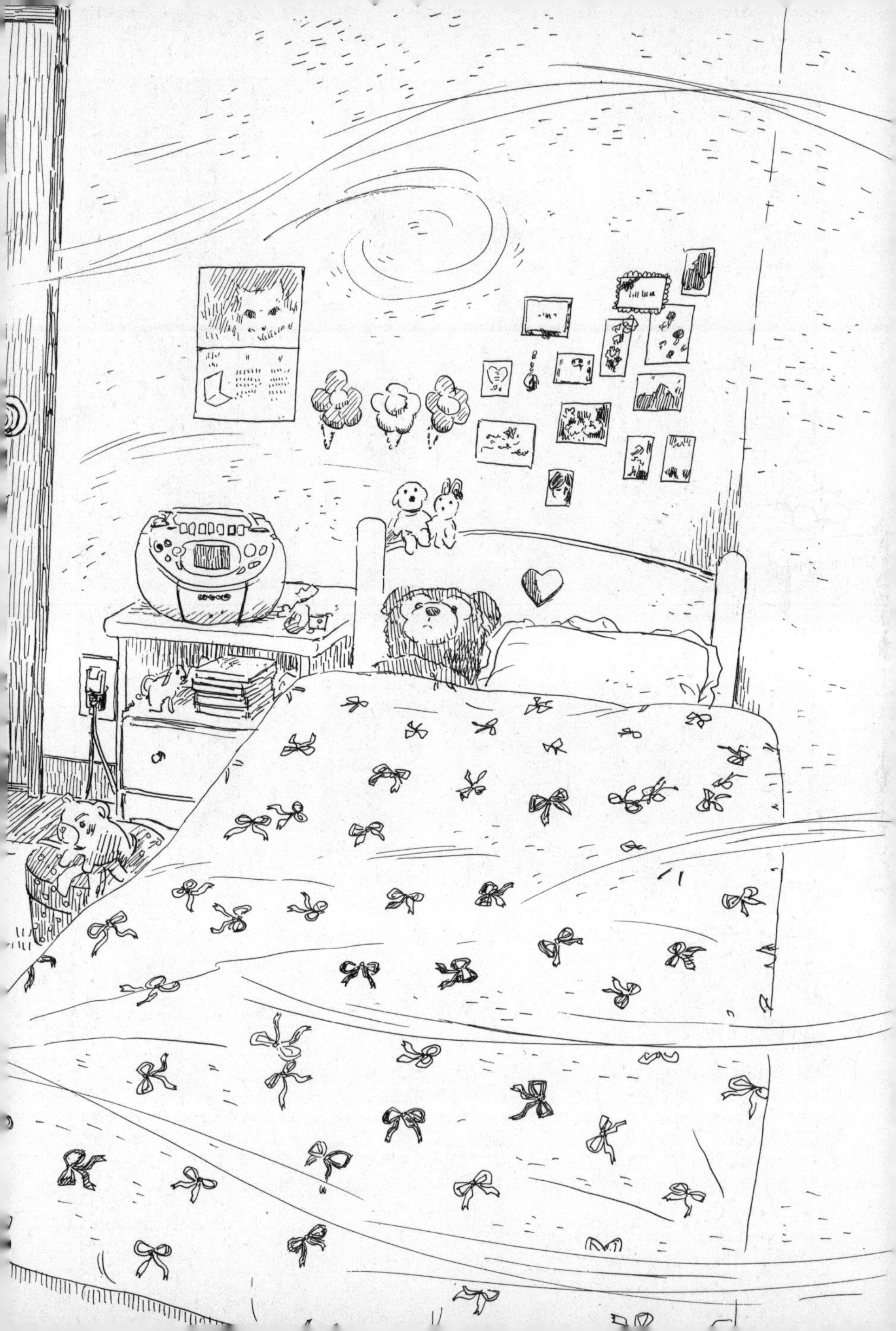

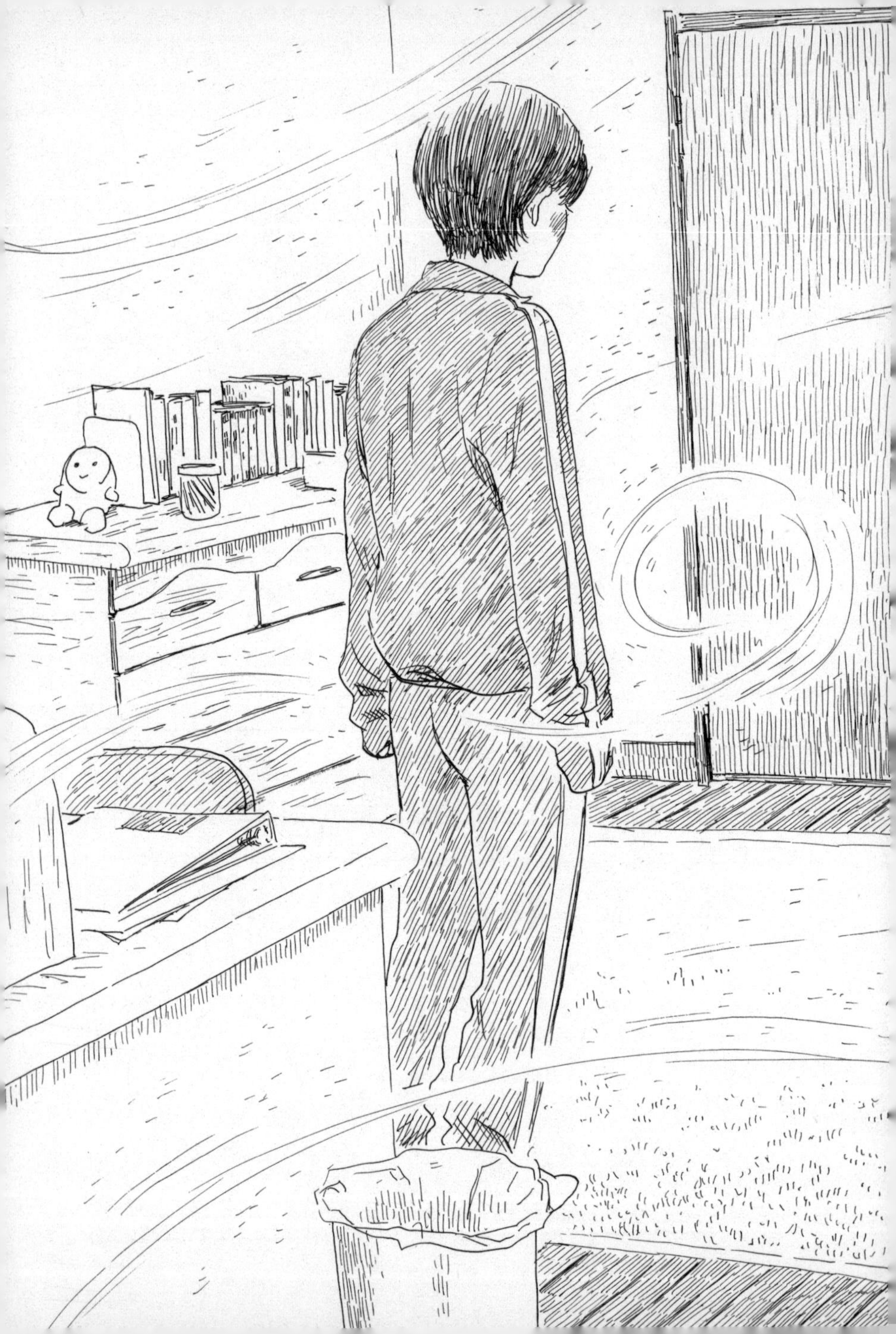

THIS WAY,
WE GET TO BE TOGETHER ALL NIGHT TOO.

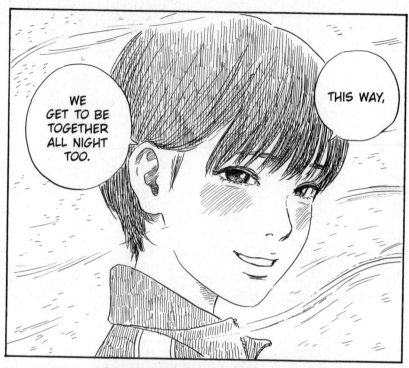

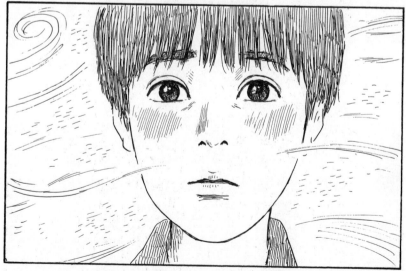

CHAPTER 35 Her Room

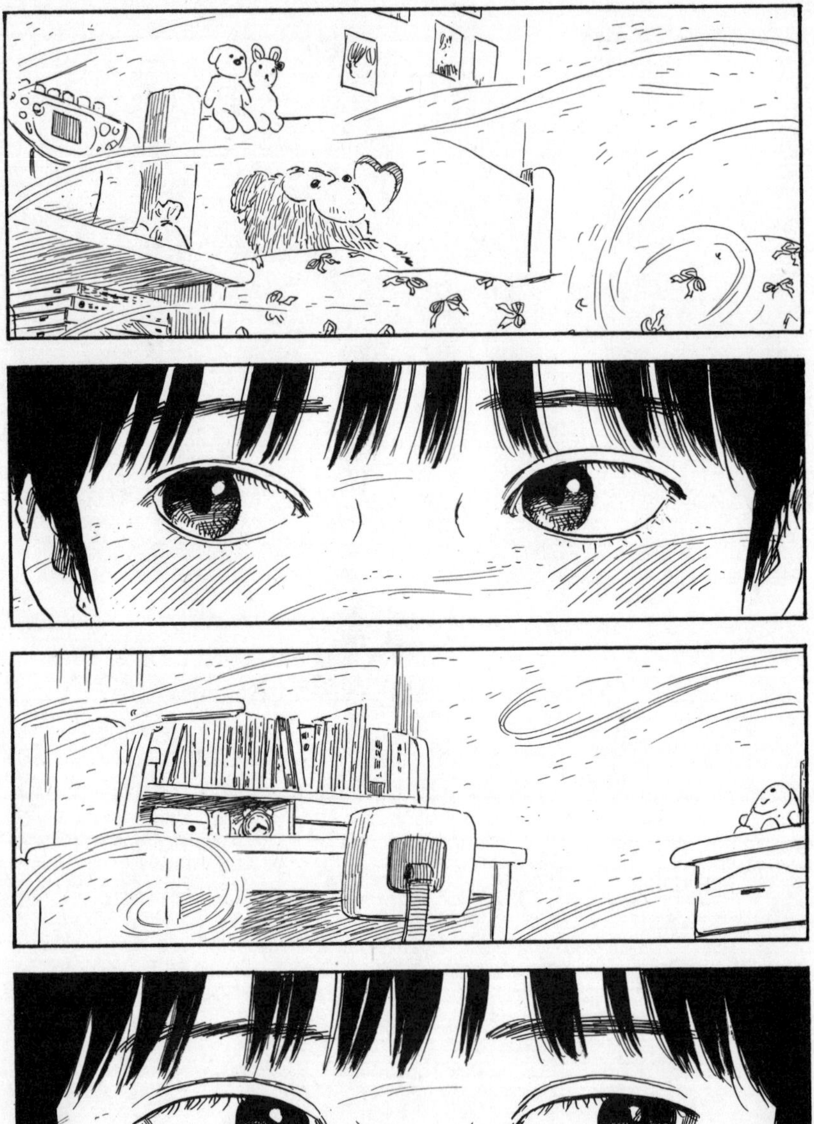

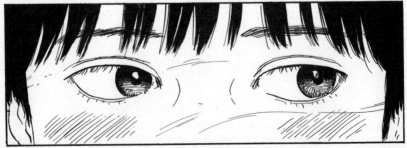

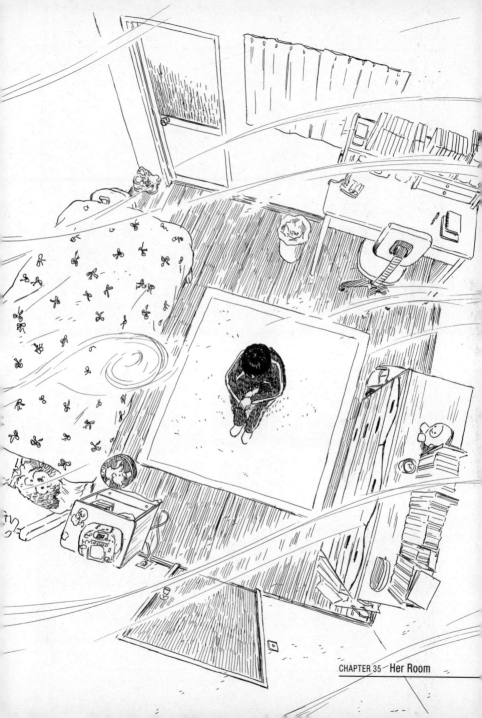

CHAPTER 35 Her Room

...
HFFF...
とて TP
とて TP
とて TP
CHIK カチャ

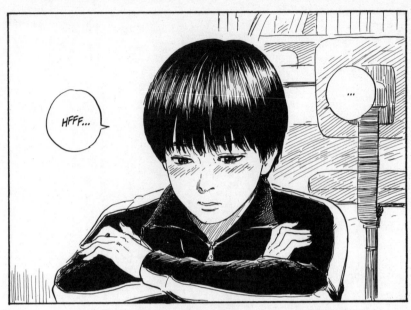

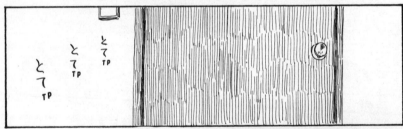

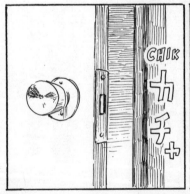

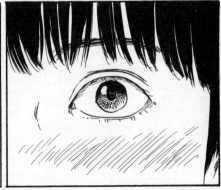

2-1
FUKIISHI
MY DAD'S
OUT DRINKING.

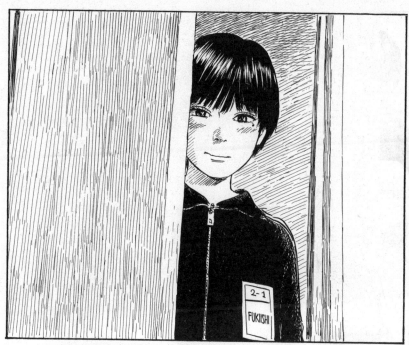

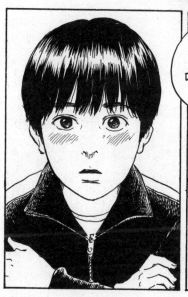

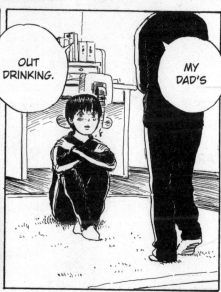

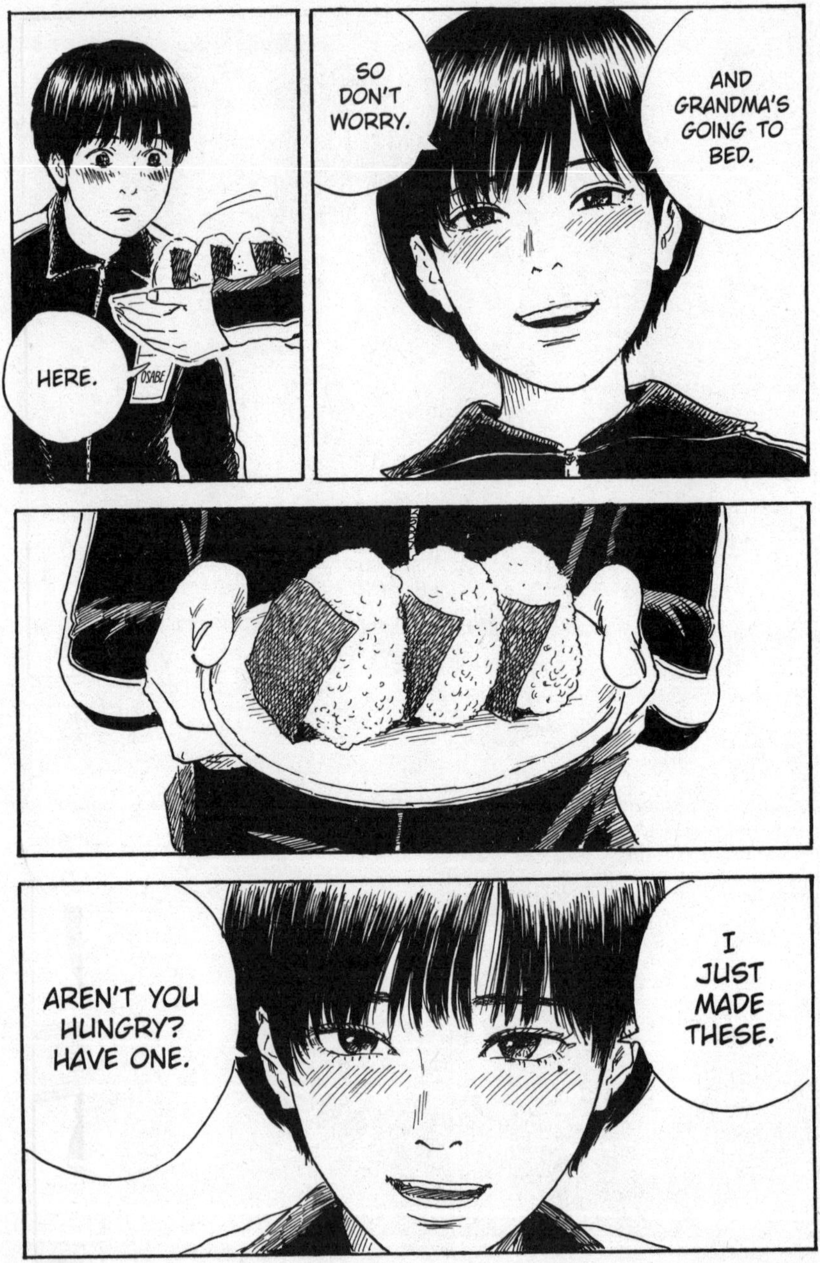
AND GRANDMA'S GOING TO BED.
SO DON'T WORRY.
HERE.
OSABE
I JUST MADE THESE.
AREN'T YOU HUNGRY? HAVE ONE.

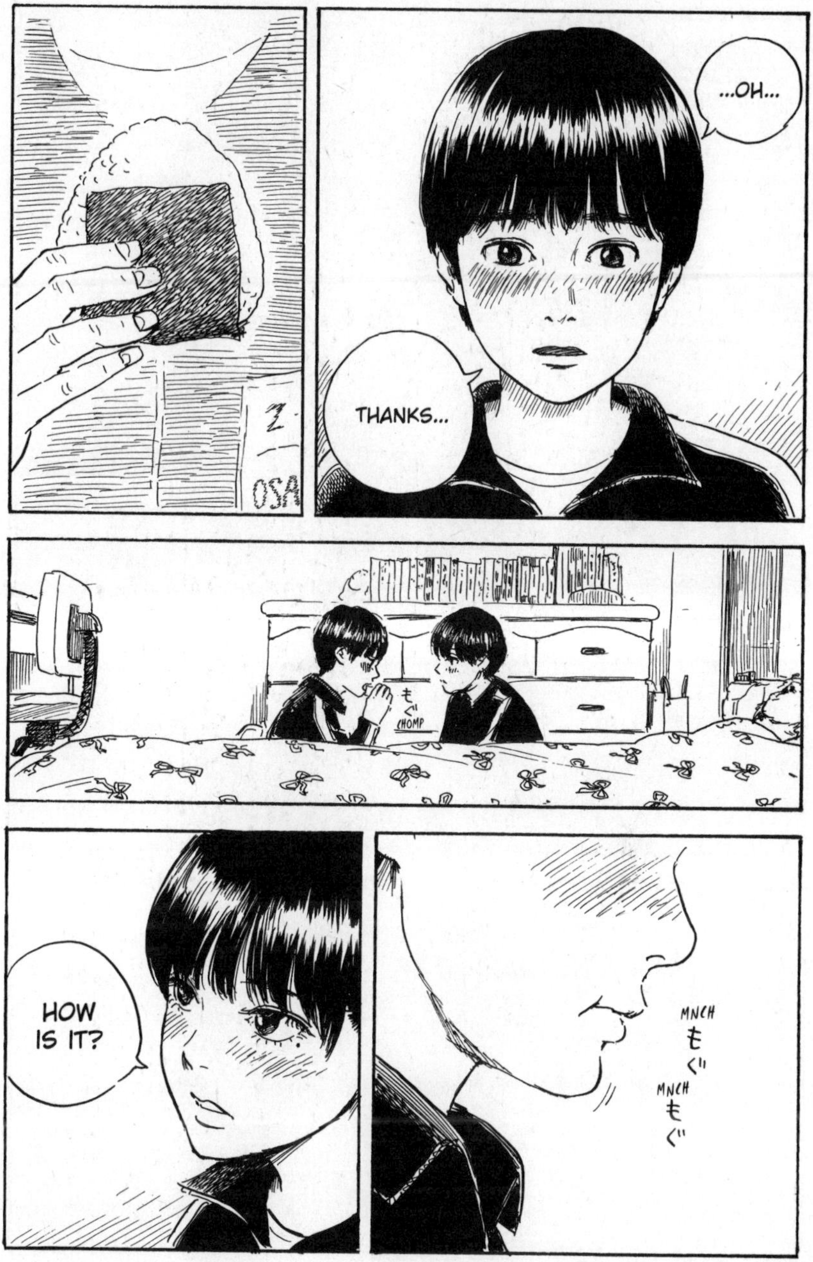
...OH...
THANKS...
もぐ
CHOMP
MNCH
もぐ
MNCH
もぐ
HOW IS IT?

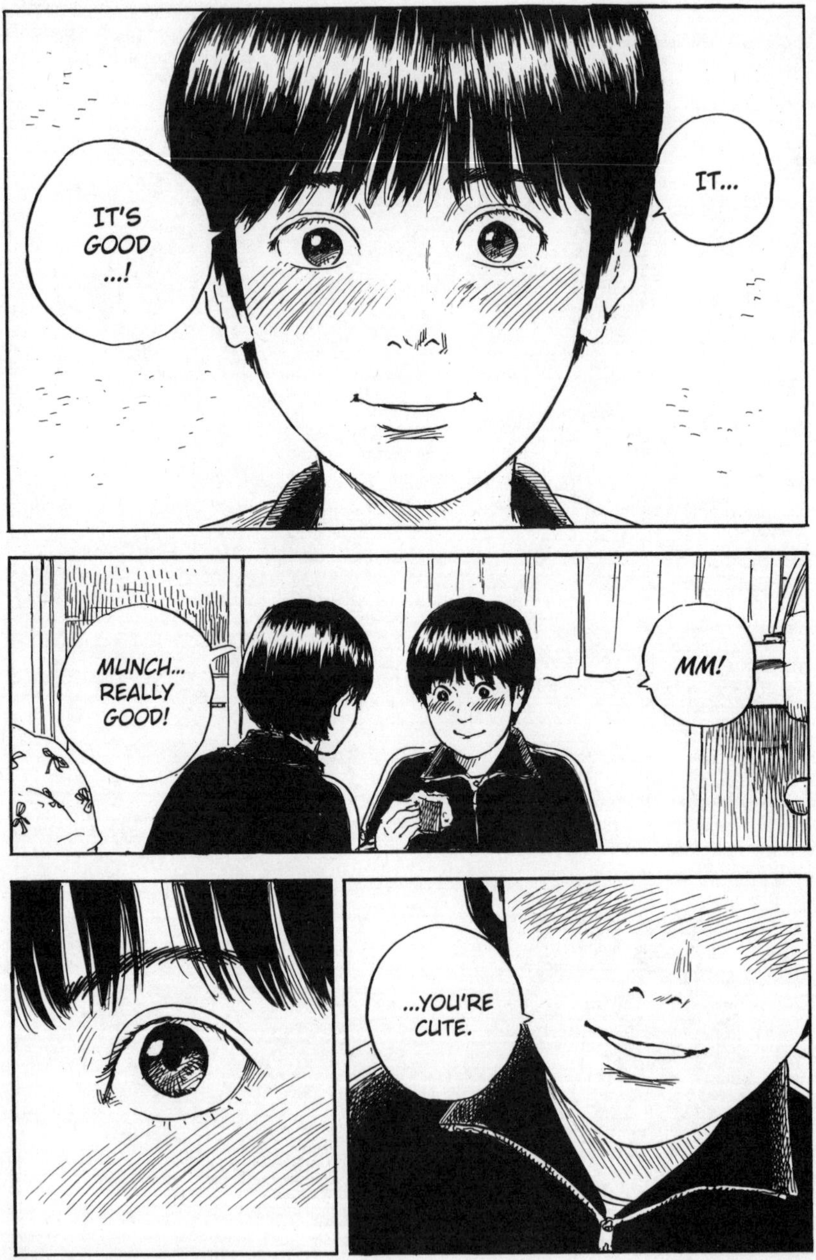
IT...
IT'S GOOD ...!
MM!
MUNCH... REALLY GOOD!
...YOU'RE CUTE.

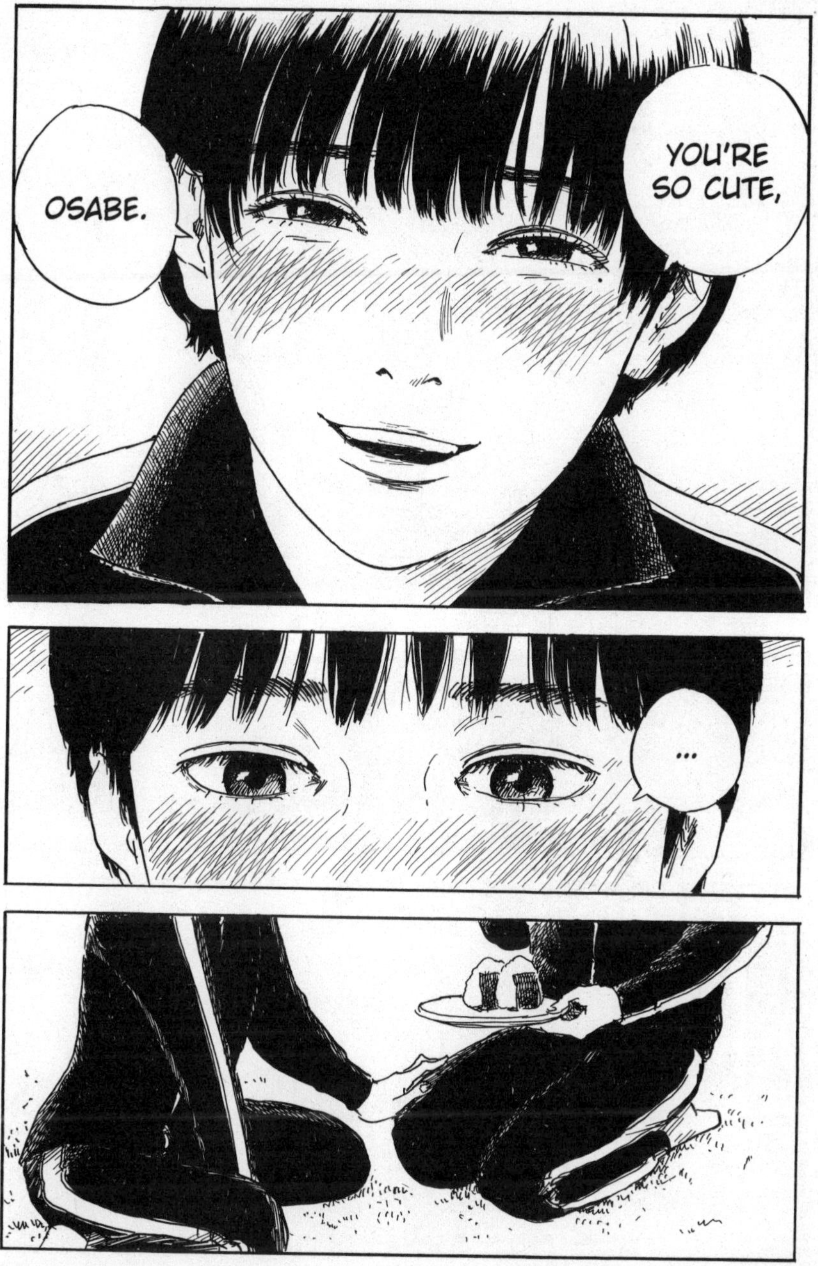
YOU'RE SO CUTE,
OSABE.
...

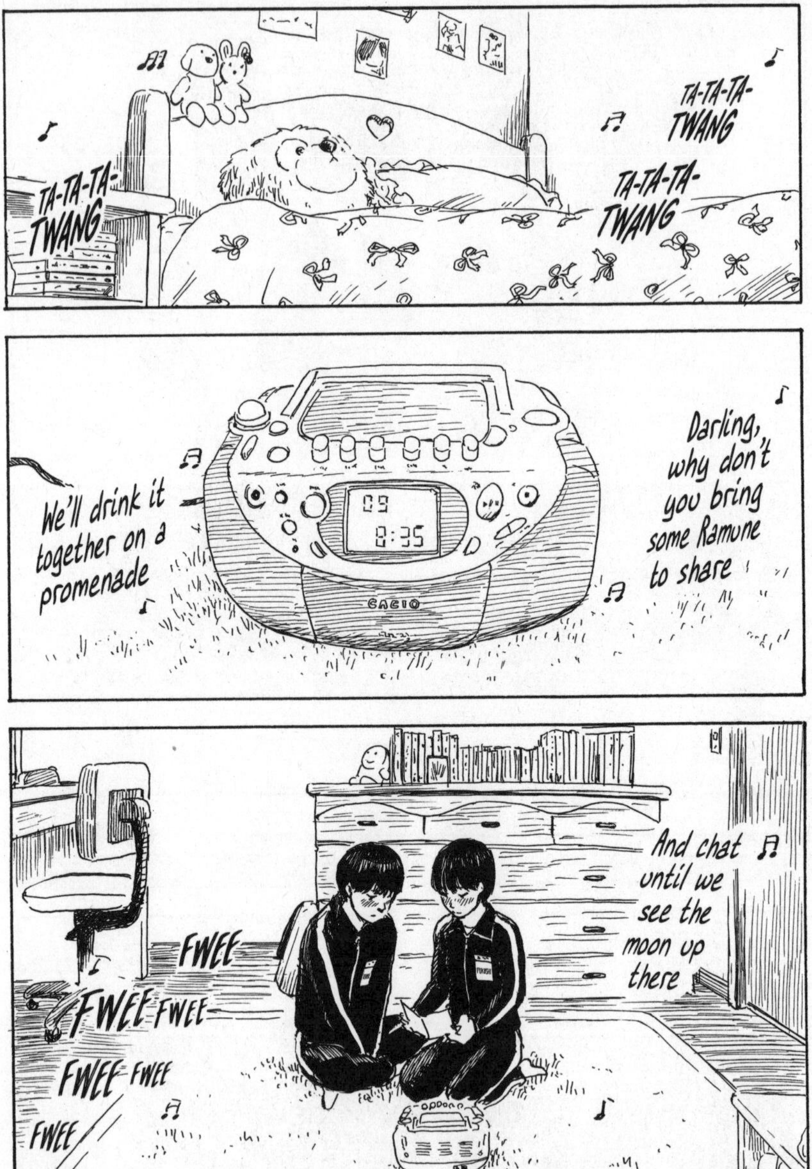
TA-TA-TA-TWANG
TA-TA-TA-TWANG
TA-TA-TA-TWANG
Darling, why don't you bring some Ramune to share
We'll drink it together on a promenade
And chat until we see the moon up there
FWEE
FWEE FWEE
FWEE FWEE
FWEE

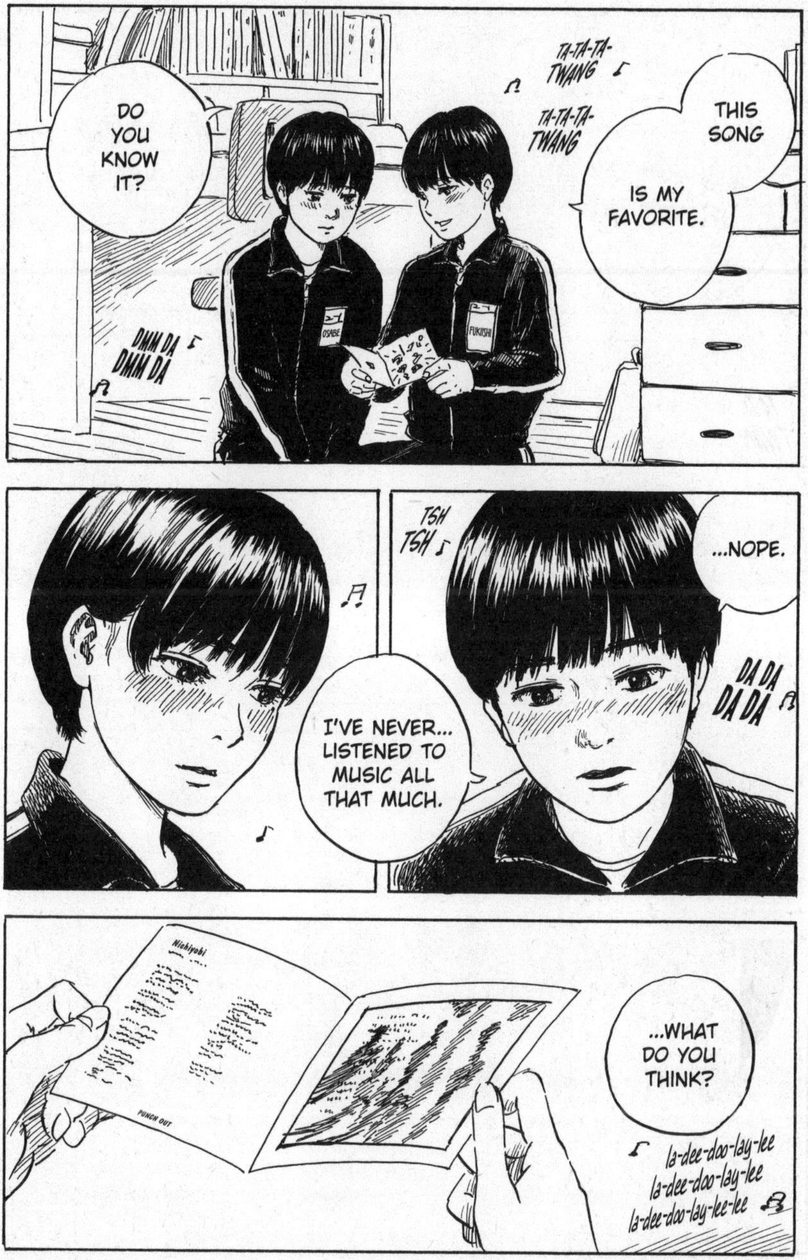
TA-TA-TA-TWANG
THIS SONG
IS MY FAVORITE.
TA-TA-TA-TWANG
DO YOU KNOW IT?
FUKIISHI
OSABE
DMM DA DMM DA
TSH TSH
...NOPE.
DA DA DA DA
I'VE NEVER... LISTENED TO MUSIC ALL THAT MUCH.
...WHAT DO YOU THINK?
la-dee-doo-lay-lee
la-dee-doo-lay-lee
la-dee-doo-lay-lee-lee
Nichiyobi
PUNCH OUT

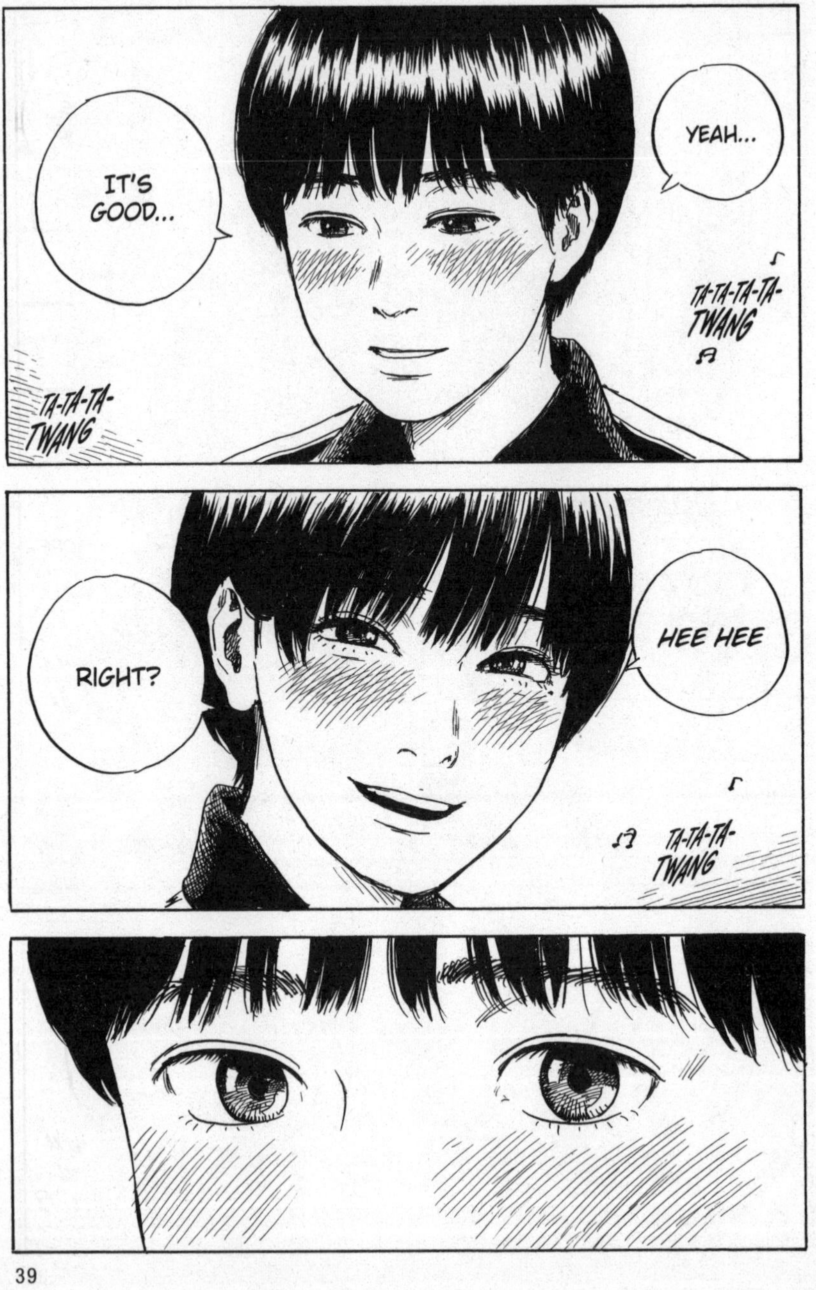
YEAH...
TA-TA-TA-TA-TWANG
IT'S GOOD...
TA-TA-TA-TWANG
HEE HEE
RIGHT?
TA-TA-TA-TWANG

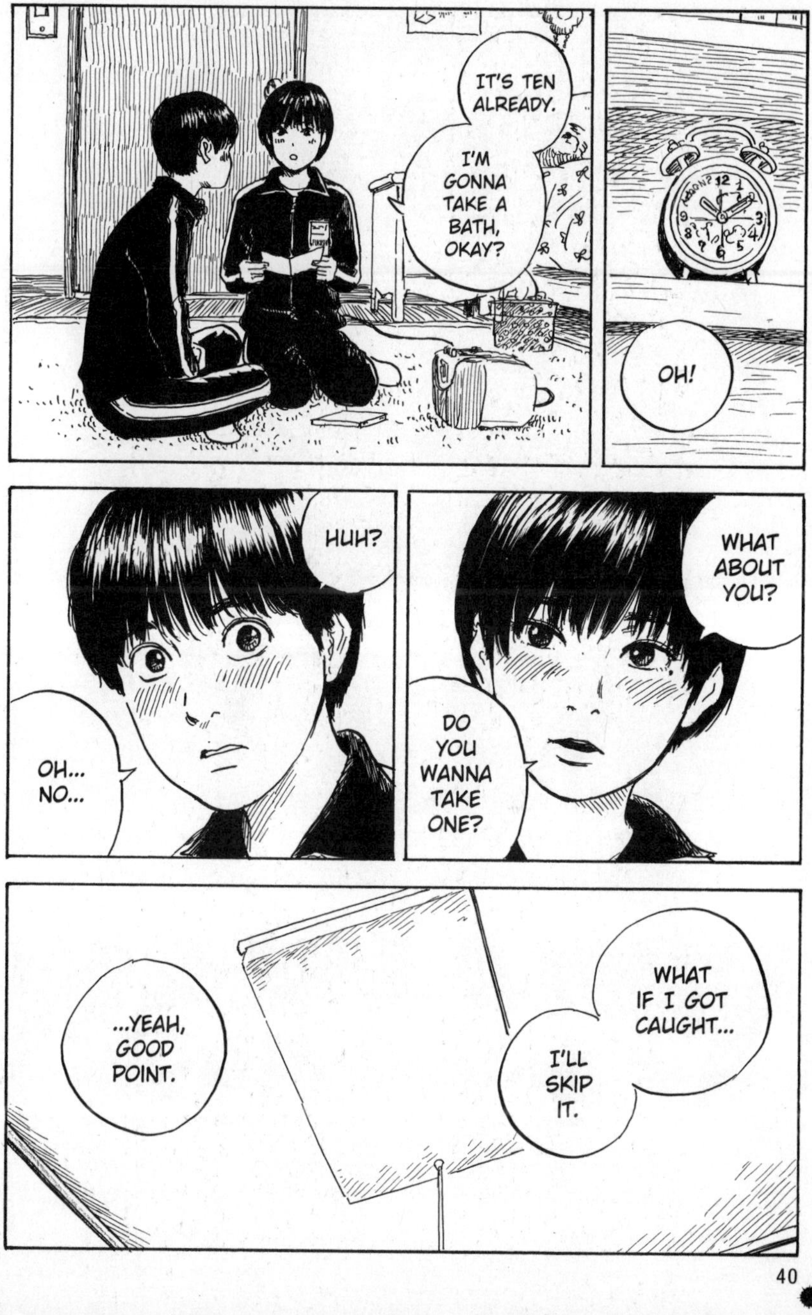
OH!
IT'S TEN ALREADY.
I'M GONNA TAKE A BATH, OKAY?
WHAT ABOUT YOU?
DO YOU WANNA TAKE ONE?
HUH?
OH... NO...
WHAT IF I GOT CAUGHT...
I'LL SKIP IT.
...YEAH, GOOD POINT.

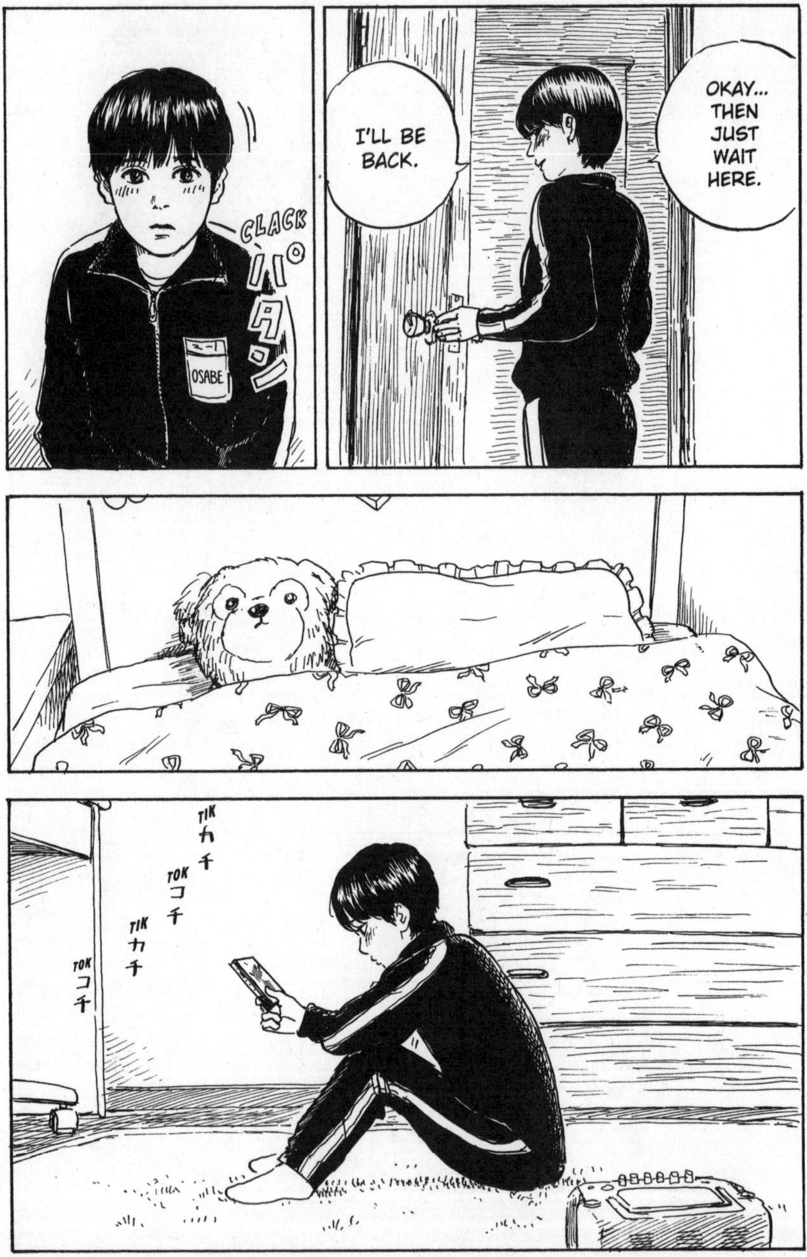
OKAY... THEN JUST WAIT HERE.
I'LL BE BACK.
CLACK
パタン
TIK カチ
TOK コチ
TIK カチ
TOK コチ

TIK
カチ
TOK
コチ
TIK
カチ
TOK
コチ
Jitterin' Jinn PUNCH OUT
シャラ
SWISH

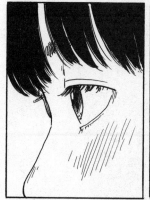

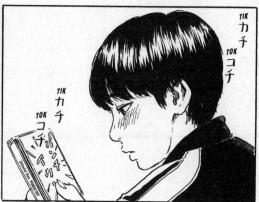

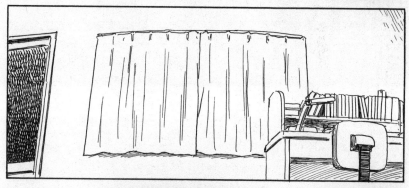

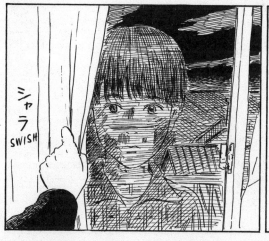

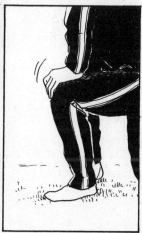

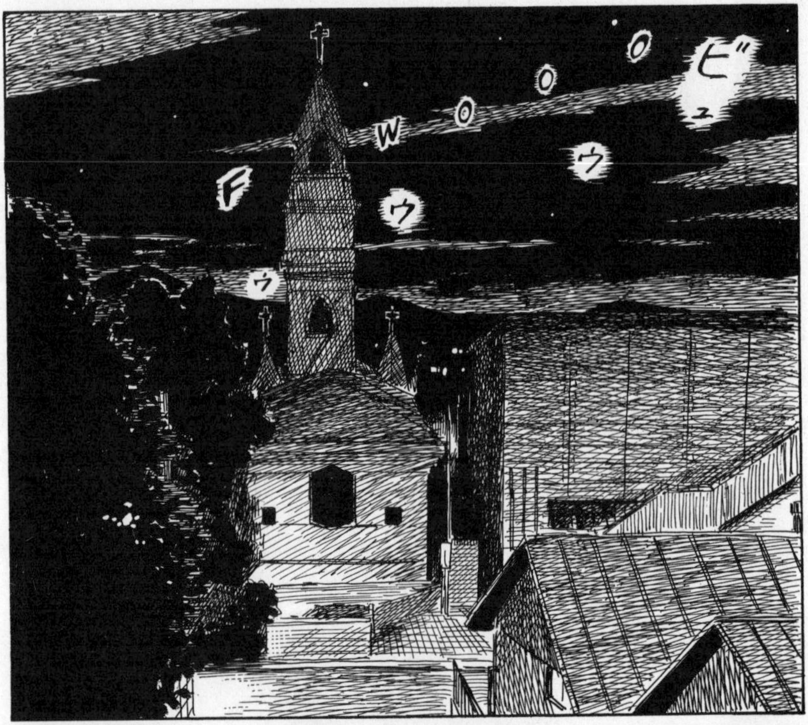
ビュ
FWOOO
ウウウ

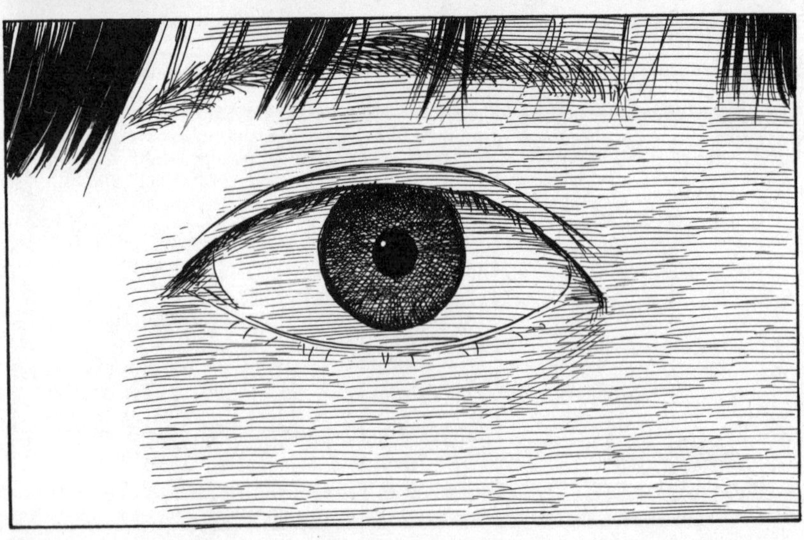

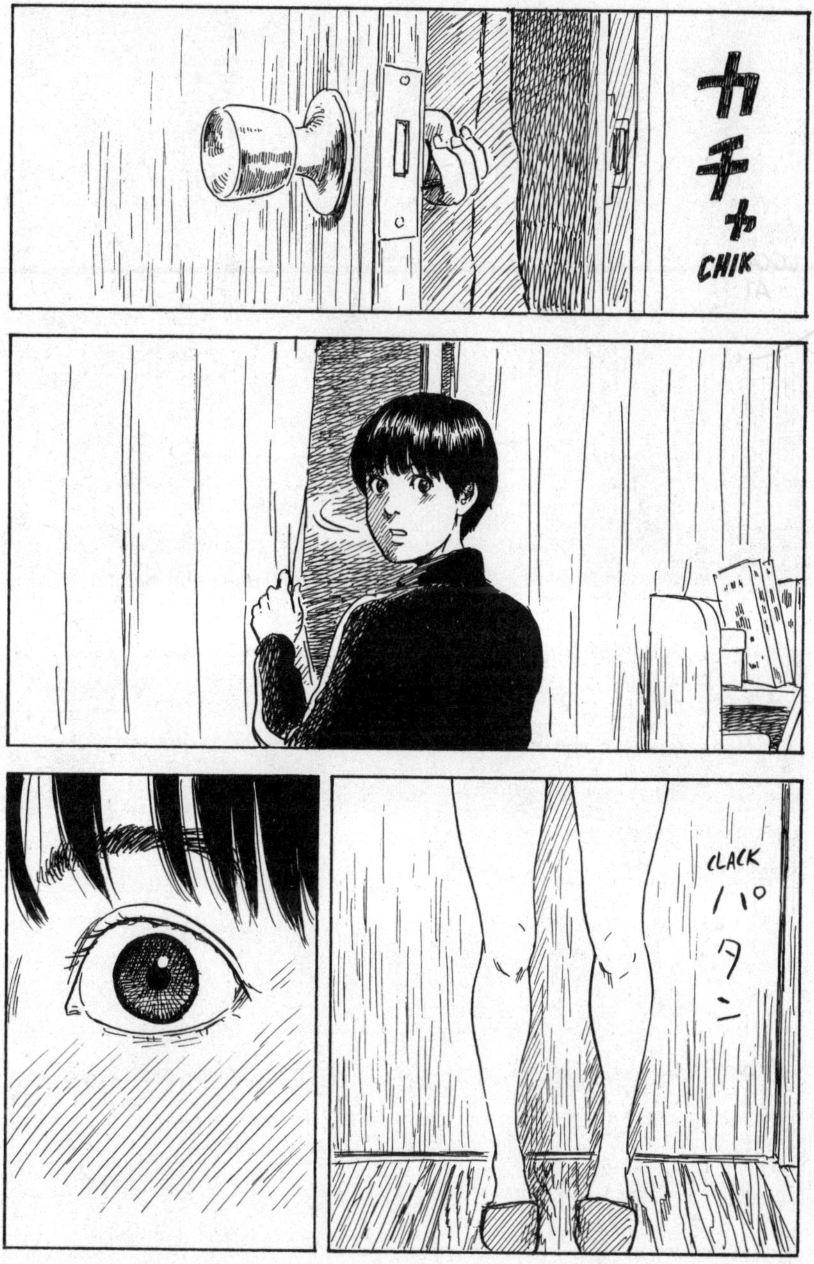
カチャ
CHIK
CLACK
パタン

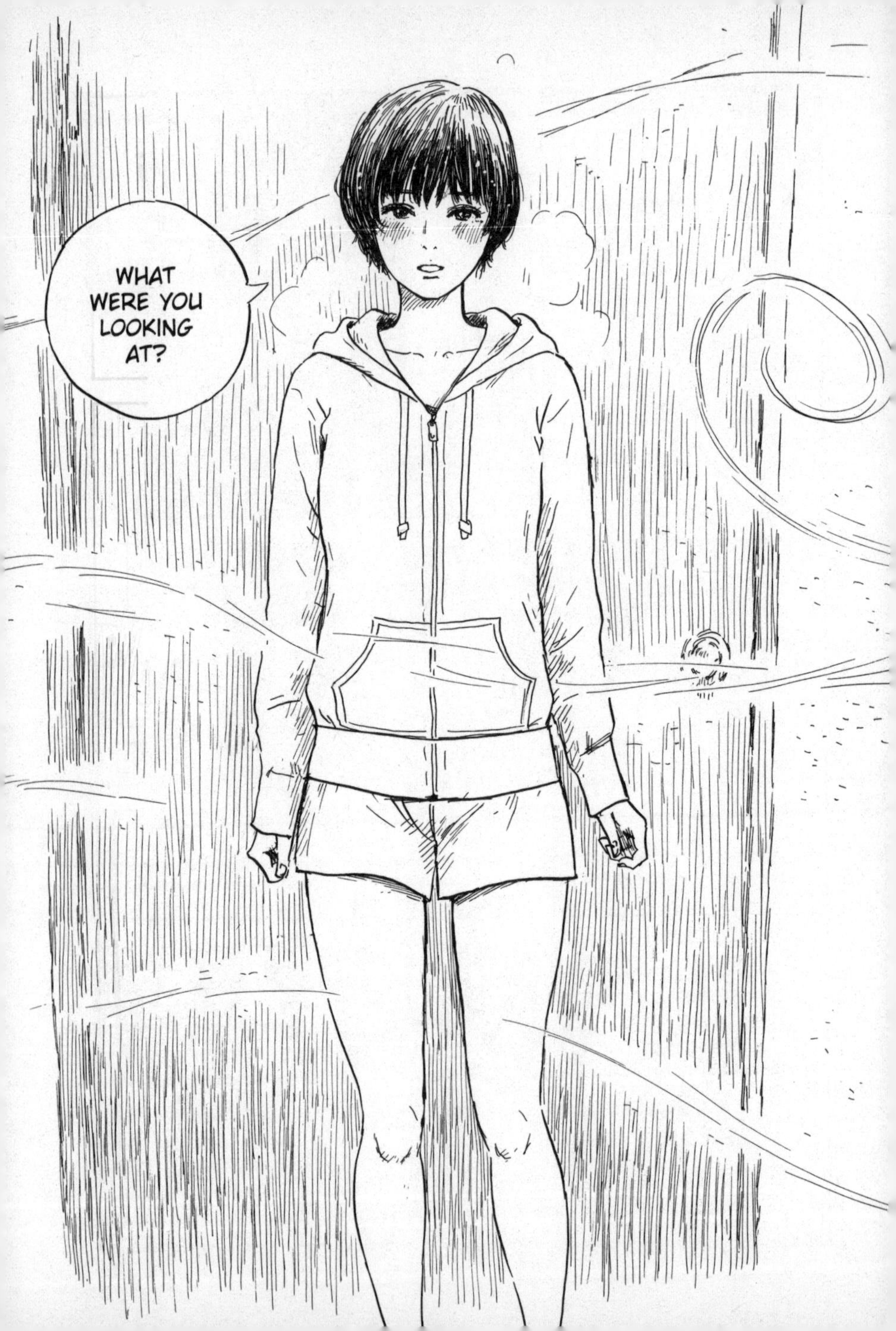
WHAT WERE YOU LOOKING AT?

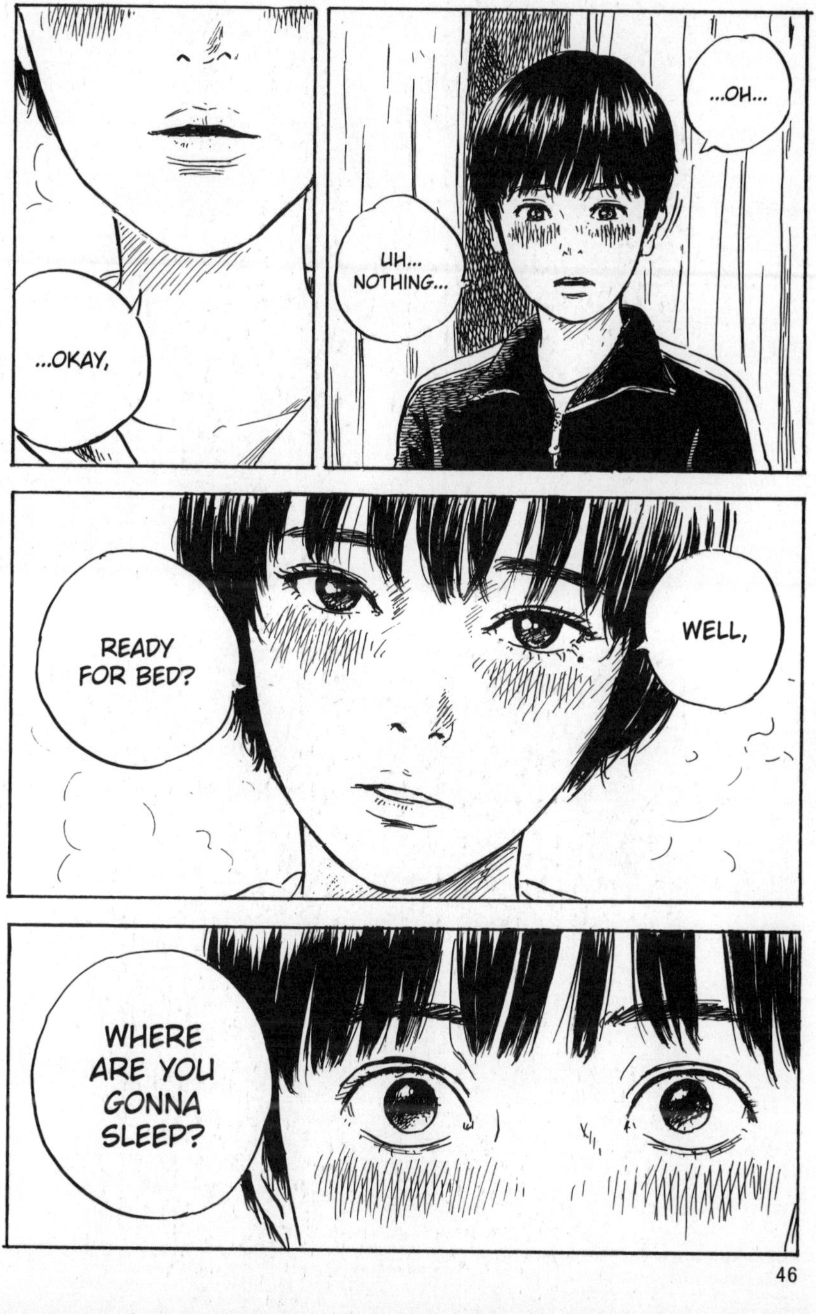
...OH...
UH... NOTHING...
...OKAY,
WELL,
READY FOR BED?
WHERE ARE YOU GONNA SLEEP?

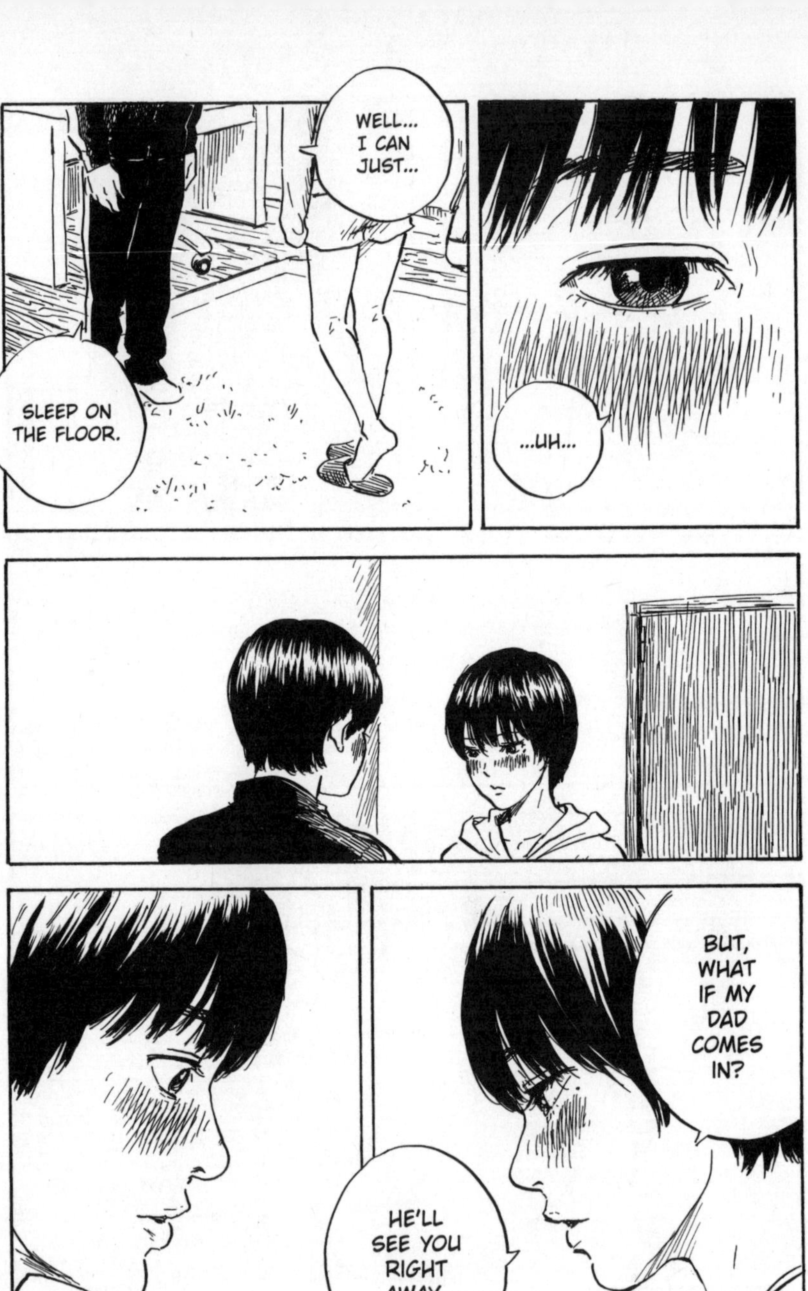
...UH...
WELL... I CAN JUST...
SLEEP ON THE FLOOR.
BUT, WHAT IF MY DAD COMES IN?
HE'LL SEE YOU RIGHT AWAY...

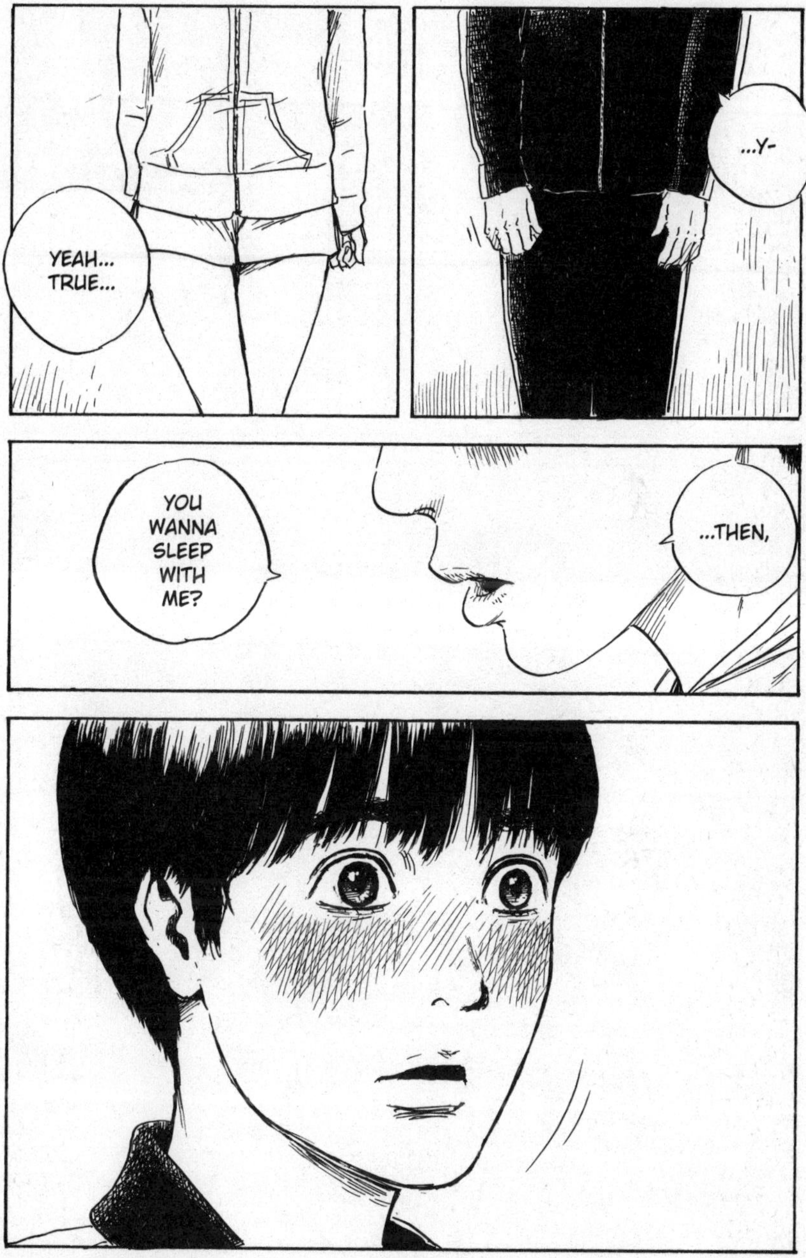
...Y-
YEAH... TRUE...
...THEN,
YOU WANNA SLEEP WITH ME?

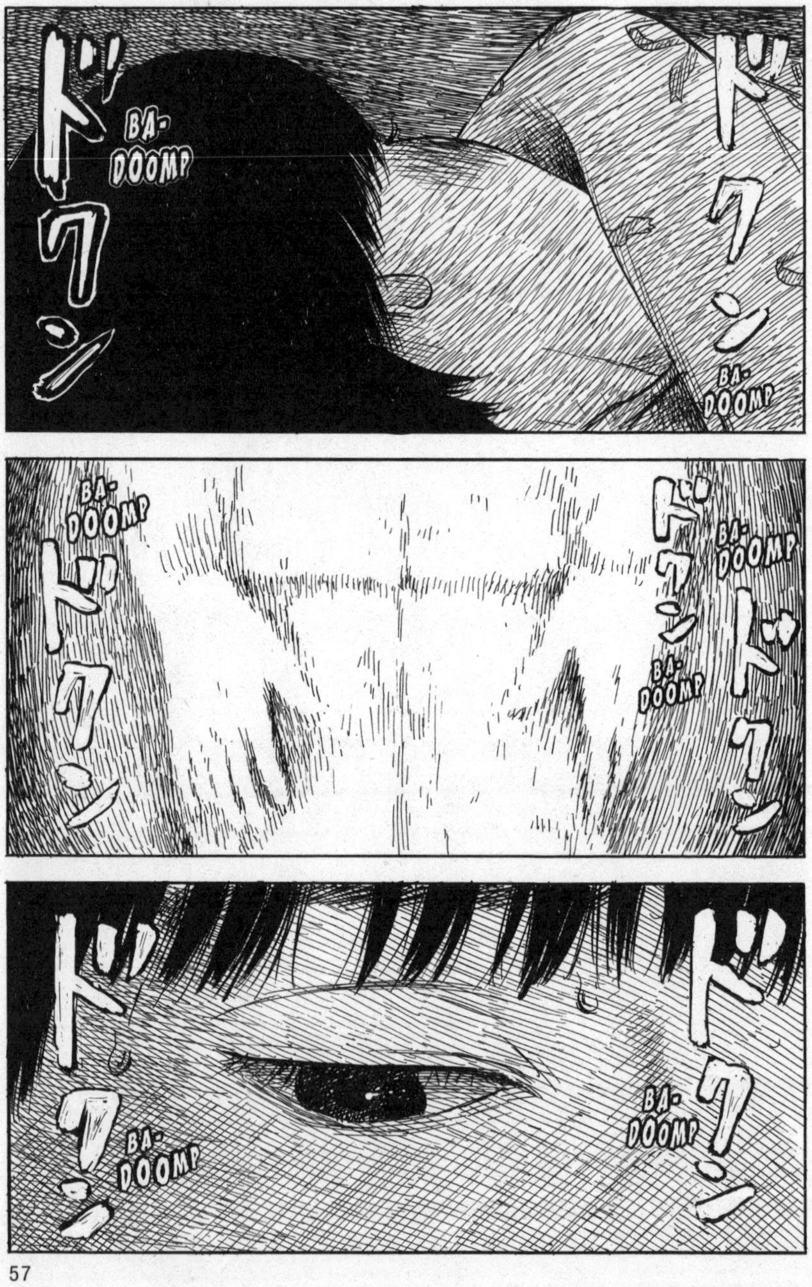
ドクン
BA-DOOMP
ドクン
BA-DOOMP
ドクン
BA-DOOMP
ドクン
BA-DOOMP
BA-DOOMP
ドクン
ドクン
BA-DOOMP
BA-DOOMP
ドクン

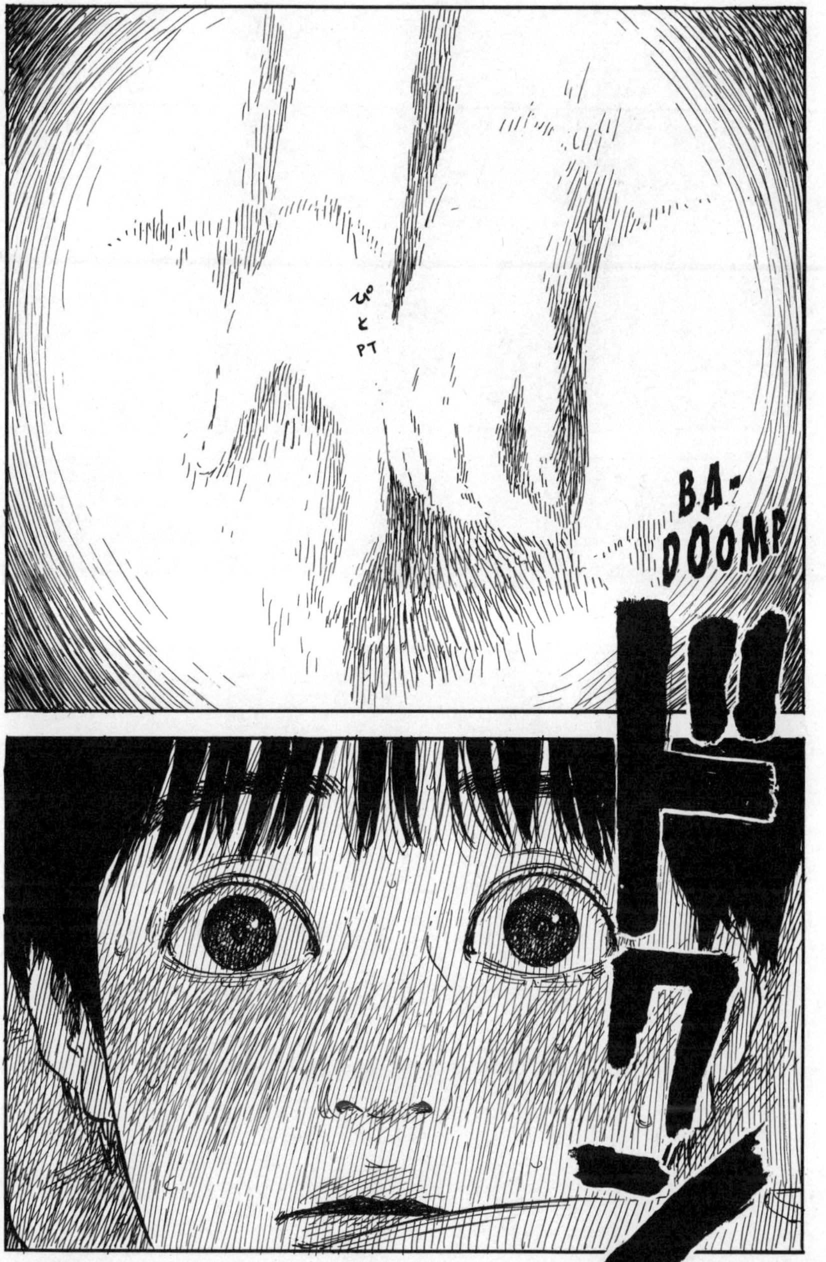
ぴと
PT
BA-DOOMP
ドクン

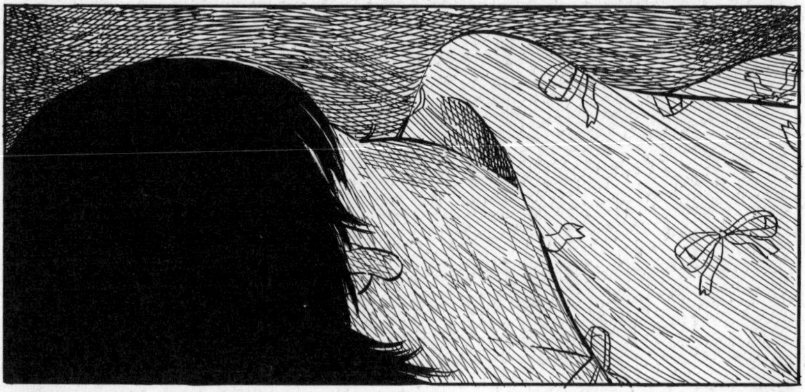

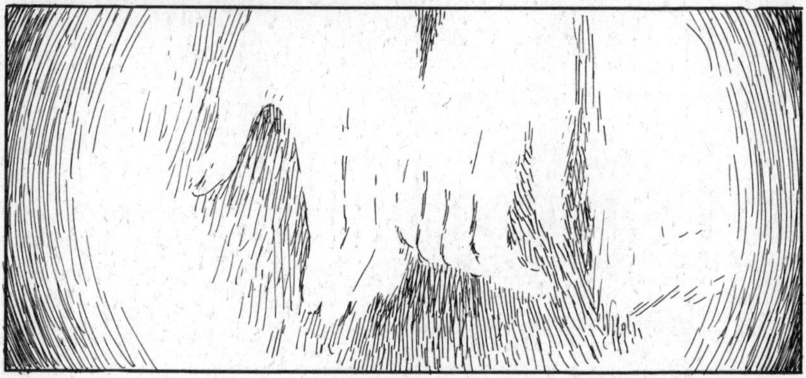

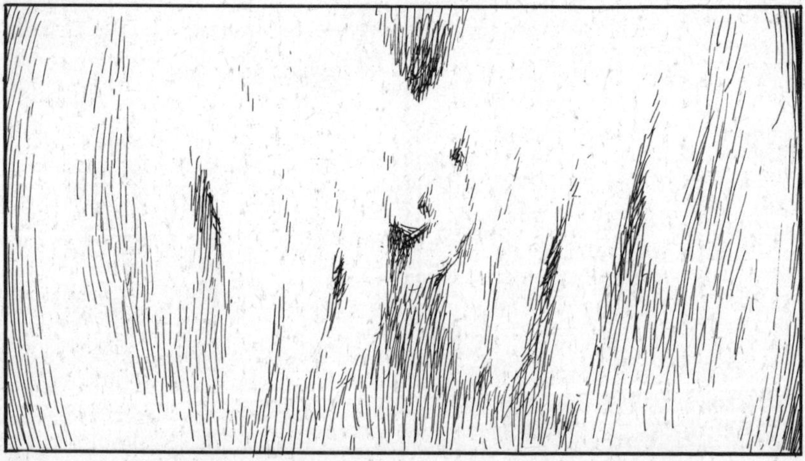

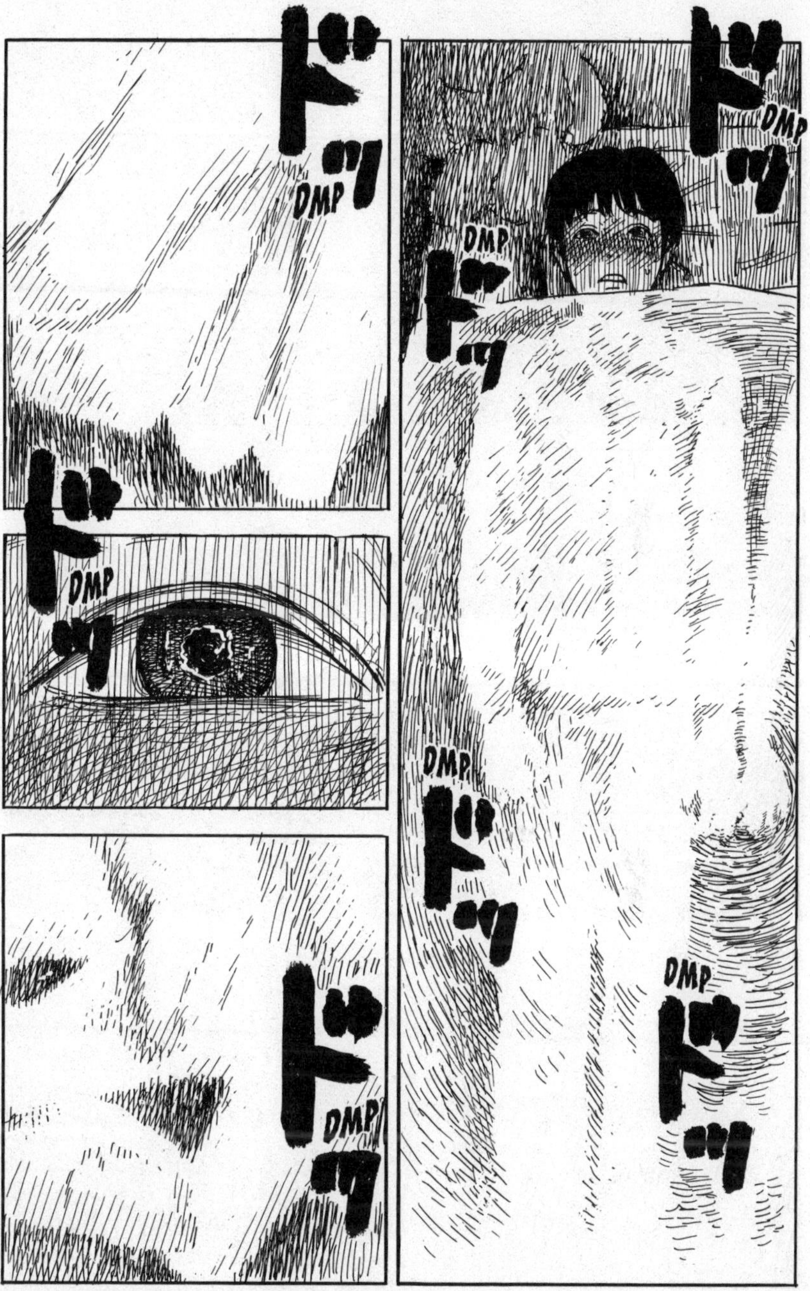
ドッ
DMP
DMP
ドッ
DMP
ドッ
DMP
ドッ
ドッ
DMP
ドッ
DMP
ドッ
DMP

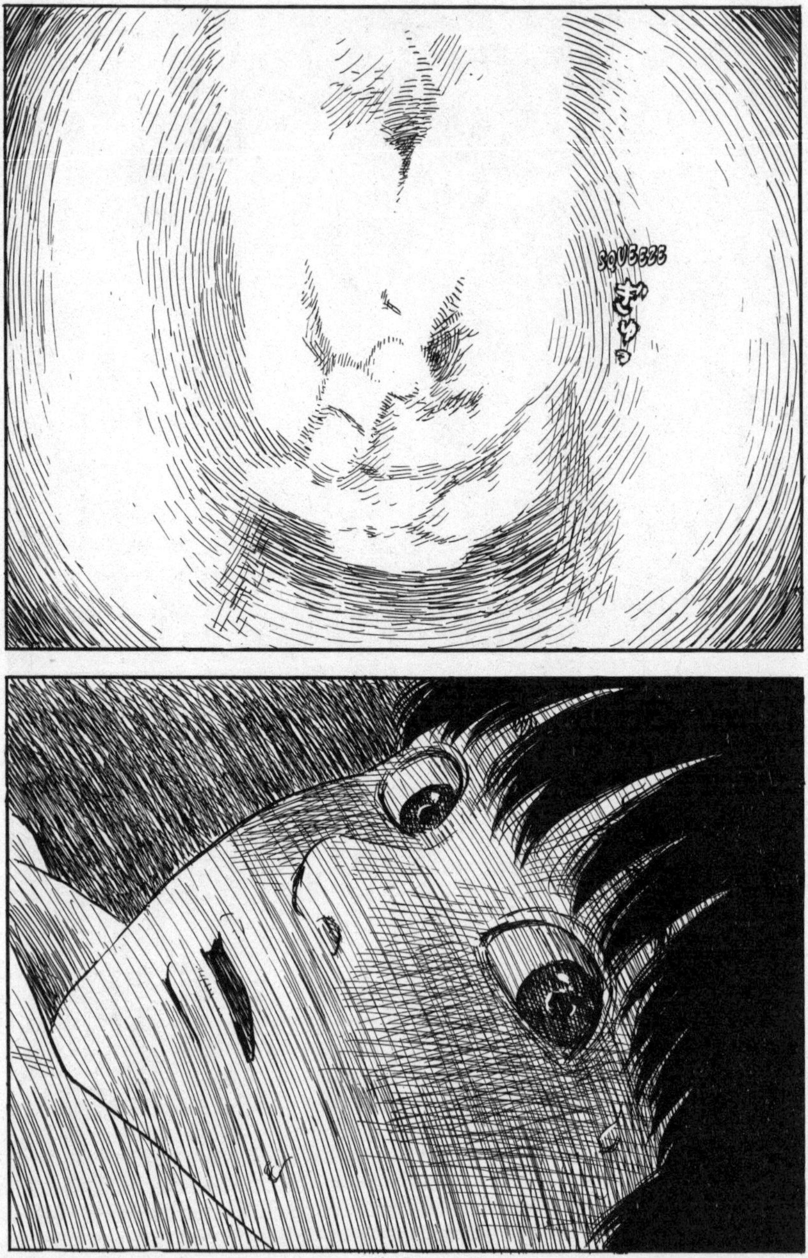
SQUEEZE
ぎゅっ

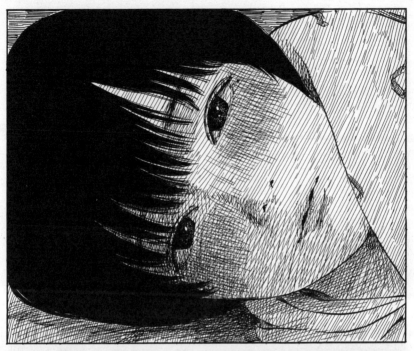

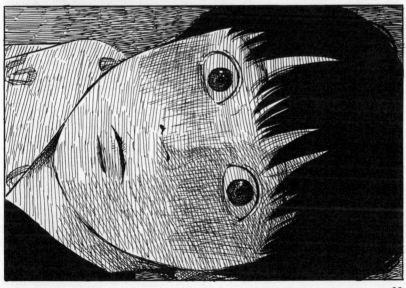

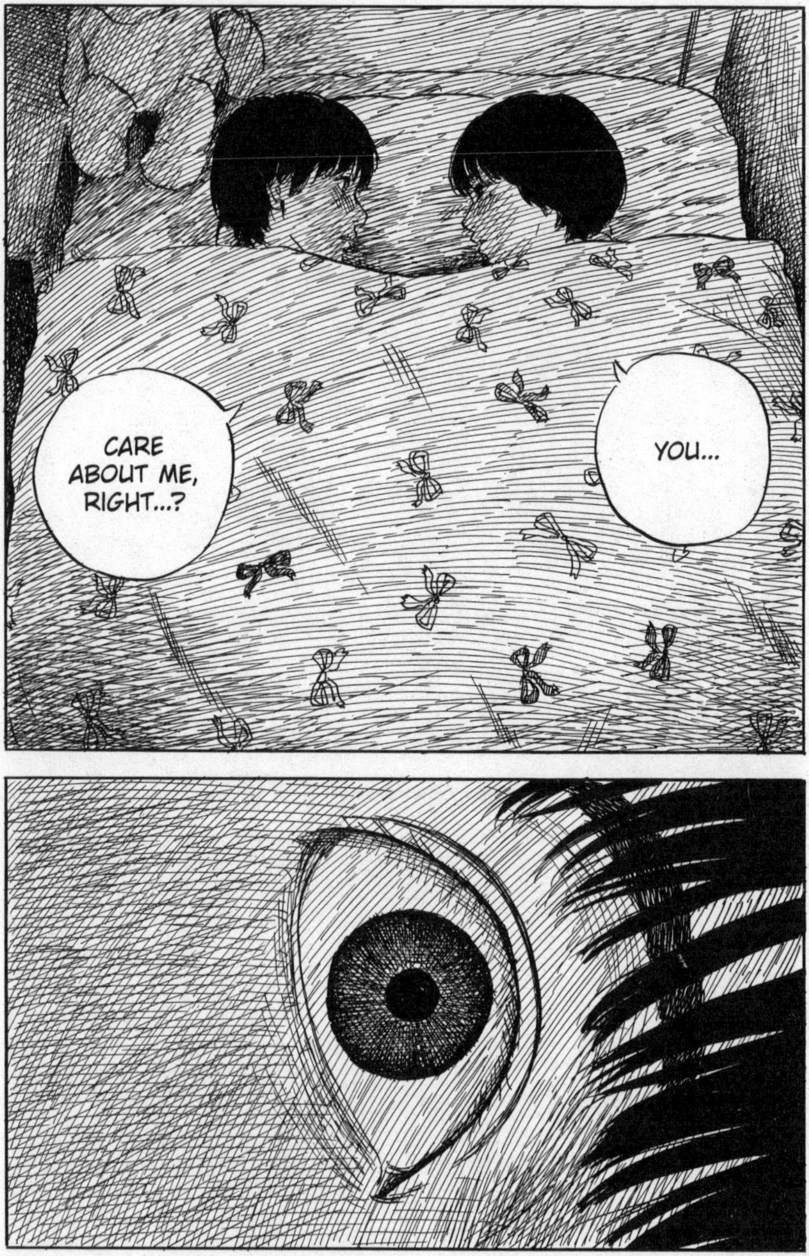
YOU...
CARE ABOUT ME, RIGHT...?

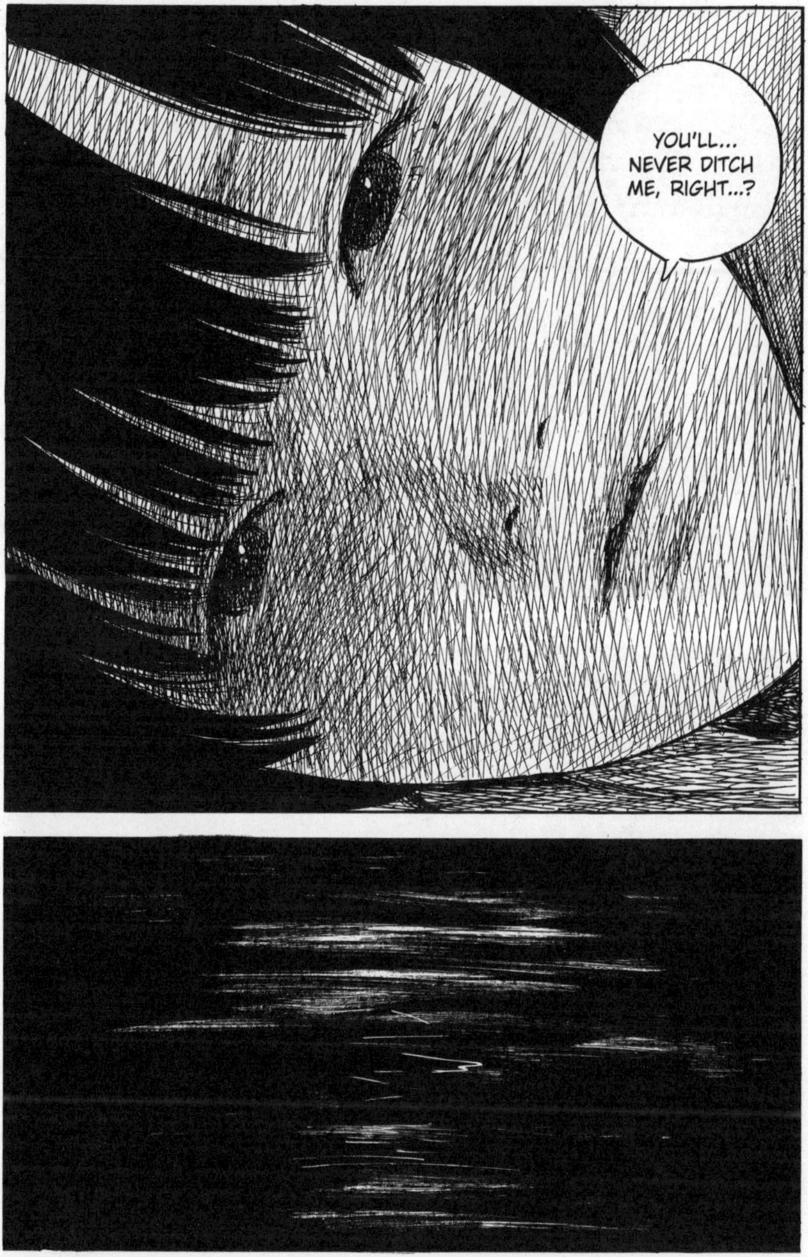
YOU'LL... NEVER DITCH ME, RIGHT...?

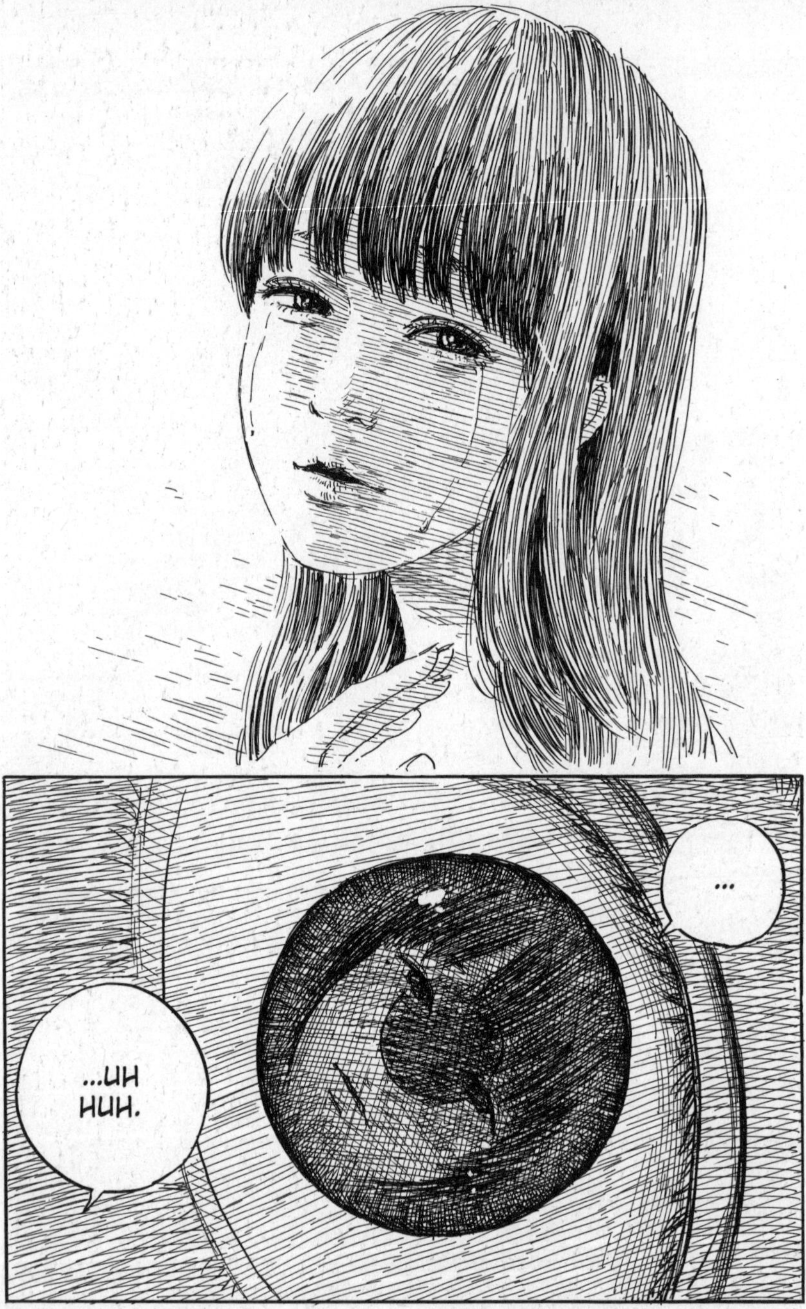
...
...UH HUH.

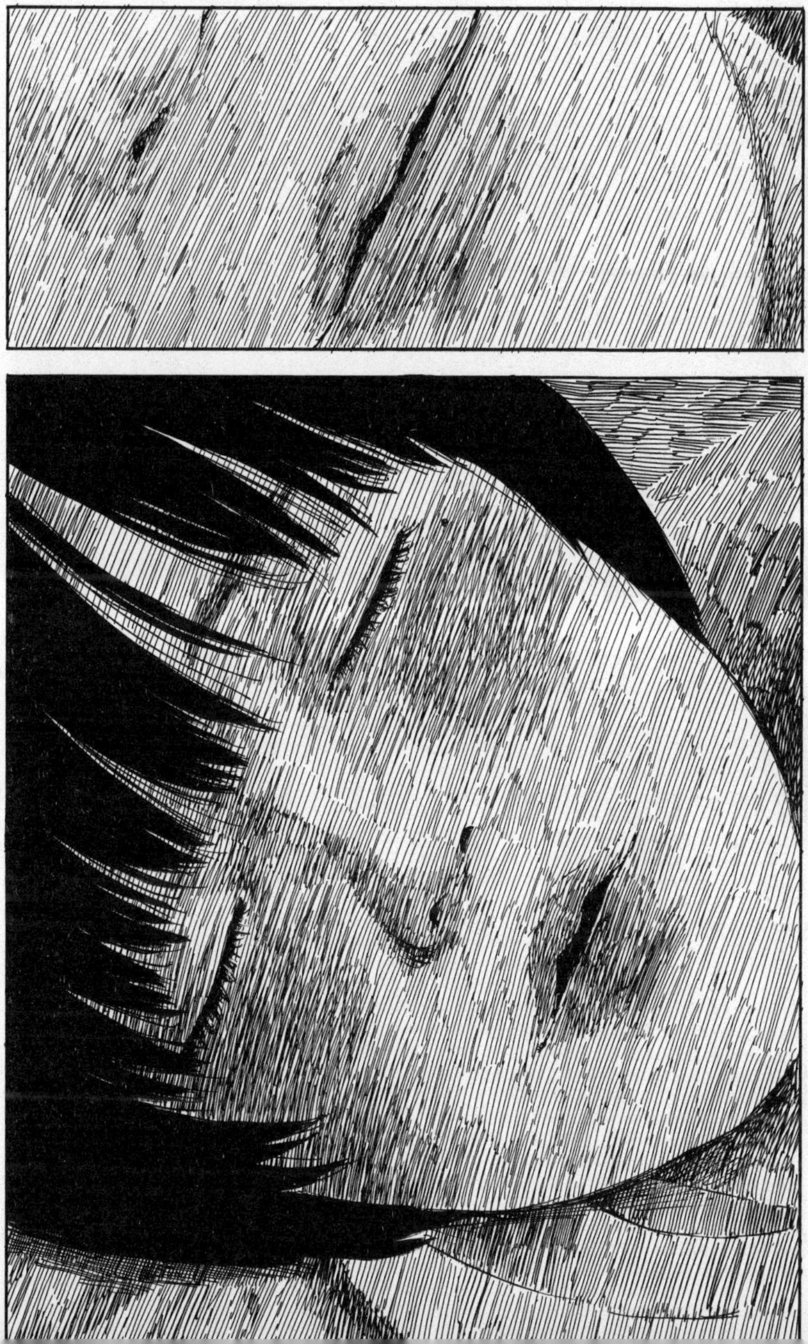

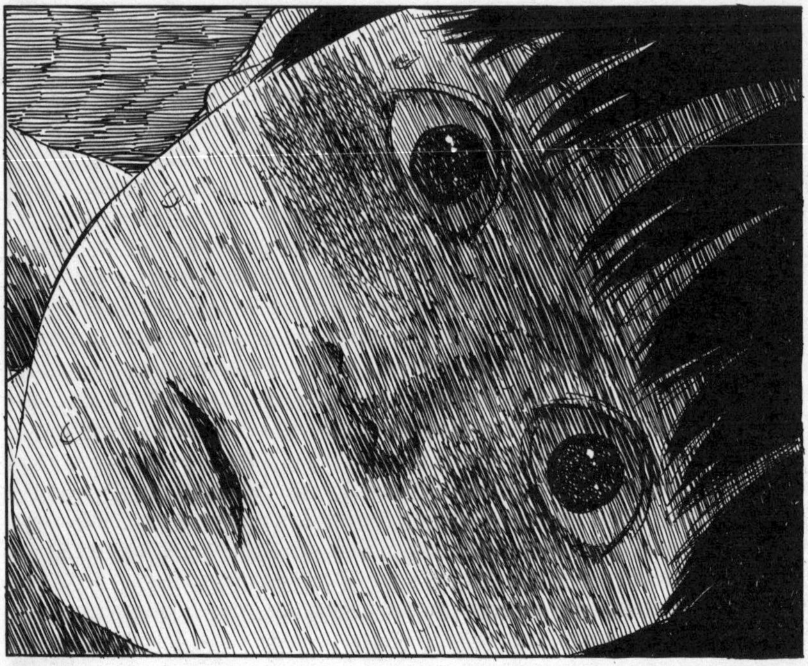

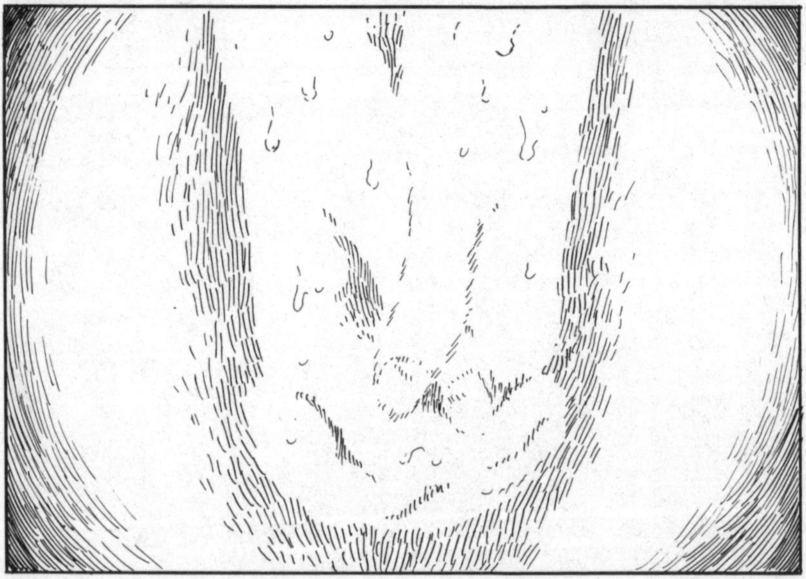

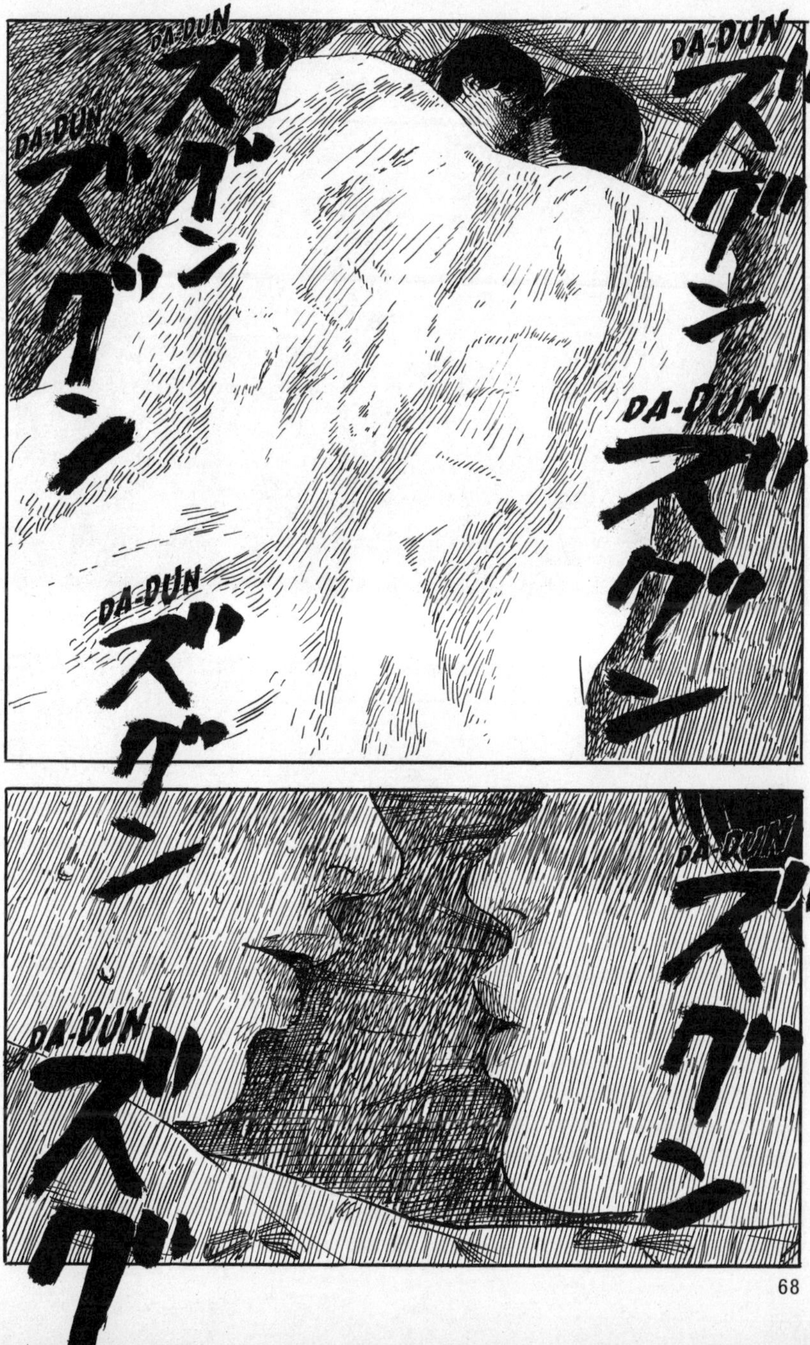
DA-DUN
ズグン
DA-DUN
ズグン
DA-DUN
ズグン
DA-DUN
ズグン
DA-DUN
ズグン
DA-DUN
ズグン
DA-DUN
ズグ

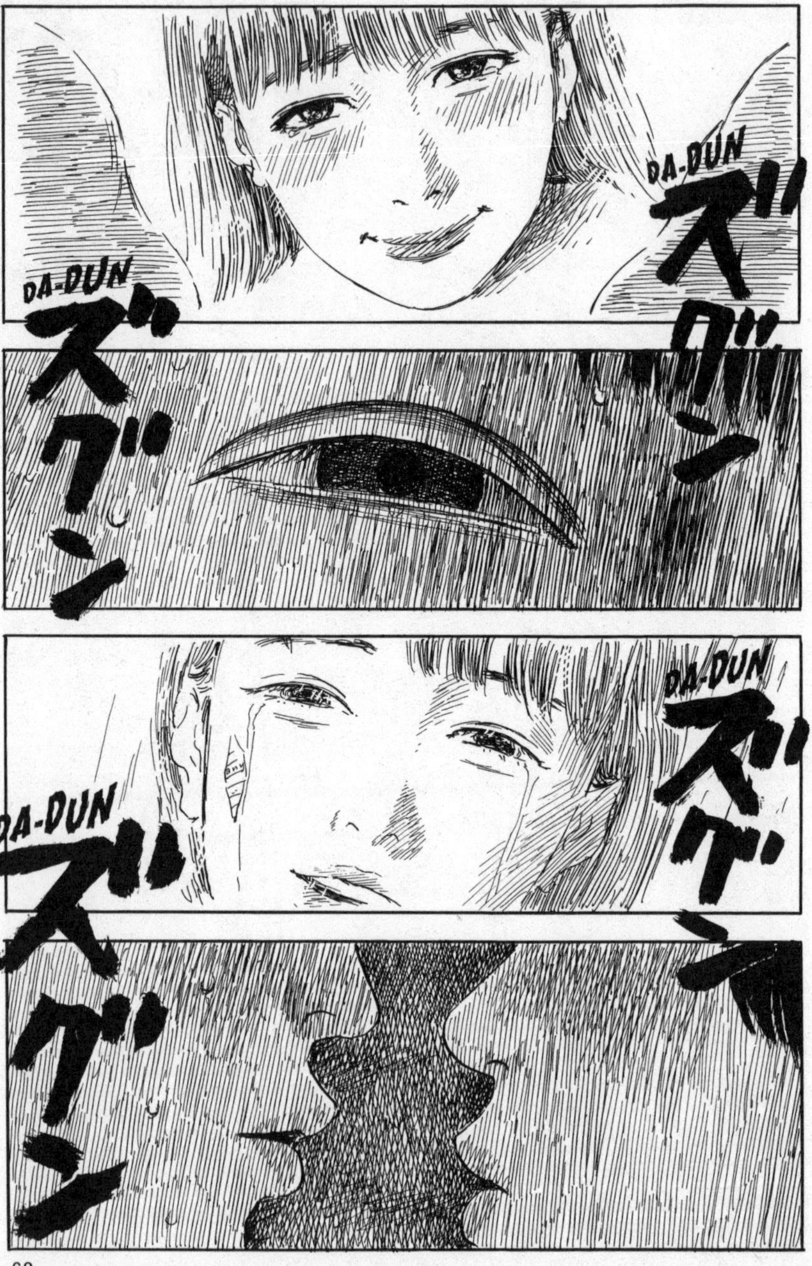
DA-DUN
ズグン
DA-DUN
ズグン
DA-DUN
ズグン
DA-DUN
ズグン

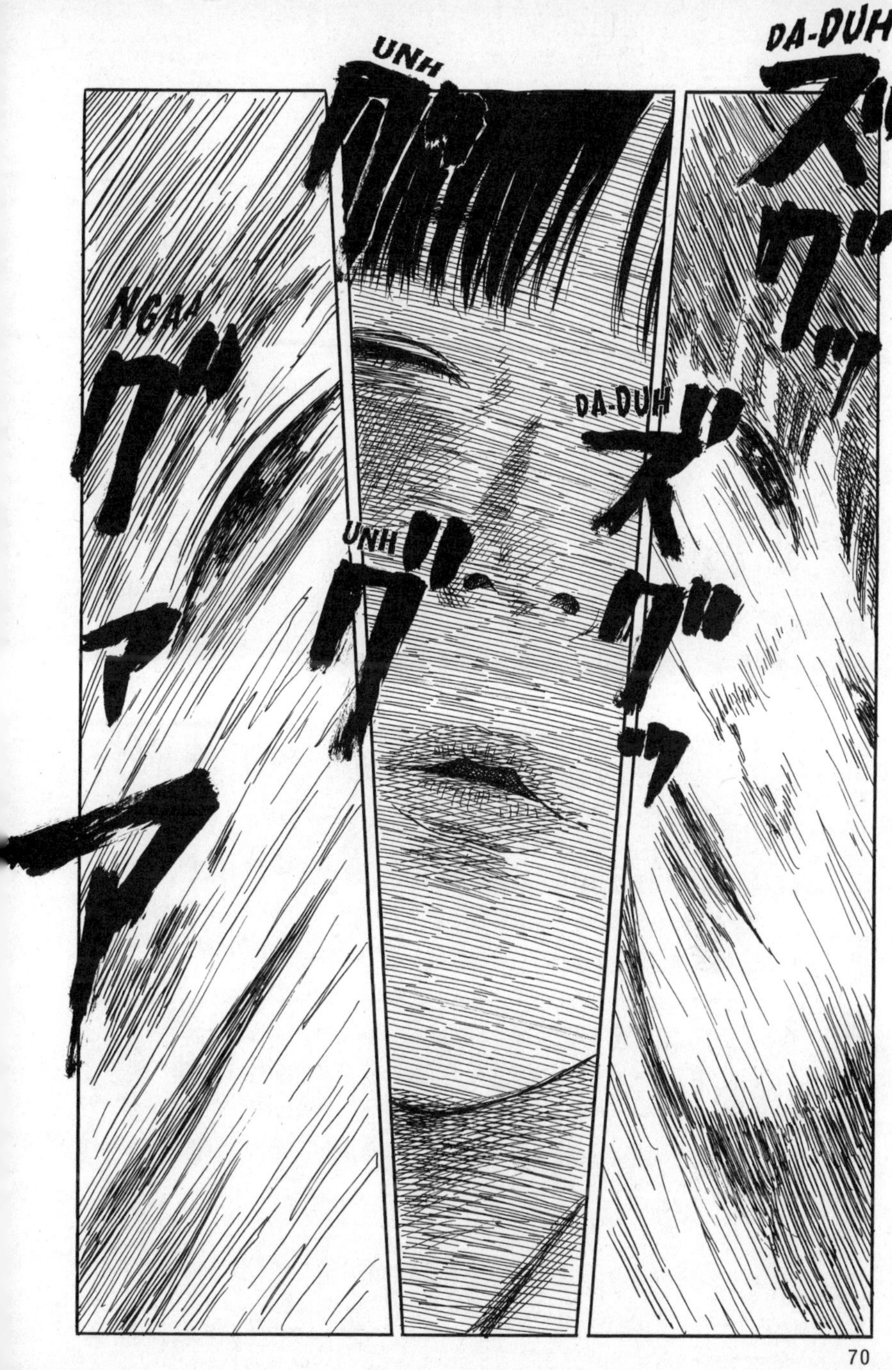
DA-DUH
DA-DUH
UNH
UNH
NGAA

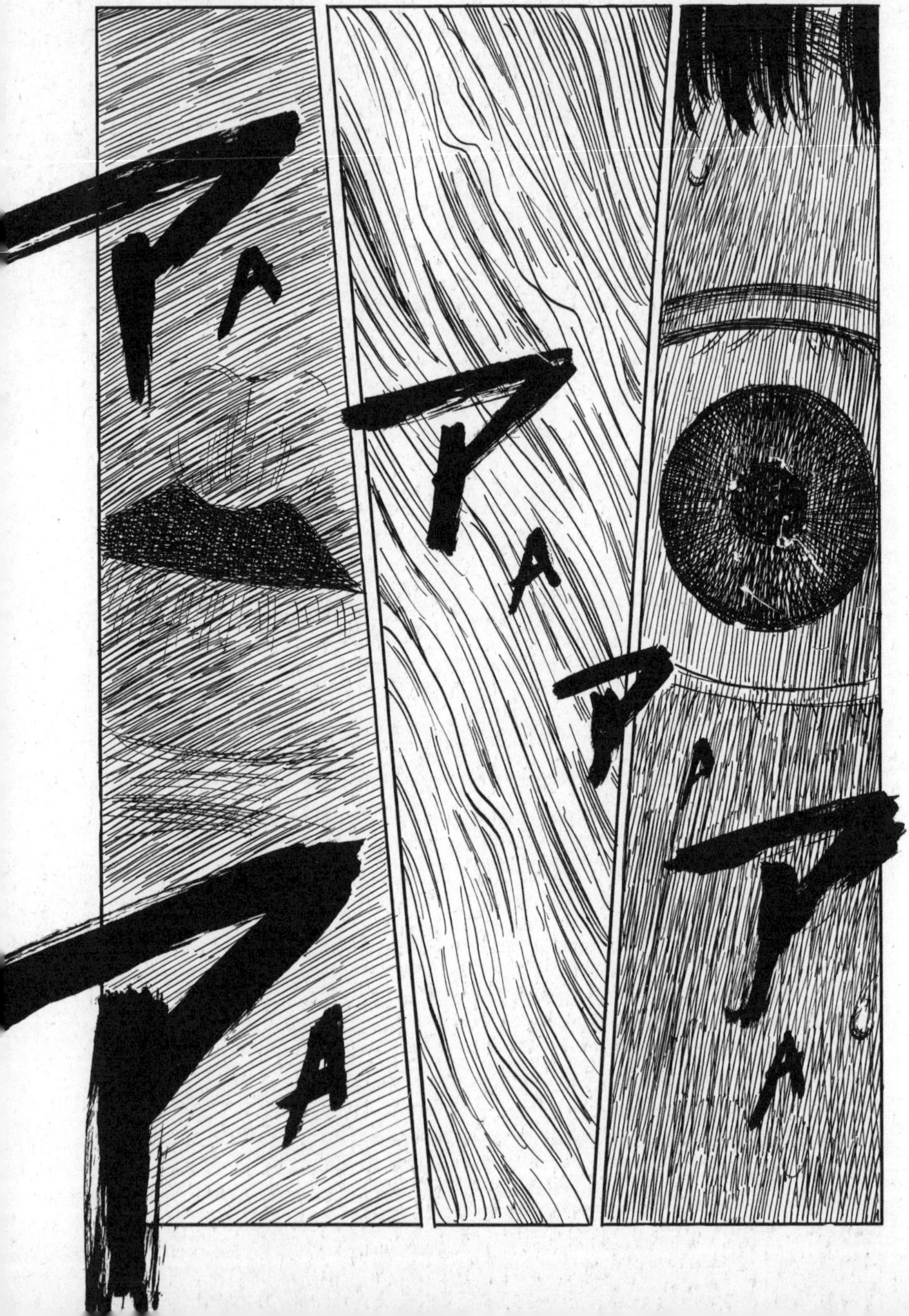
AA
AA
AA
AA
AA

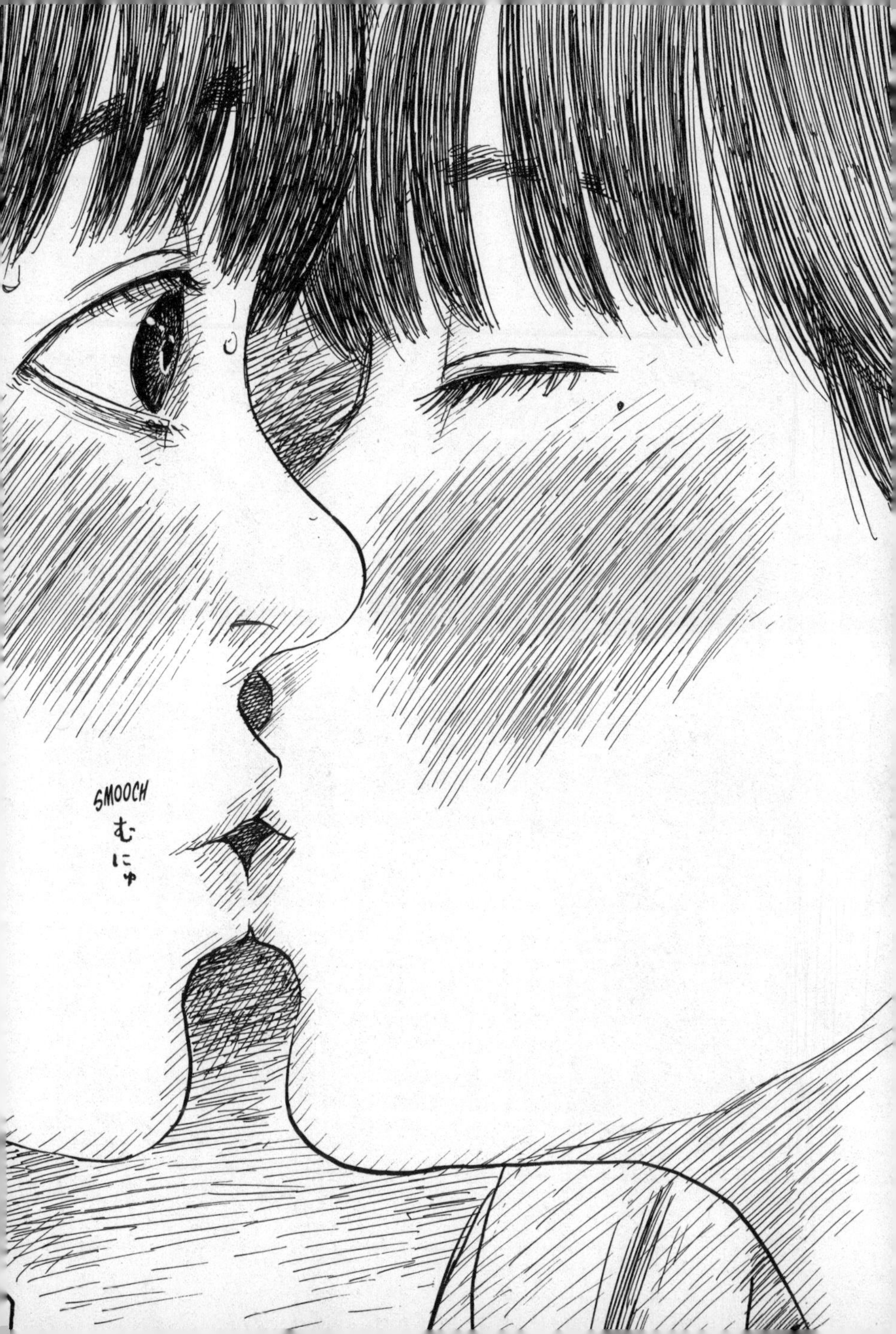
SMOOCH
むにゅ

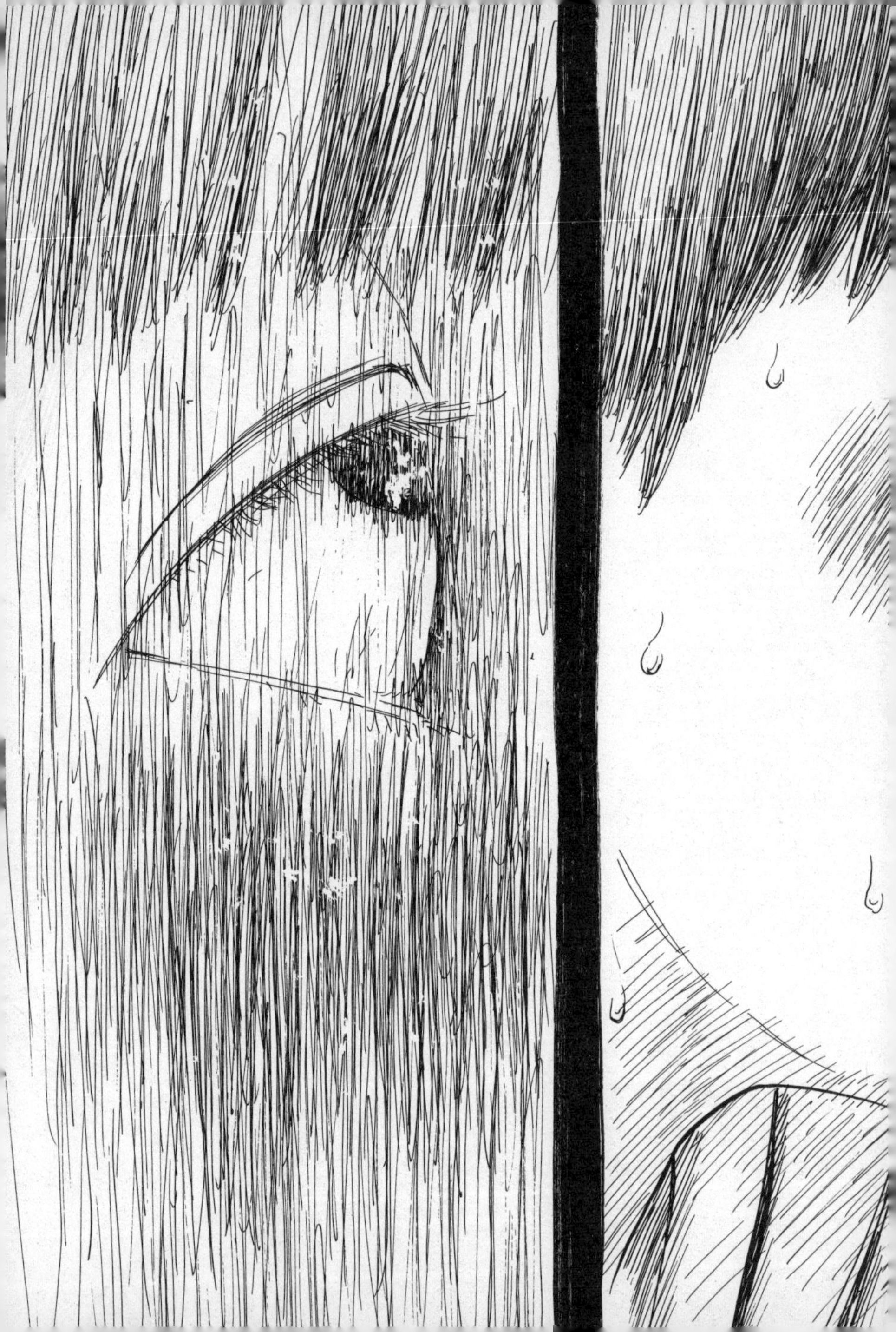

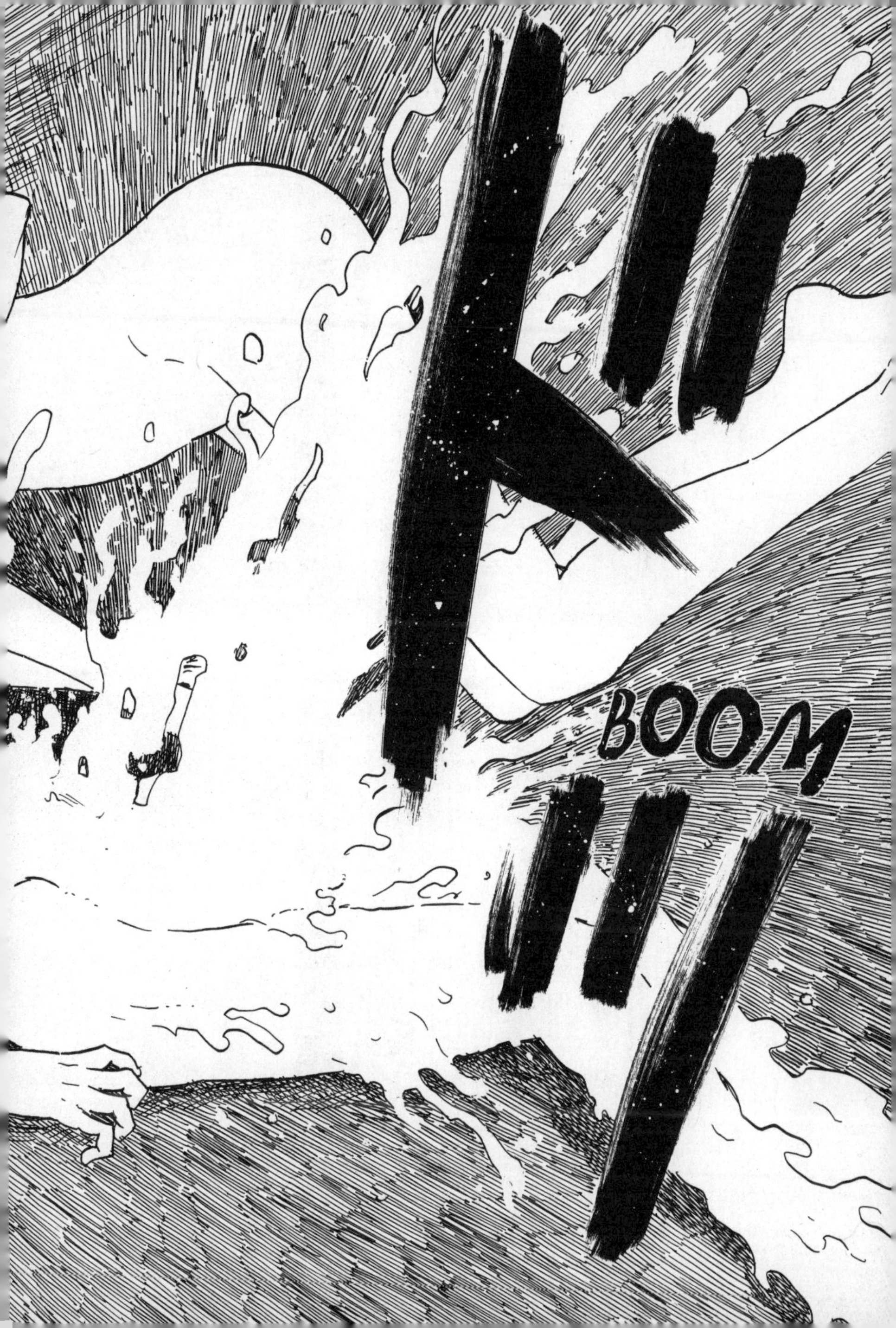
BOOM

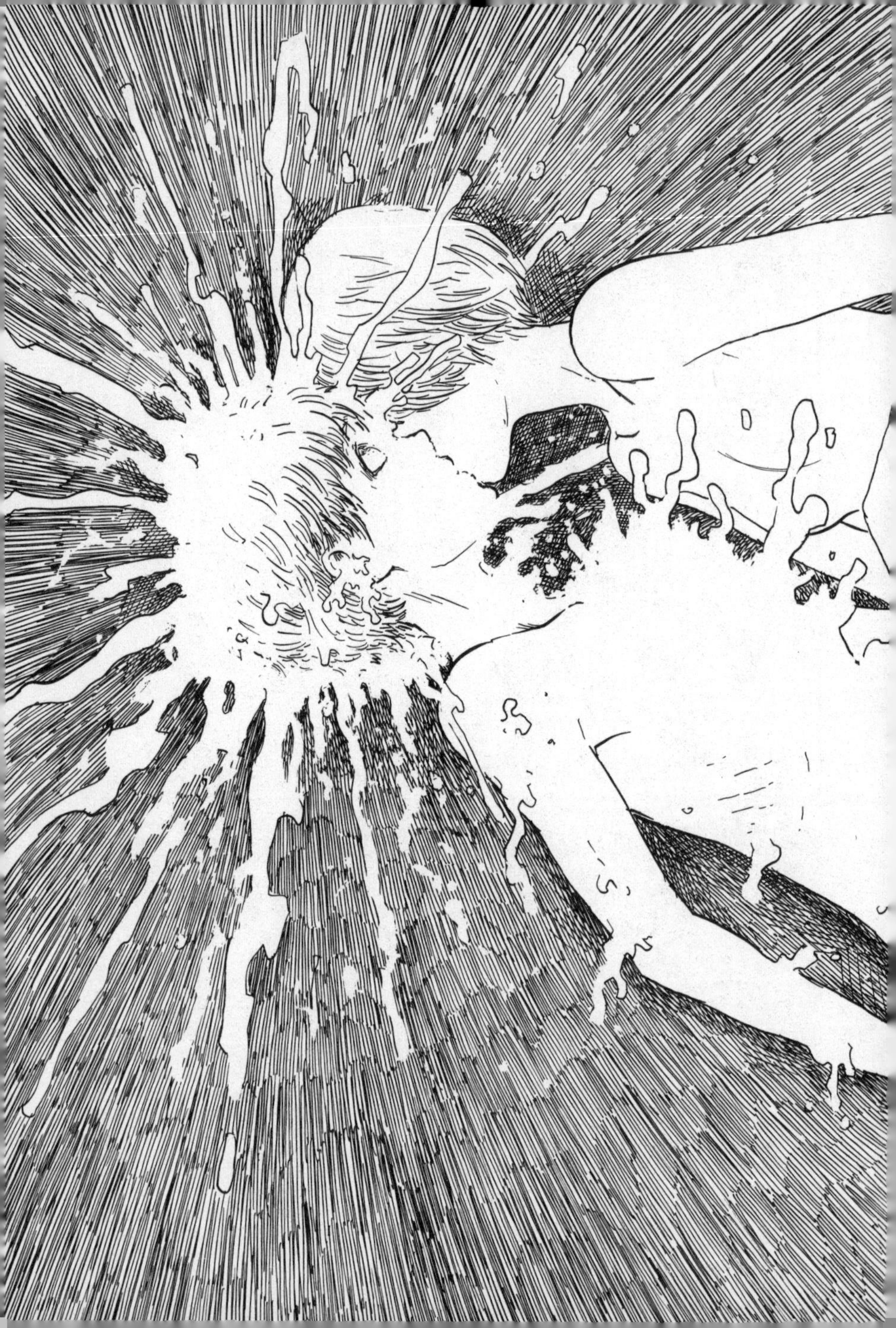

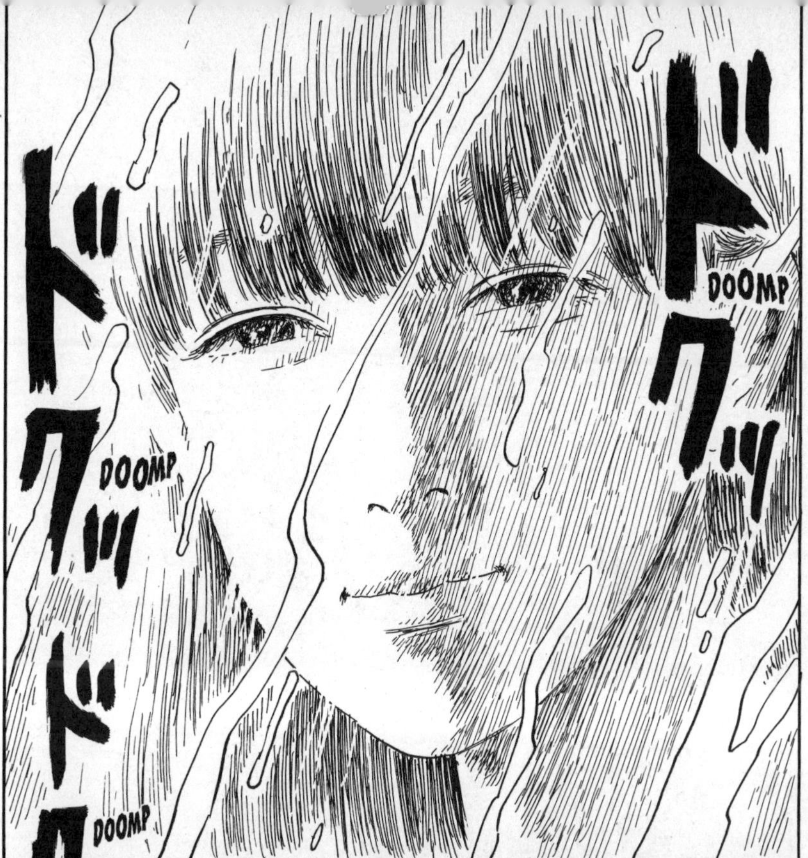
ドクッ
DOOMP
ドクッ
DOOMP
ドクッ
DOOMP

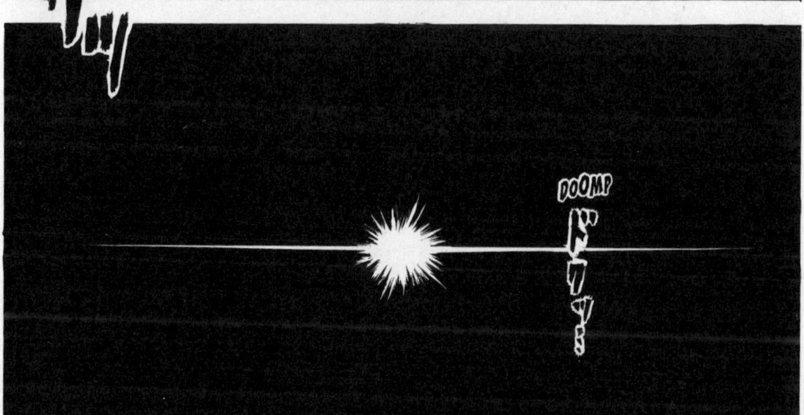
DOOMP
ドクッ

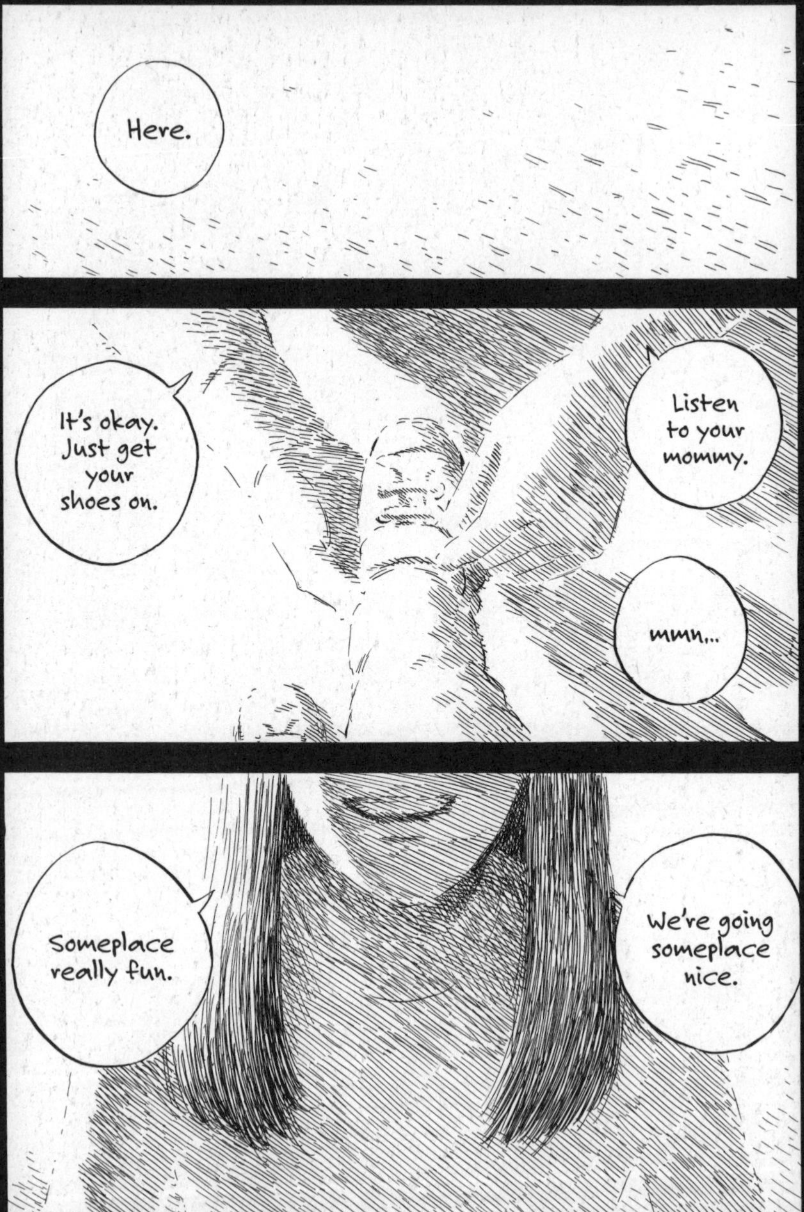
Here.
Listen to your mommy.
mmn...
It's okay. Just get your shoes on.
We're going someplace nice.
Someplace really fun.

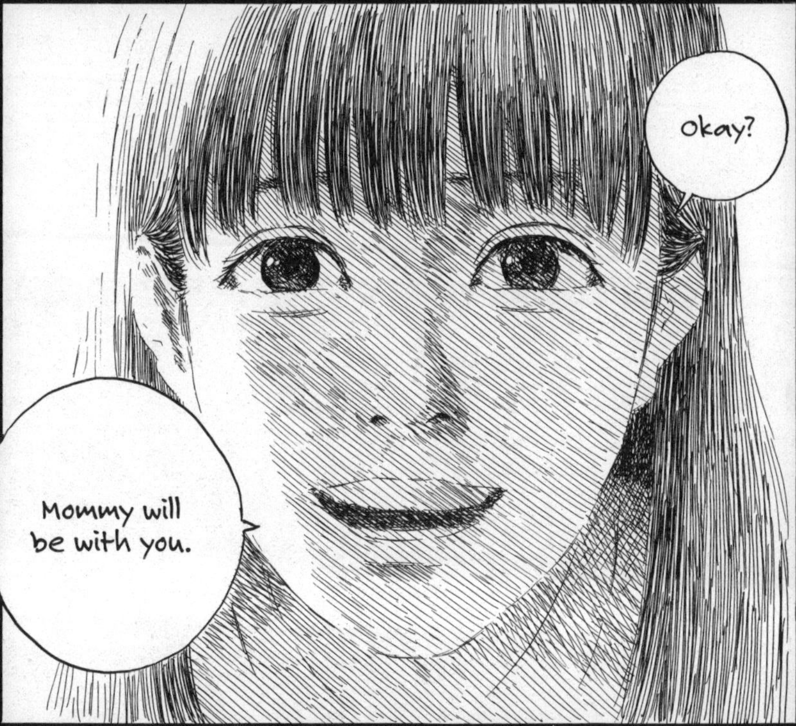
Okay?
Mommy will be with you.

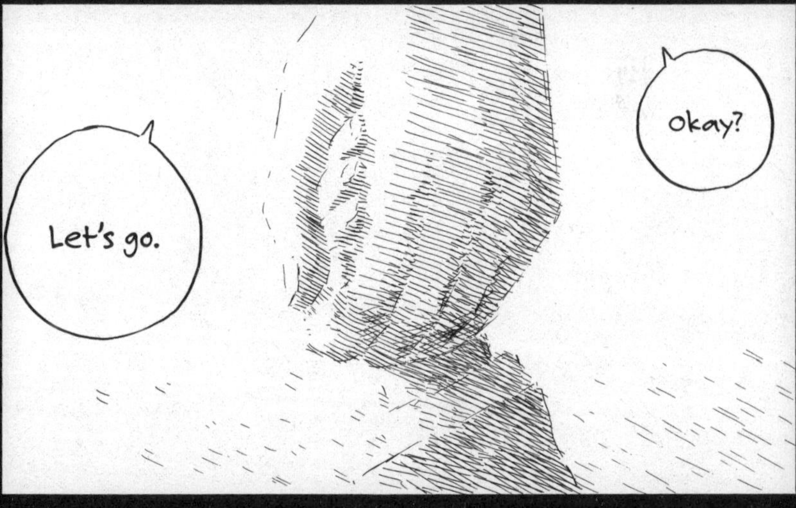
Okay?
Let's go.

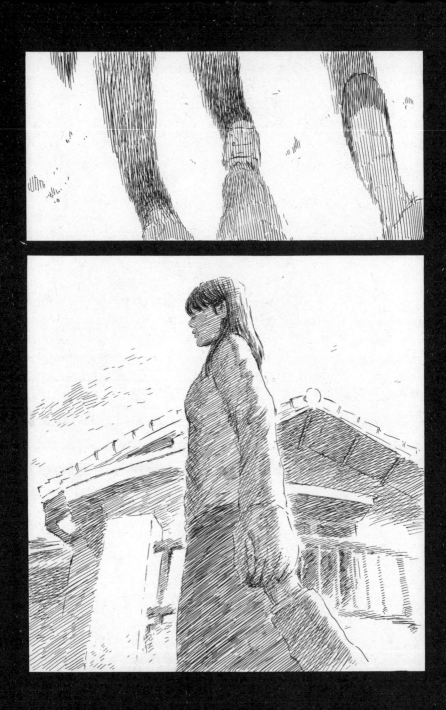

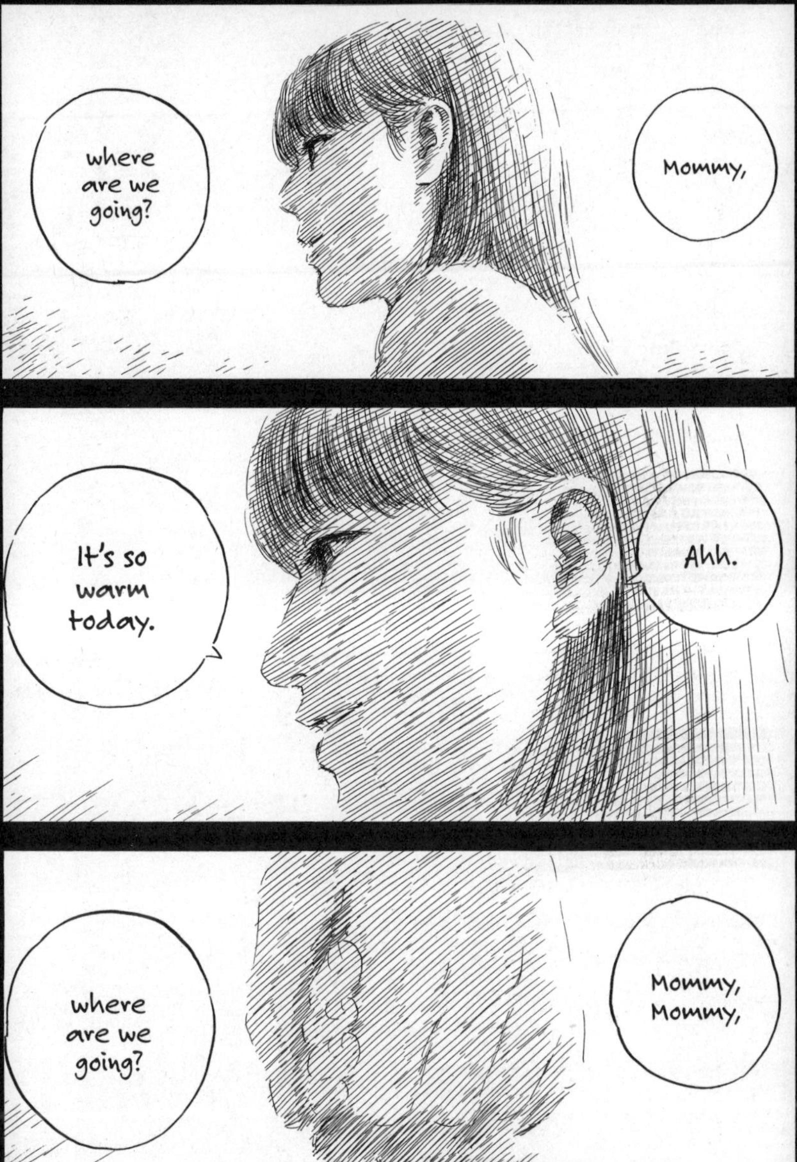
Mommy,
where are we going?
Ahh.
It's so warm today.
Mommy, Mommy,
where are we going?

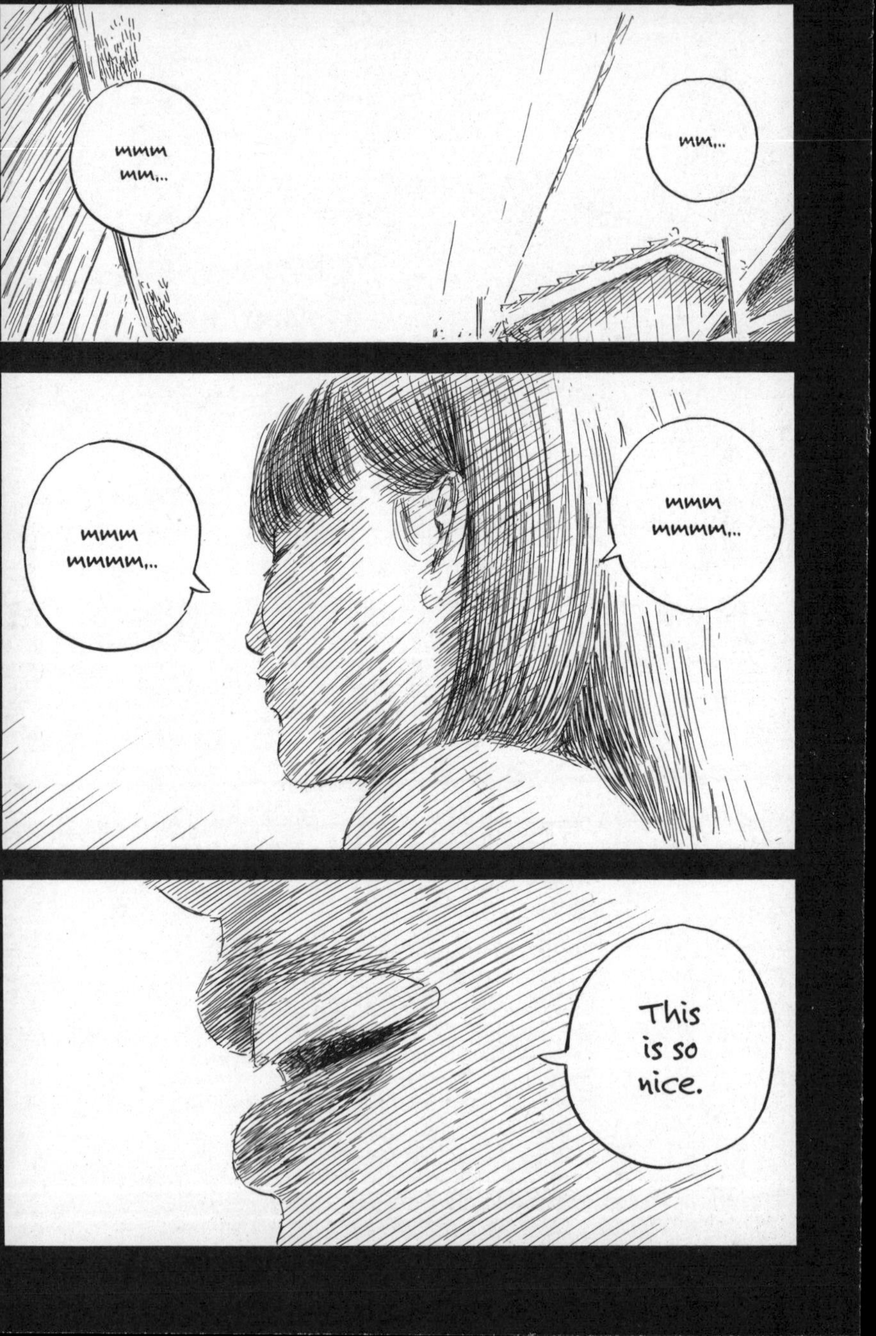
mm...
mmm mm...
mmm mmmm...
mmm mmmm...
This is so nice.

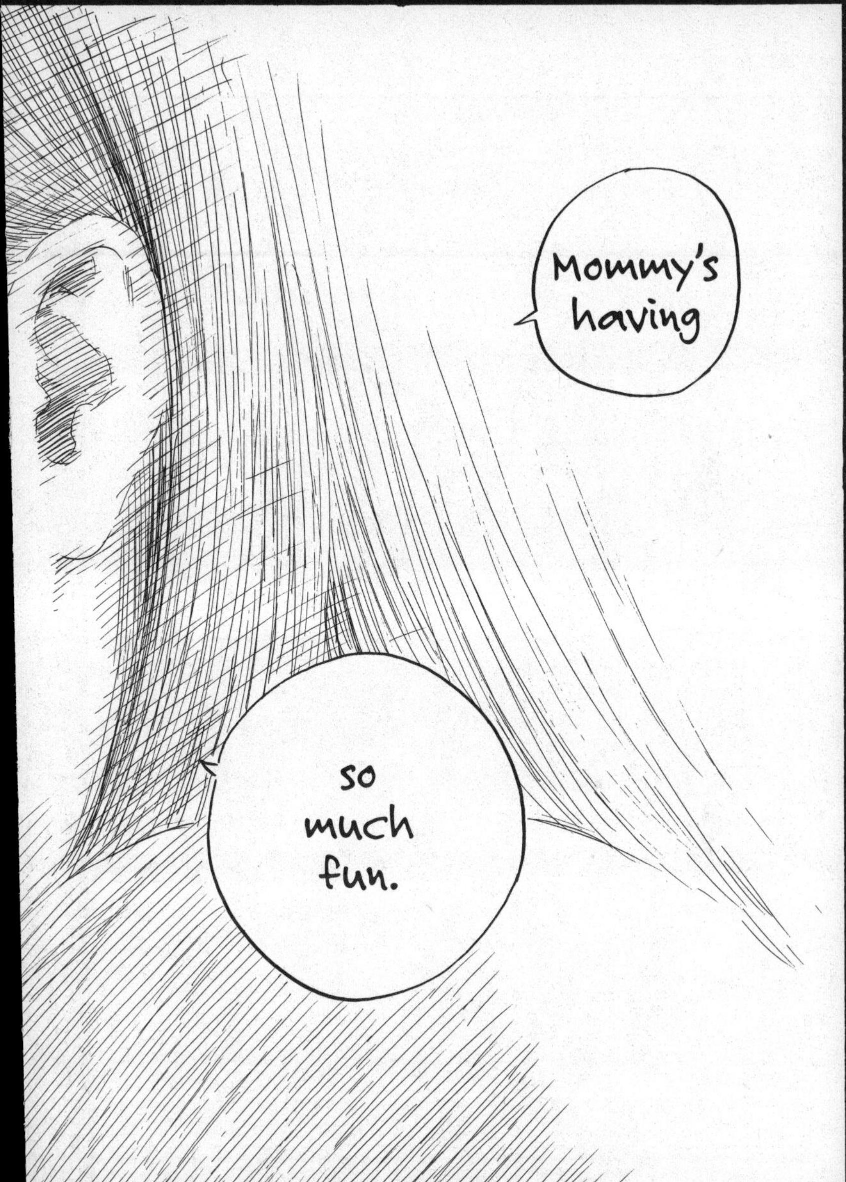
Mommy's having
so much fun.

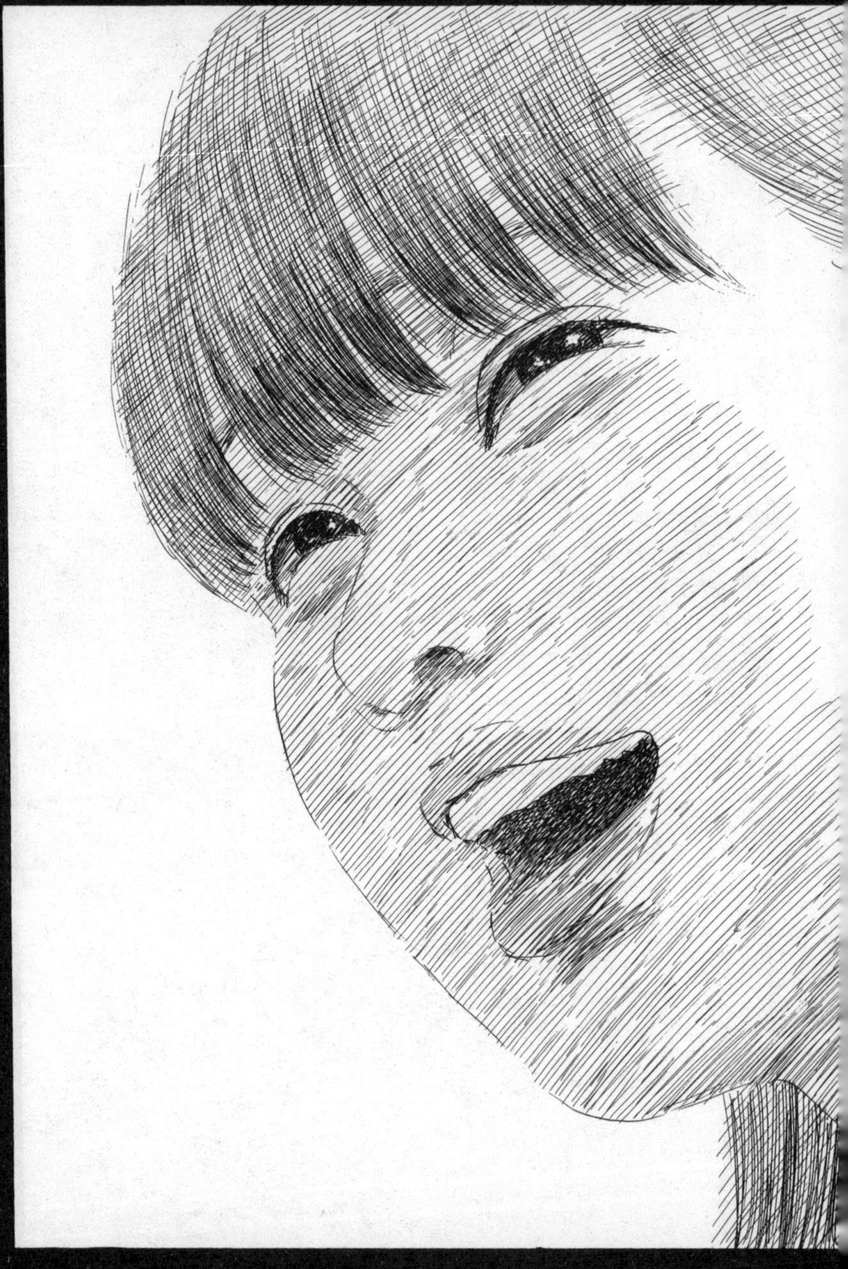

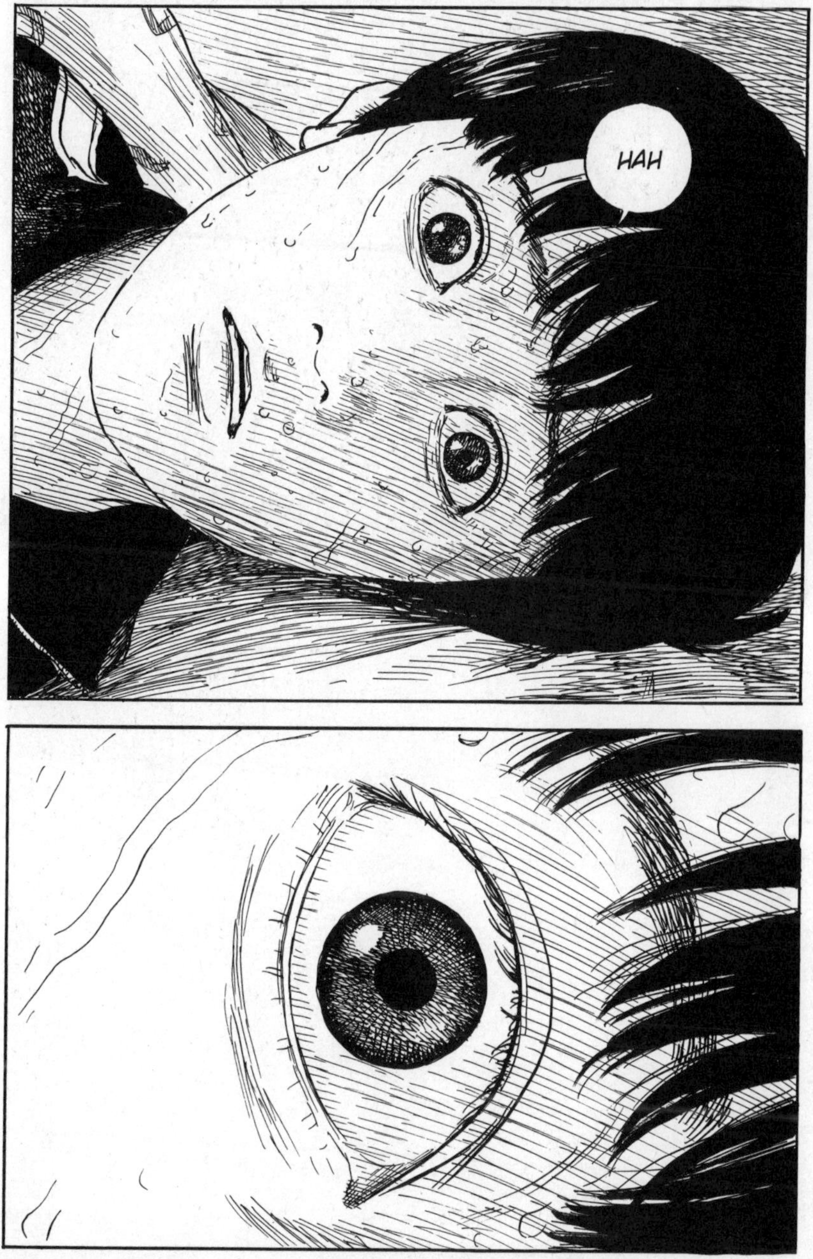
HAH

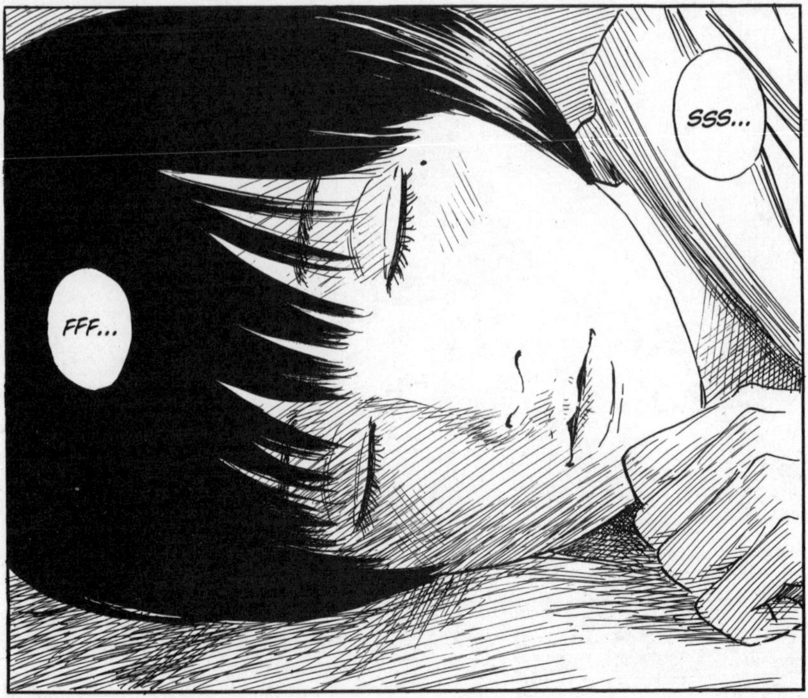
SSS...
FFF...
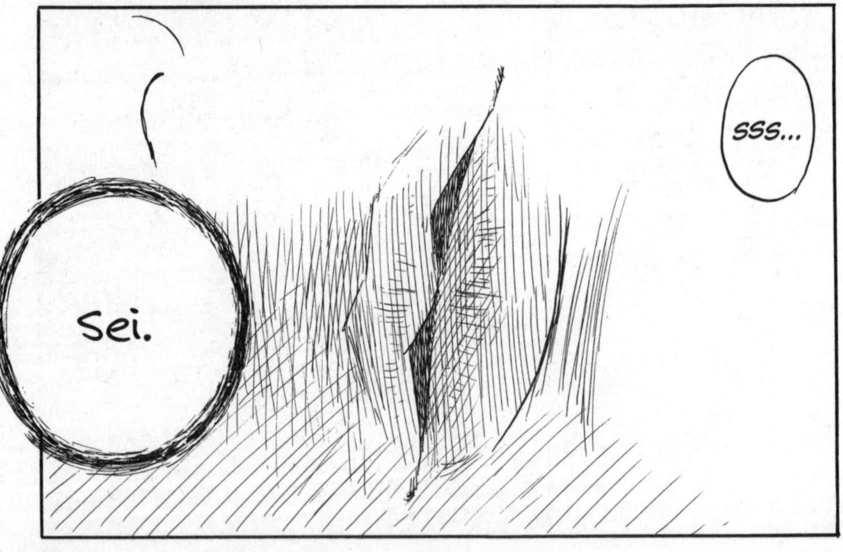
SSS...
Sei.

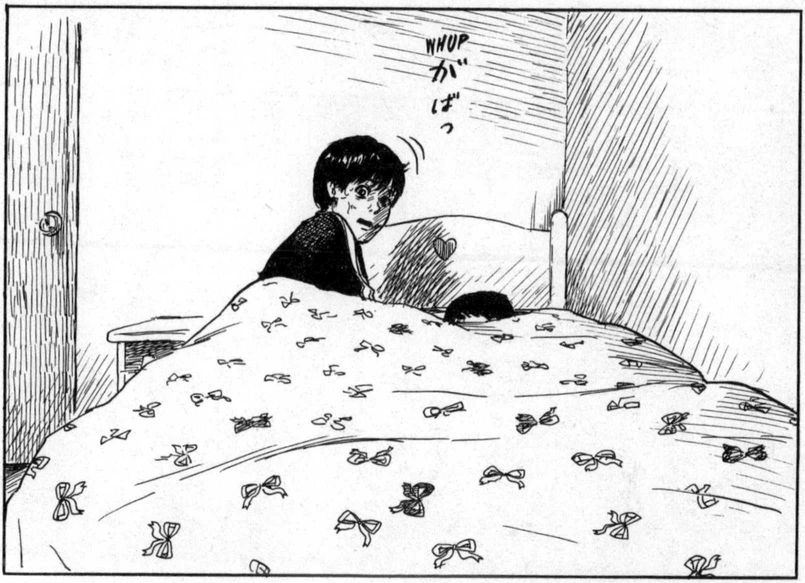
WHUP
がばっ

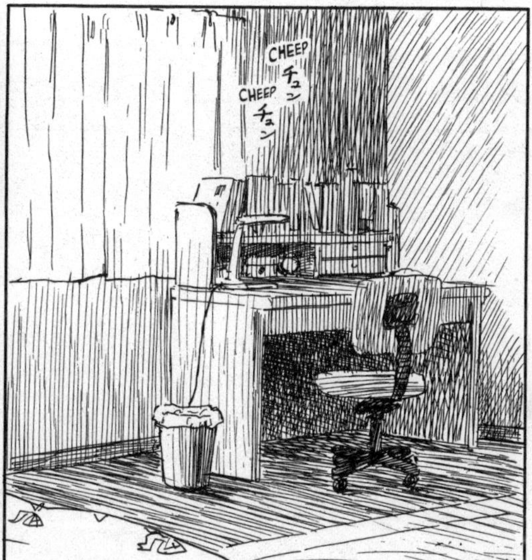
CHEEP
チュン
CHEEP
チュン

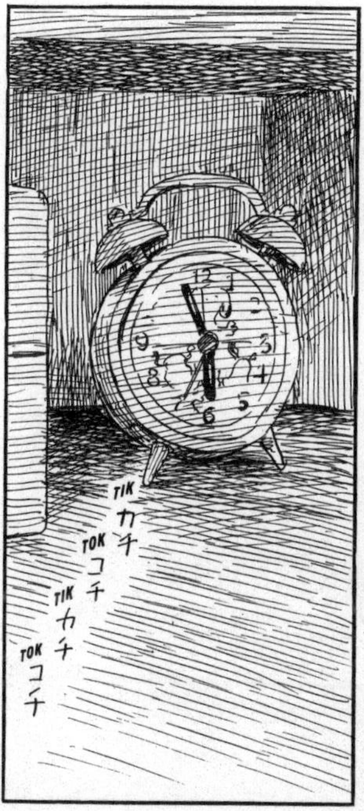
TIK
カチ
TOK
コチ
TIK
カチ
TOK
コチ

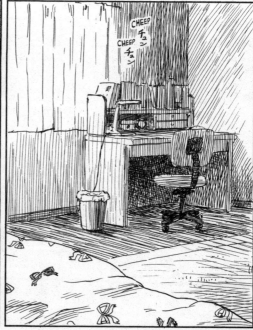

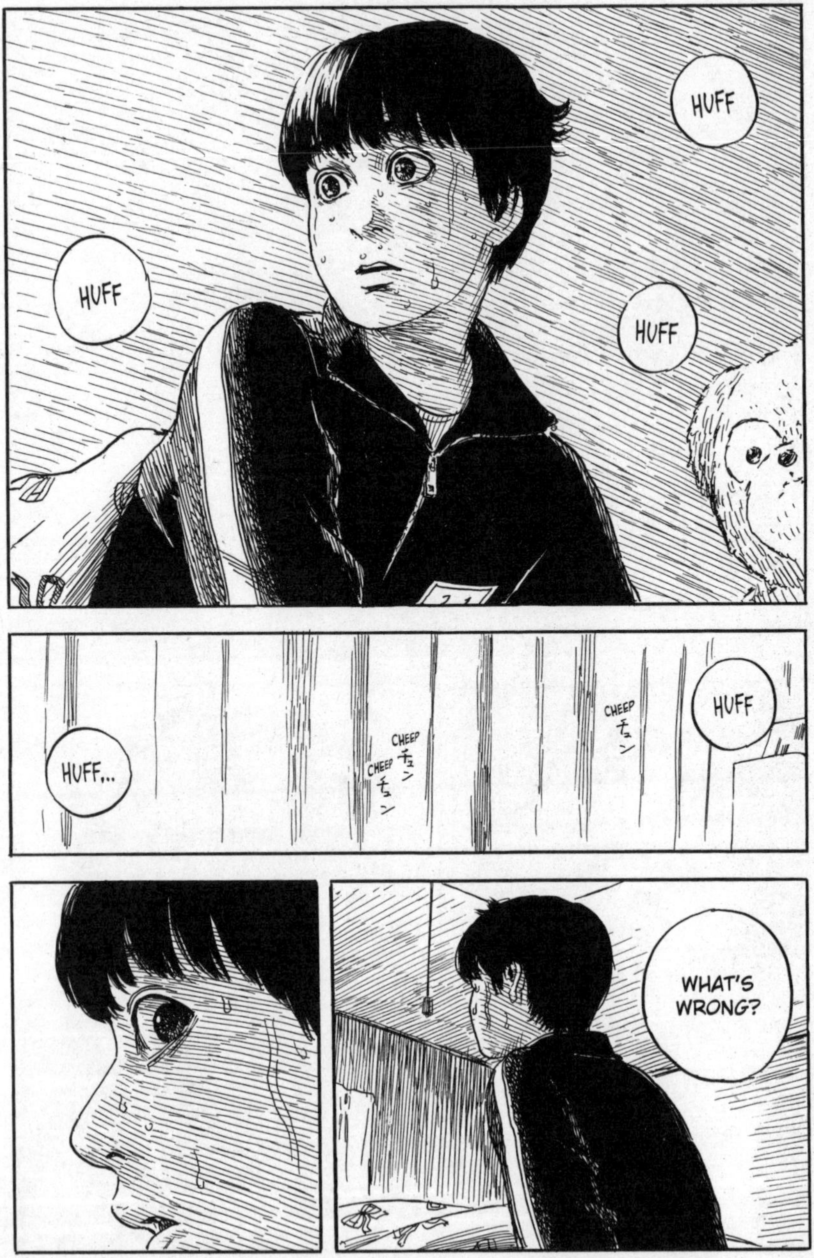
HUFF
HUFF
HUFF
HUFF
CHEEP チュン
CHEEP チュン
CHEEP チュン
HUFF...
WHAT'S WRONG?

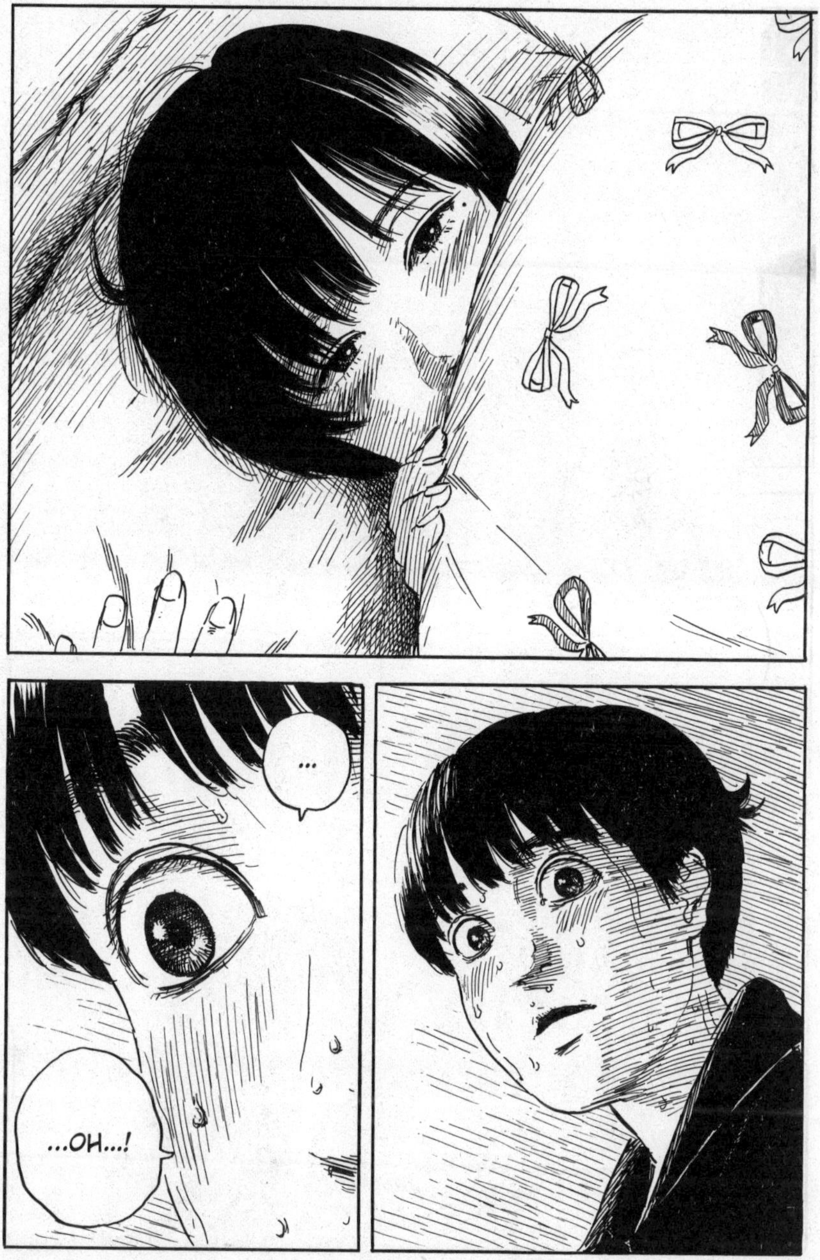
...
...OH...!

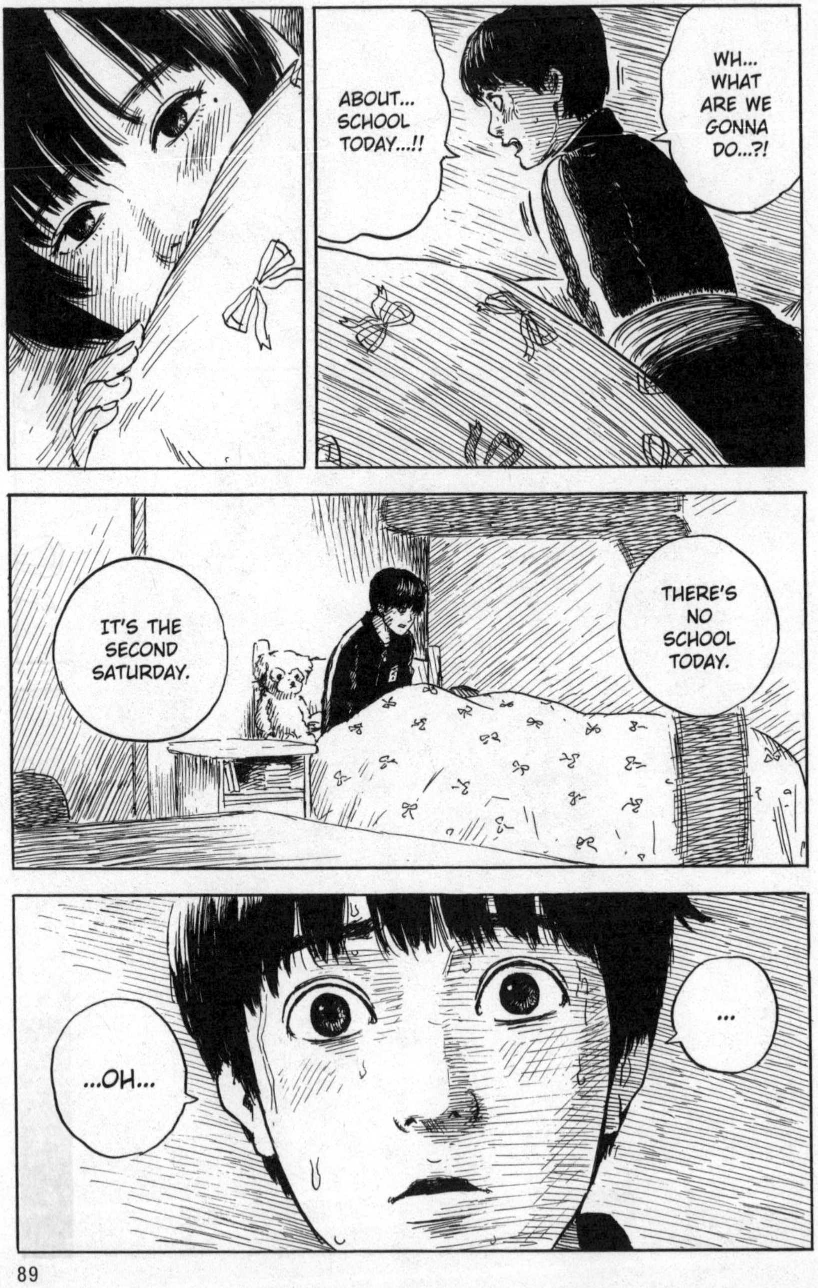
WH... WHAT ARE WE GONNA DO...?!
ABOUT... SCHOOL TODAY...!!
THERE'S NO SCHOOL TODAY.
IT'S THE SECOND SATURDAY.
...
...OH...

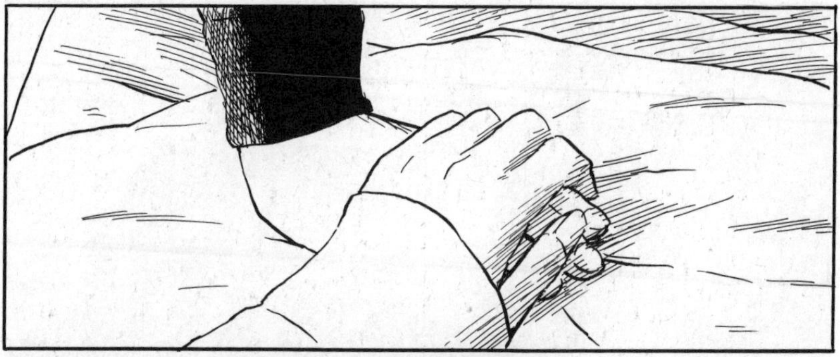

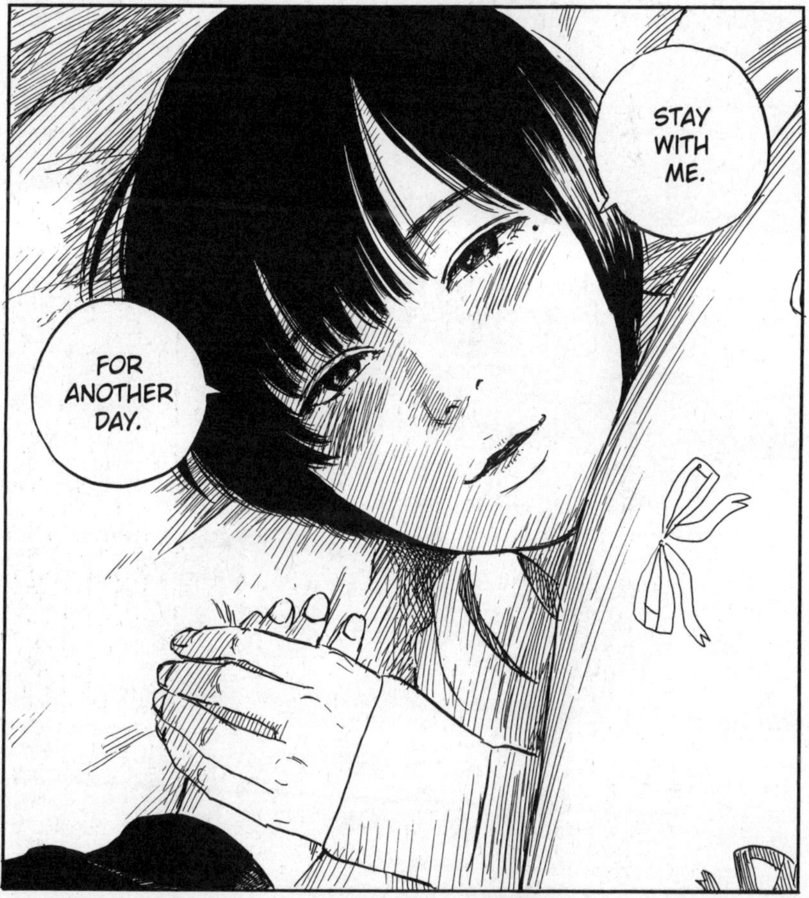
STAY WITH ME.
FOR ANOTHER DAY.

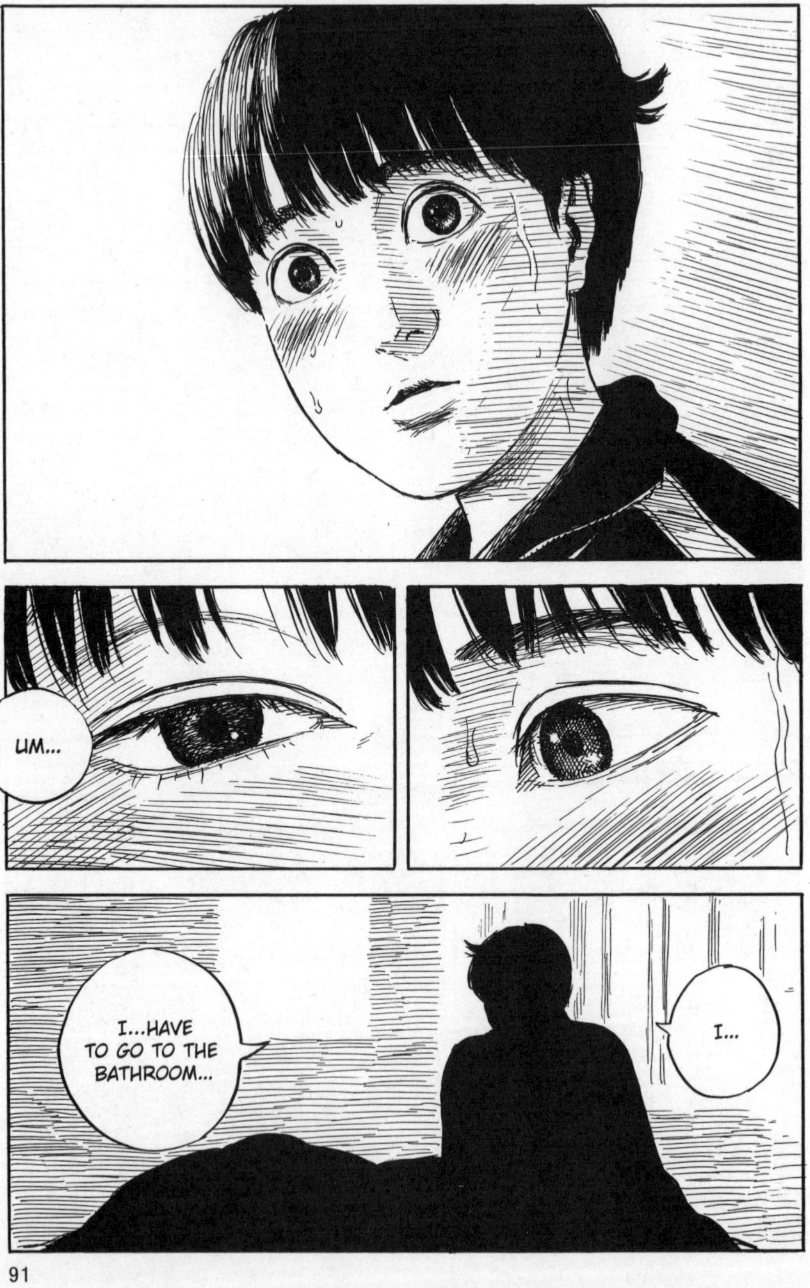
UM...
I...
I...HAVE TO GO TO THE BATHROOM...

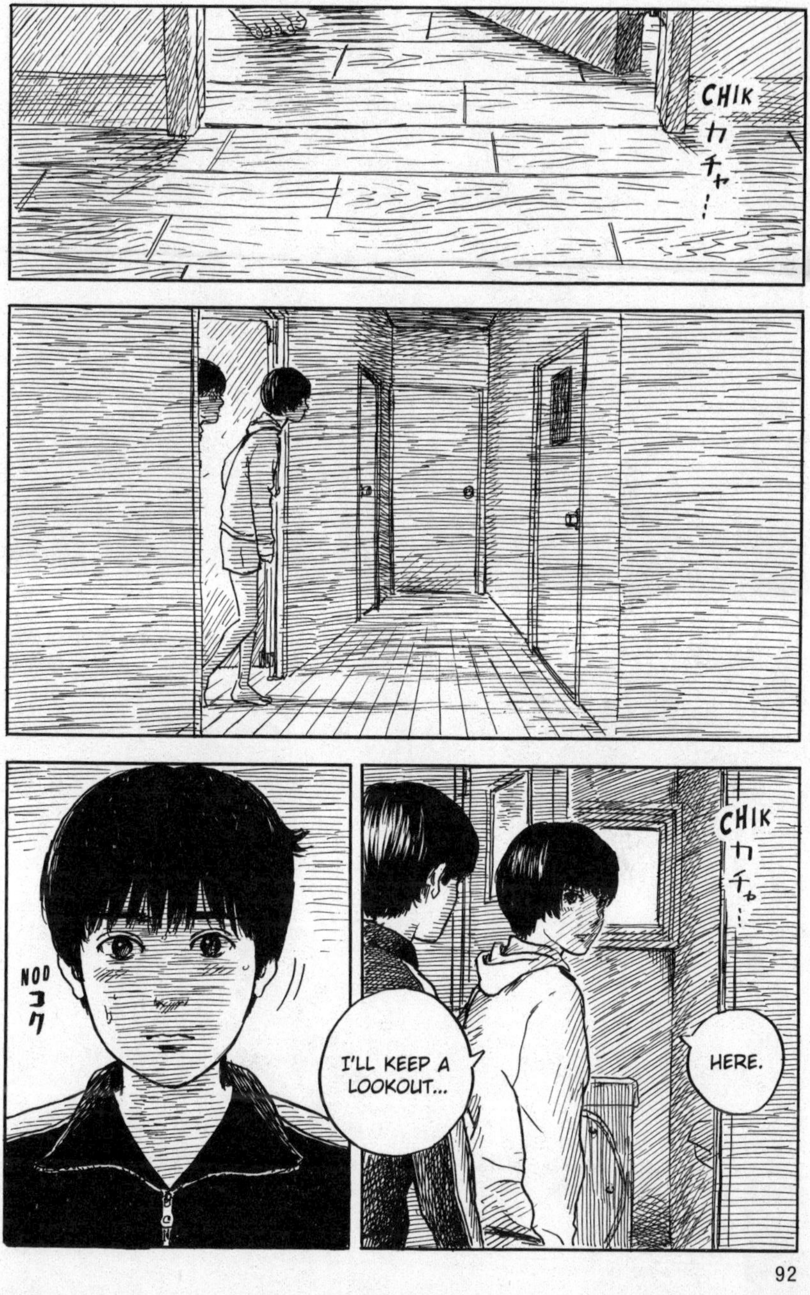
CHIK
カチャ…
CHIK
カチャ…
HERE.
I'LL KEEP A LOOKOUT...
NOD
コク

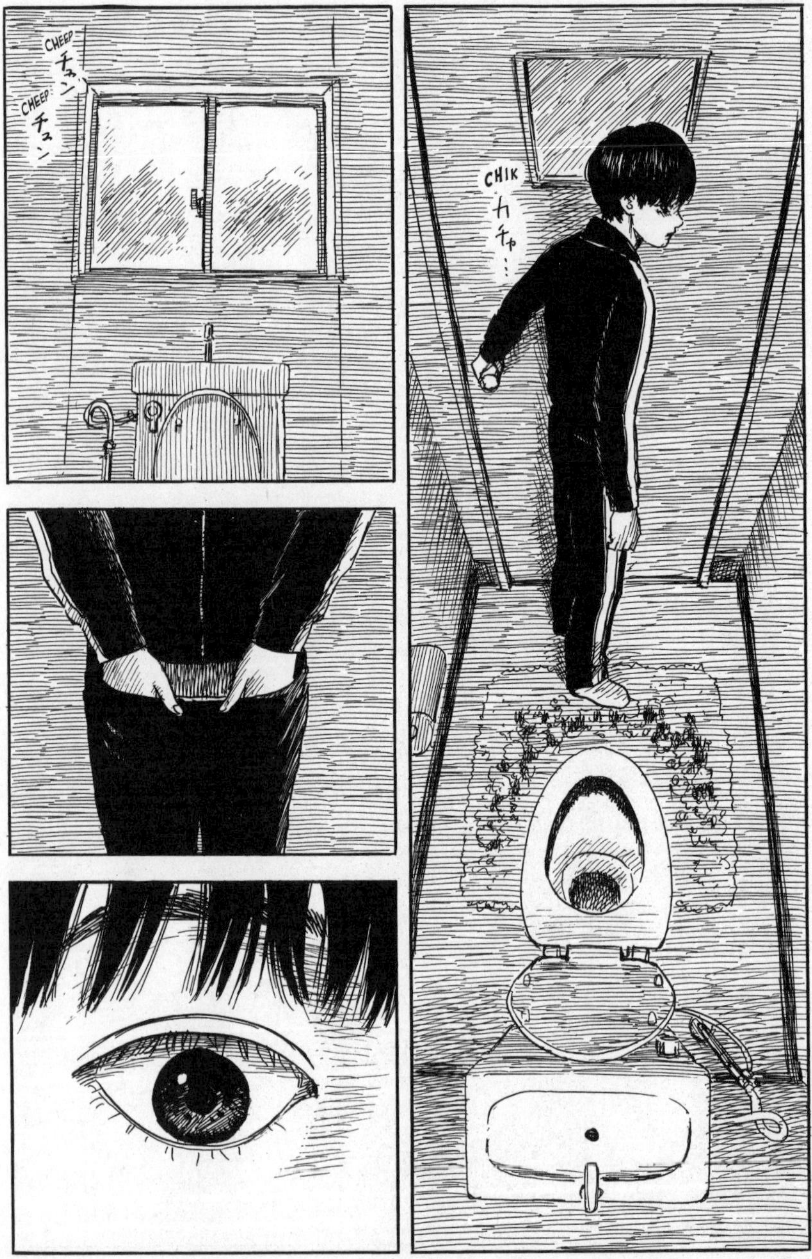
CHIK
カチャ…
CHEEP
チュン、
CHEEP
チュン

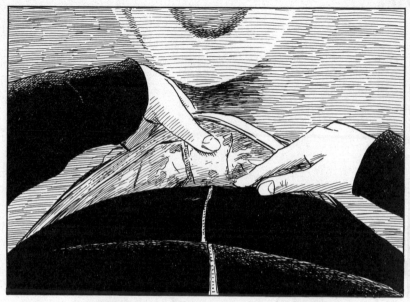

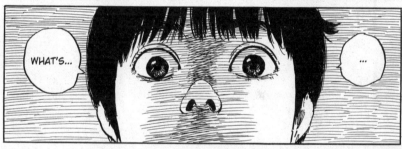

WHAT'S...

...

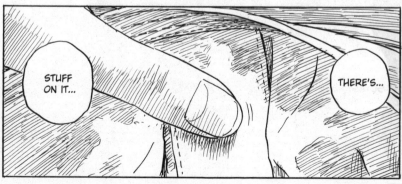

STUFF
ON IT...

THERE'S...

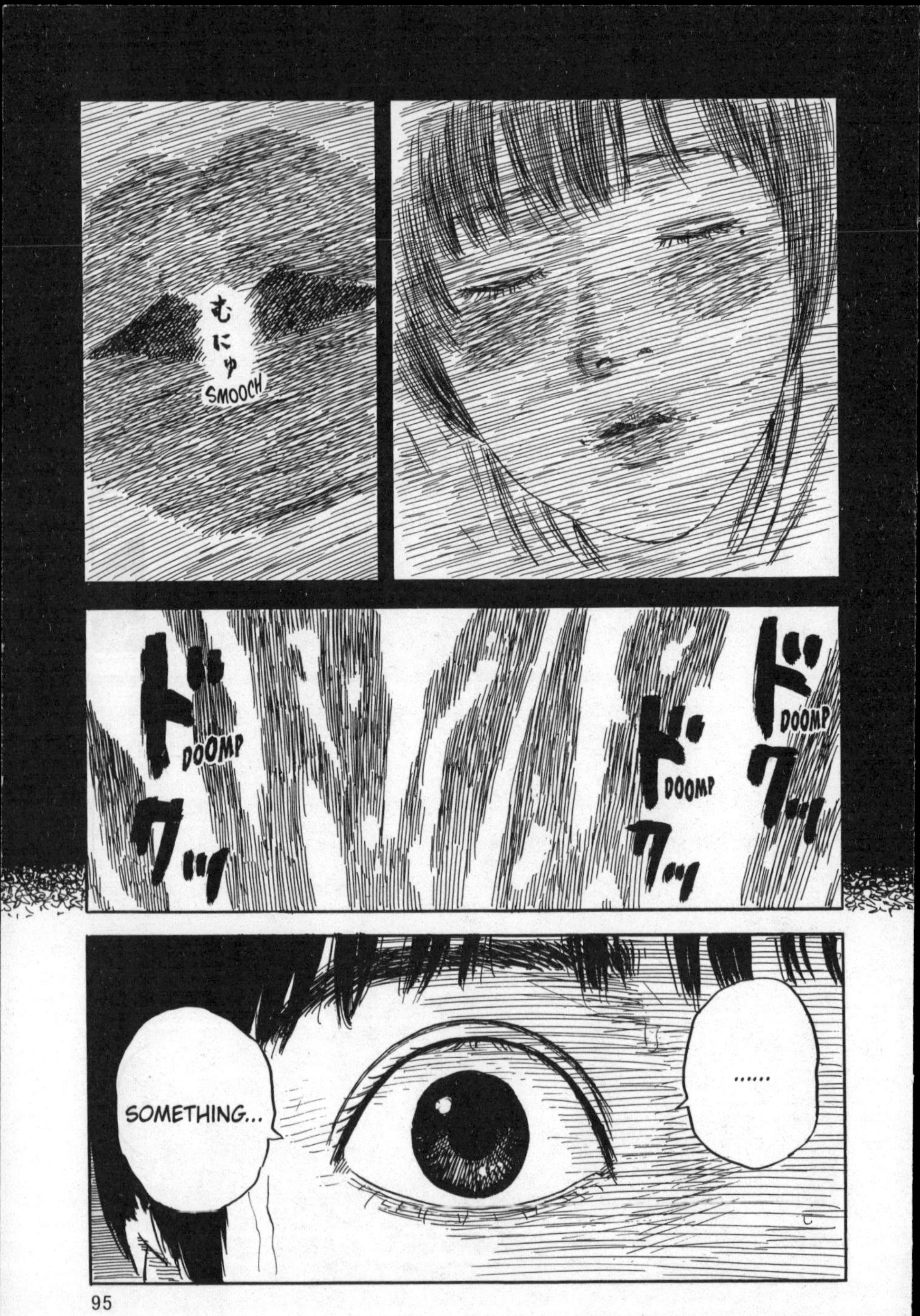
むにゅ
SMOOCH
ドクッ
DOOMP
ドクッ
DOOMP
ドクッ
DOOMP
......
SOMETHING...

SOMETHING...
CAME OUT WHEN...
WHAT... IS IT?
WHAT IS IT?
WHAT IS IT?

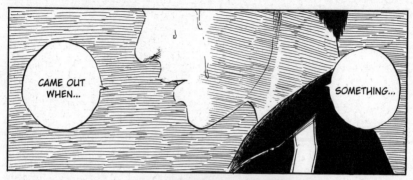

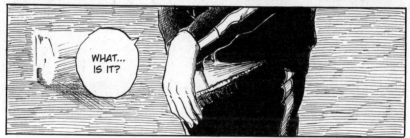

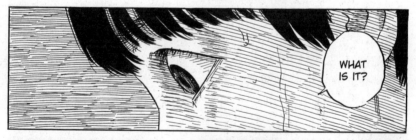

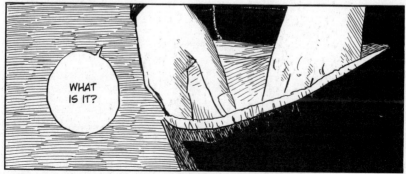

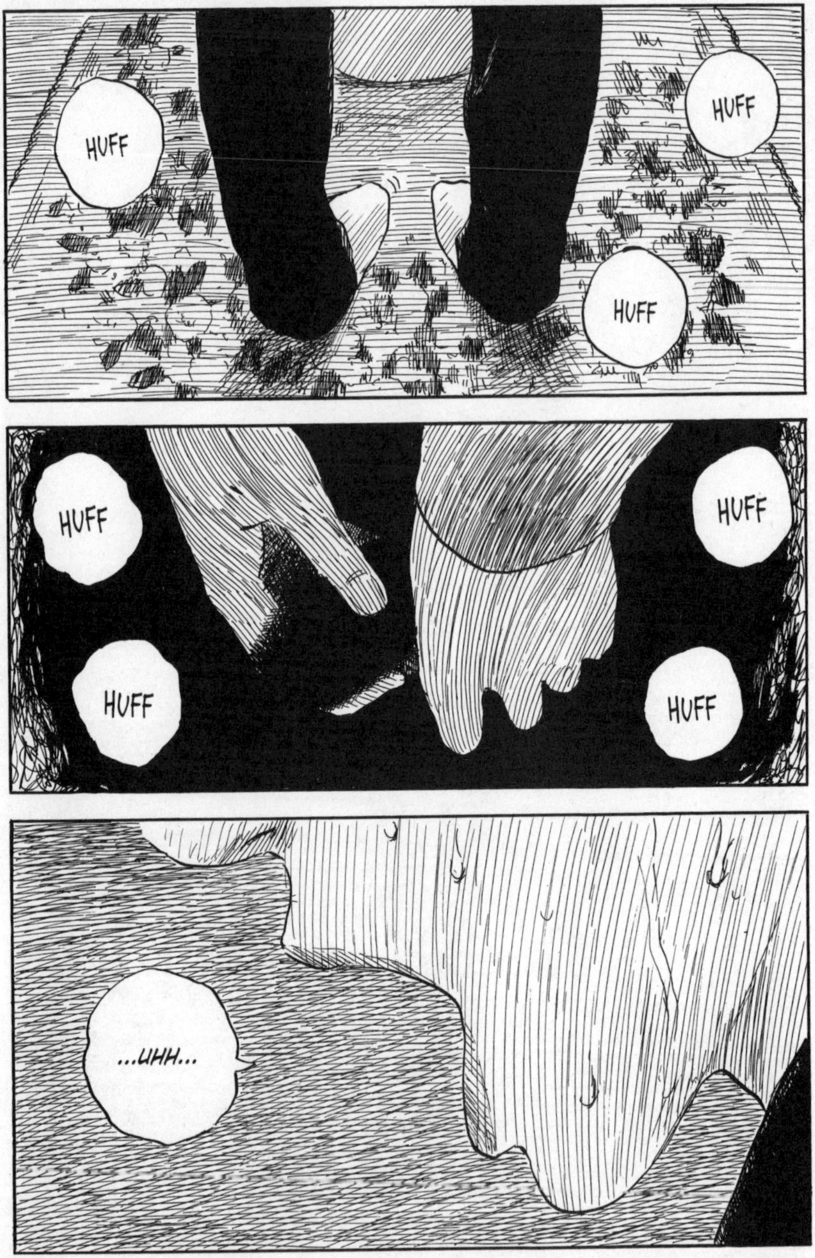
HUFF
HUFF
HUFF
HUFF
HUFF
HUFF
HUFF
...UHH...

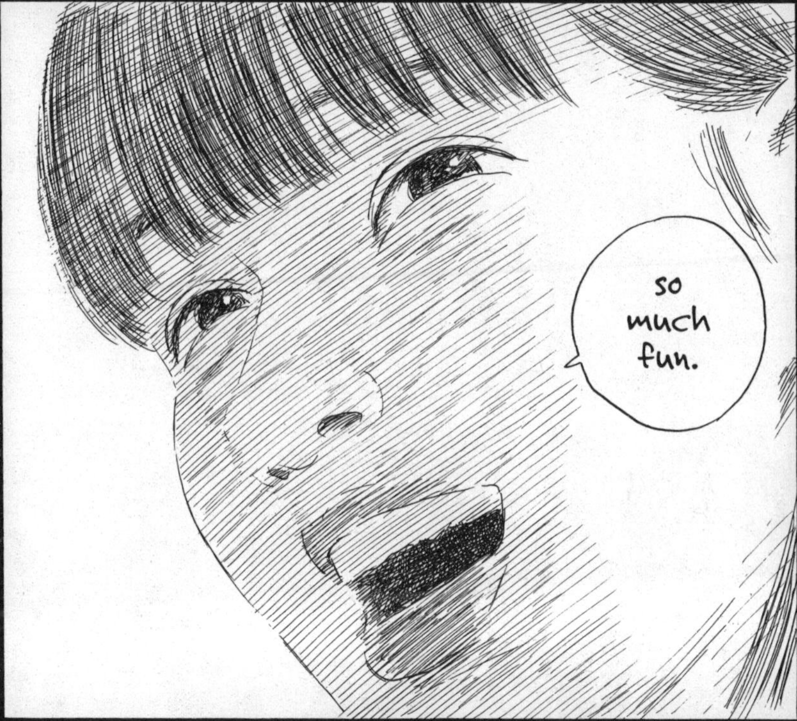
so much fun.
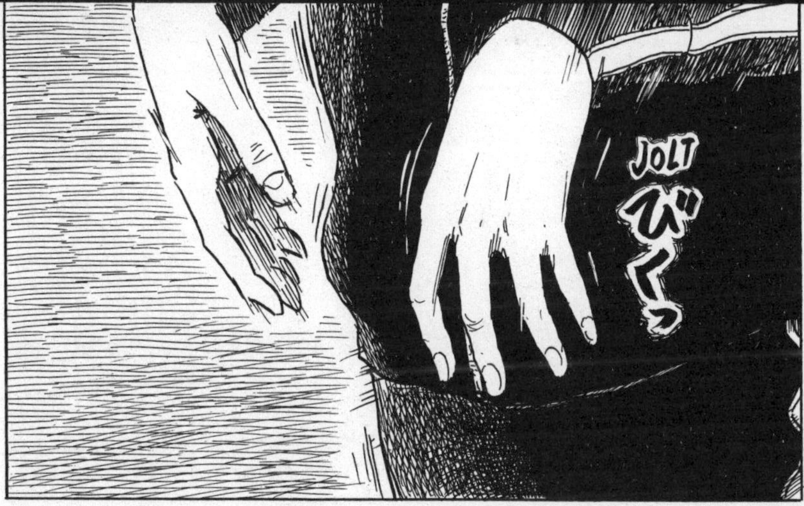
JOLT
びくっ

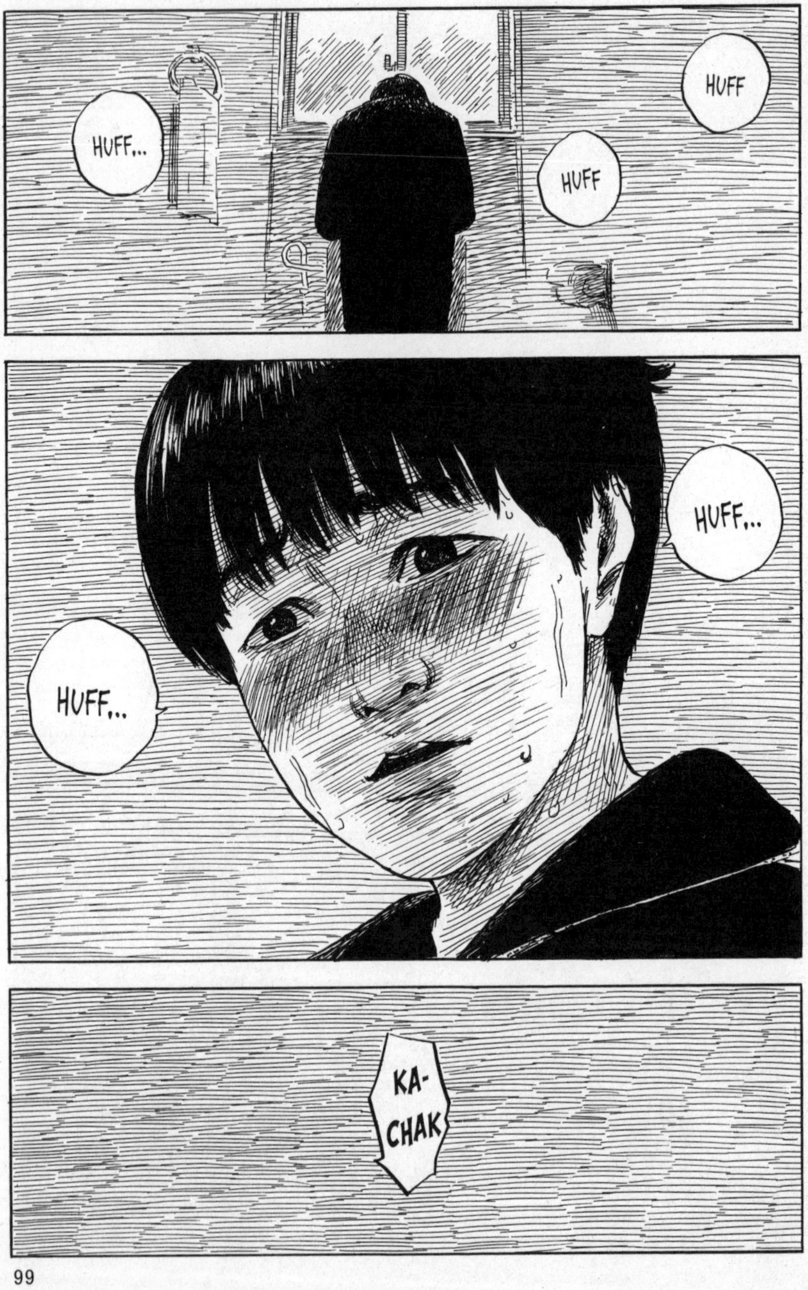
HUFF
HUFF
HUFF...
HUFF...
HUFF...
KA-CHAK

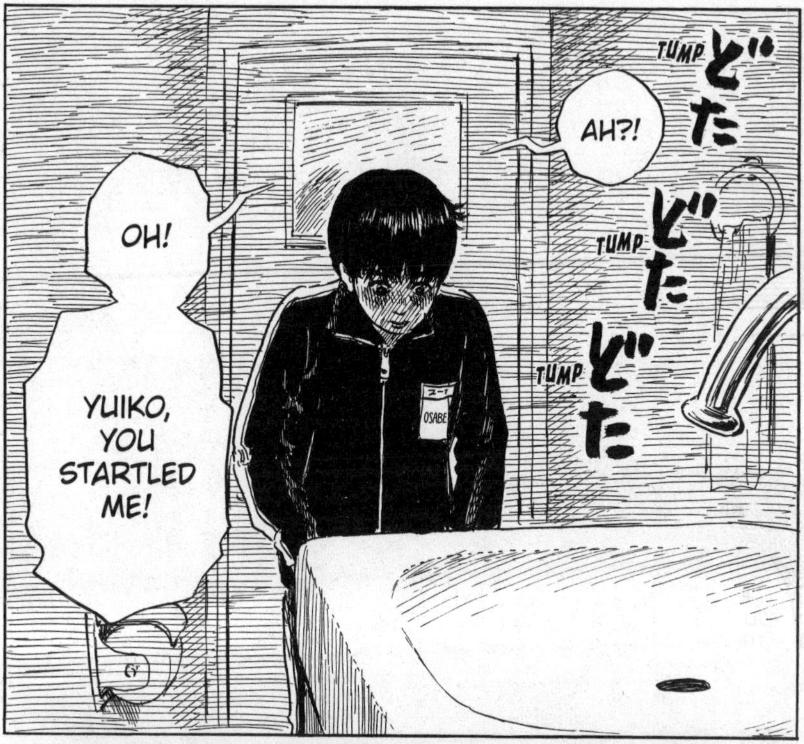
TUMP どた
AH?!
TUMP どた
TUMP どた
OH!
YUIKO, YOU STARTLED ME!
OSABE

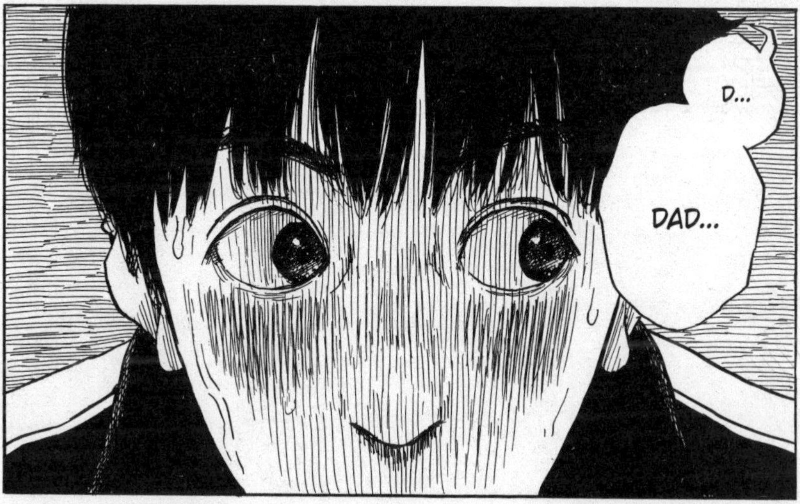
D...
DAD...

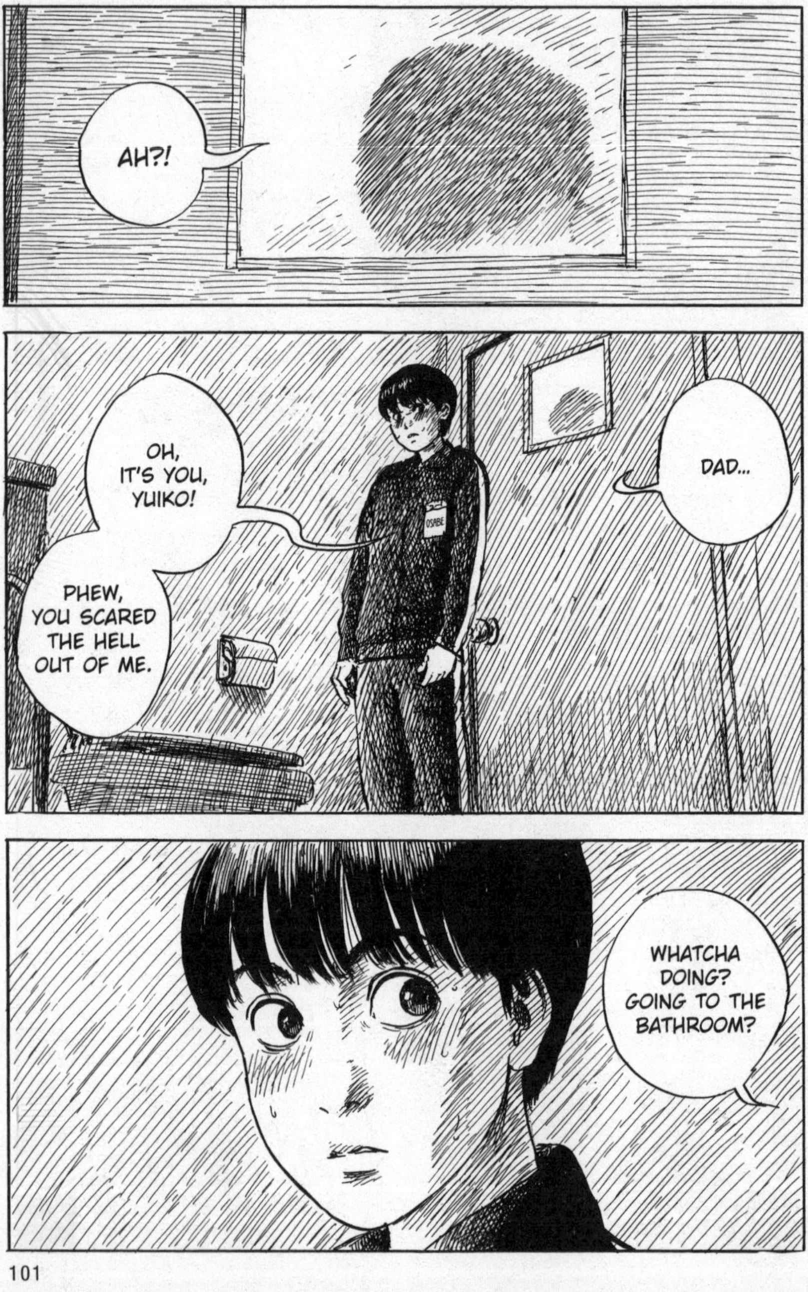
AH?!
DAD...
OSABE
OH, IT'S YOU, YUIKO!
PHEW, YOU SCARED THE HELL OUT OF ME.
WHATCHA DOING? GOING TO THE BATHROOM?

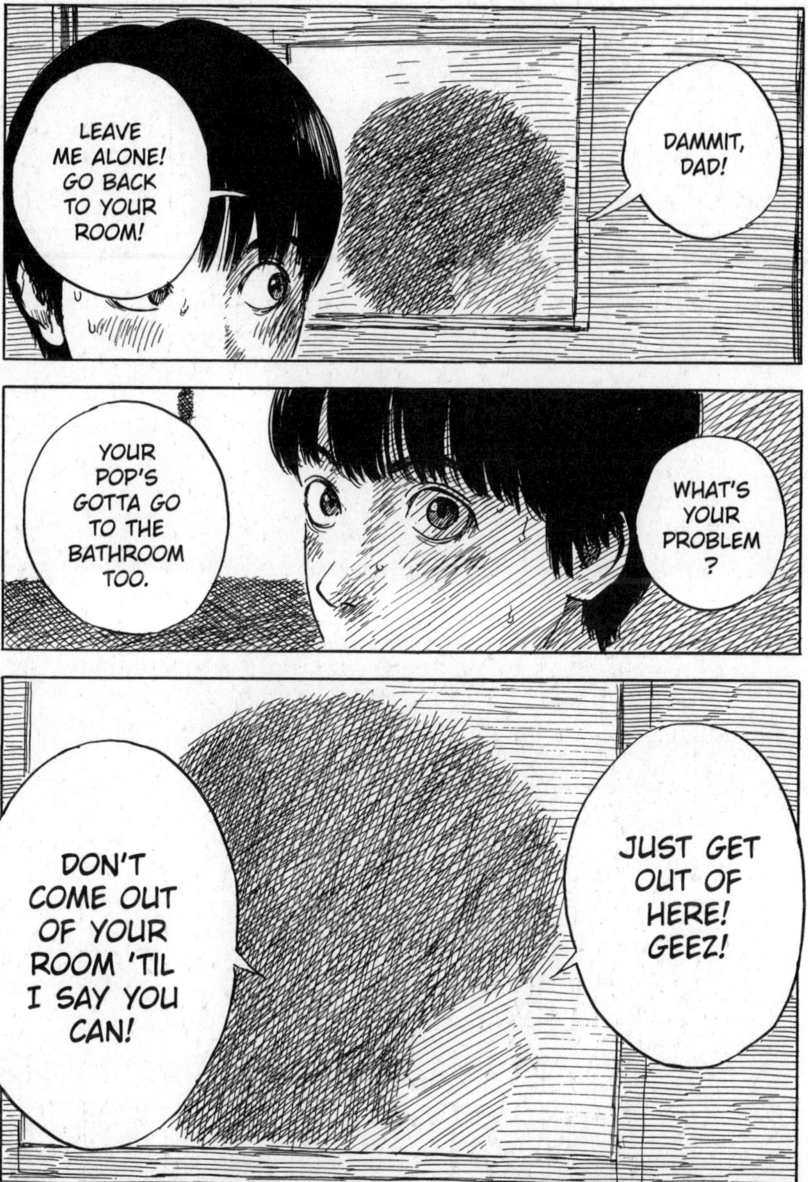
DAMMIT, DAD!
LEAVE ME ALONE! GO BACK TO YOUR ROOM!
WHAT'S YOUR PROBLEM ?
YOUR POP'S GOTTA GO TO THE BATHROOM TOO.
JUST GET OUT OF HERE! GEEZ!
DON'T COME OUT OF YOUR ROOM 'TIL I SAY YOU CAN!

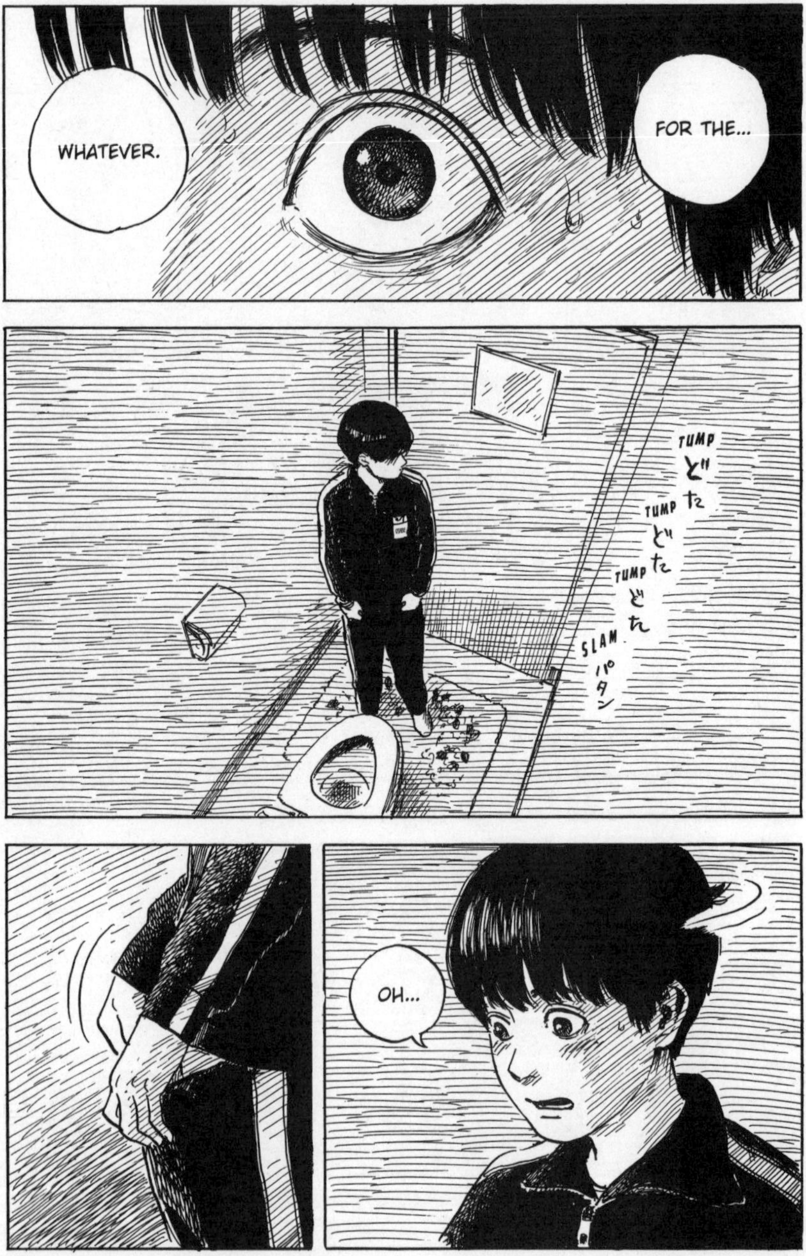
FOR THE...
WHATEVER.
TUMP どた
TUMP どた
TUMP どた
SLAM パタン
OH...

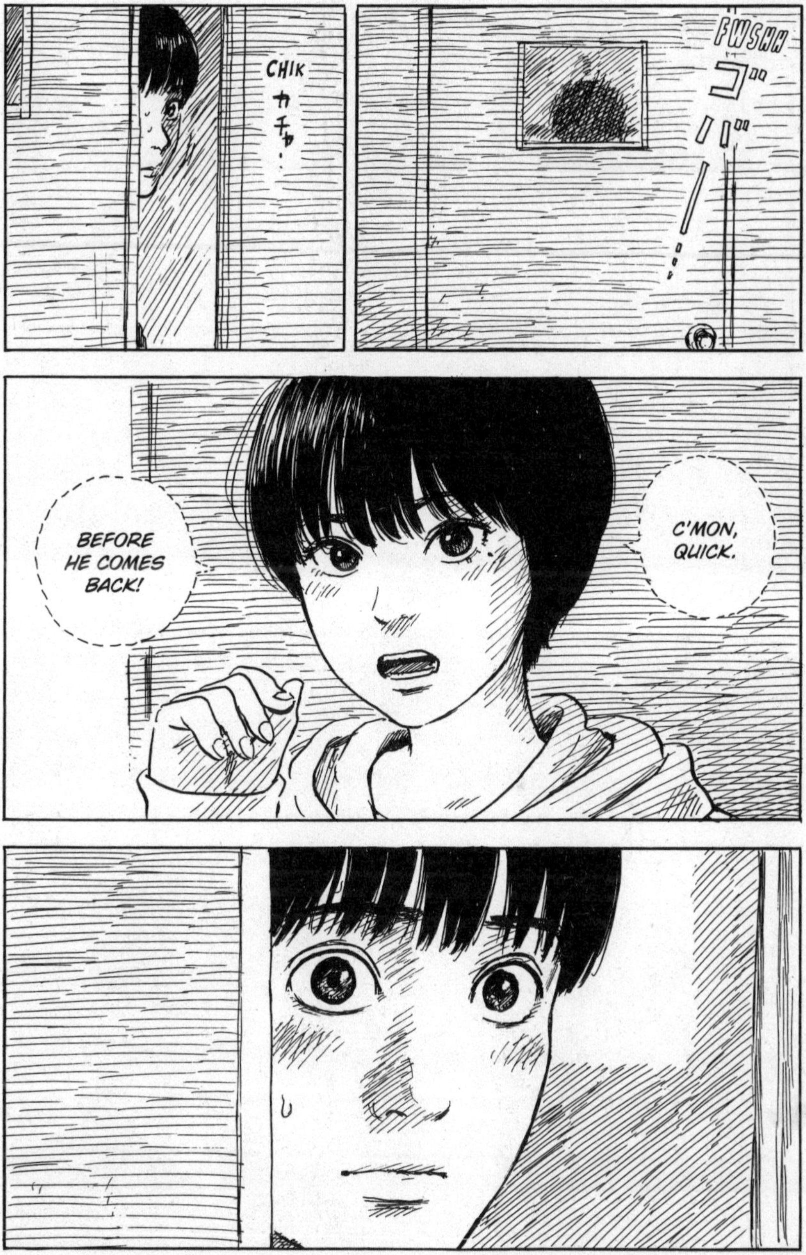
FWSHH
ゴバー
CHIK
カチャ
C'MON, QUICK.
BEFORE HE COMES BACK!

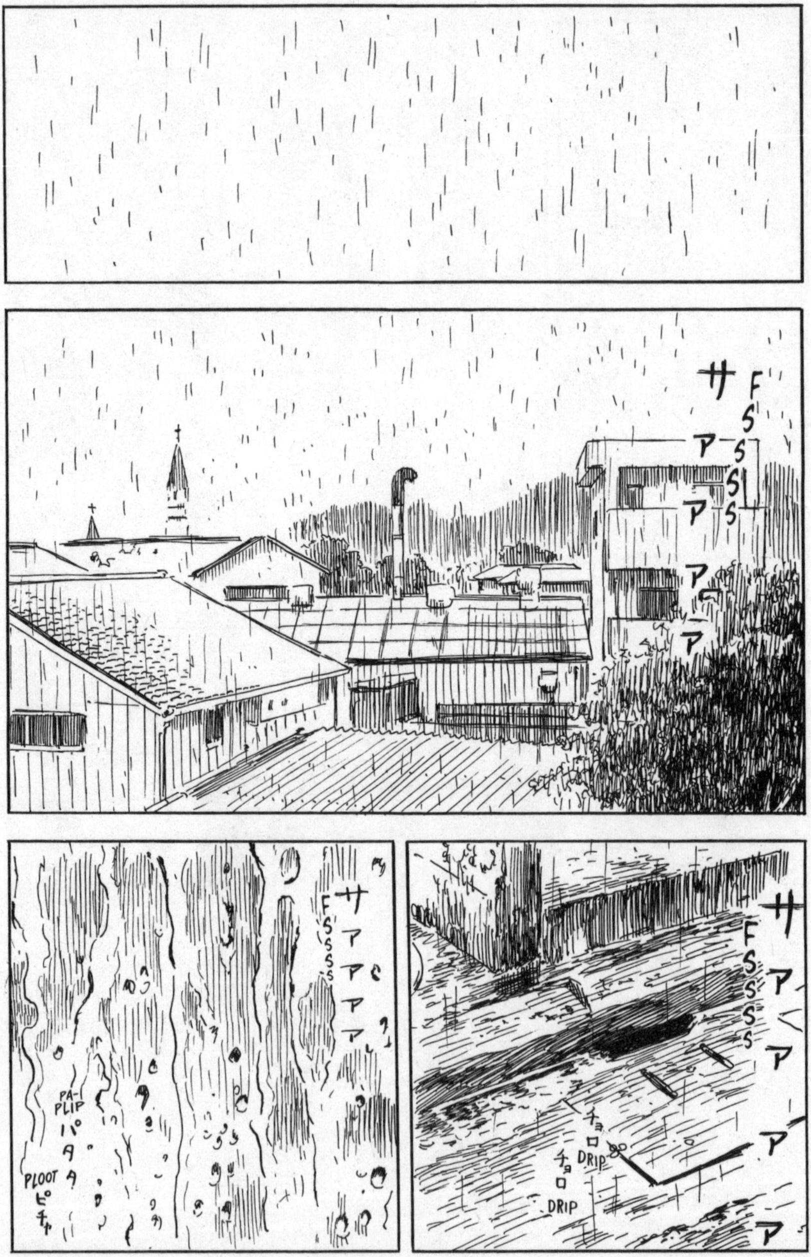
サアアアア
FSSSSS
サアアアア
FSSSSS
チョロ
DRIP
チョロ
DRIP
サアアアア
FSSSS
PA-PLIP
パタタ
PLOOT
ピチャ

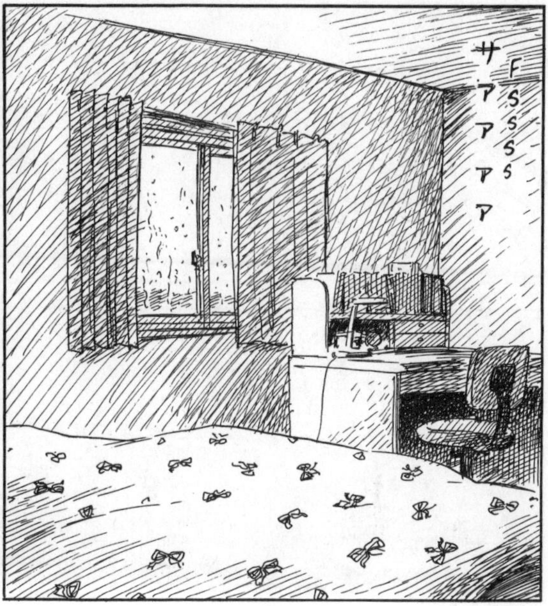
サアアアア
FSSSS
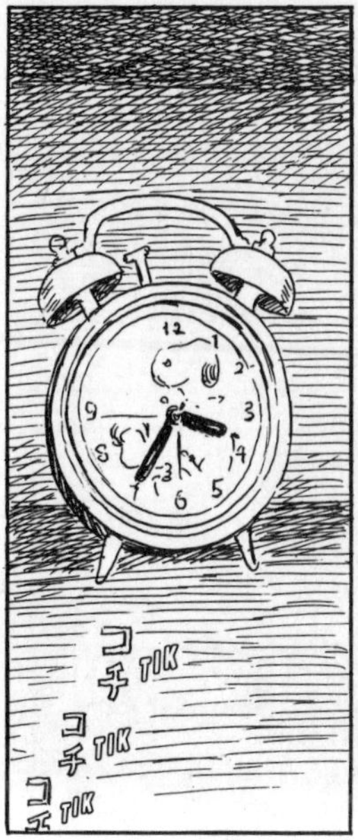
コチ TIK
コチ TIK
コチ TIK
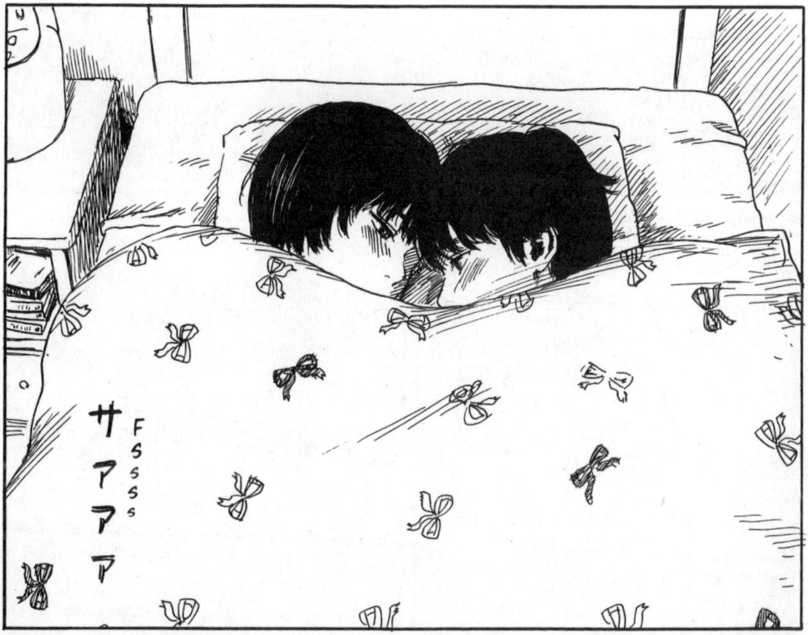
サアア
FSSS

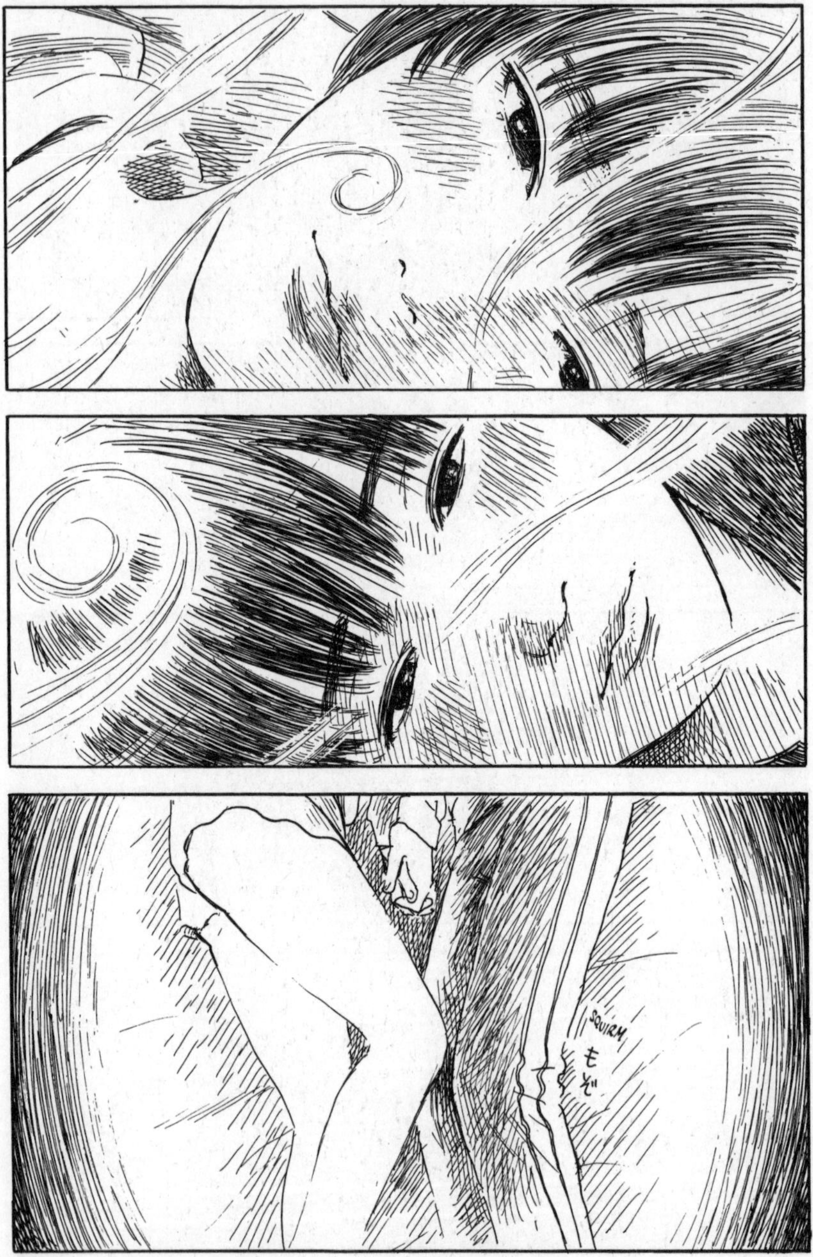
SQUIRM
もぞ

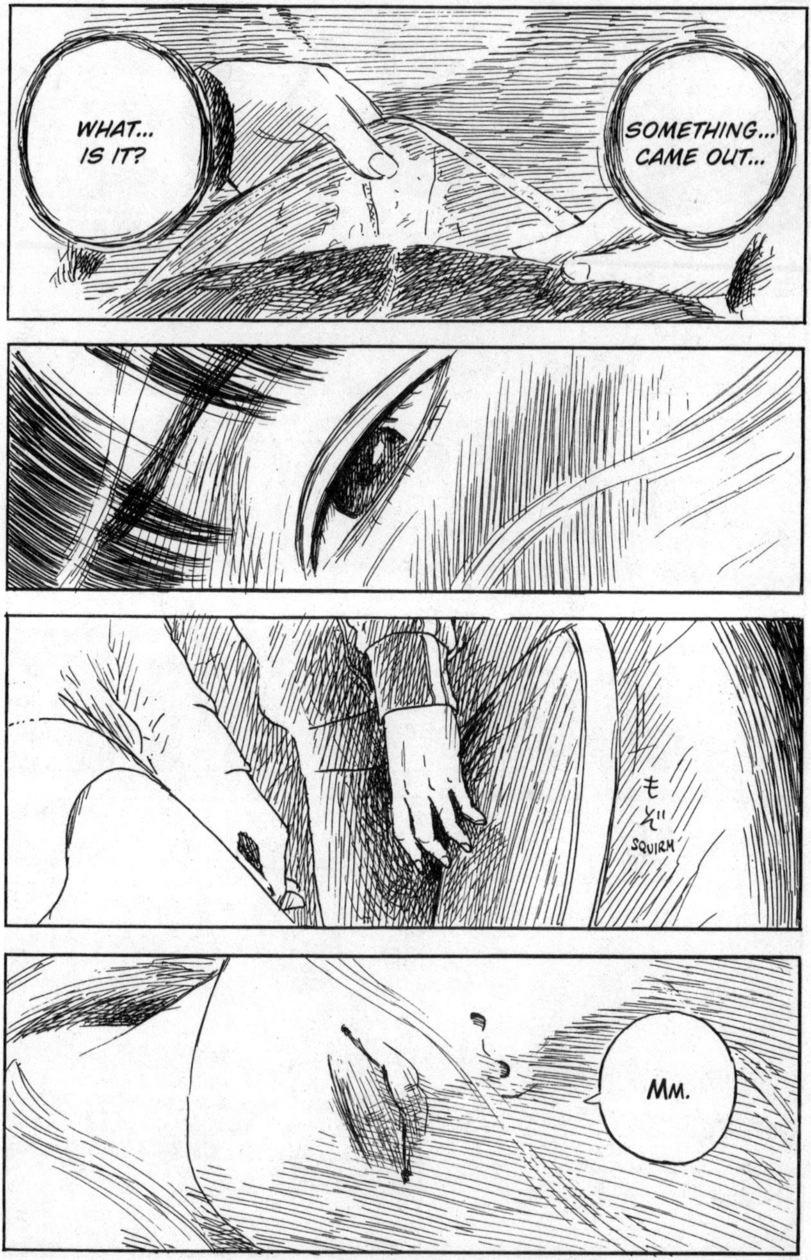
SOMETHING... CAME OUT...
WHAT... IS IT?
もぞ
SQUIRM
MM.

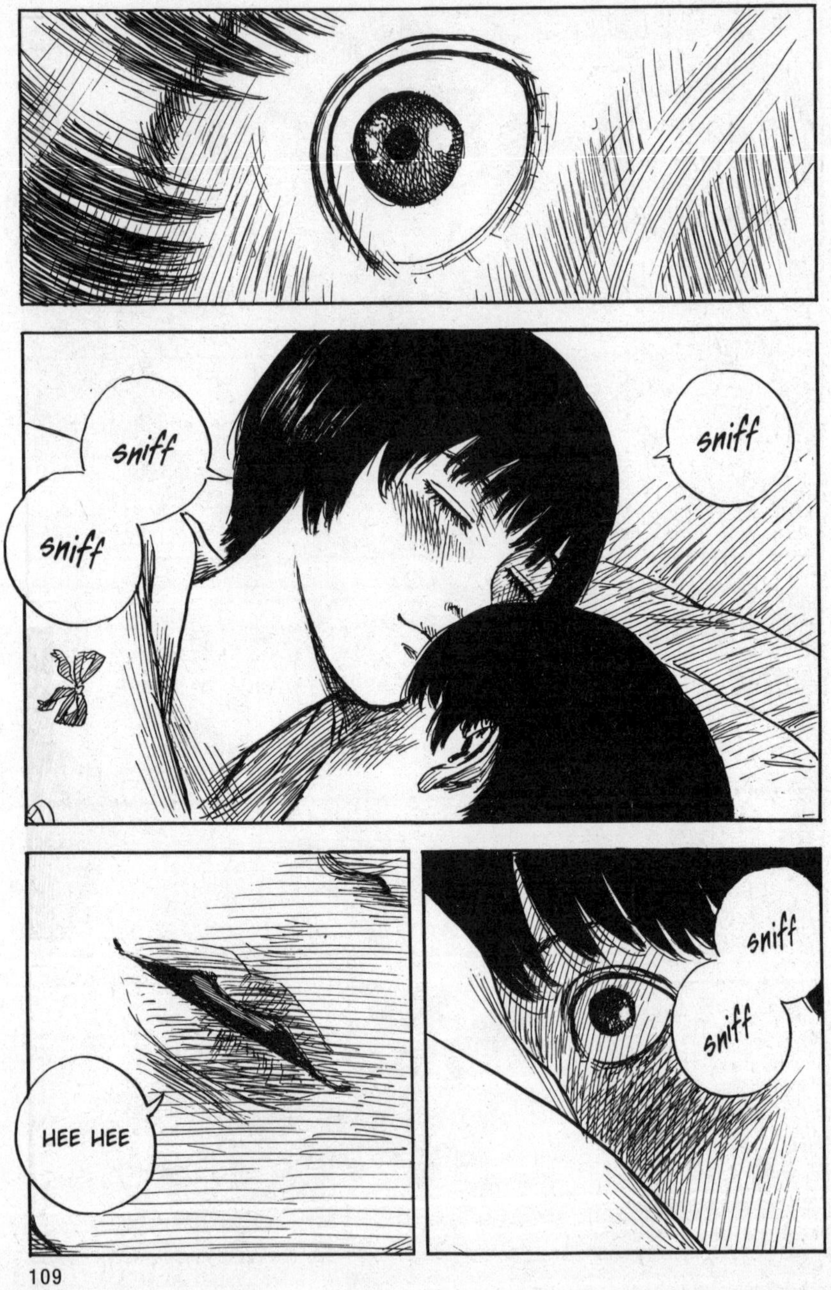

sniff
sniff
sniff
sniff
sniff
HEE HEE

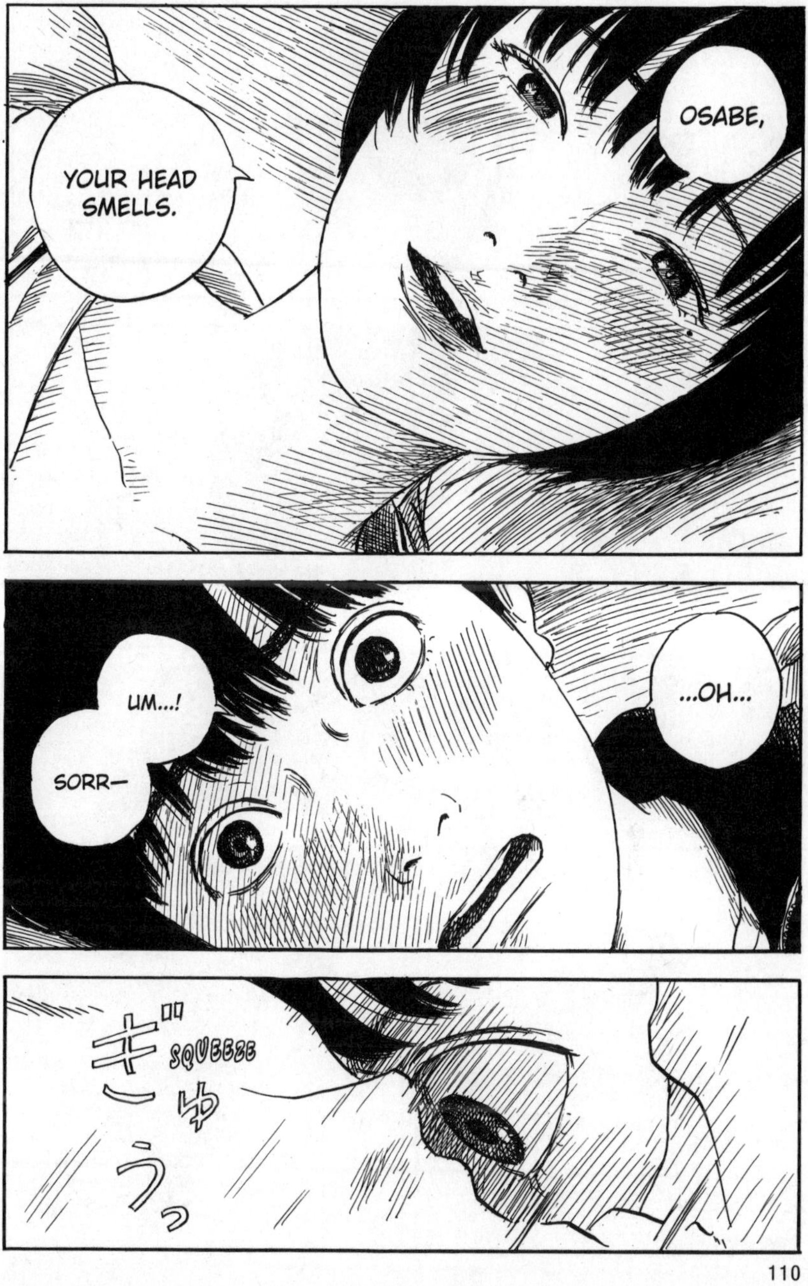
OSABE,
YOUR HEAD SMELLS.
...OH...
UM...!
SORR—
ギュウッ
SQUEEZE

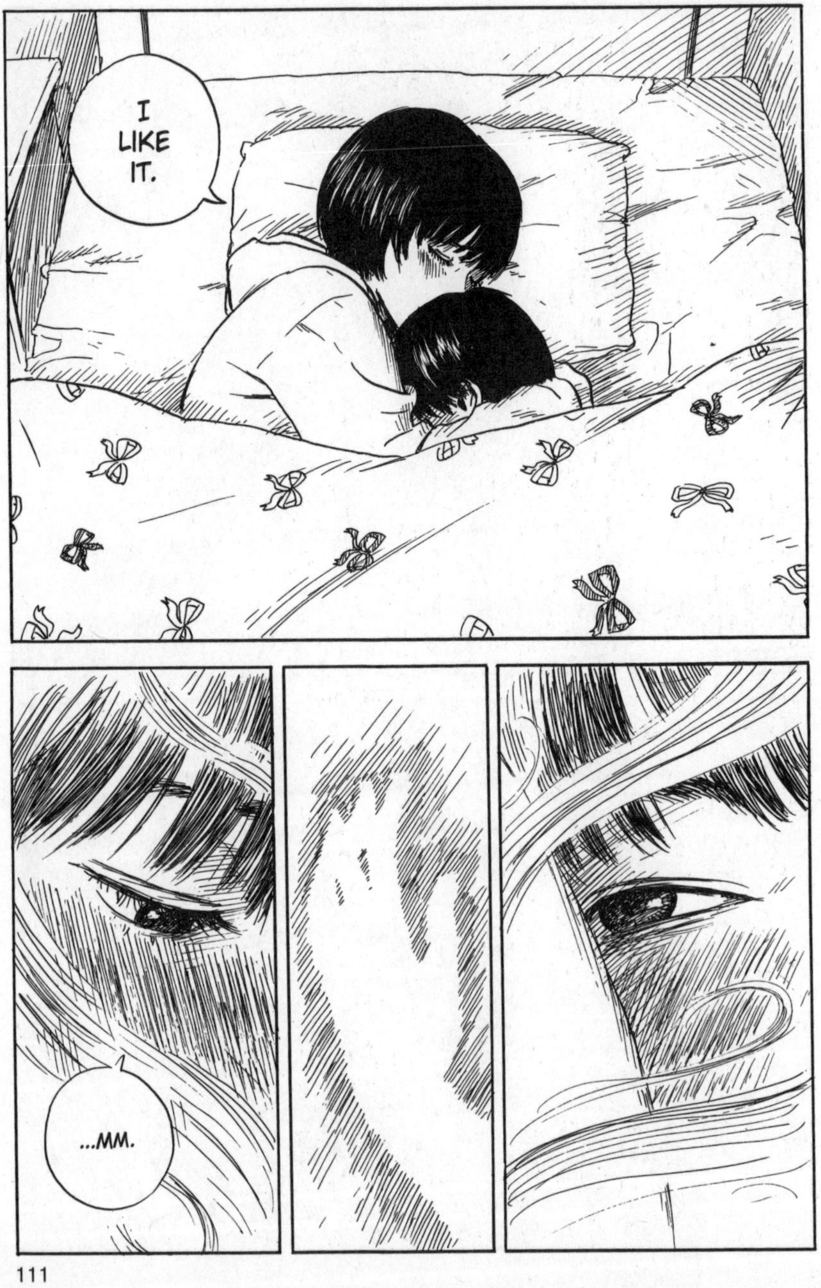
I LIKE IT.
...MM.

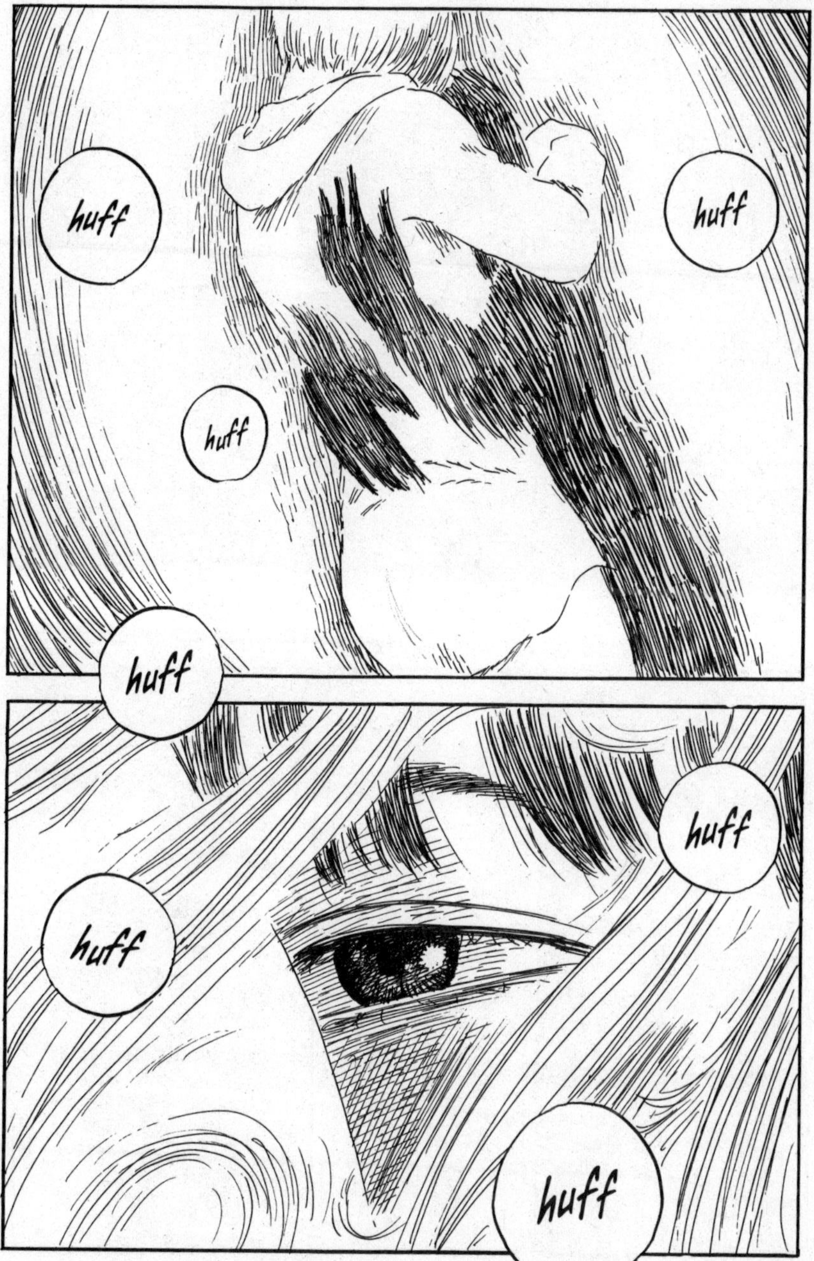
huff
huff
huff
huff
huff
huff
huff

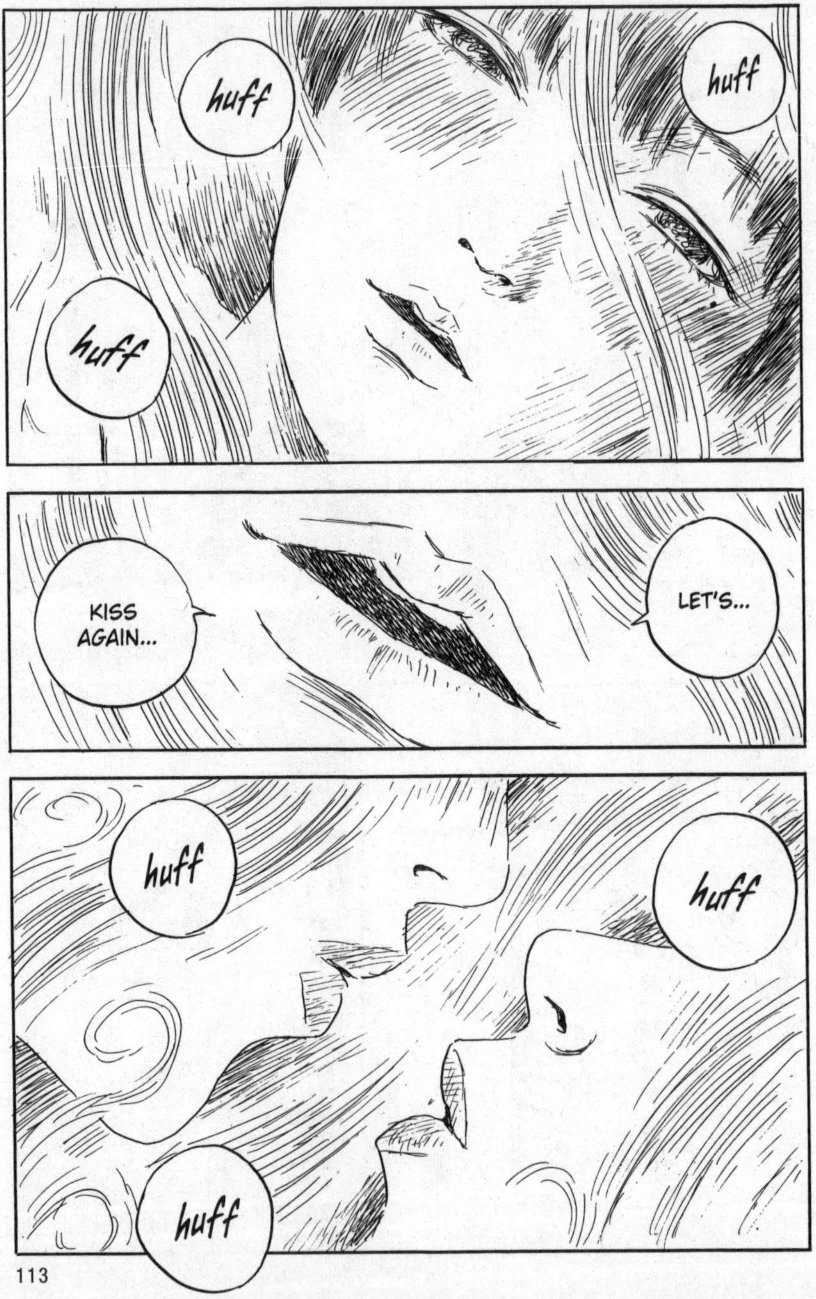
huff
huff
huff
LET'S...
KISS AGAIN...
huff
huff
huff

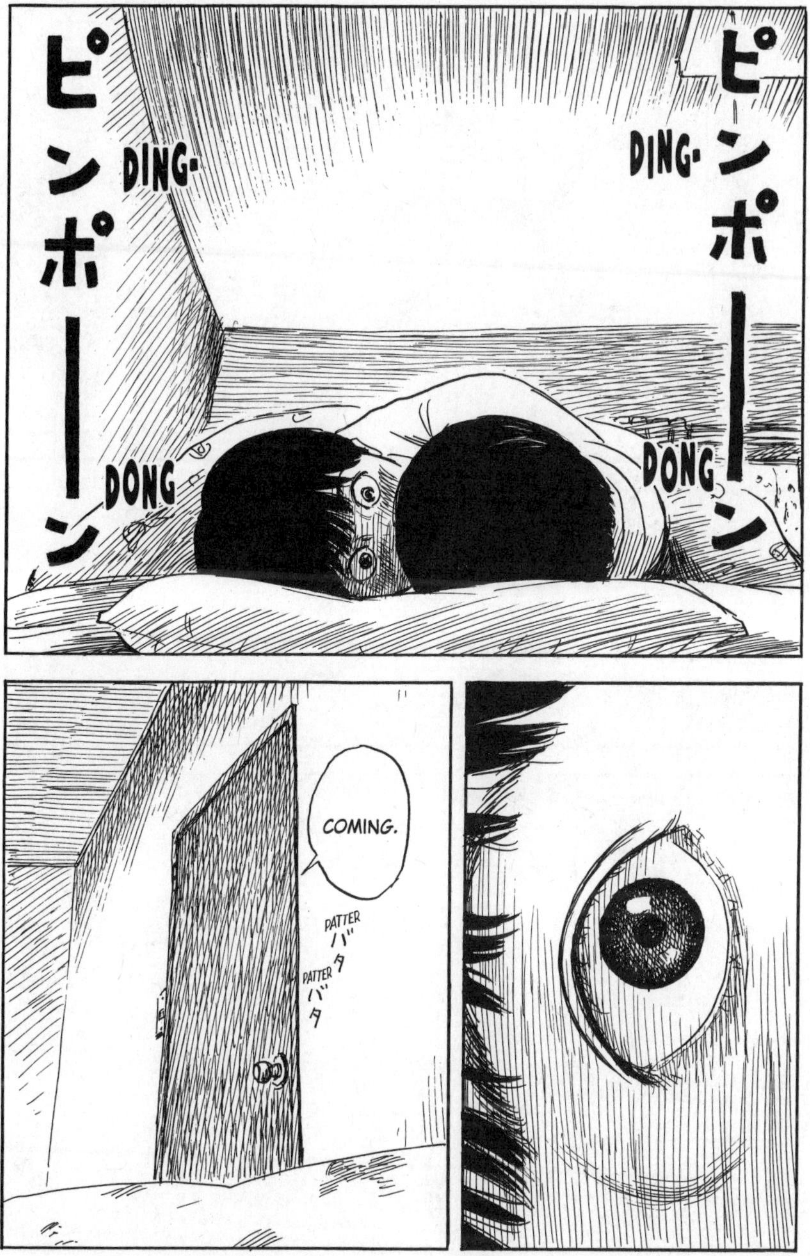
ピンポーン
DING-
DONG
ピンポーン
DING-
DONG
COMING.
PATTER
バタ
PATTER
バタ

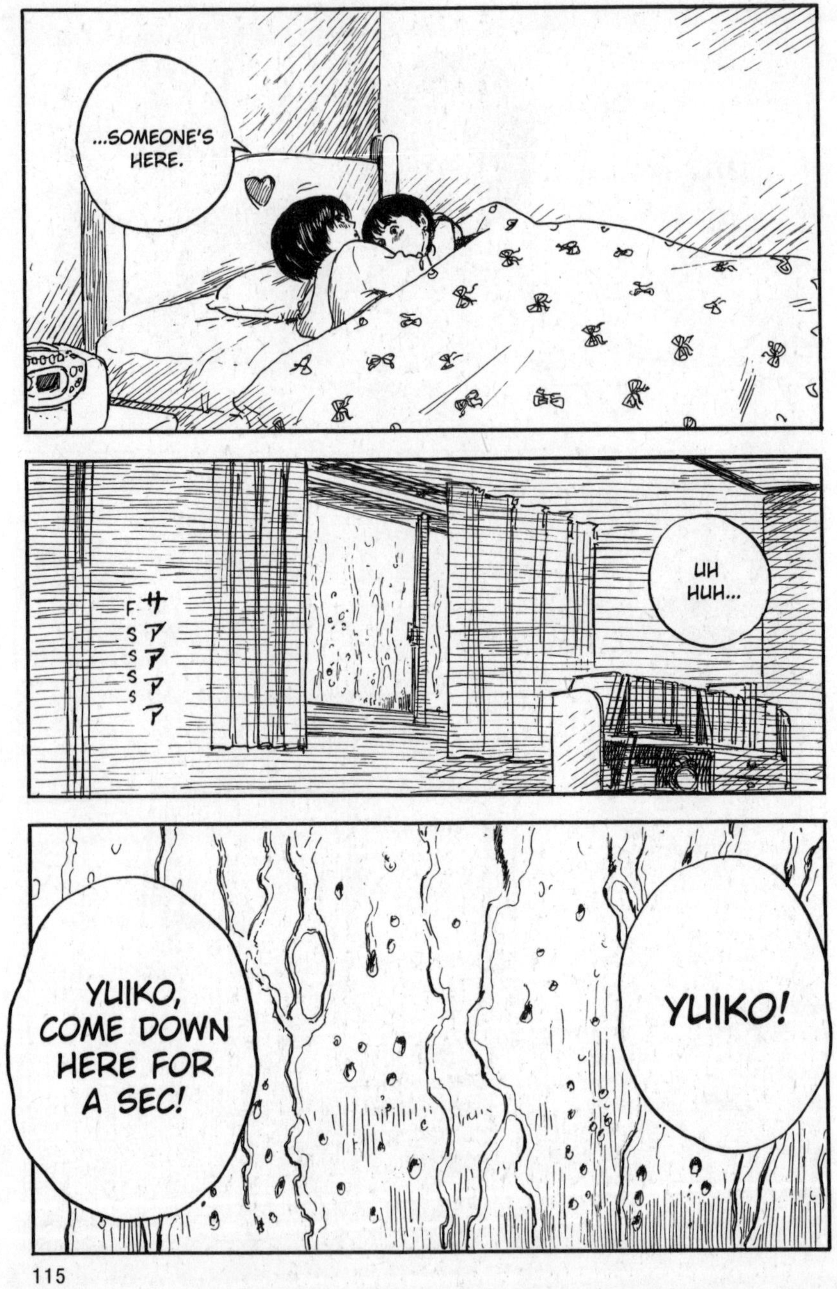

...SOMEONE'S HERE.
FSSSS
UH HUH...
YUIKO!
YUIKO, COME DOWN HERE FOR A SEC!

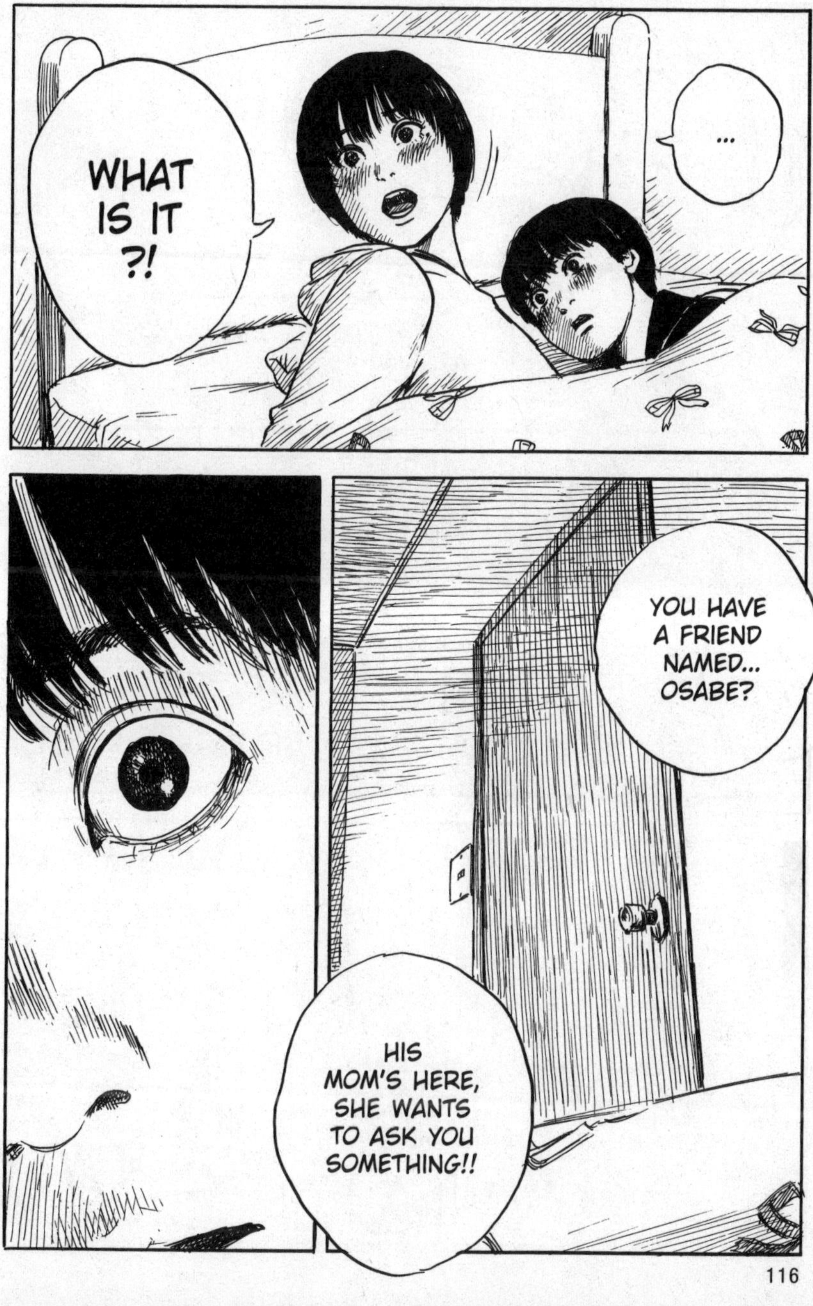
...
WHAT IS IT ?!
YOU HAVE A FRIEND NAMED... OSABE?
HIS MOM'S HERE, SHE WANTS TO ASK YOU SOMETHING!!

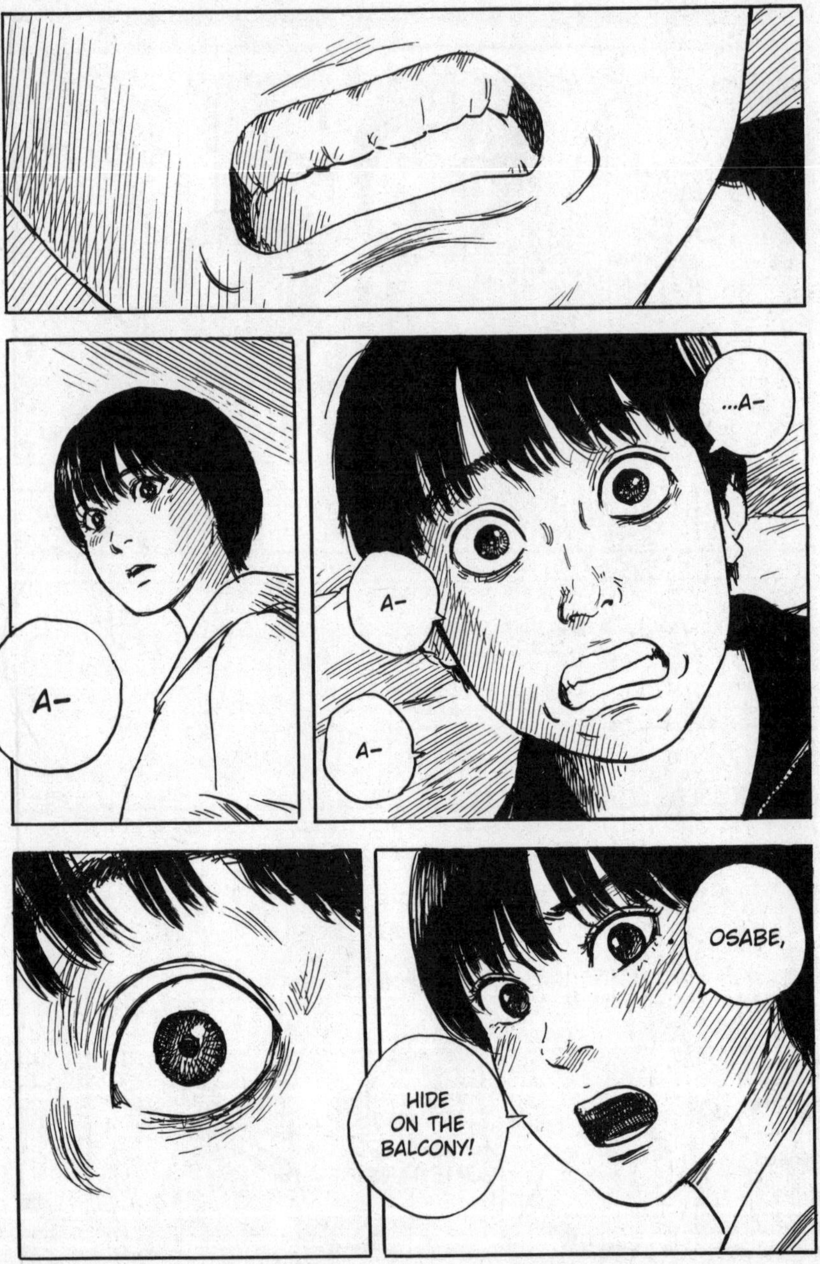

...A-
A-
A-
A-
OSABE,
HIDE ON THE BALCONY!

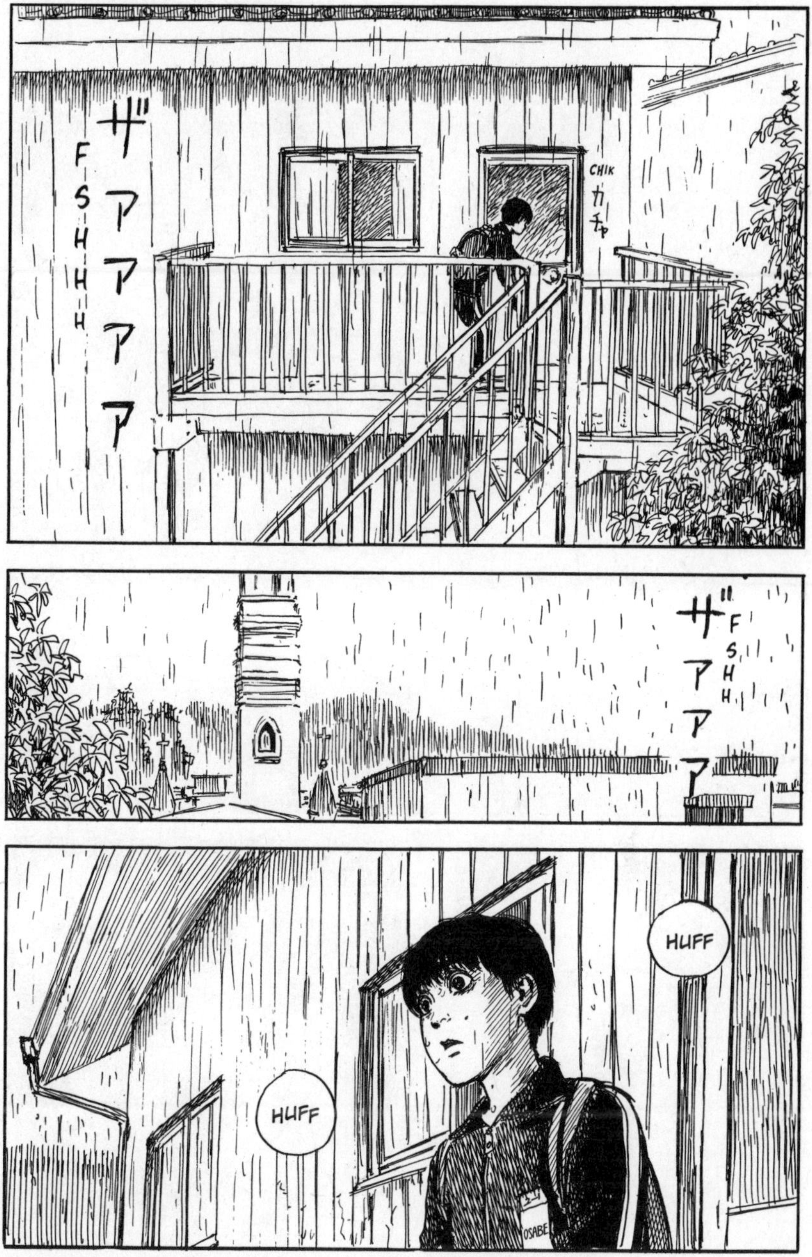
CHIK
カチャ
ザアアア
FSHHHH
ザアアア
FSHH
HUFF
HUFF
OSABE

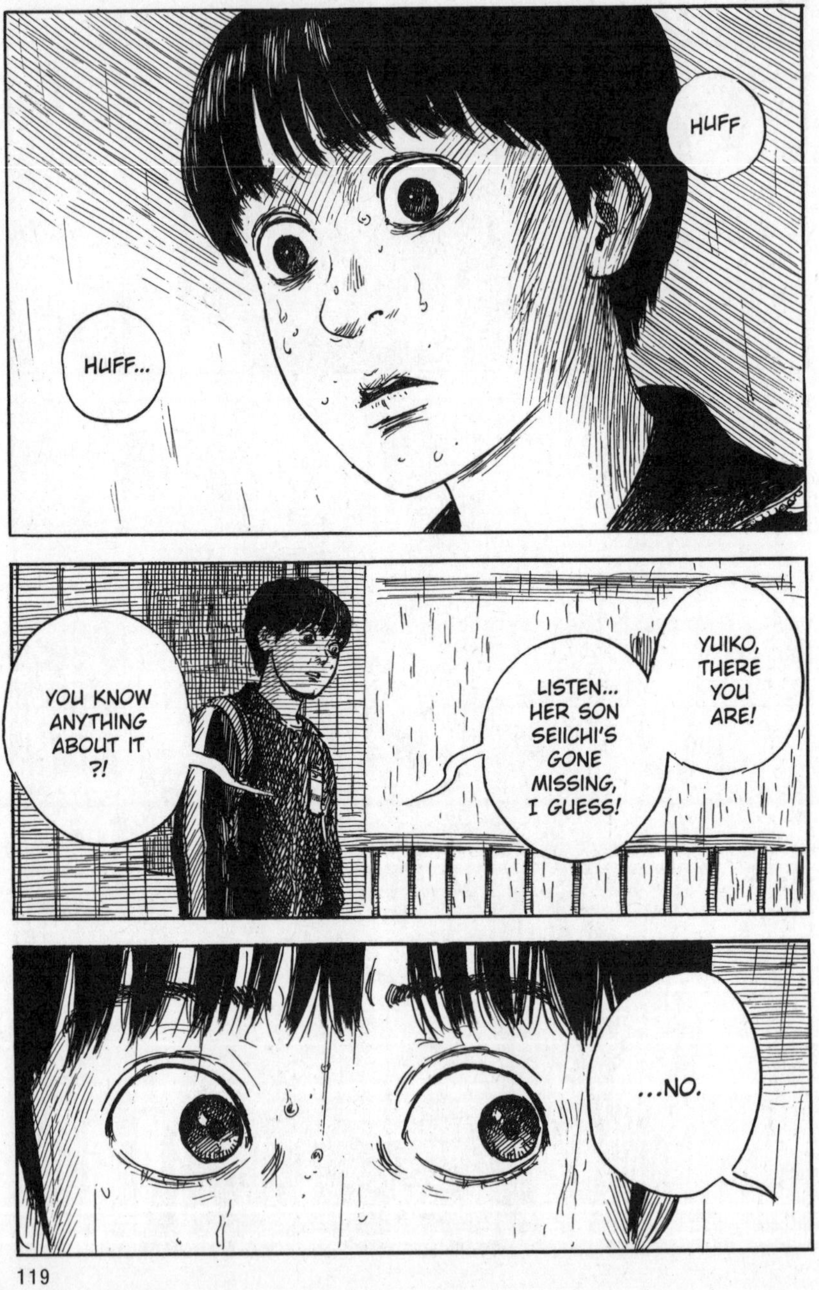
HUFF
HUFF...
YUIKO, THERE YOU ARE!
LISTEN... HER SON SEIICHI'S GONE MISSING, I GUESS!
YOU KNOW ANYTHING ABOUT IT ?!
...NO.

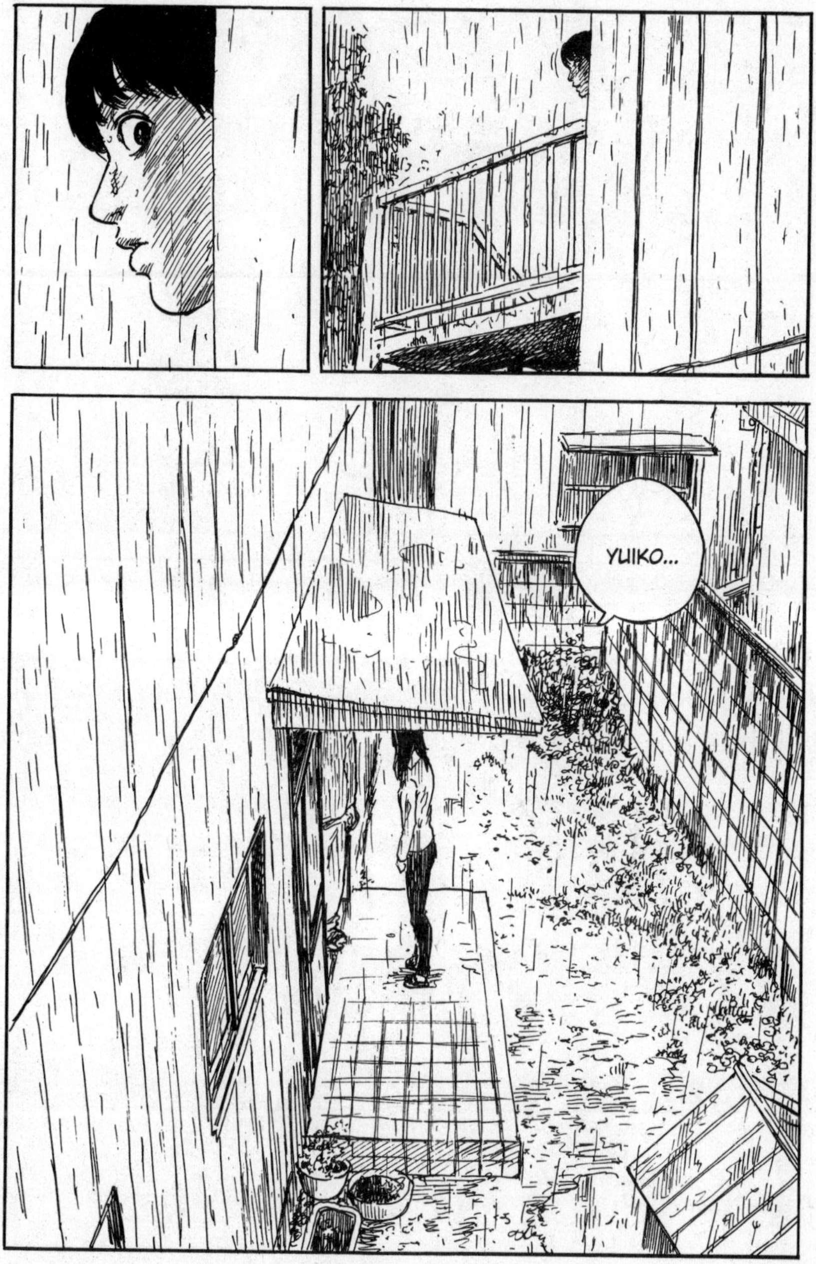
YUIKO...

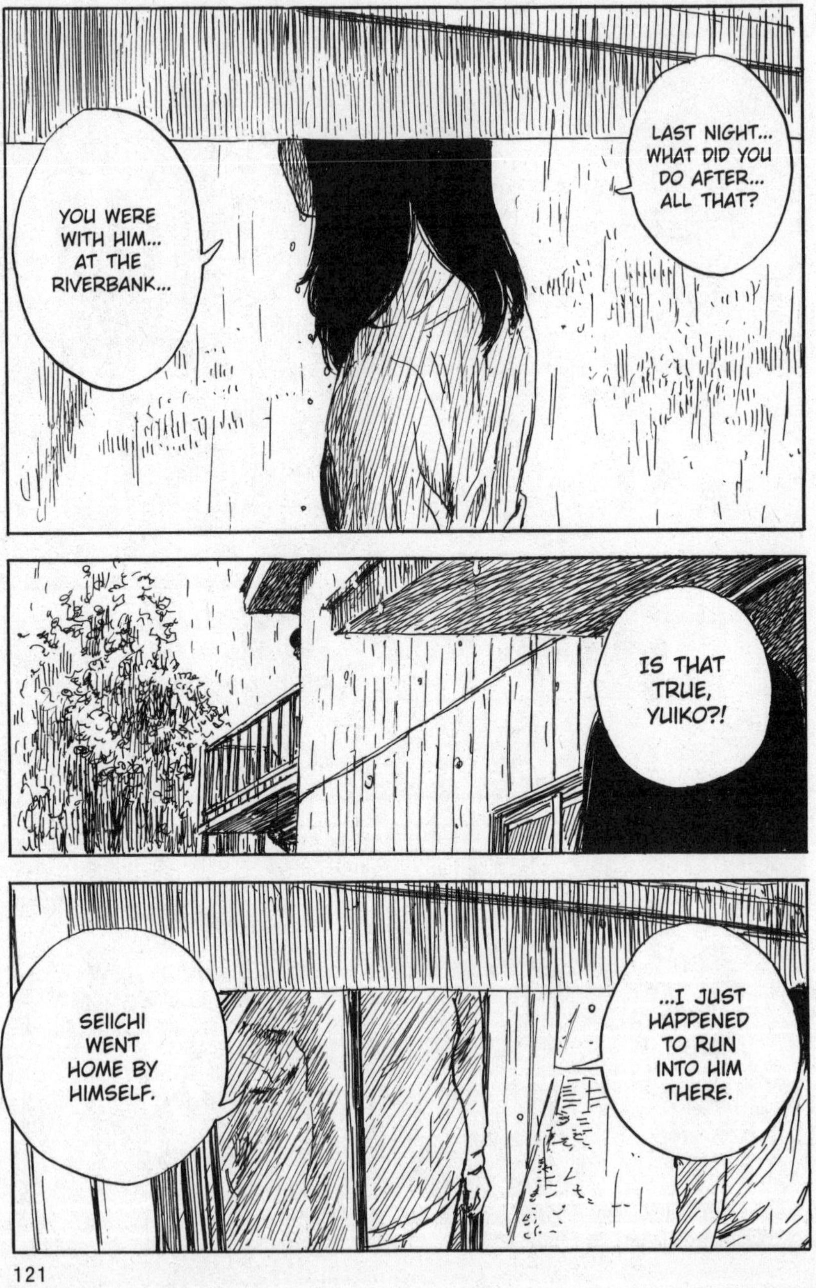
LAST NIGHT... WHAT DID YOU DO AFTER... ALL THAT?
YOU WERE WITH HIM... AT THE RIVERBANK...
IS THAT TRUE, YUIKO?!
...I JUST HAPPENED TO RUN INTO HIM THERE.
SEIICHI WENT HOME BY HIMSELF.

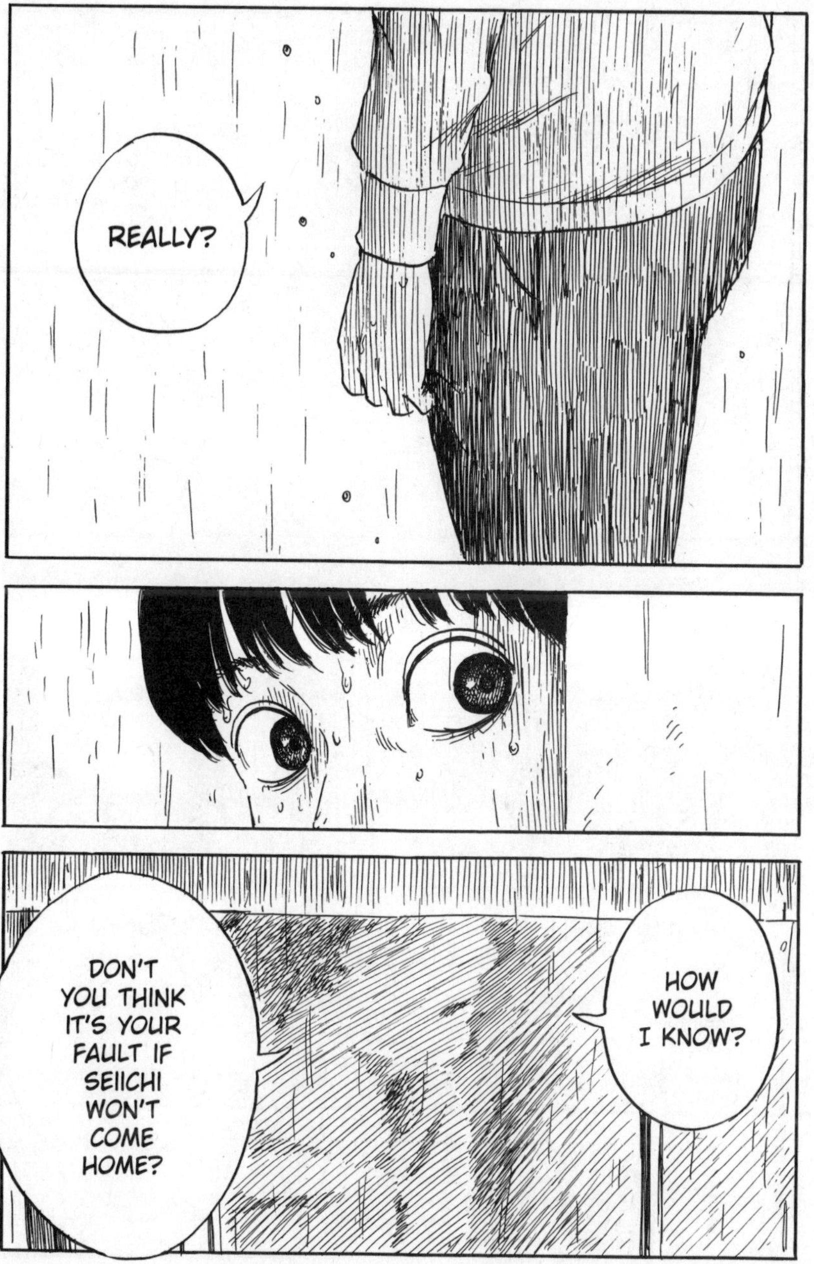
REALLY?
HOW WOULD I KNOW?
DON'T YOU THINK IT'S YOUR FAULT IF SEIICHI WON'T COME HOME?

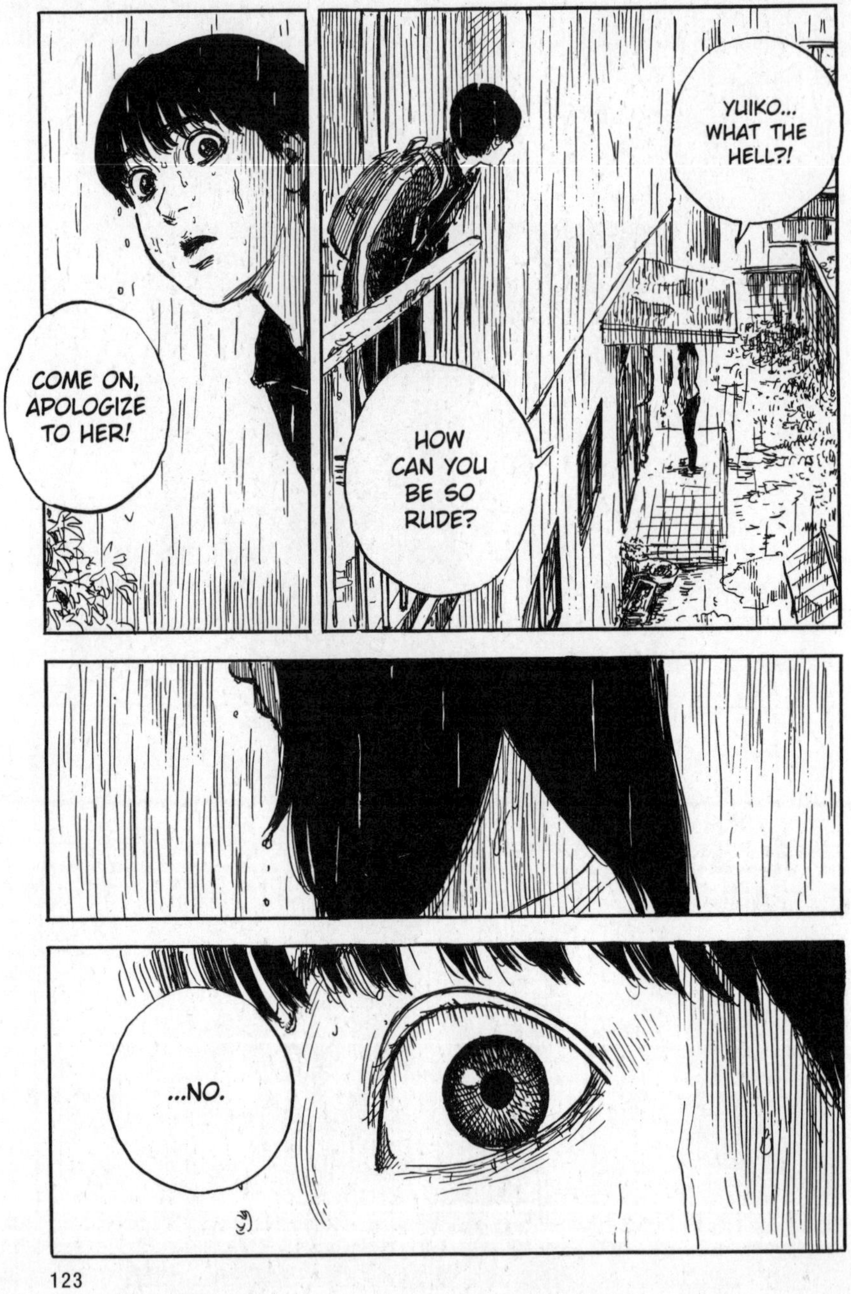
YUIKO... WHAT THE HELL?!
HOW CAN YOU BE SO RUDE?
COME ON, APOLOGIZE TO HER!
...NO.

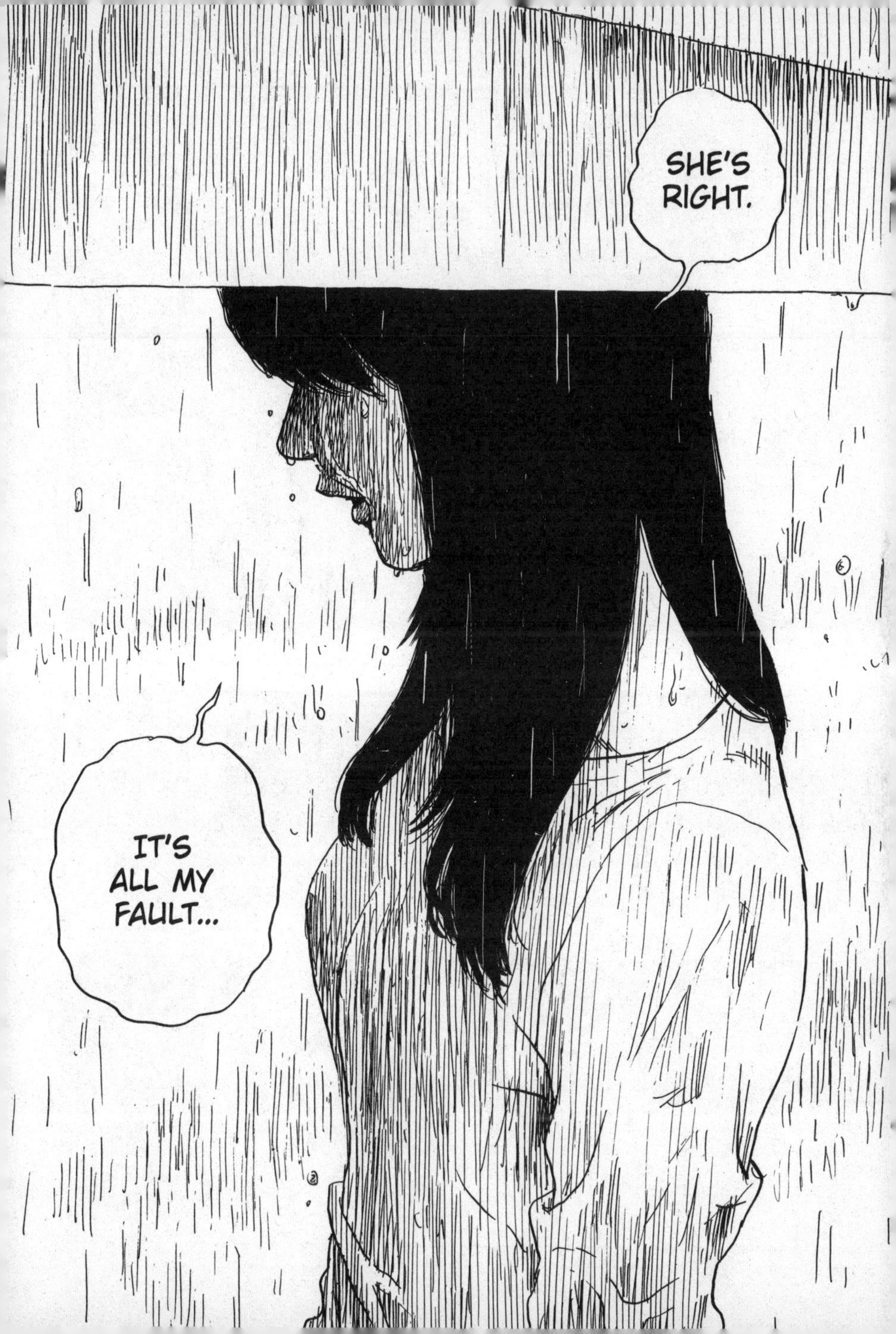
SHE'S RIGHT.
IT'S ALL MY FAULT...

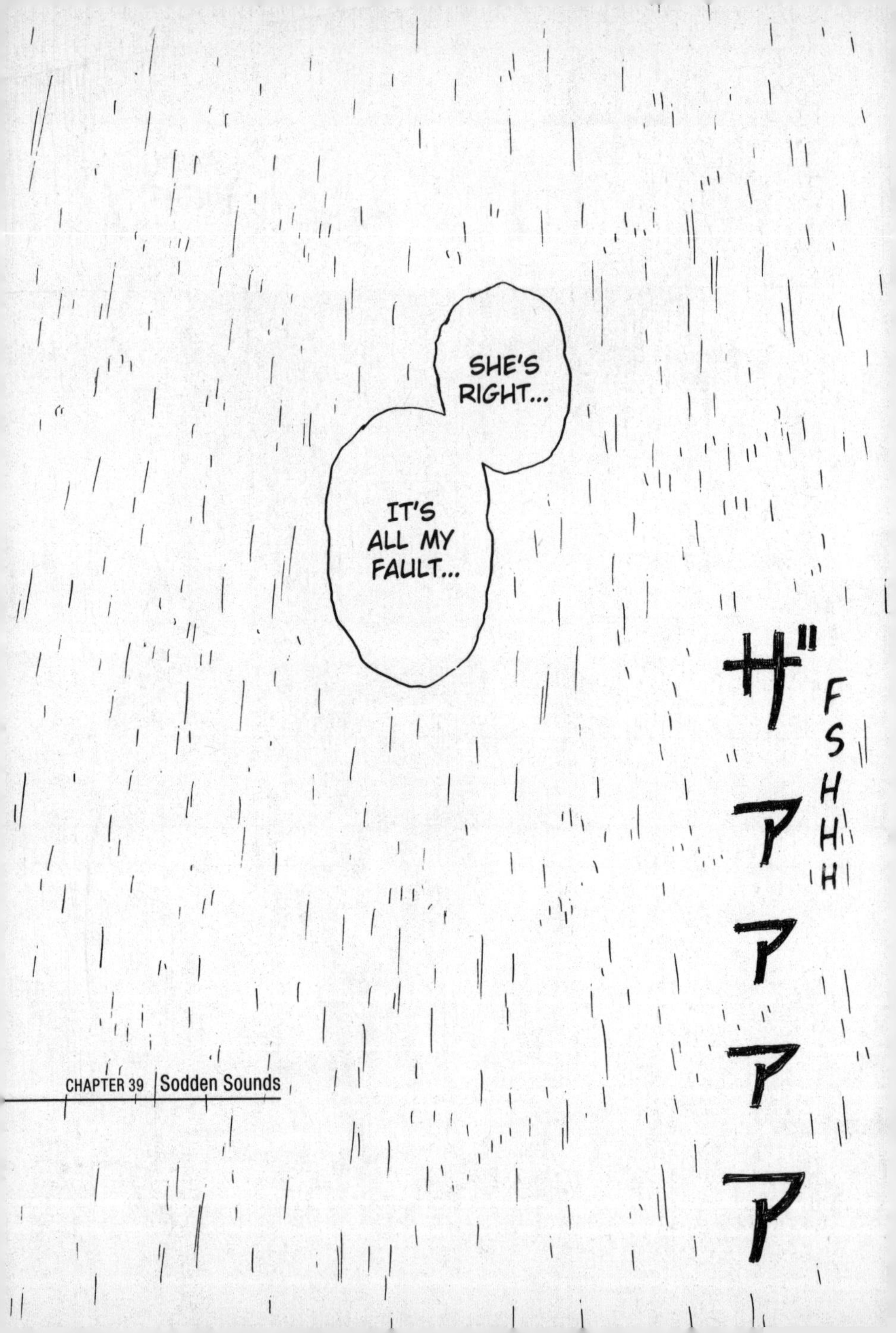
ザァァァァ
FSHHH
SHE'S RIGHT...
IT'S ALL MY FAULT...
CHAPTER 39 Sodden Sounds

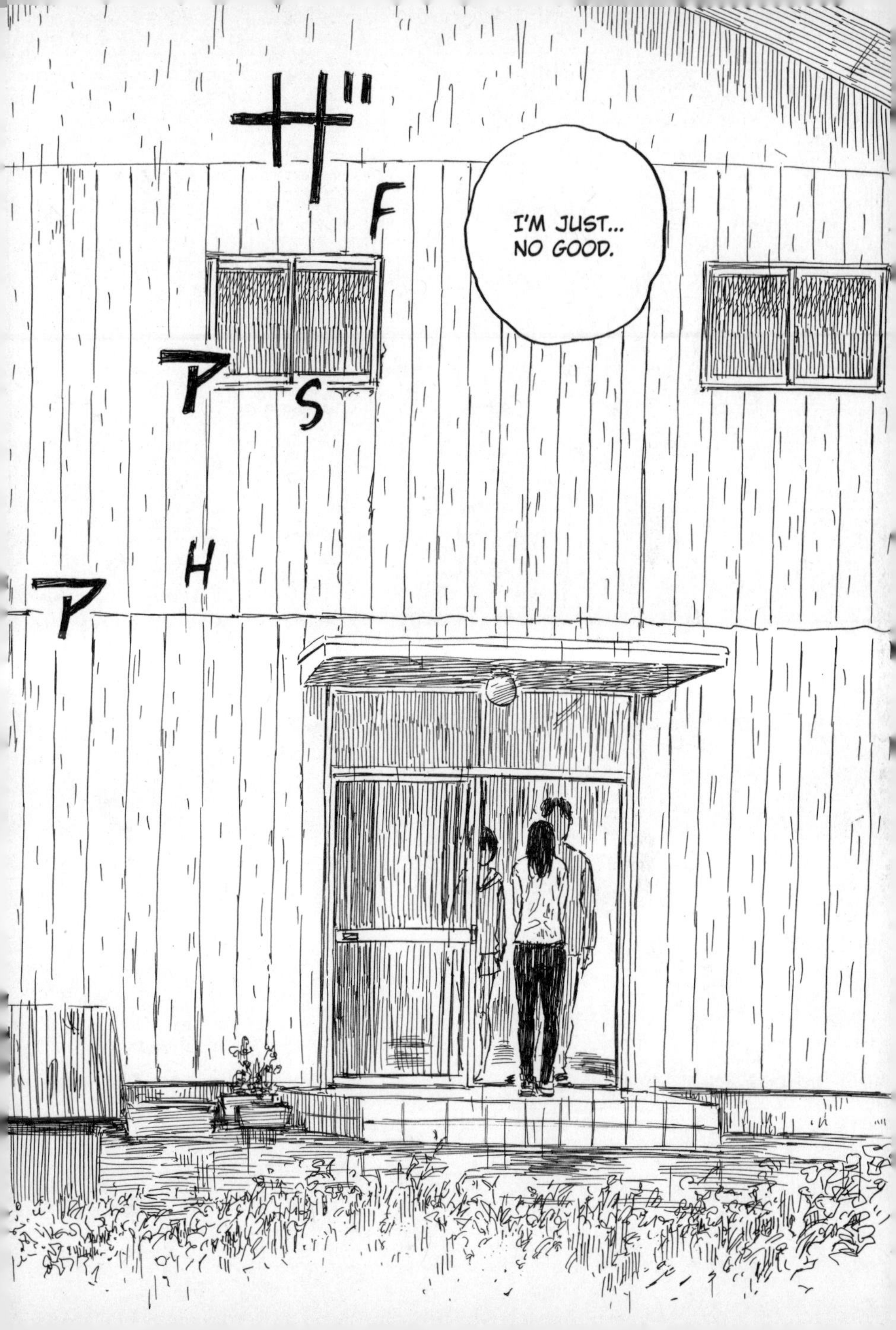
ザ
F
ア
S
ア
H
I'M JUST... NO GOOD.

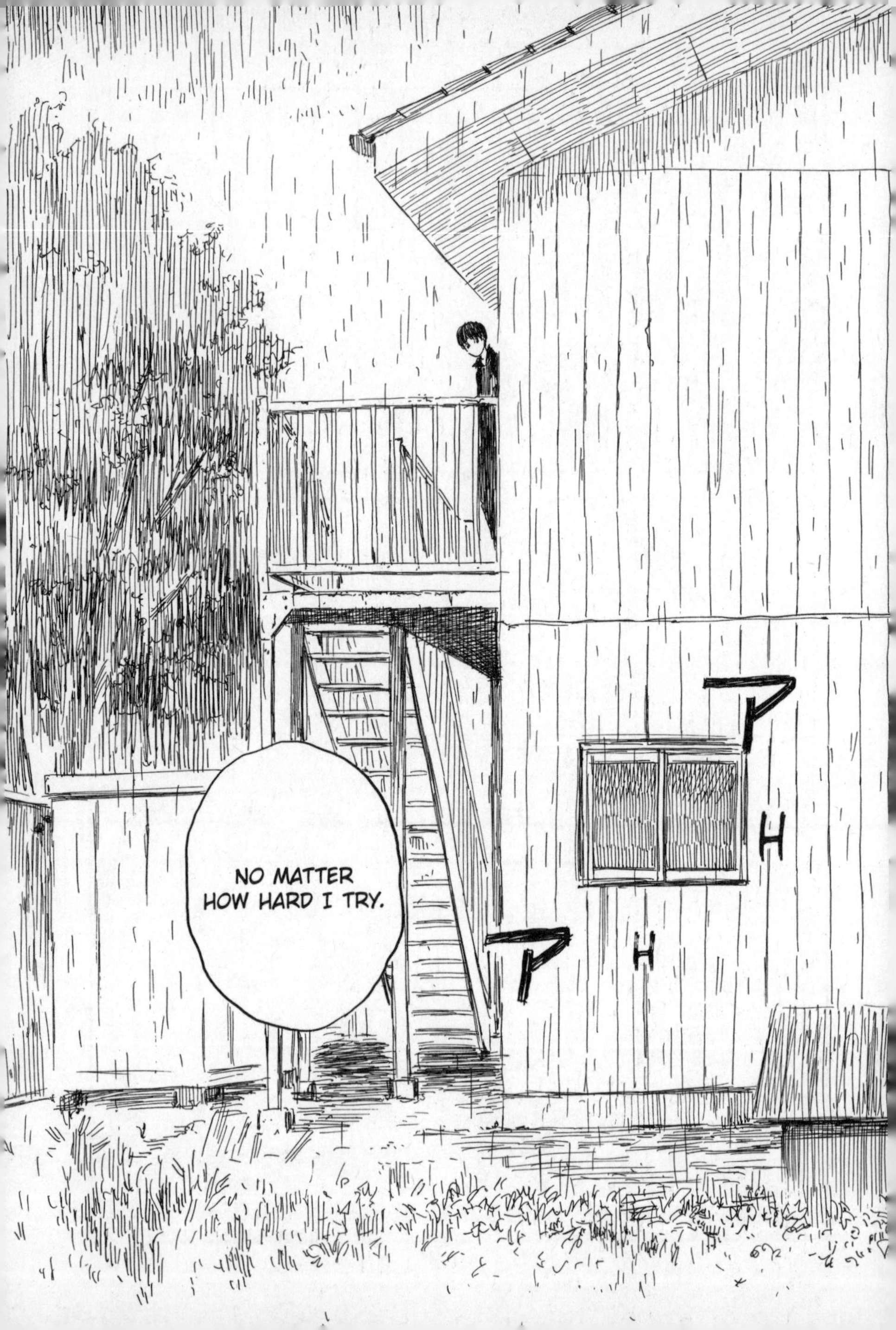
NO MATTER HOW HARD I TRY.
ア
ハ
ア
ハ

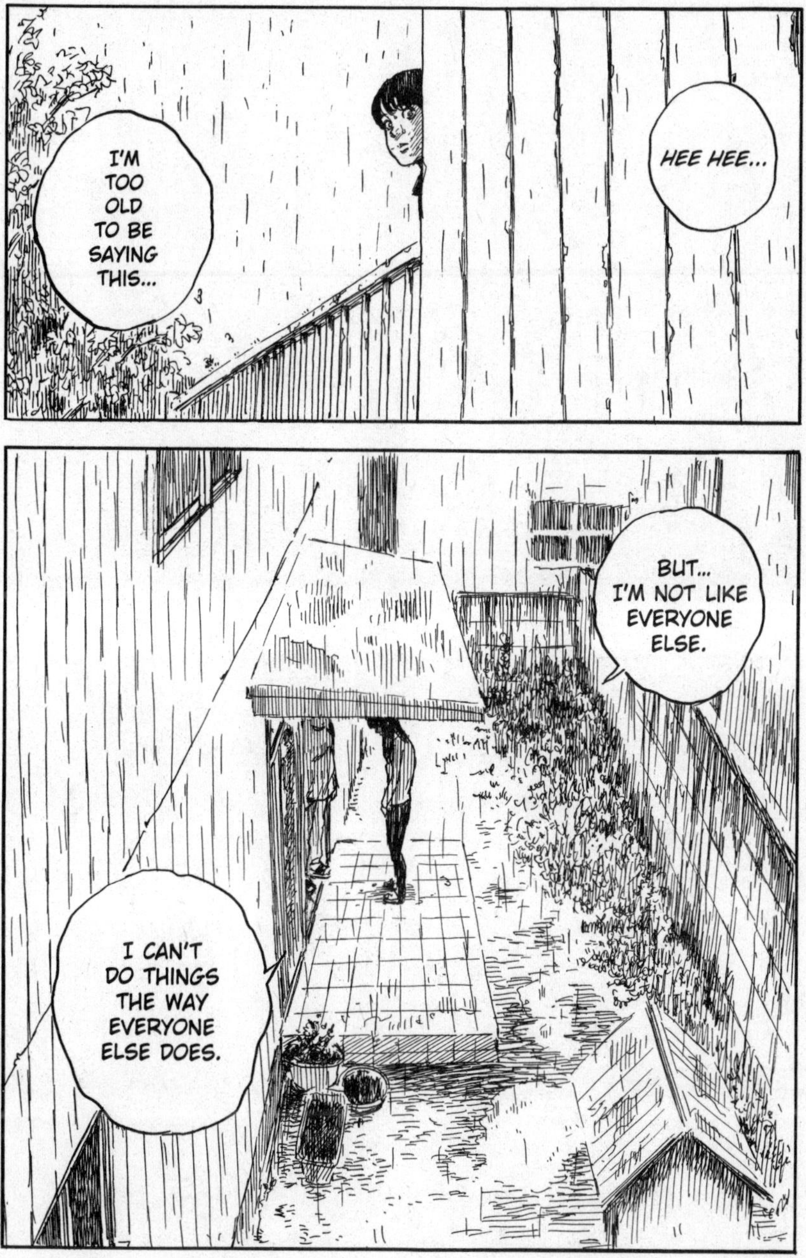
HEE HEE...
I'M TOO OLD TO BE SAYING THIS...
BUT... I'M NOT LIKE EVERYONE ELSE.
I CAN'T DO THINGS THE WAY EVERYONE ELSE DOES.

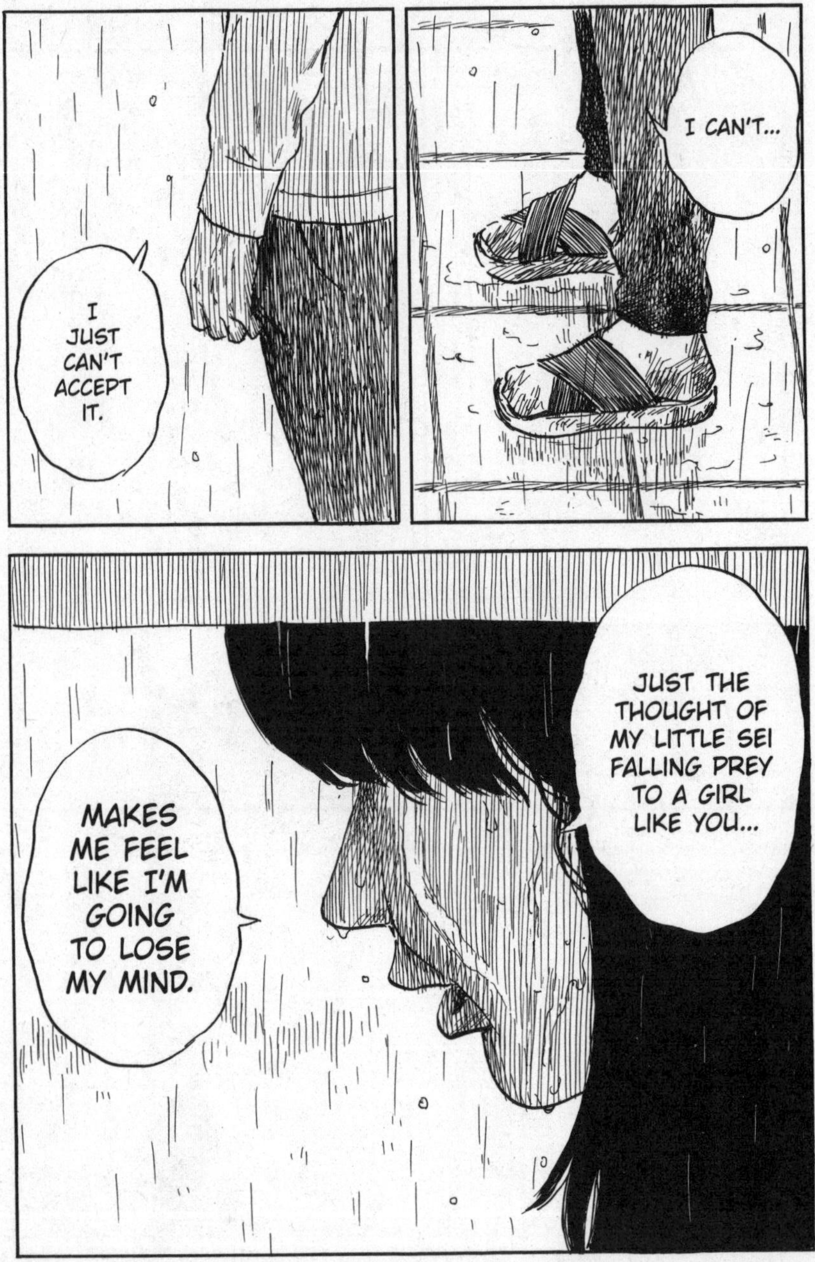
I CAN'T...
I JUST CAN'T ACCEPT IT.
JUST THE THOUGHT OF MY LITTLE SEI FALLING PREY TO A GIRL LIKE YOU...
MAKES ME FEEL LIKE I'M GOING TO LOSE MY MIND.

HUH...?
FORGIVE ME.

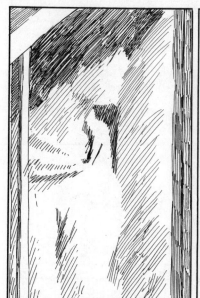

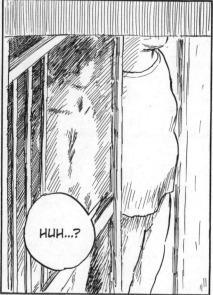

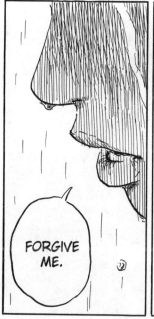

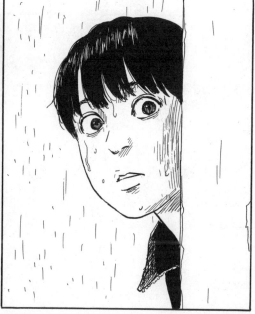

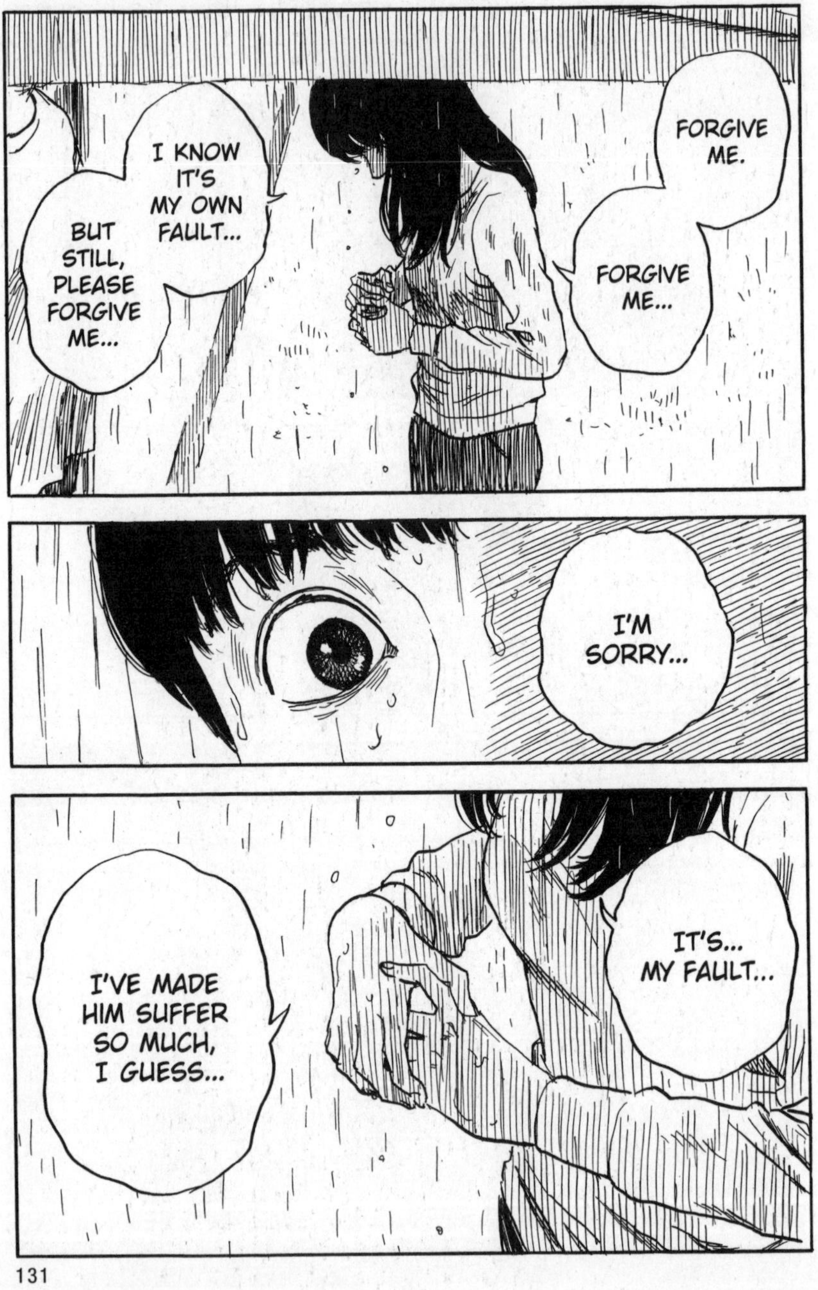
FORGIVE ME.
FORGIVE ME...
I KNOW IT'S MY OWN FAULT...
BUT STILL, PLEASE FORGIVE ME...
I'M SORRY...
IT'S... MY FAULT...
I'VE MADE HIM SUFFER SO MUCH, I GUESS...

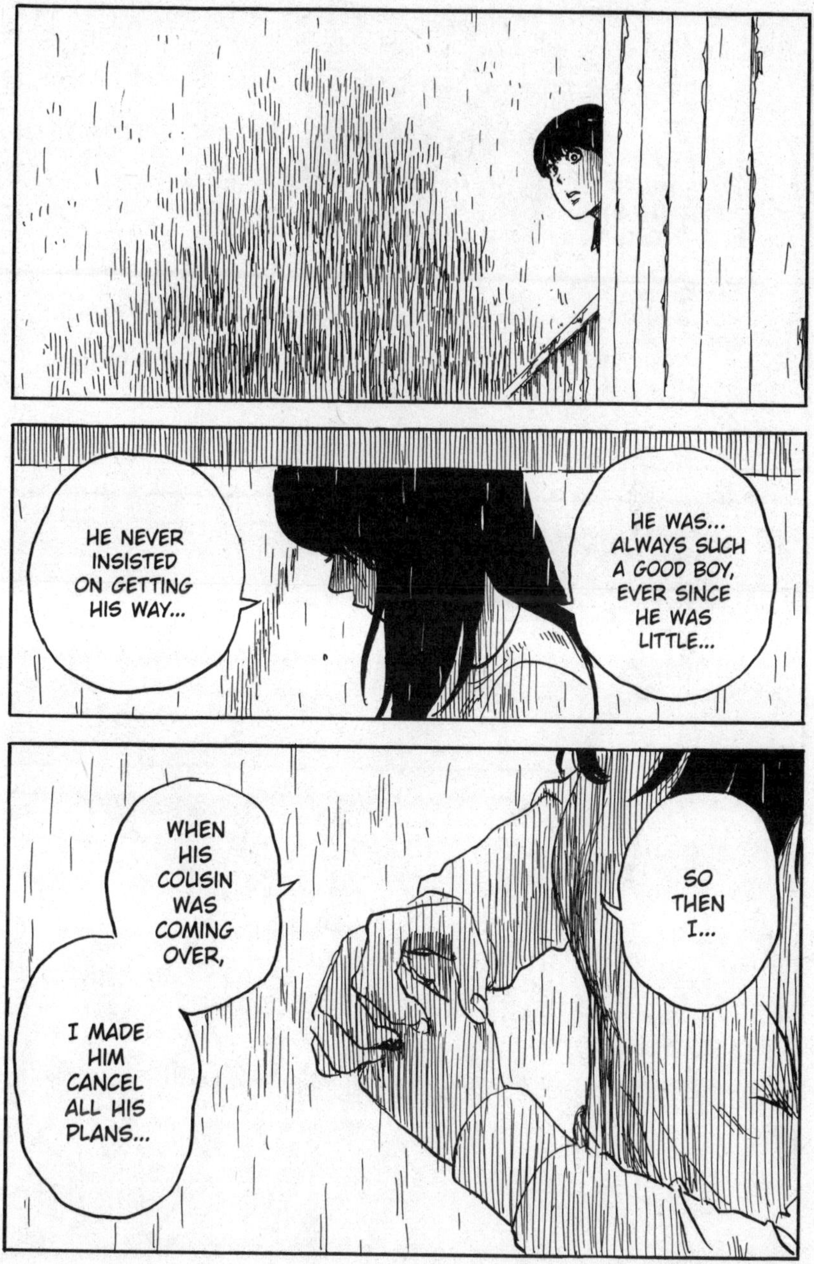
HE WAS... ALWAYS SUCH A GOOD BOY, EVER SINCE HE WAS LITTLE...
HE NEVER INSISTED ON GETTING HIS WAY...
SO THEN I...
WHEN HIS COUSIN WAS COMING OVER,
I MADE HIM CANCEL ALL HIS PLANS...

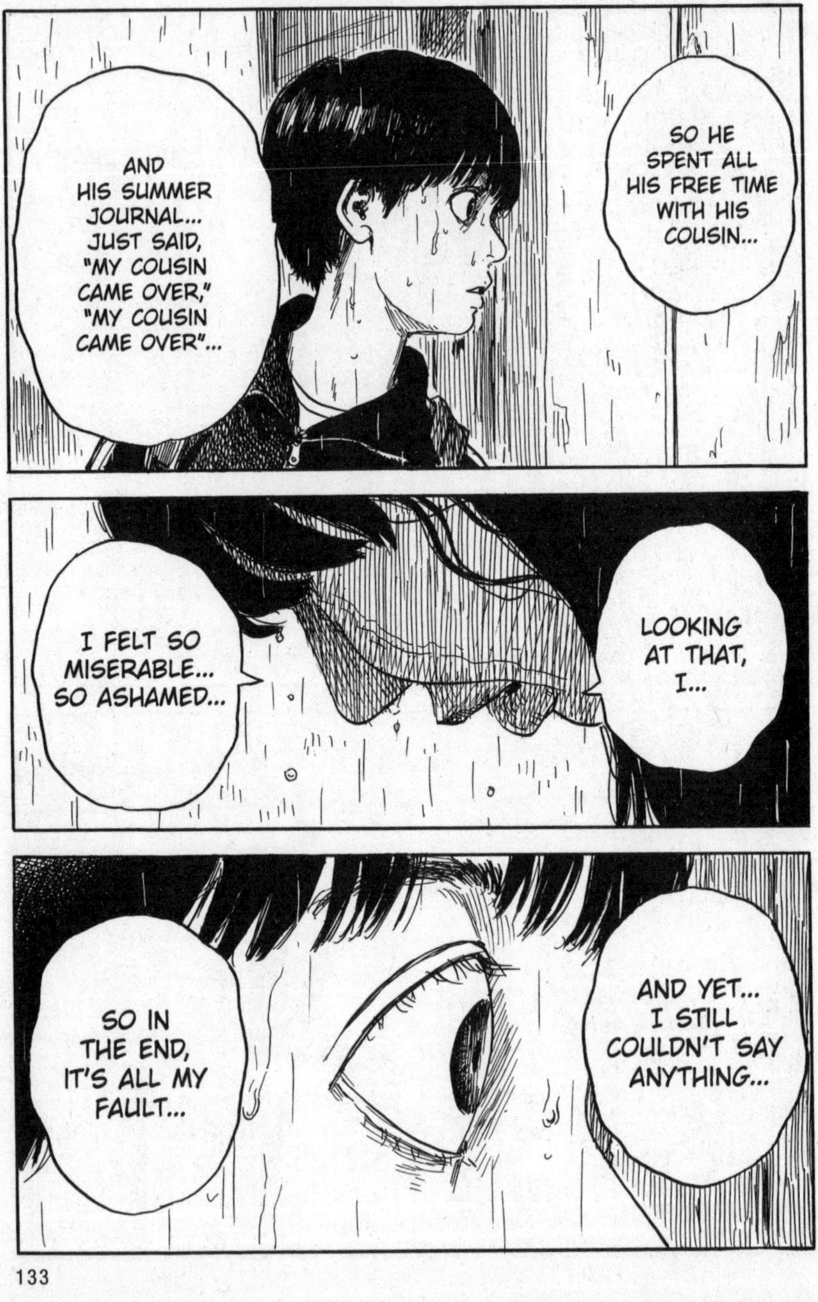
SO HE SPENT ALL HIS FREE TIME WITH HIS COUSIN...
AND HIS SUMMER JOURNAL... JUST SAID, "MY COUSIN CAME OVER," "MY COUSIN CAME OVER"...
LOOKING AT THAT, I...
I FELT SO MISERABLE... SO ASHAMED...
AND YET... I STILL COULDN'T SAY ANYTHING...
SO IN THE END, IT'S ALL MY FAULT...

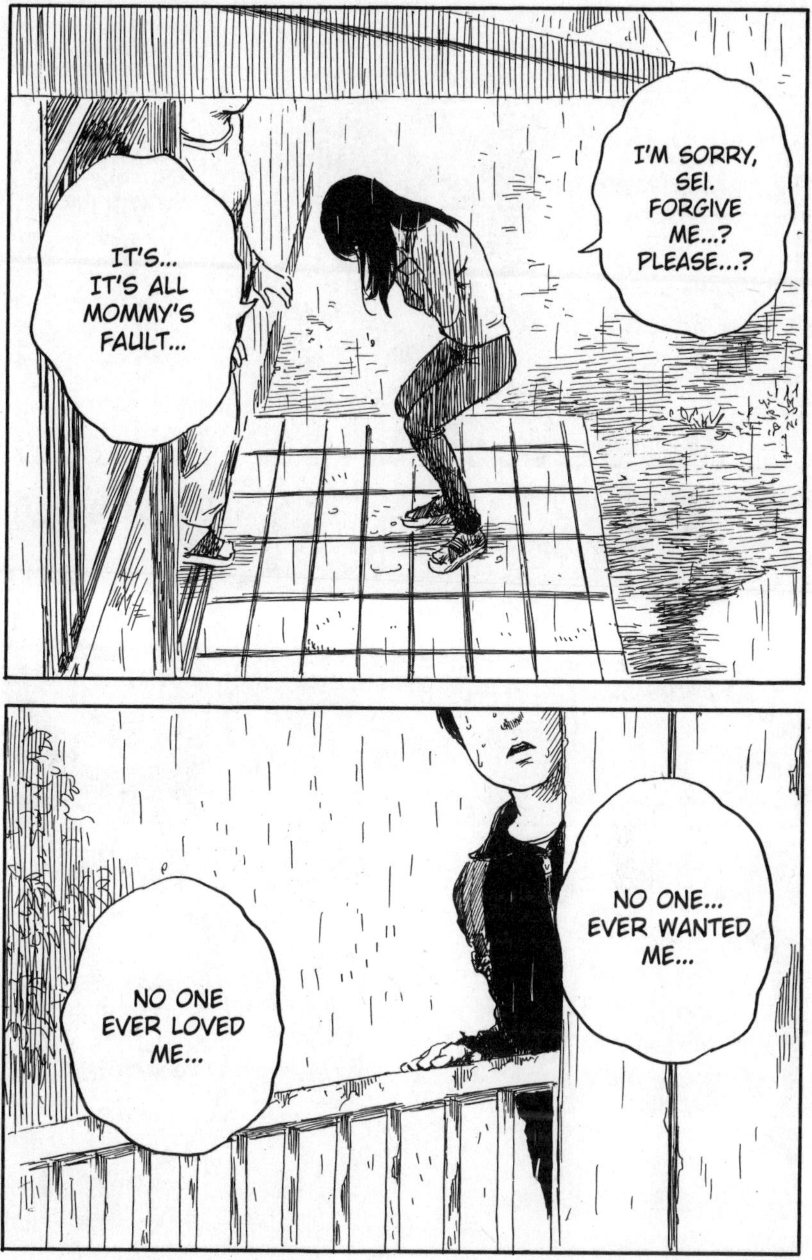
I'M SORRY, SEI. FORGIVE ME...? PLEASE...?
IT'S... IT'S ALL MOMMY'S FAULT...
NO ONE... EVER WANTED ME...
NO ONE EVER LOVED ME...

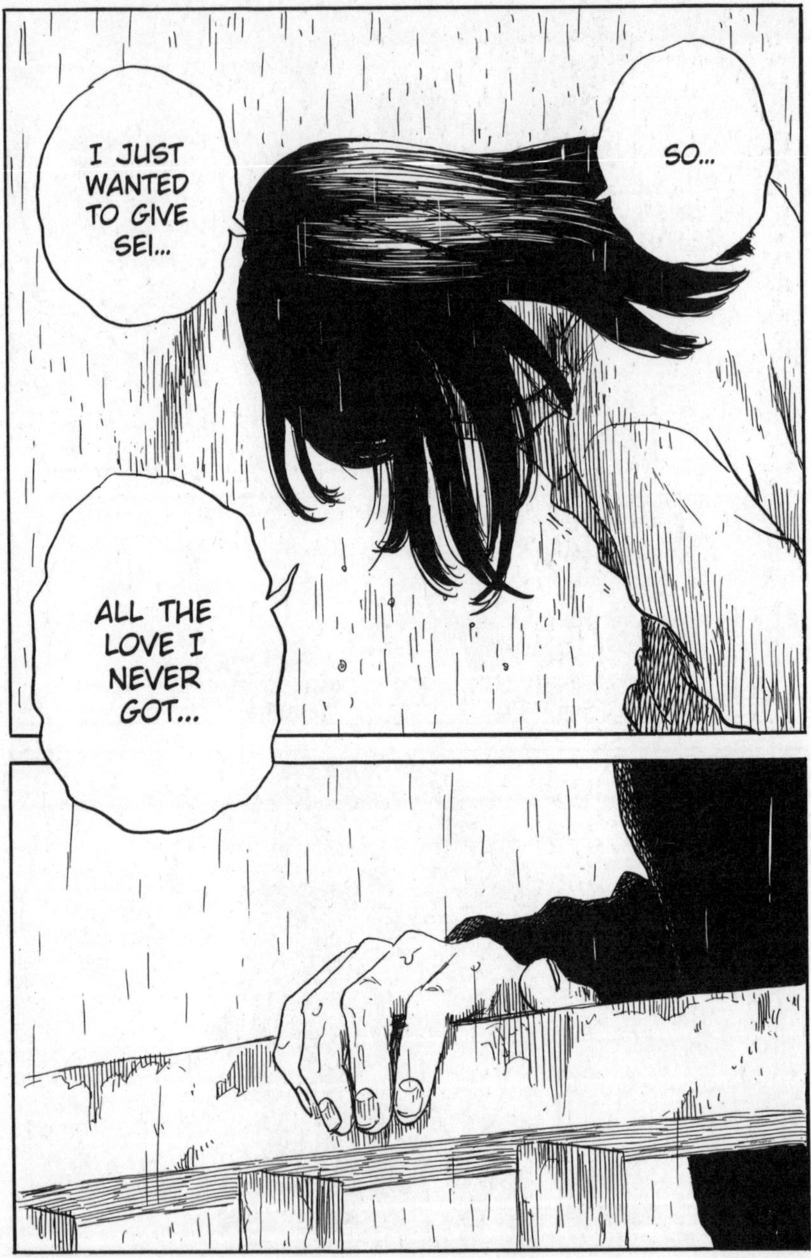
SO...
I JUST WANTED TO GIVE SEI...
ALL THE LOVE I NEVER GOT...

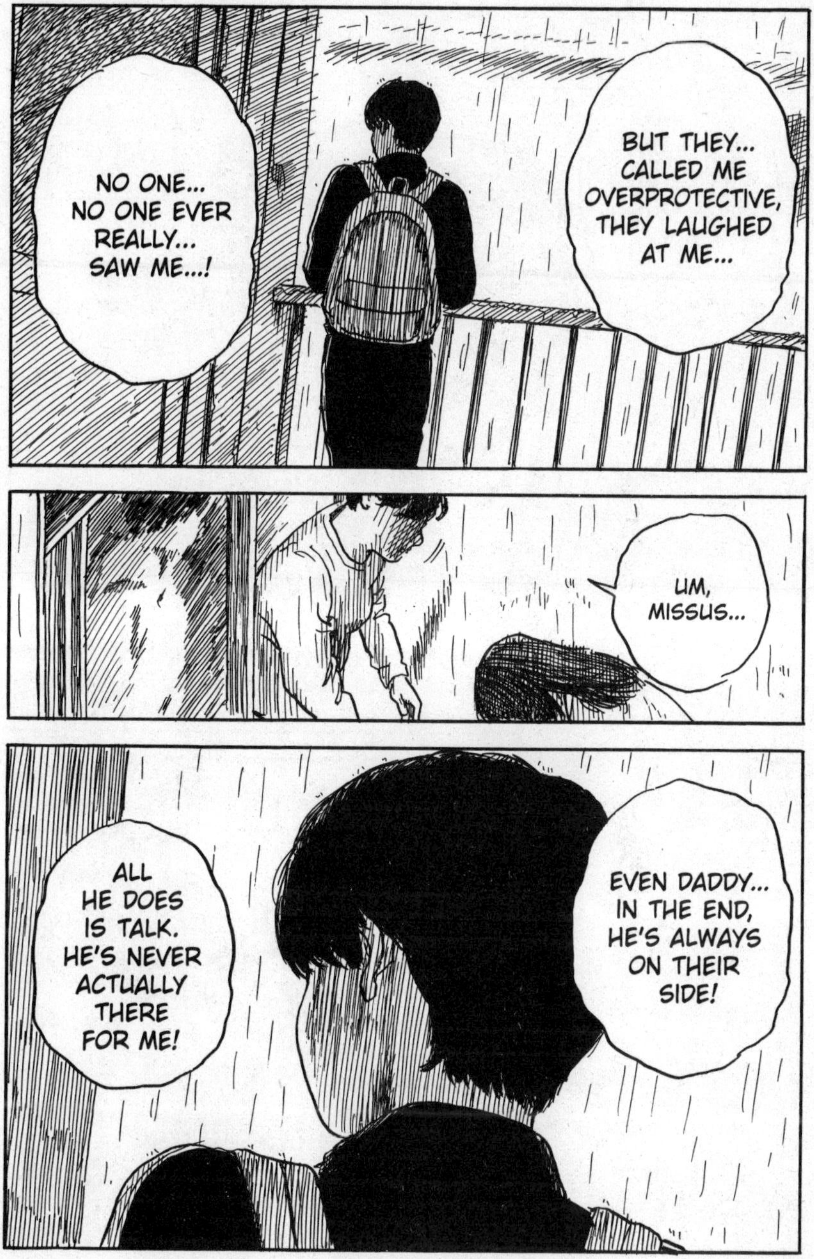
BUT THEY... CALLED ME OVERPROTECTIVE, THEY LAUGHED AT ME...
NO ONE... NO ONE EVER REALLY... SAW ME...!
UM, MISSUS...
EVEN DADDY... IN THE END, HE'S ALWAYS ON THEIR SIDE!
ALL HE DOES IS TALK. HE'S NEVER ACTUALLY THERE FOR ME!

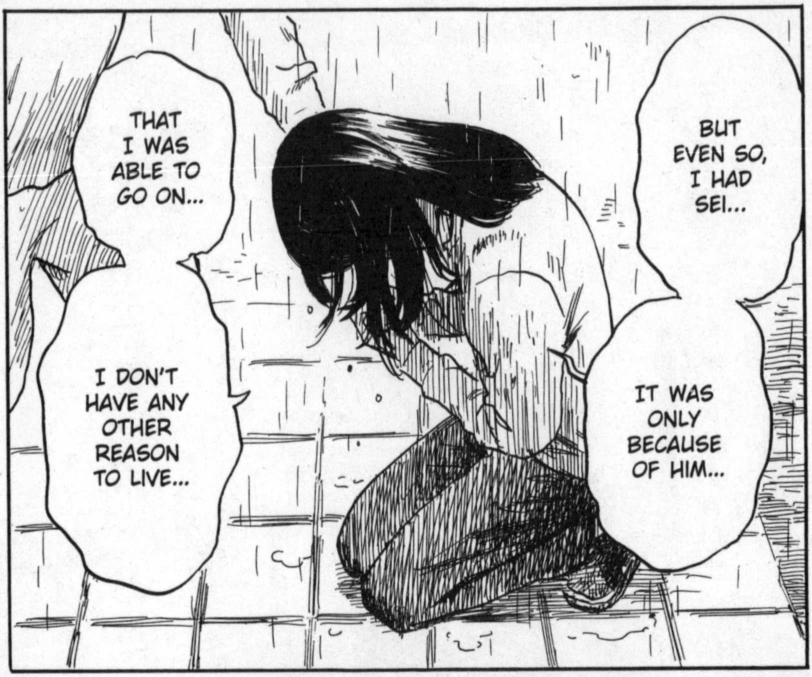
BUT EVEN SO, I HAD SEI...
IT WAS ONLY BECAUSE OF HIM...
THAT I WAS ABLE TO GO ON...
I DON'T HAVE ANY OTHER REASON TO LIVE...

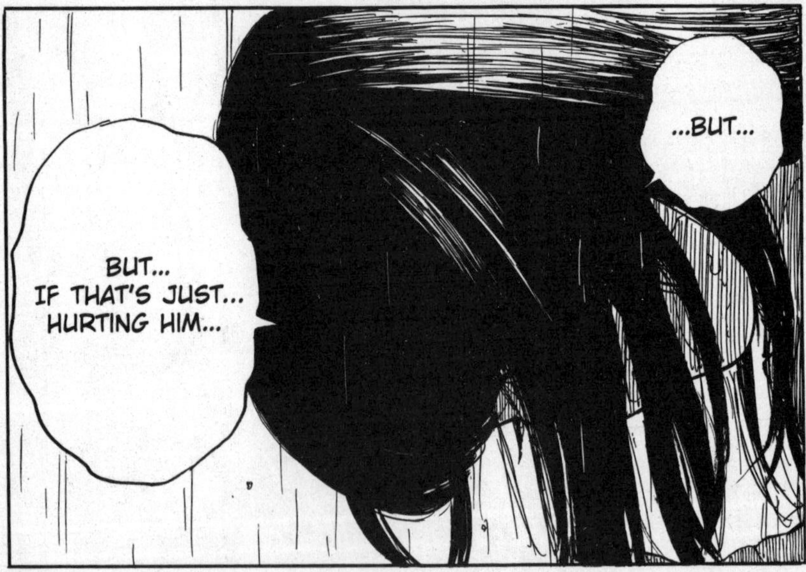
...BUT...
BUT... IF THAT'S JUST... HURTING HIM...

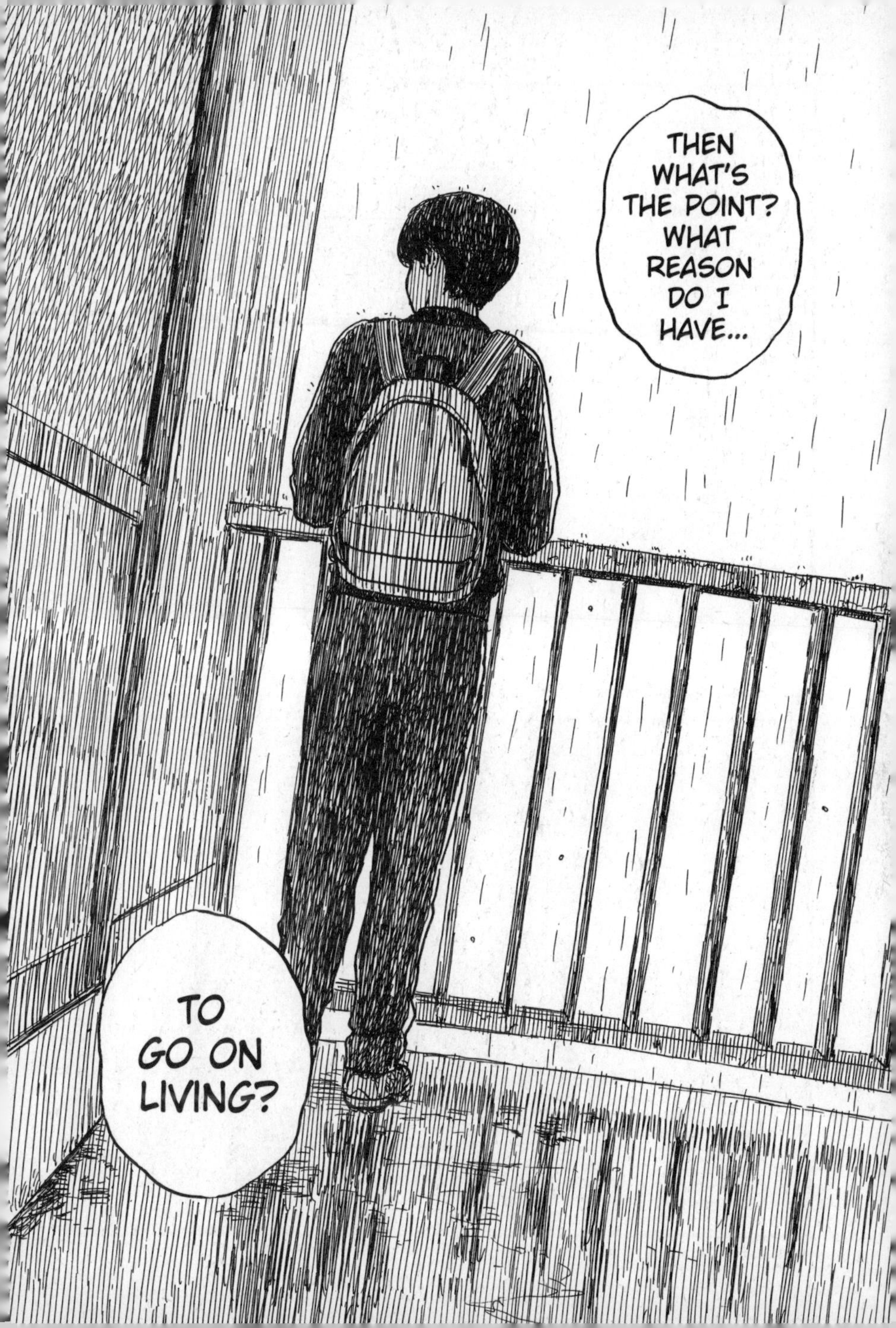
THEN WHAT'S THE POINT? WHAT REASON DO I HAVE...
TO GO ON LIVING?

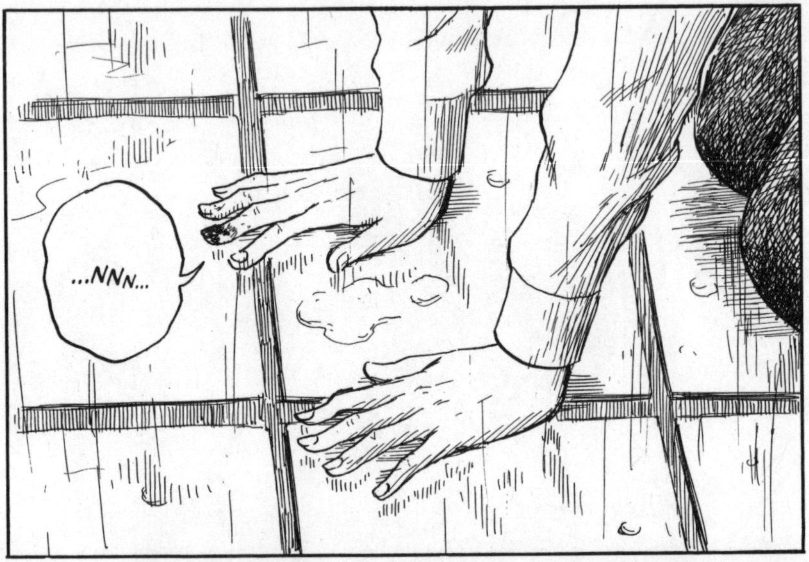
...NNN...
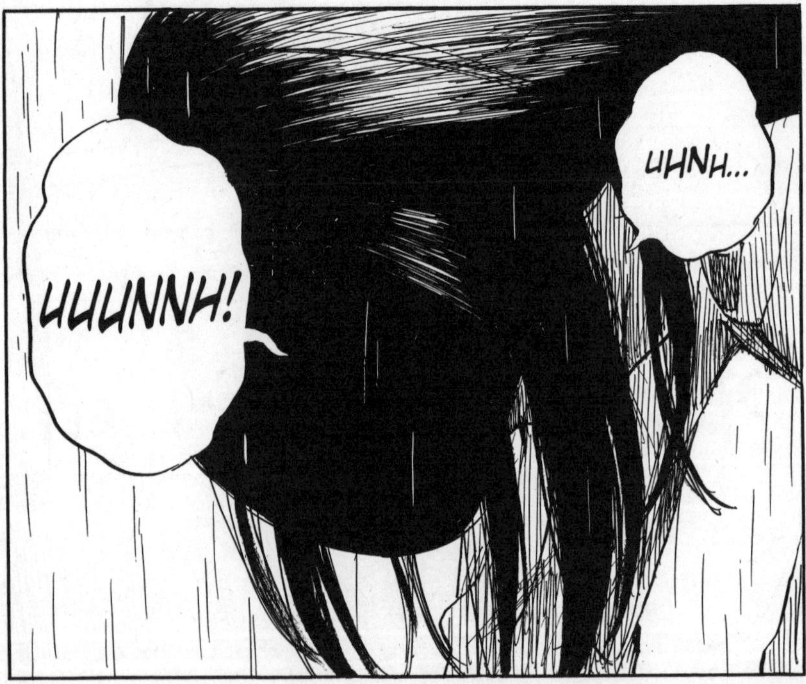
UHNH...
UUUNNH!

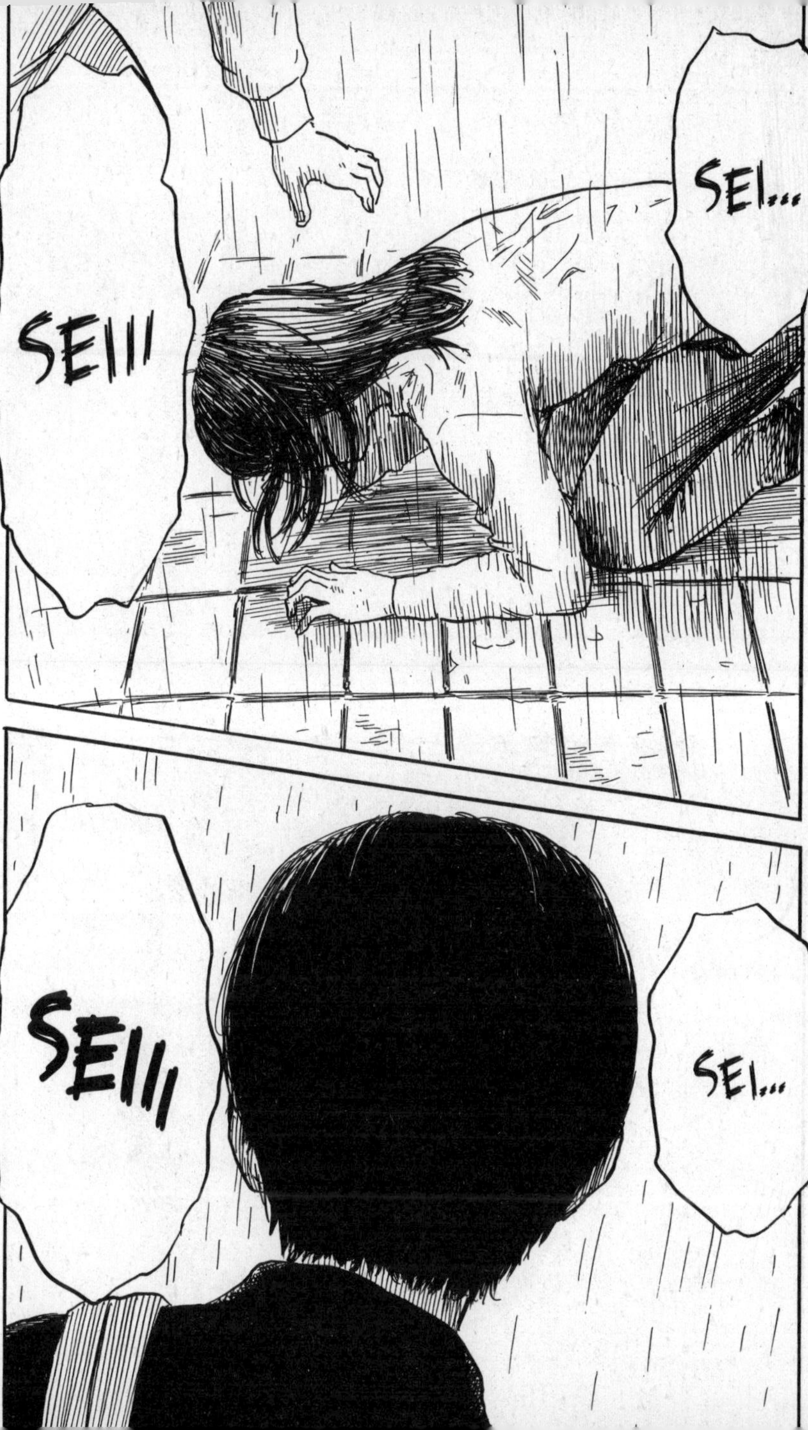
SEI...
SEI!!!
SEI...
SEI!!!

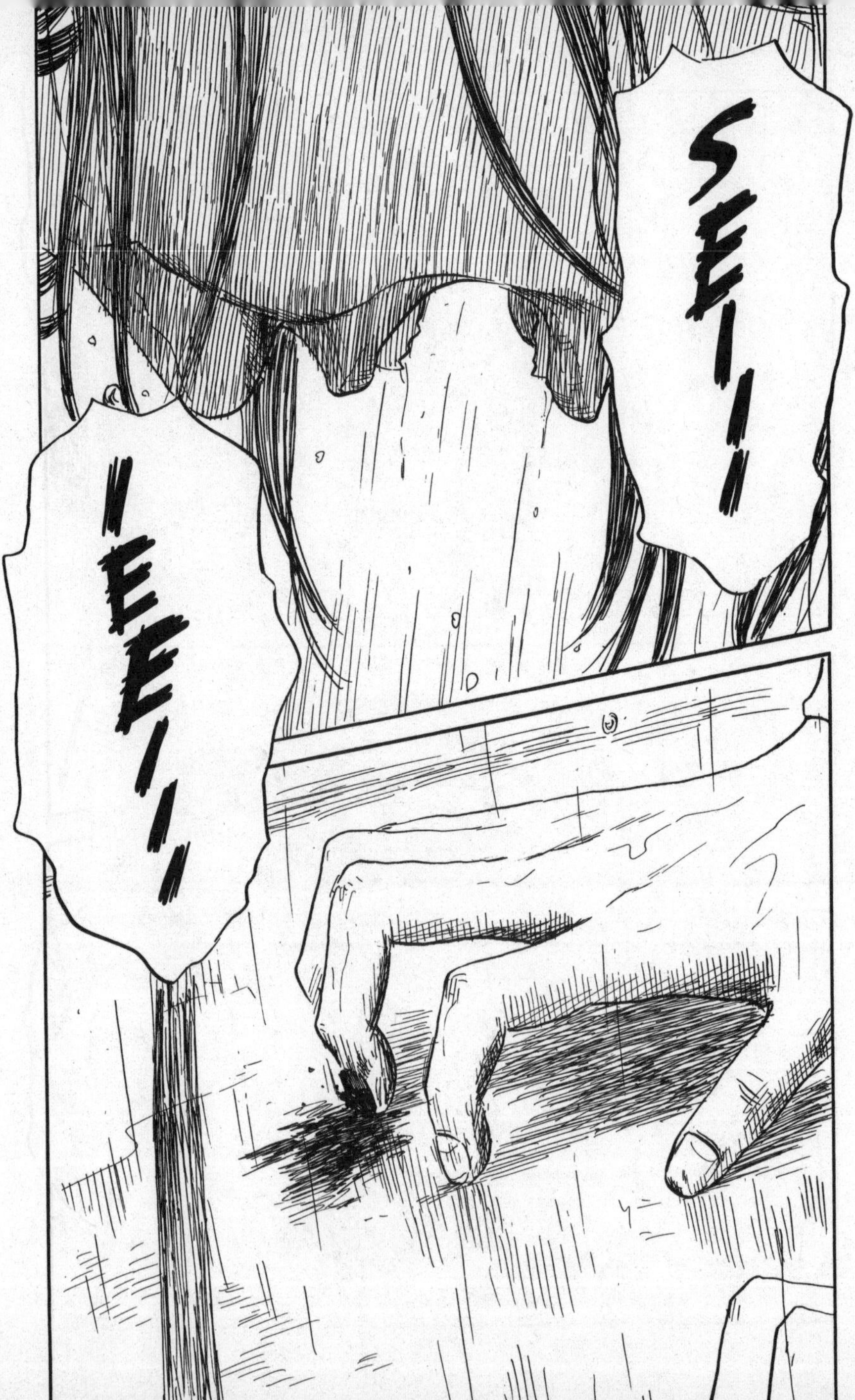
SEE
EE

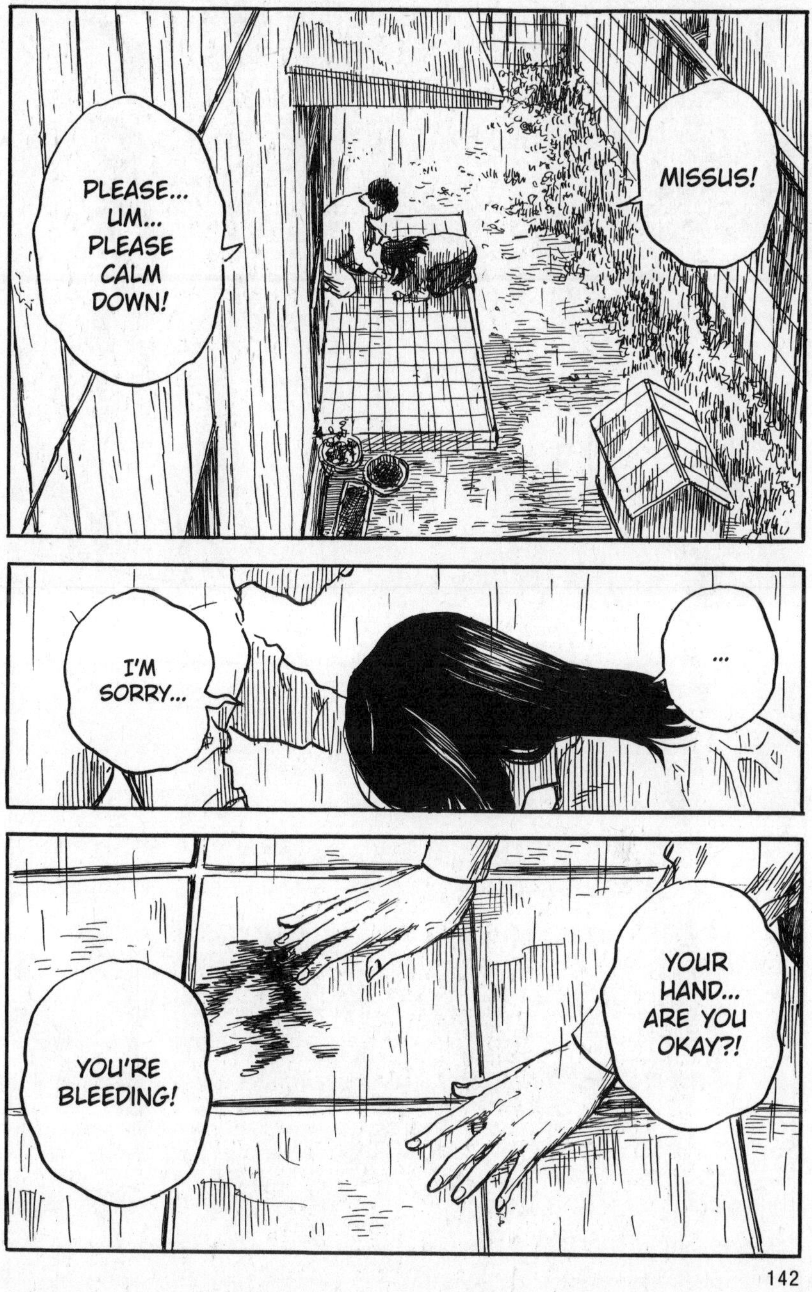
MISSUS!
PLEASE... UM... PLEASE CALM DOWN!
...
I'M SORRY...
YOUR HAND... ARE YOU OKAY?!
YOU'RE BLEEDING!

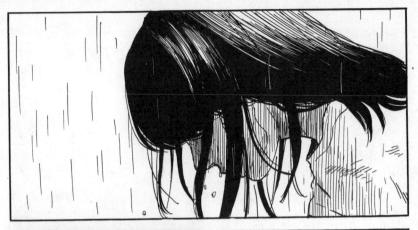

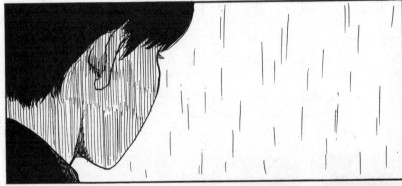

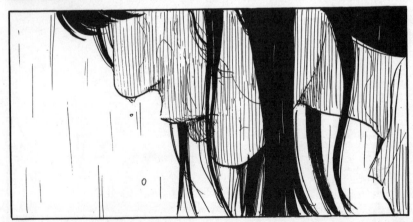

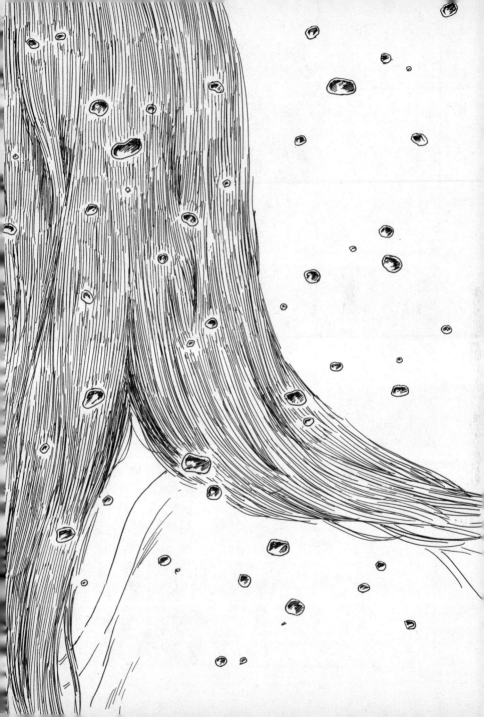

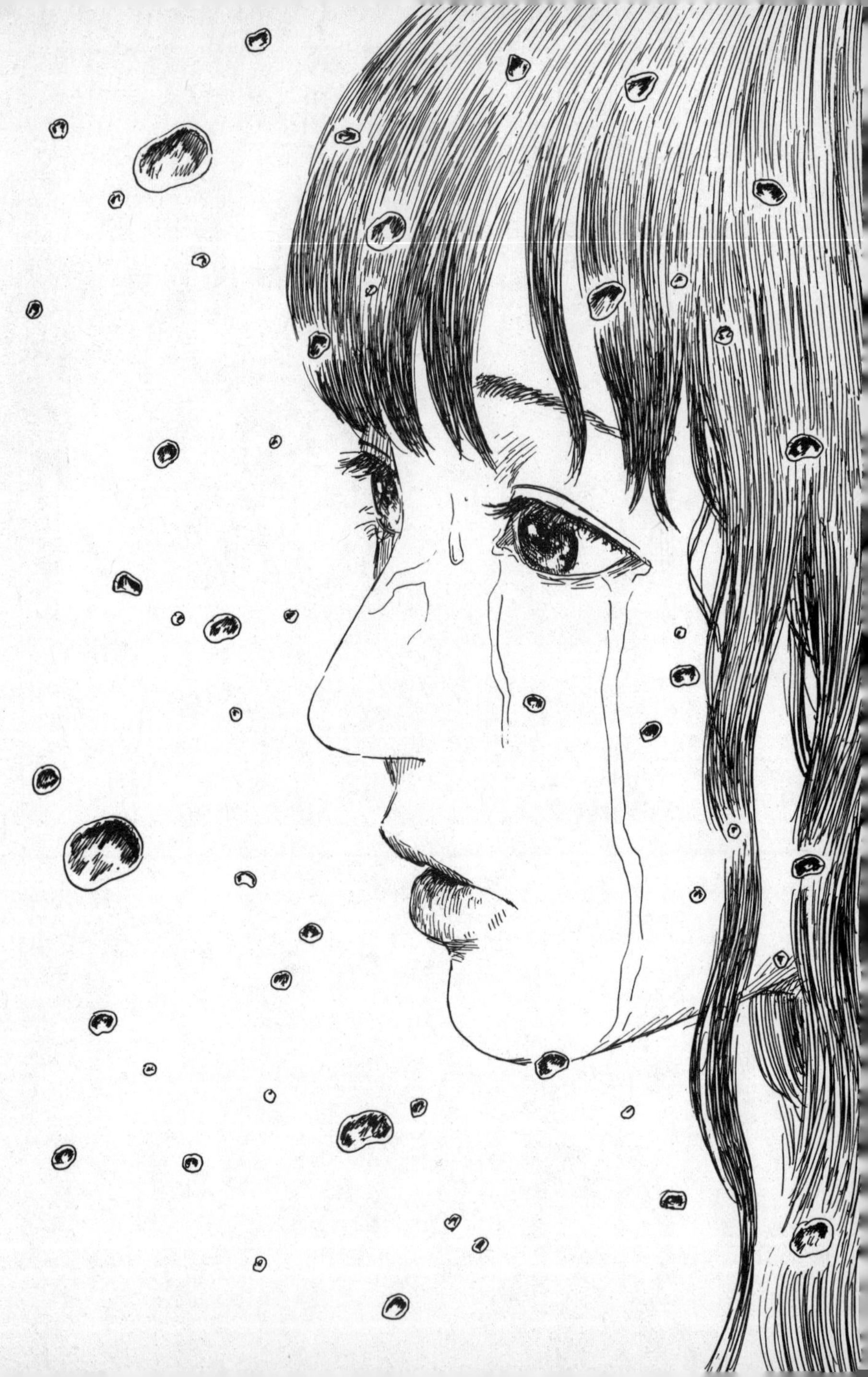

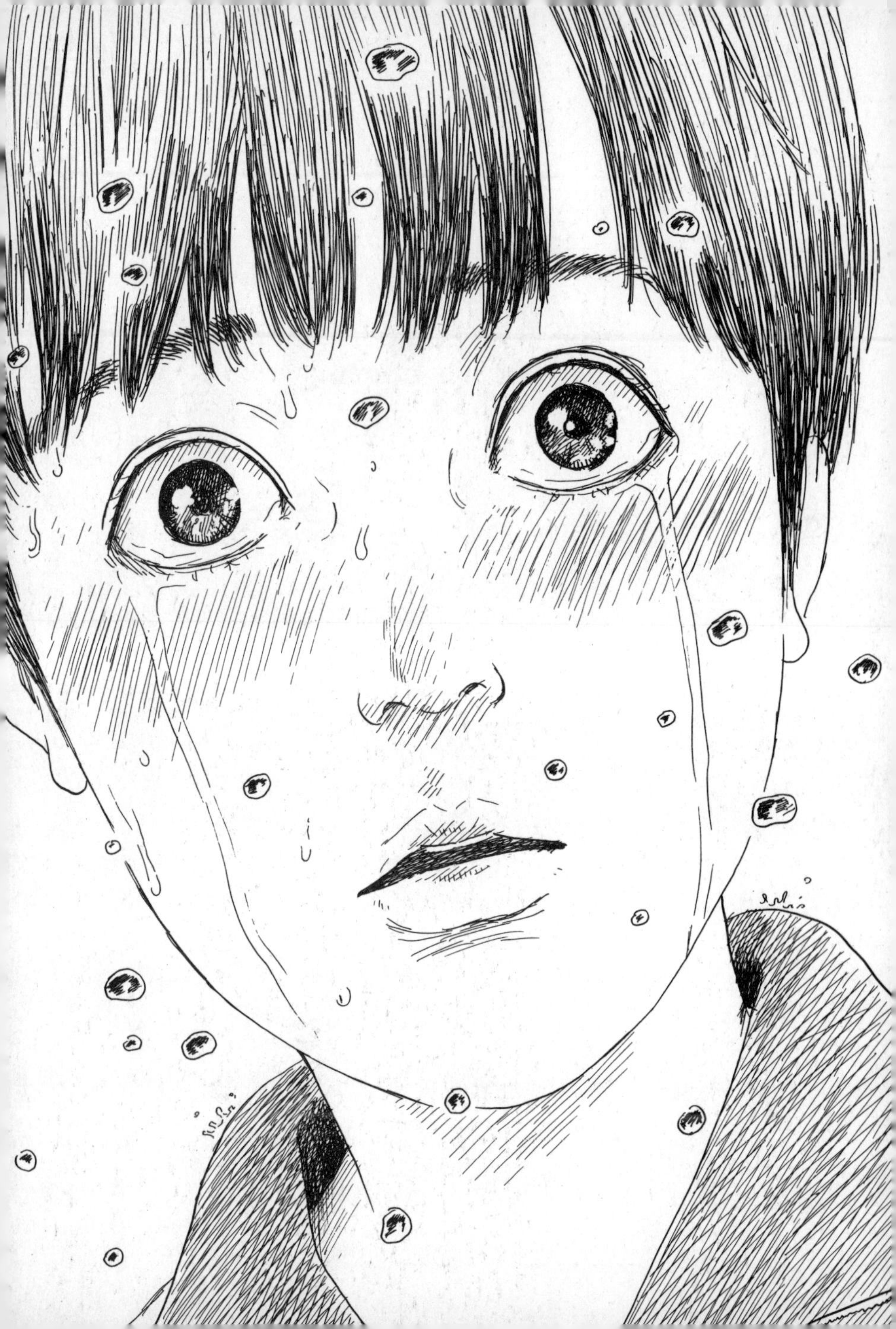

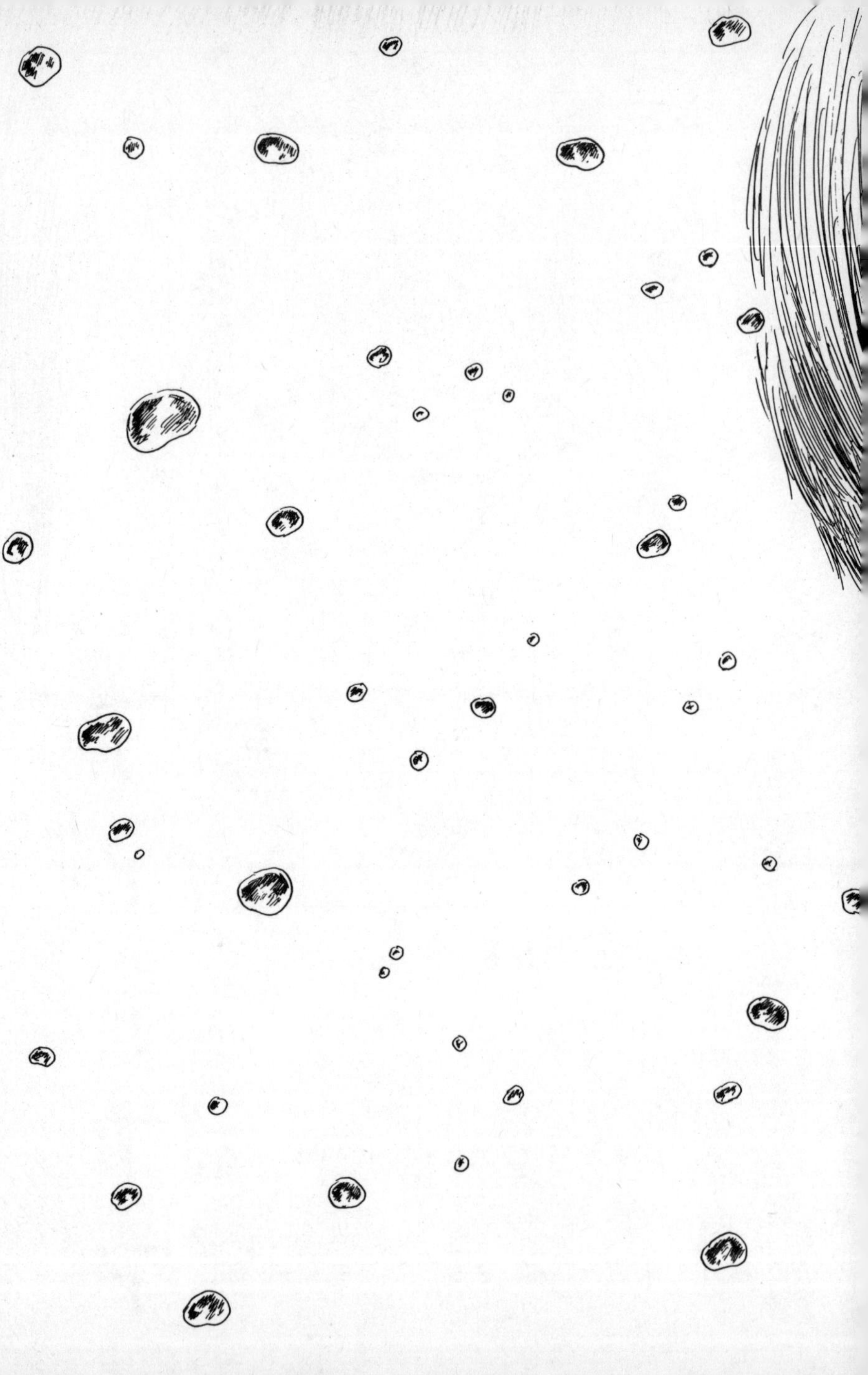

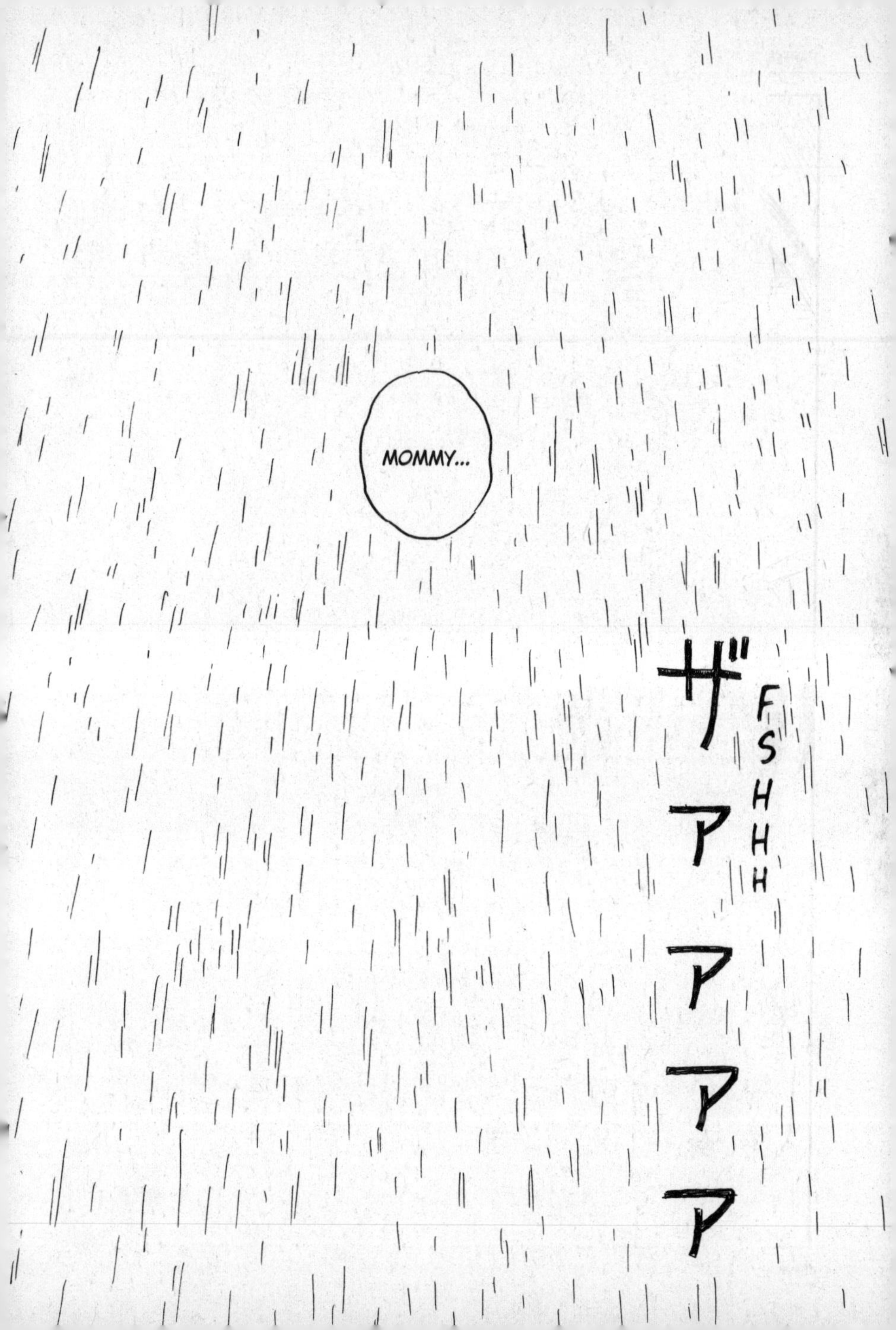
MOMMY...
ザアアアア
FSHHH

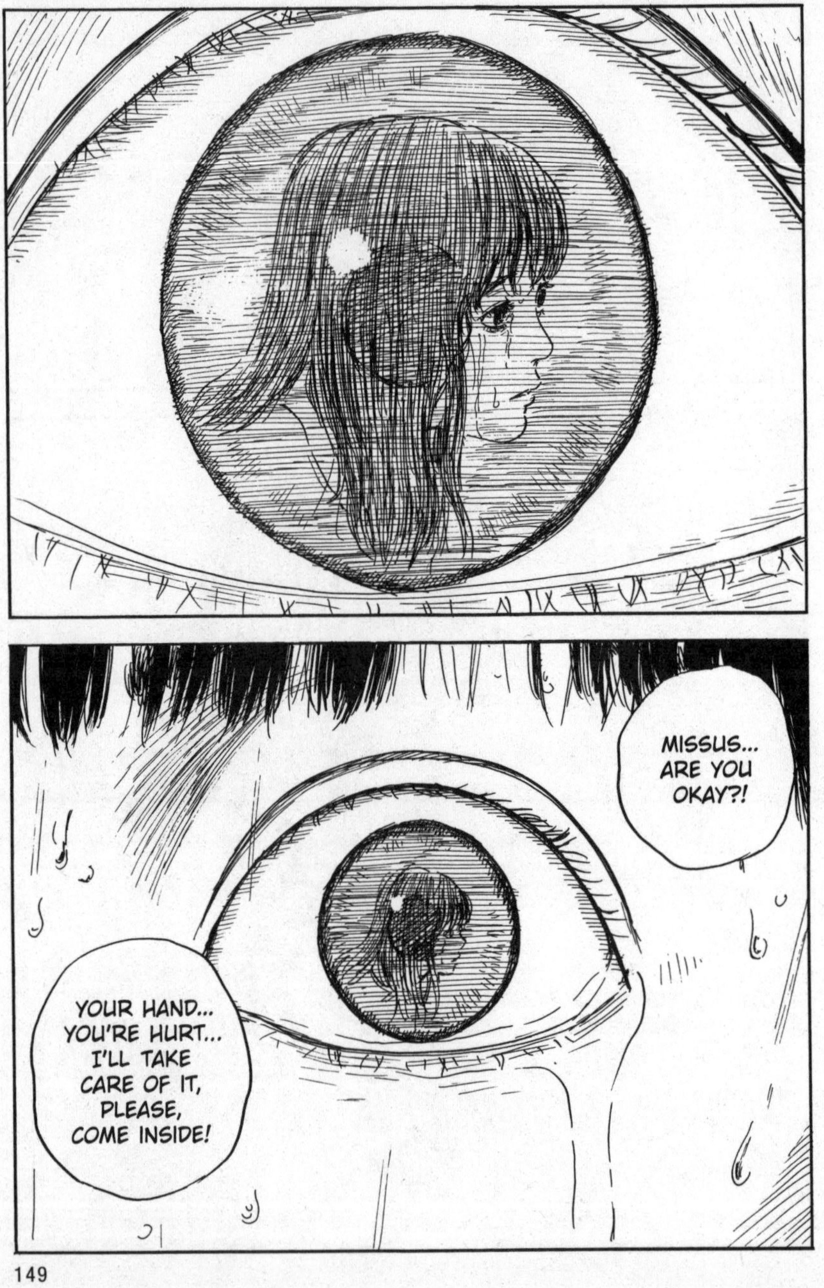
MISSUS... ARE YOU OKAY?!
YOUR HAND... YOU'RE HURT... I'LL TAKE CARE OF IT, PLEASE, COME INSIDE!

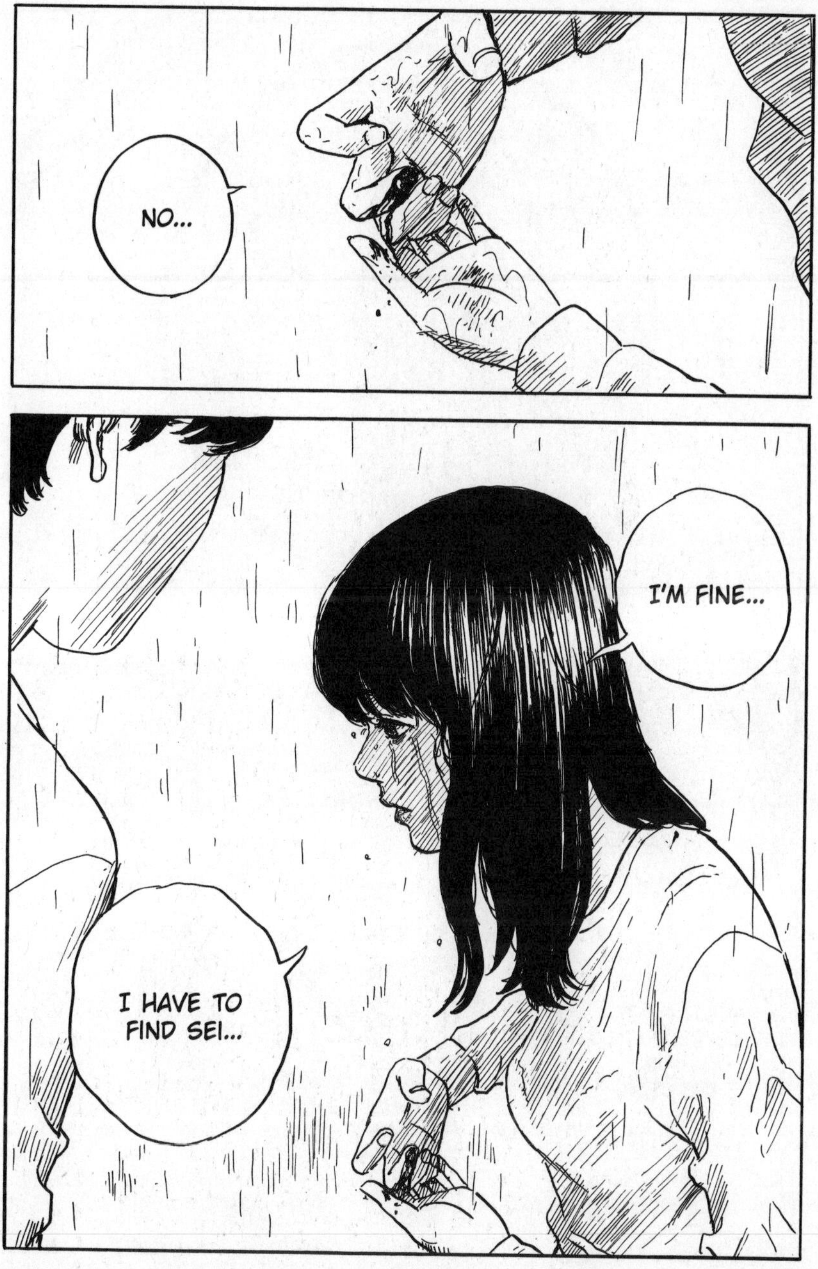
NO...
I'M FINE...
I HAVE TO FIND SEI...

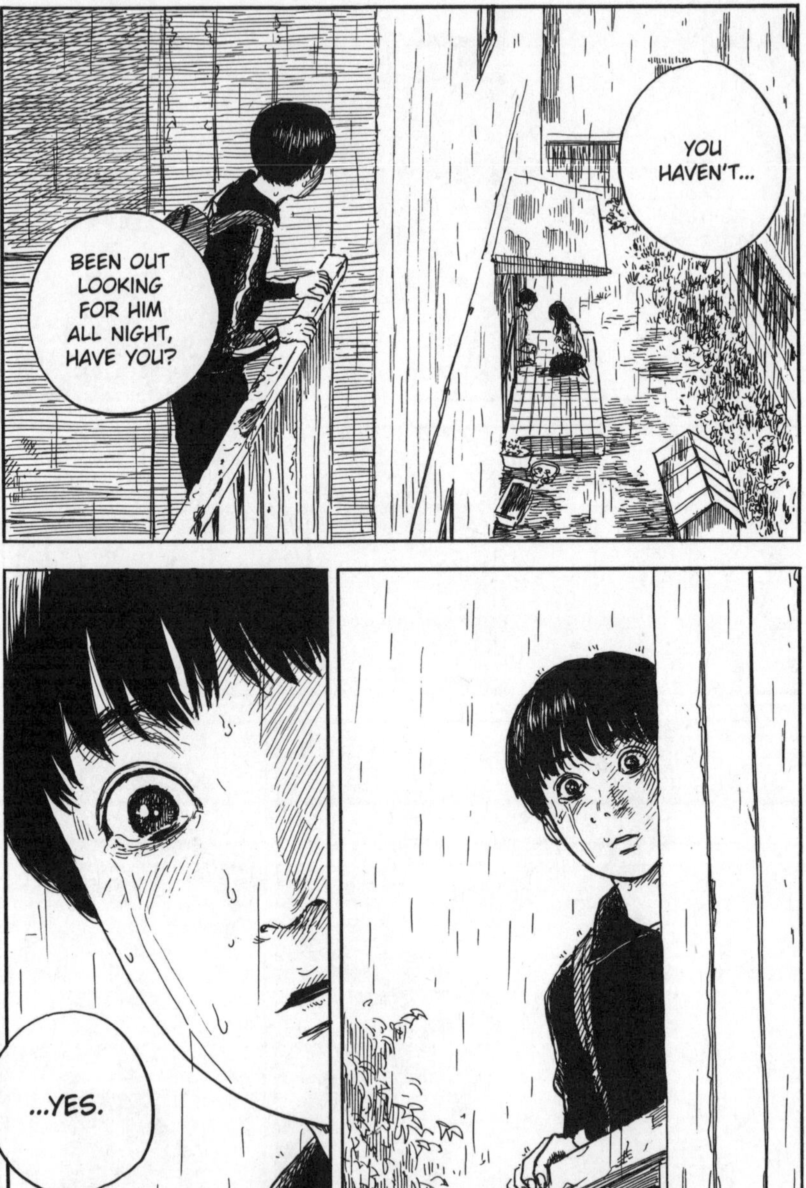
YOU HAVEN'T...
BEEN OUT LOOKING FOR HIM ALL NIGHT, HAVE YOU?
...YES.

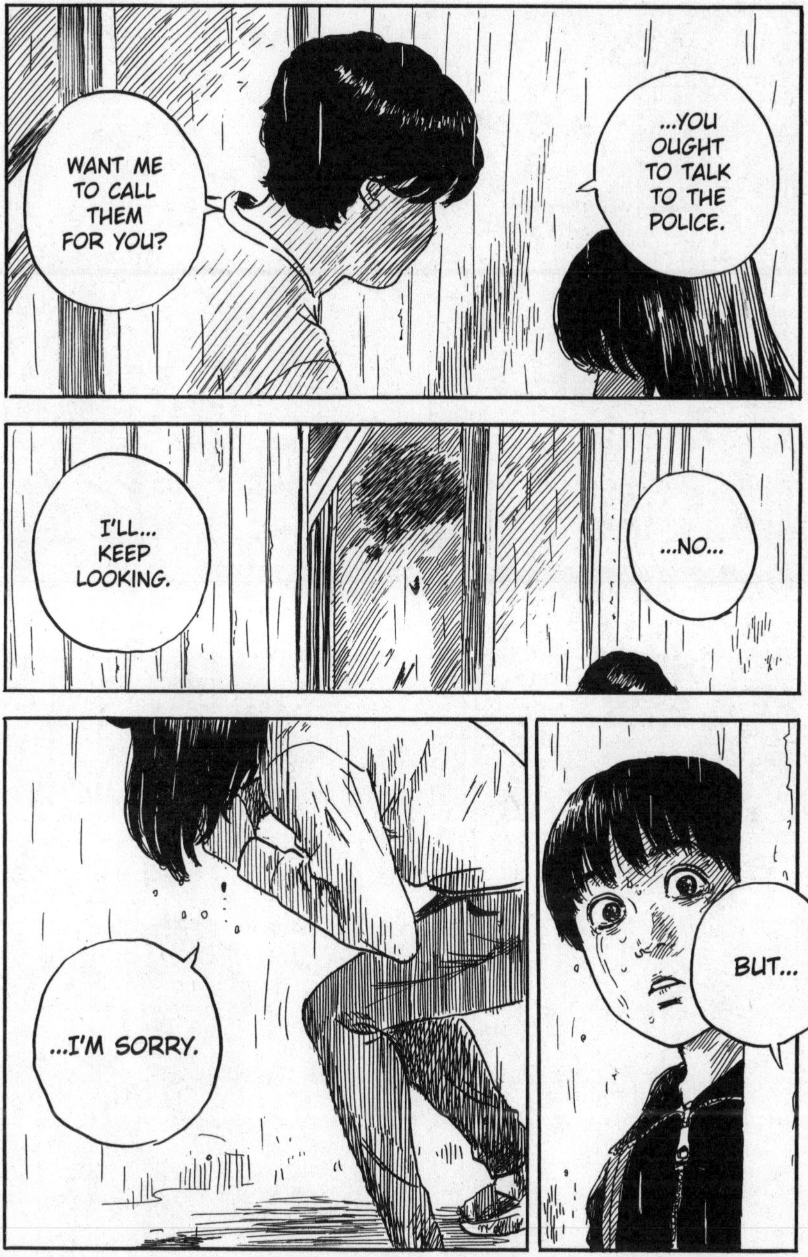
...YOU OUGHT TO TALK TO THE POLICE.
WANT ME TO CALL THEM FOR YOU?
...NO...
I'LL... KEEP LOOKING.
BUT...
...I'M SORRY.

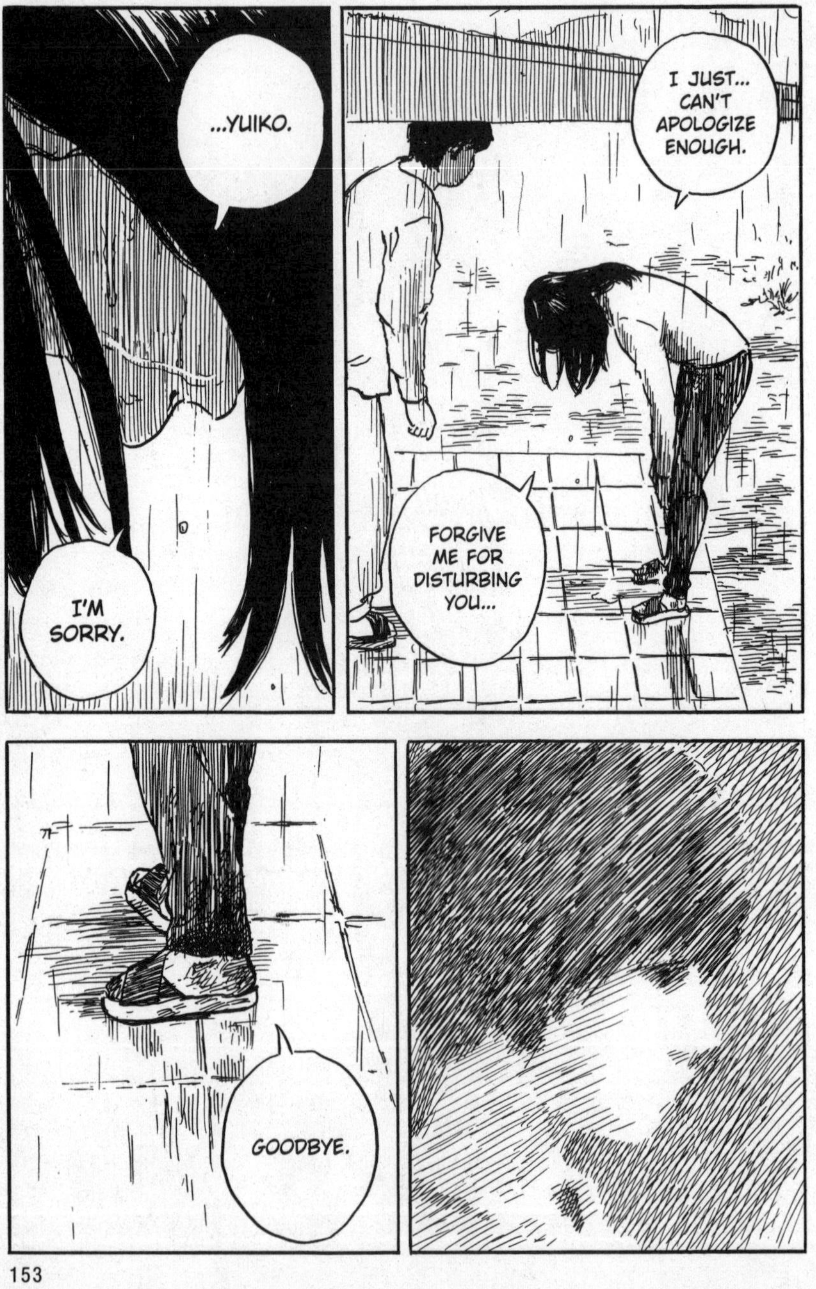
I JUST... CAN'T APOLOGIZE ENOUGH.
FORGIVE ME FOR DISTURBING YOU...
...YUIKO.
I'M SORRY.
GOODBYE.

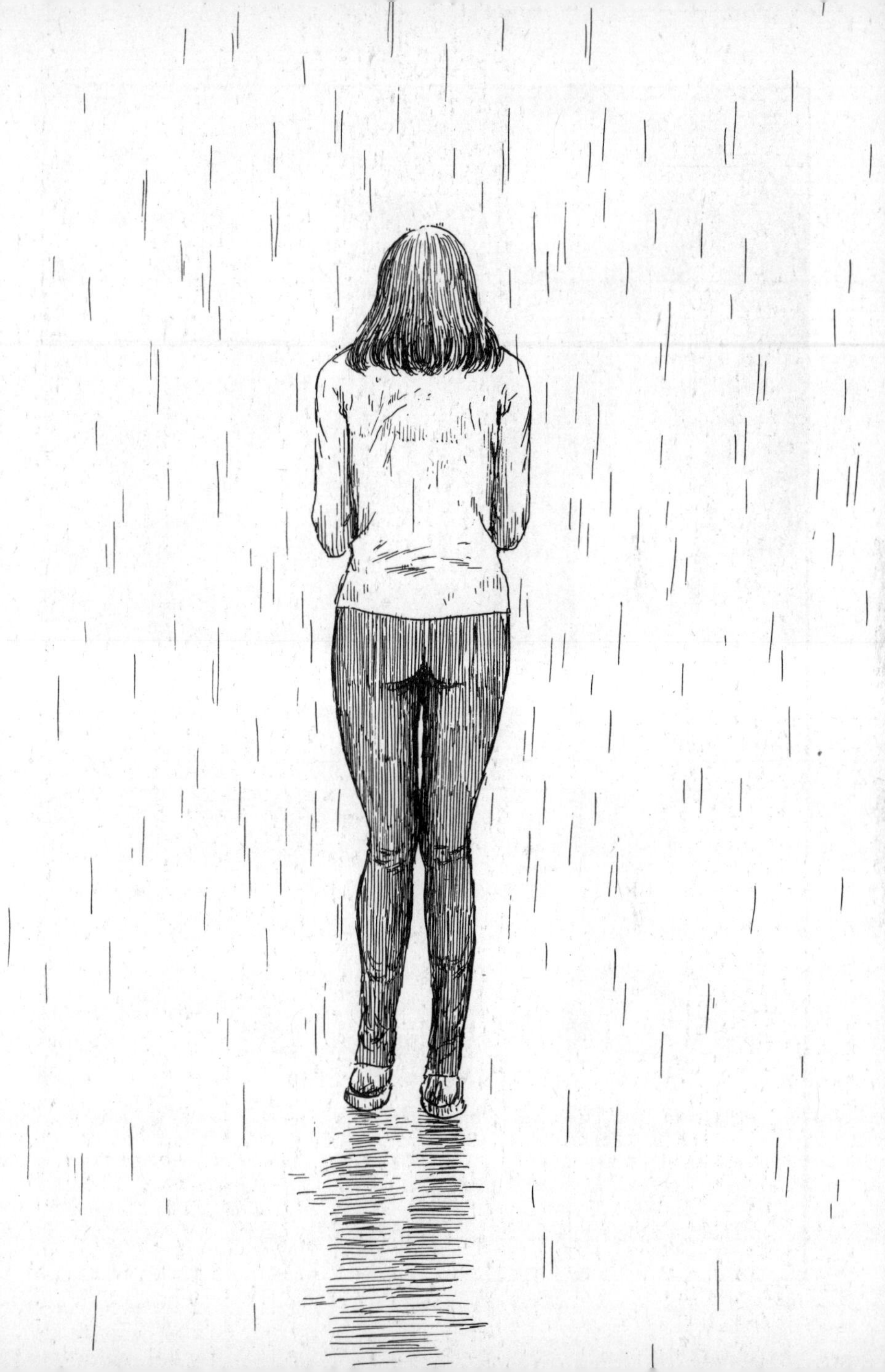

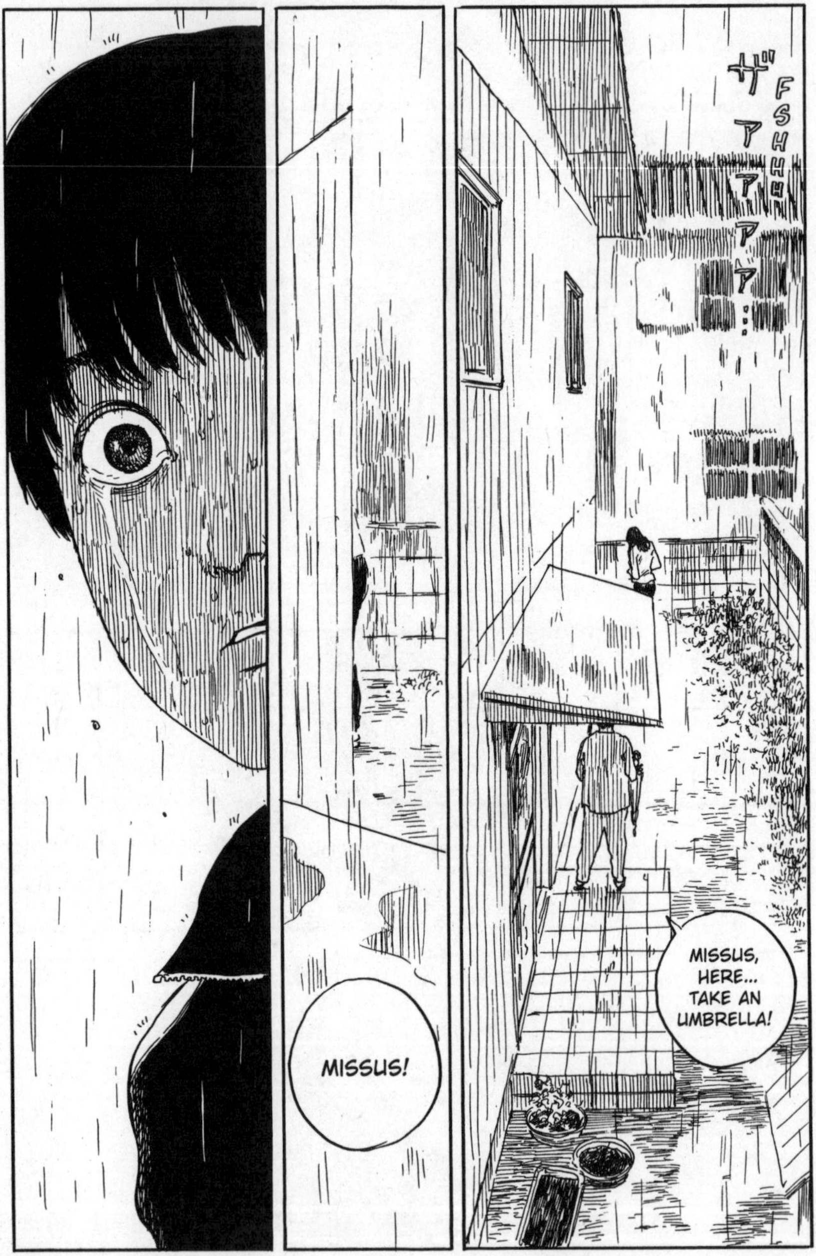
ザァァァァ…
FSHHH
MISSUS, HERE... TAKE AN UMBRELLA!
MISSUS!

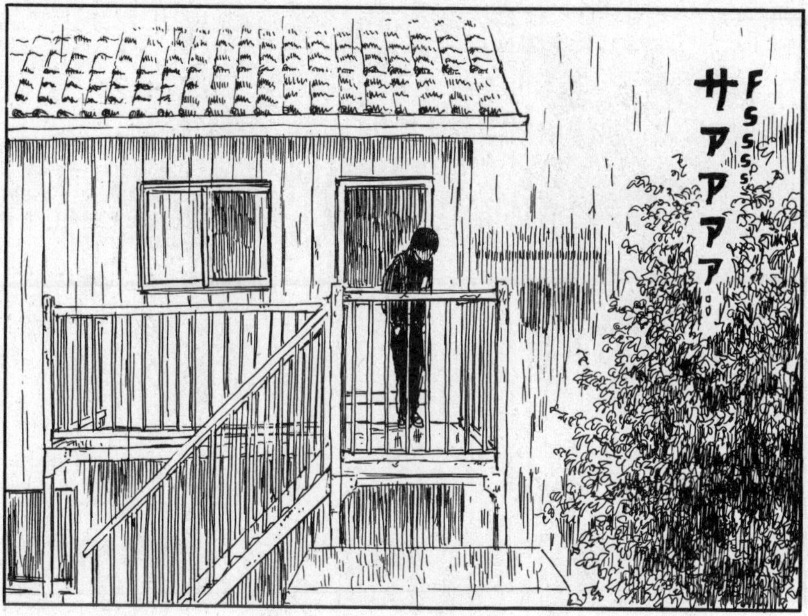
サァァァ…
FSSS
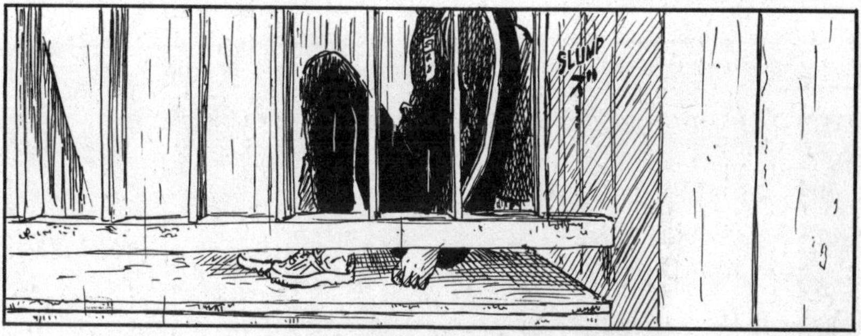
SLUMP
ズ
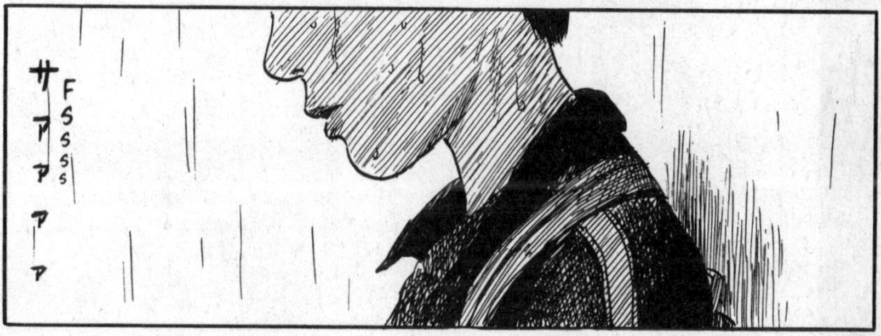
サァァァァ
FSSS

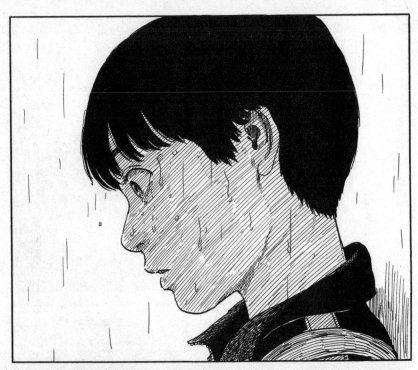

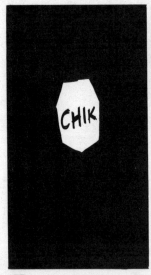

CHIK

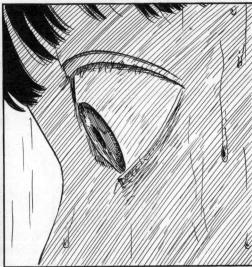

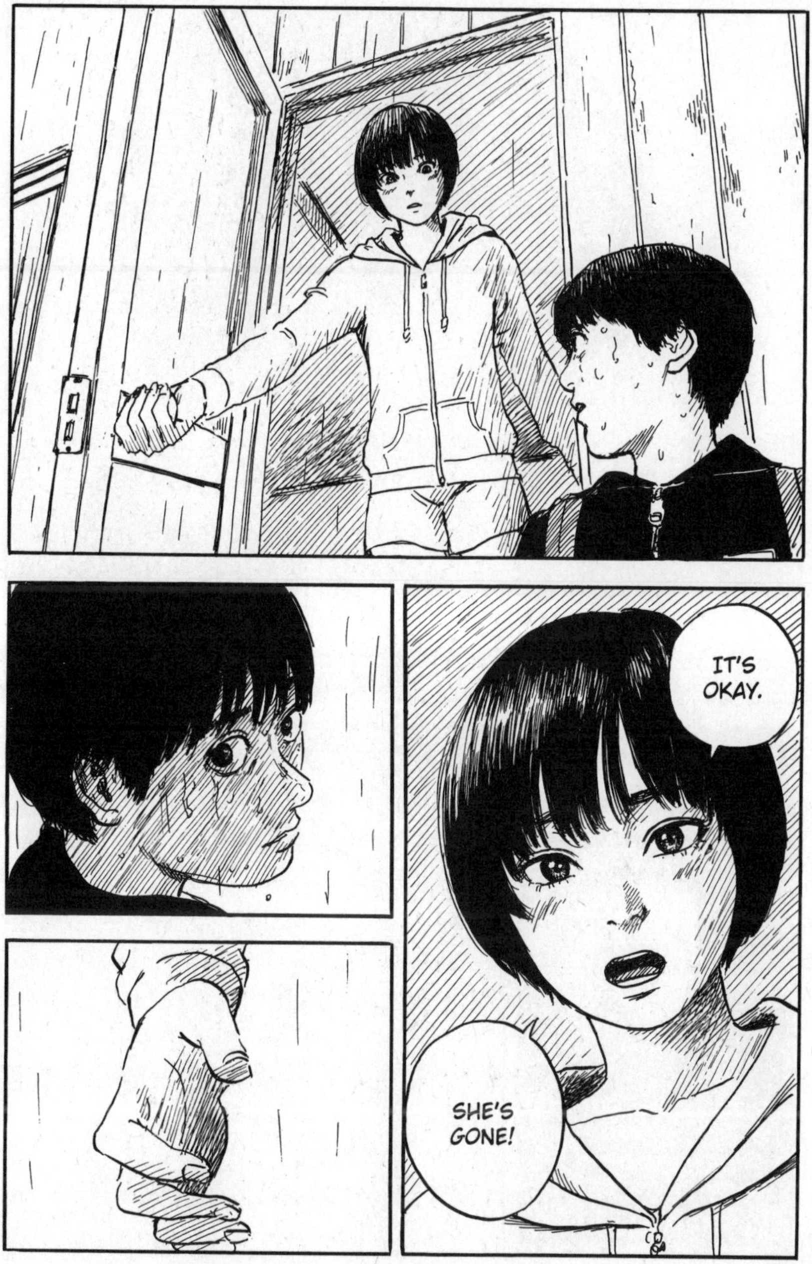
IT'S OKAY.
SHE'S GONE!

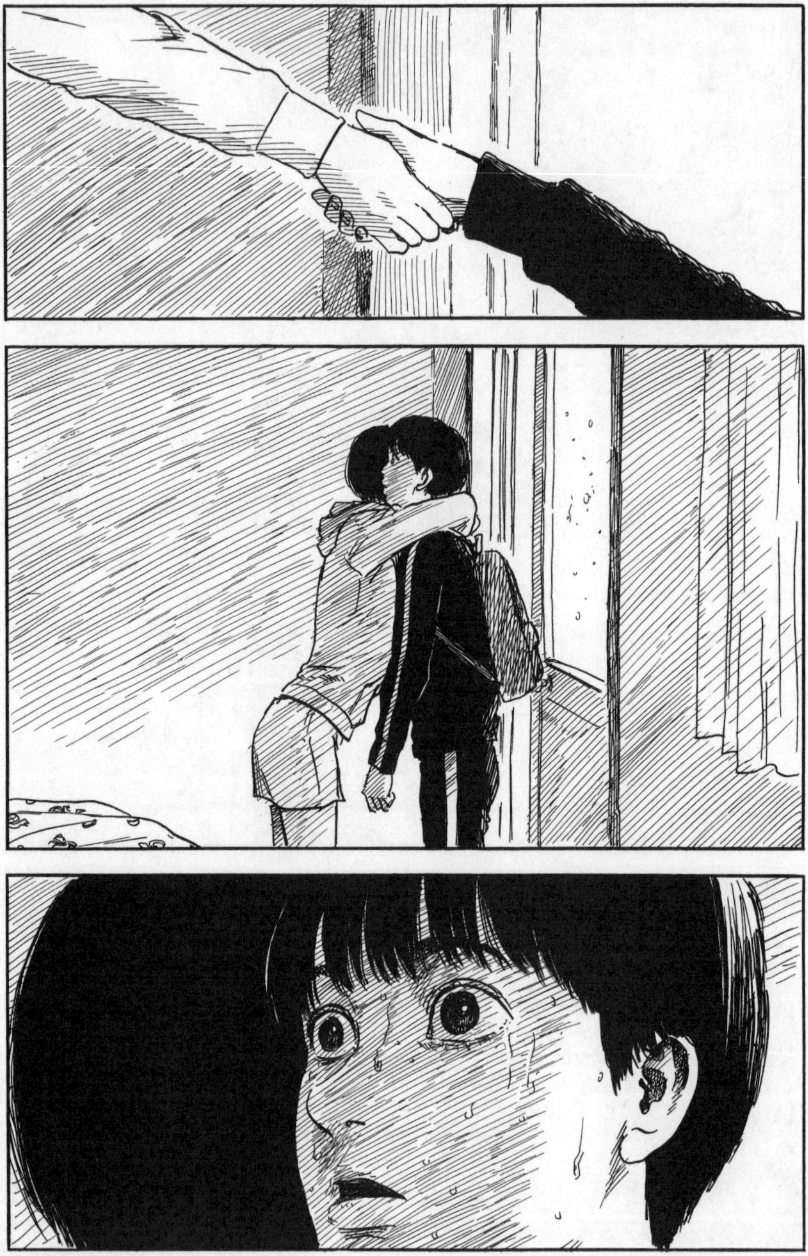

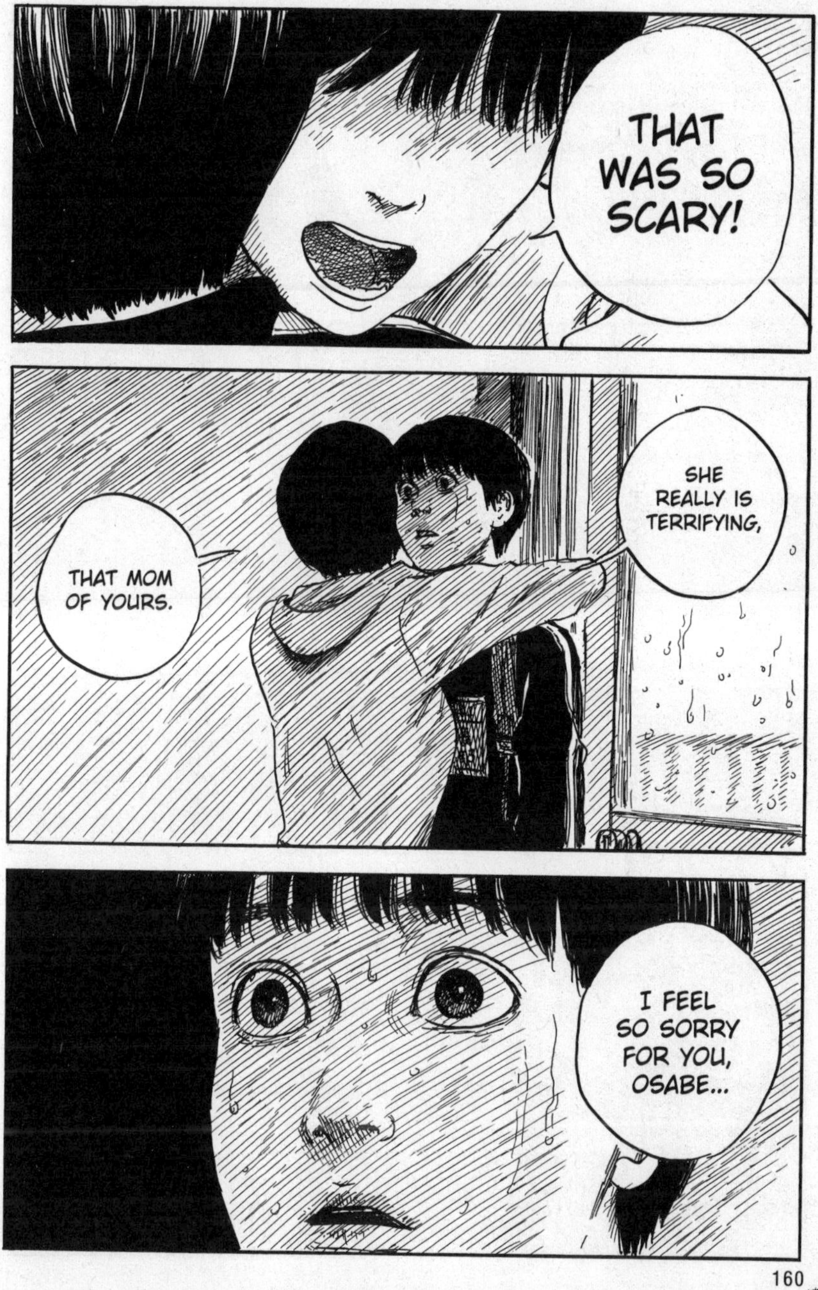
THAT WAS SO SCARY!
SHE REALLY IS TERRIFYING,
THAT MOM OF YOURS.
I FEEL SO SORRY FOR YOU, OSABE...

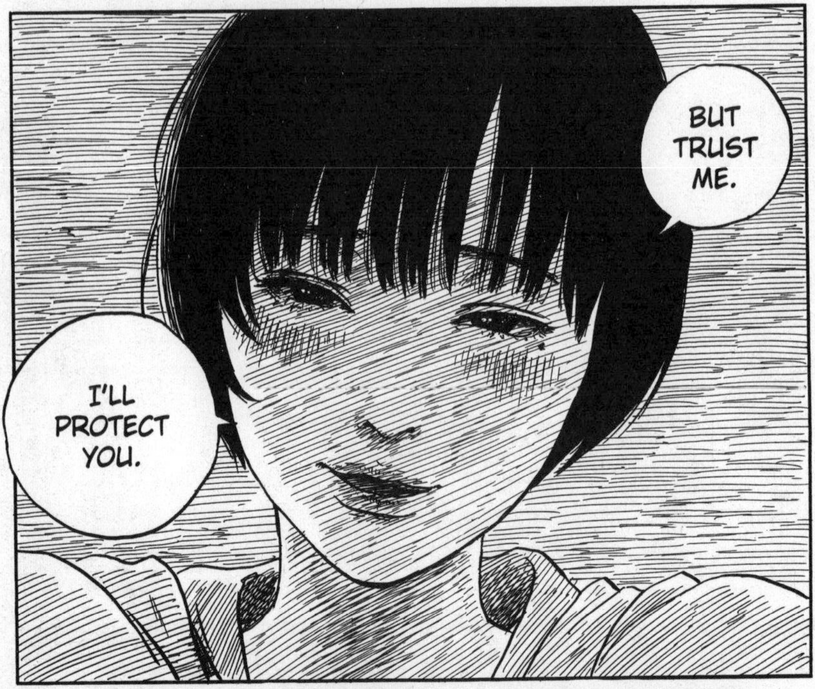
BUT TRUST ME.
I'LL PROTECT YOU.

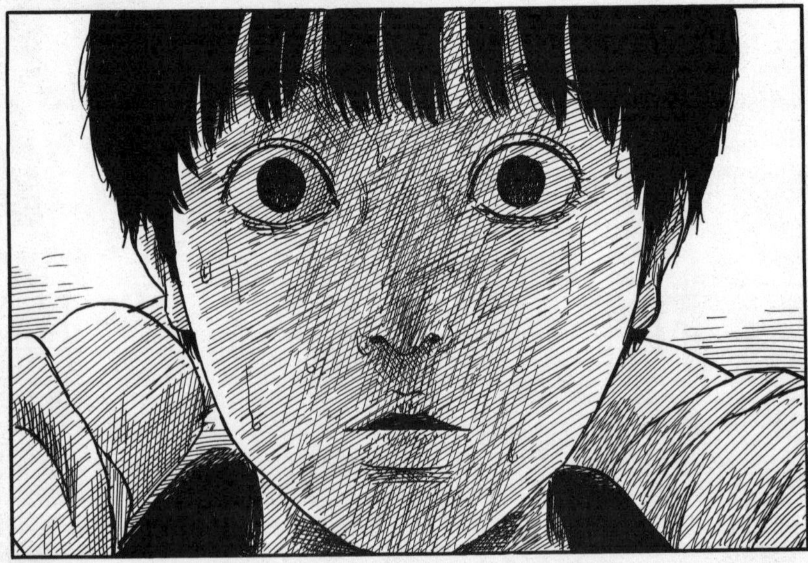

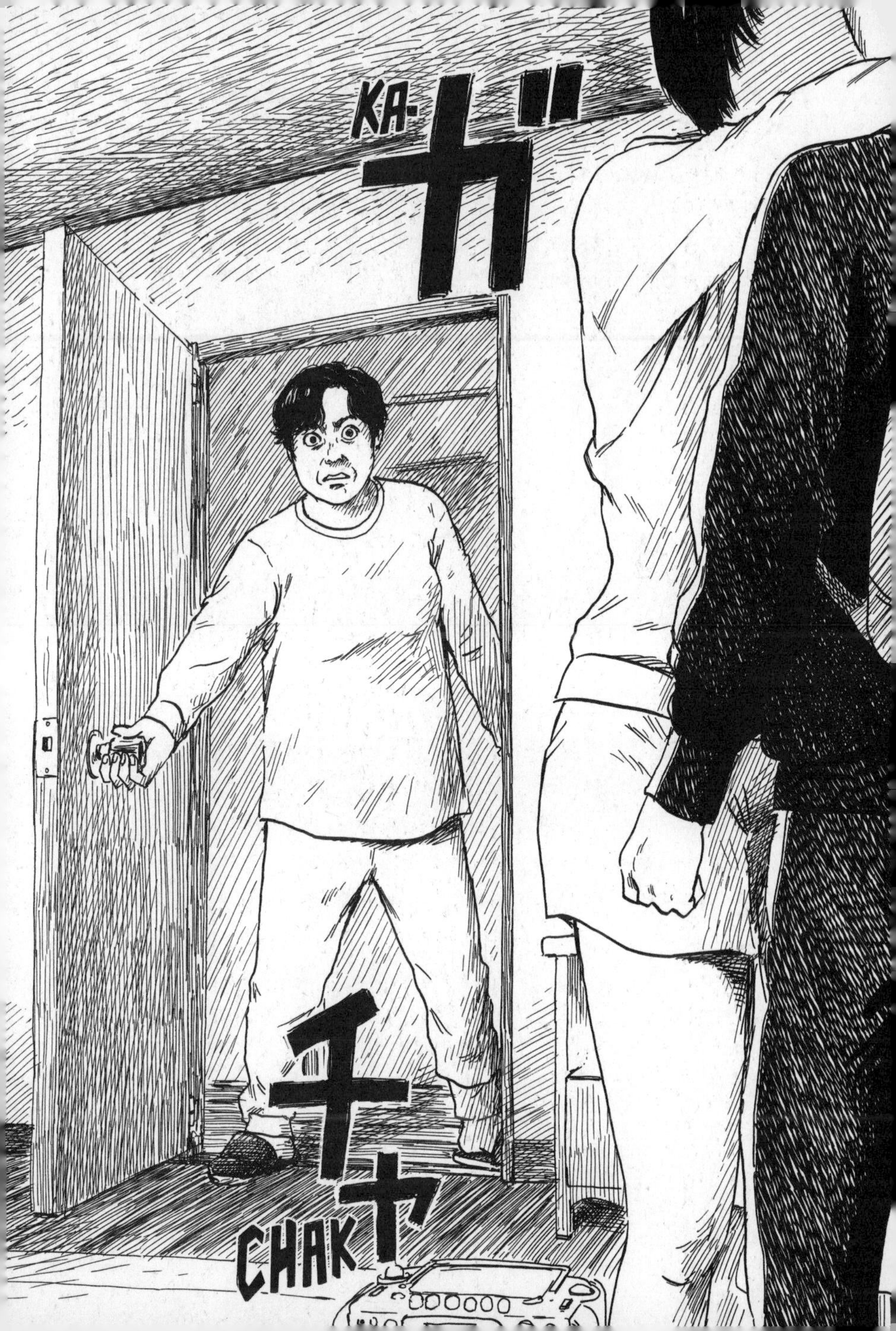
KA-
ガ
チャ
CHAK

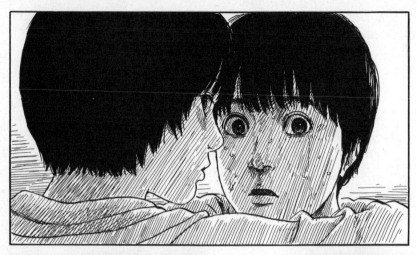

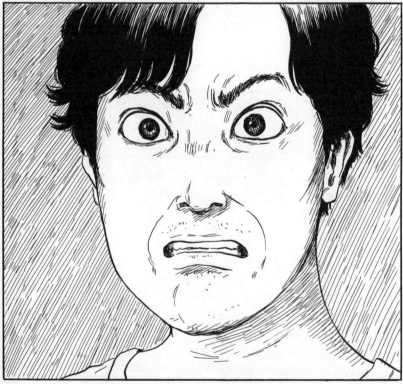

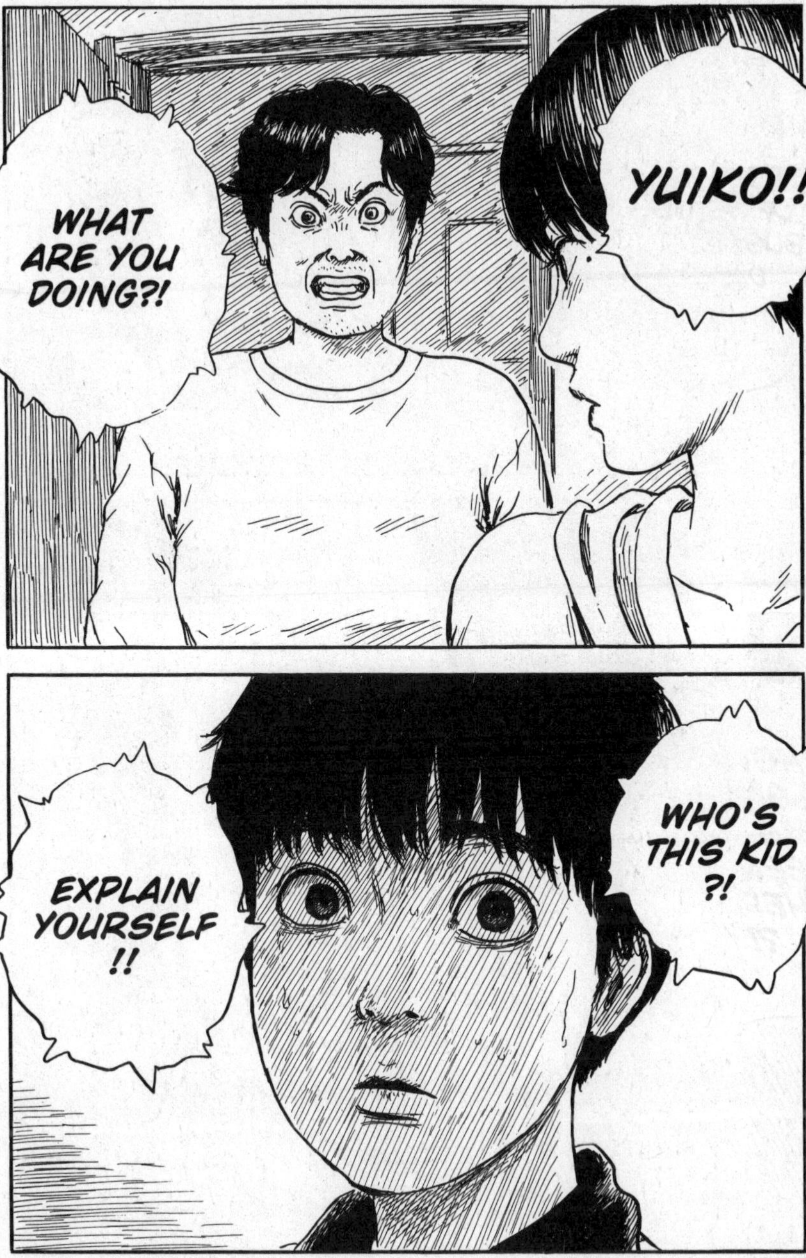
YUIKO!!
WHAT ARE YOU DOING?!
WHO'S THIS KID ?!
EXPLAIN YOURSELF !!

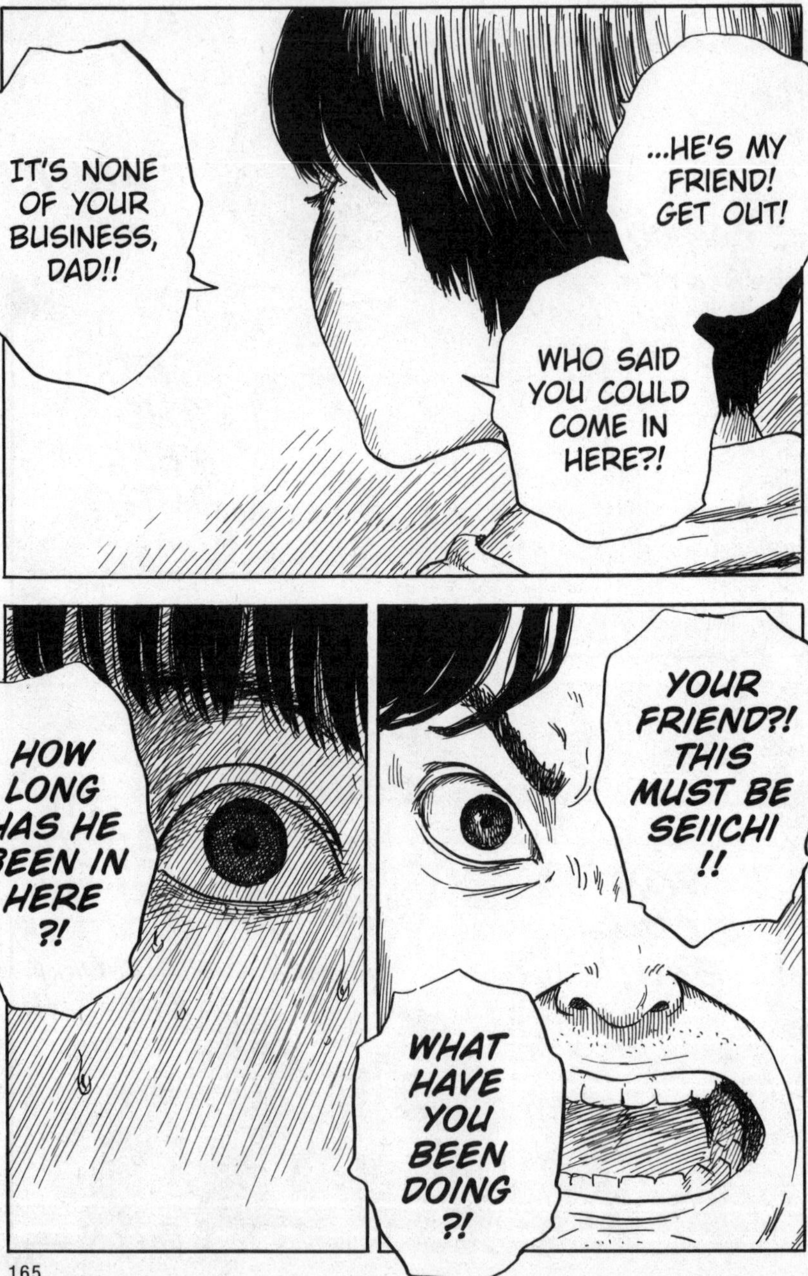
...HE'S MY FRIEND! GET OUT!
WHO SAID YOU COULD COME IN HERE?!
IT'S NONE OF YOUR BUSINESS, DAD!!
YOUR FRIEND?! THIS MUST BE SEIICHI!!
WHAT HAVE YOU BEEN DOING?!
HOW LONG HAS HE BEEN IN HERE?!

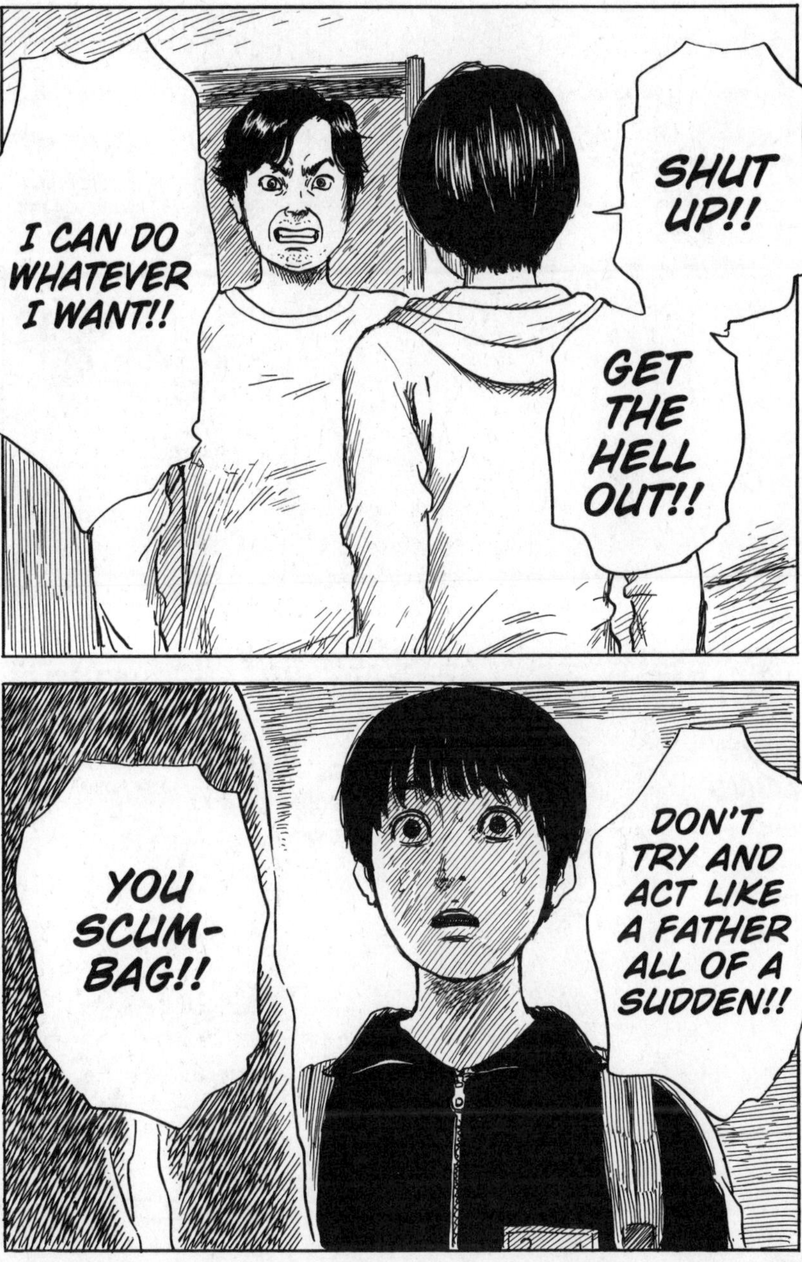
SHUT UP!!
GET THE HELL OUT!!
I CAN DO WHATEVER I WANT!!
DON'T TRY AND ACT LIKE A FATHER ALL OF A SUDDEN!!
YOU SCUM-BAG!!

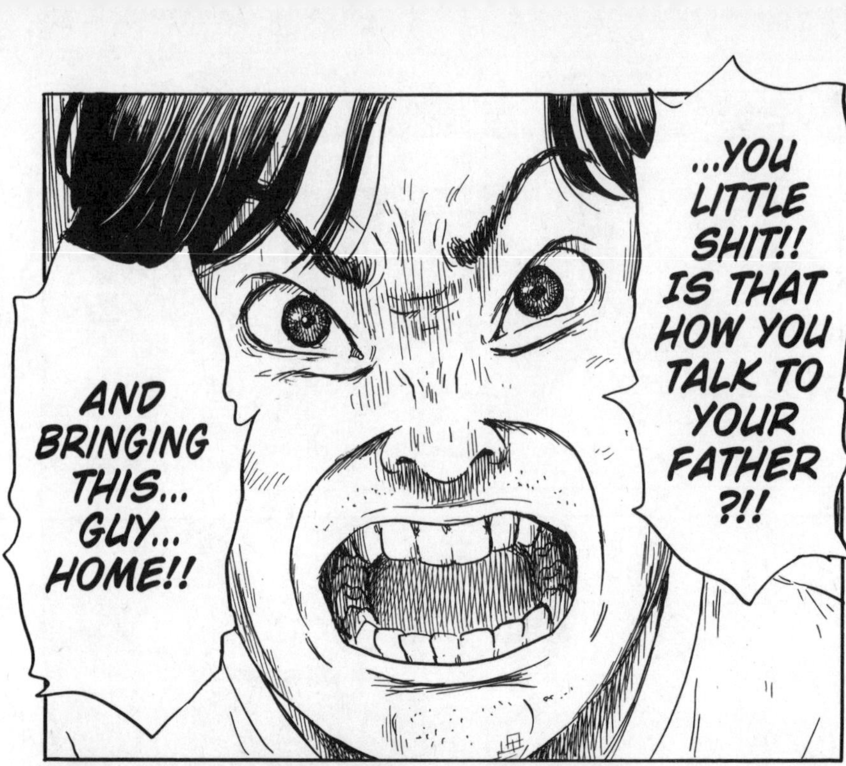
...YOU LITTLE SHIT!! IS THAT HOW YOU TALK TO YOUR FATHER ?!!
AND BRINGING THIS... GUY... HOME!!

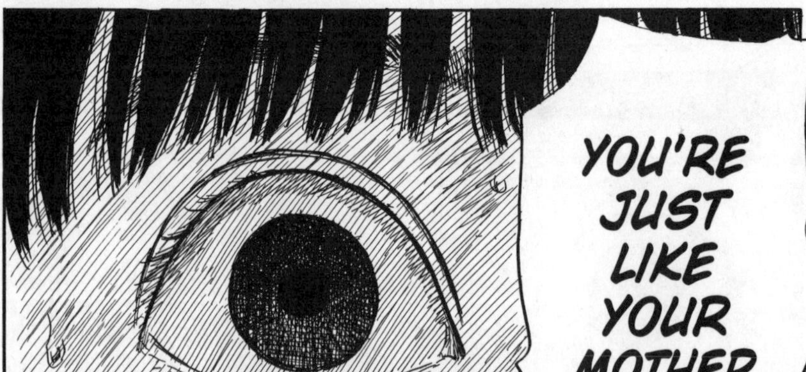
YOU'RE JUST LIKE YOUR MOTHER !!!

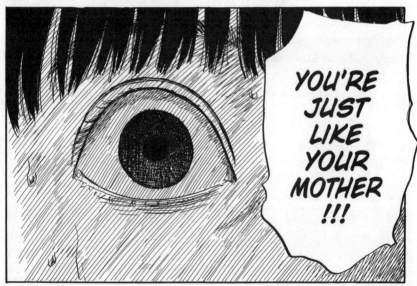

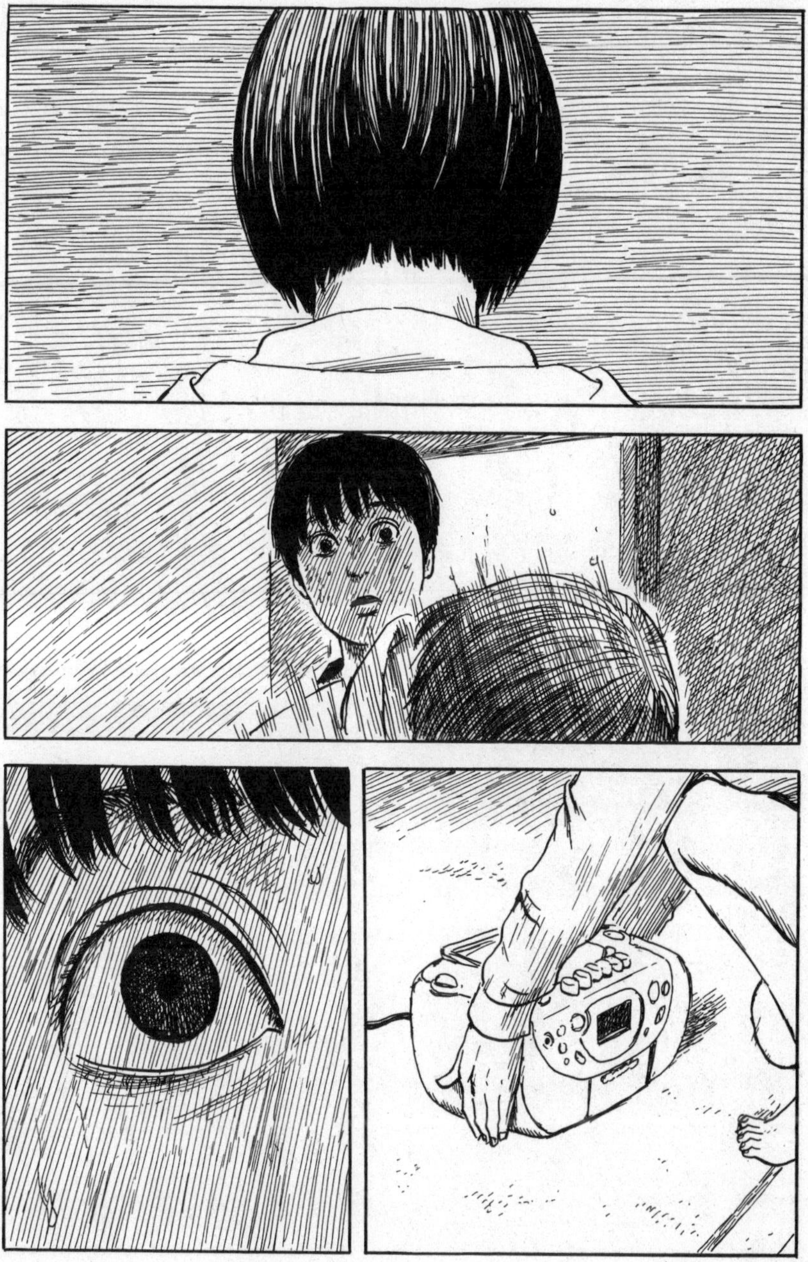

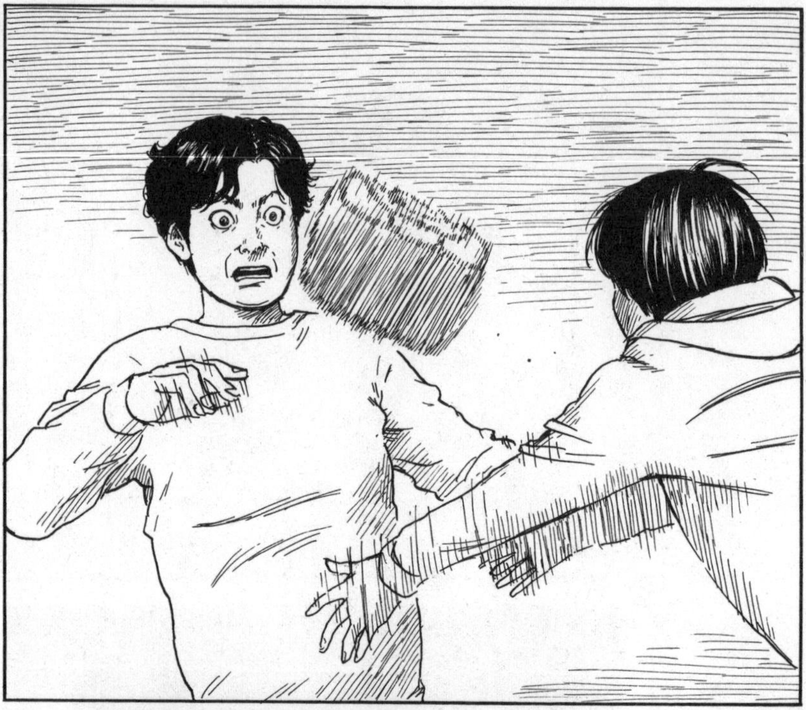

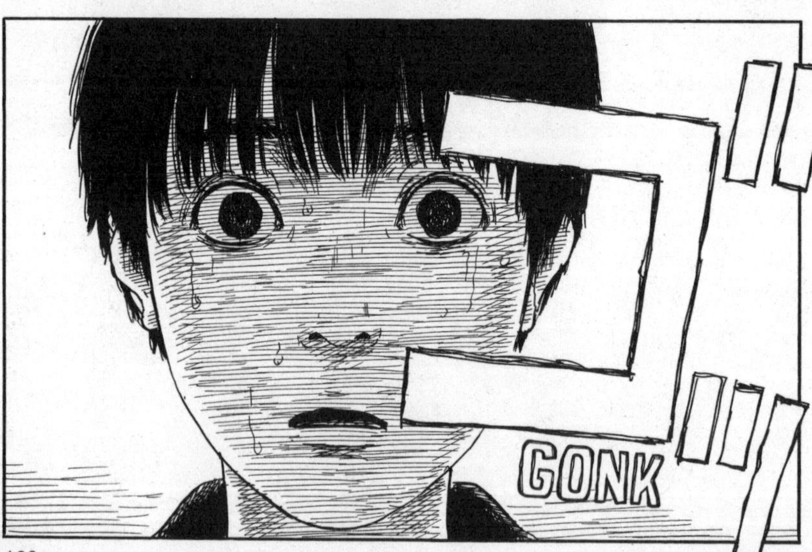
GONK

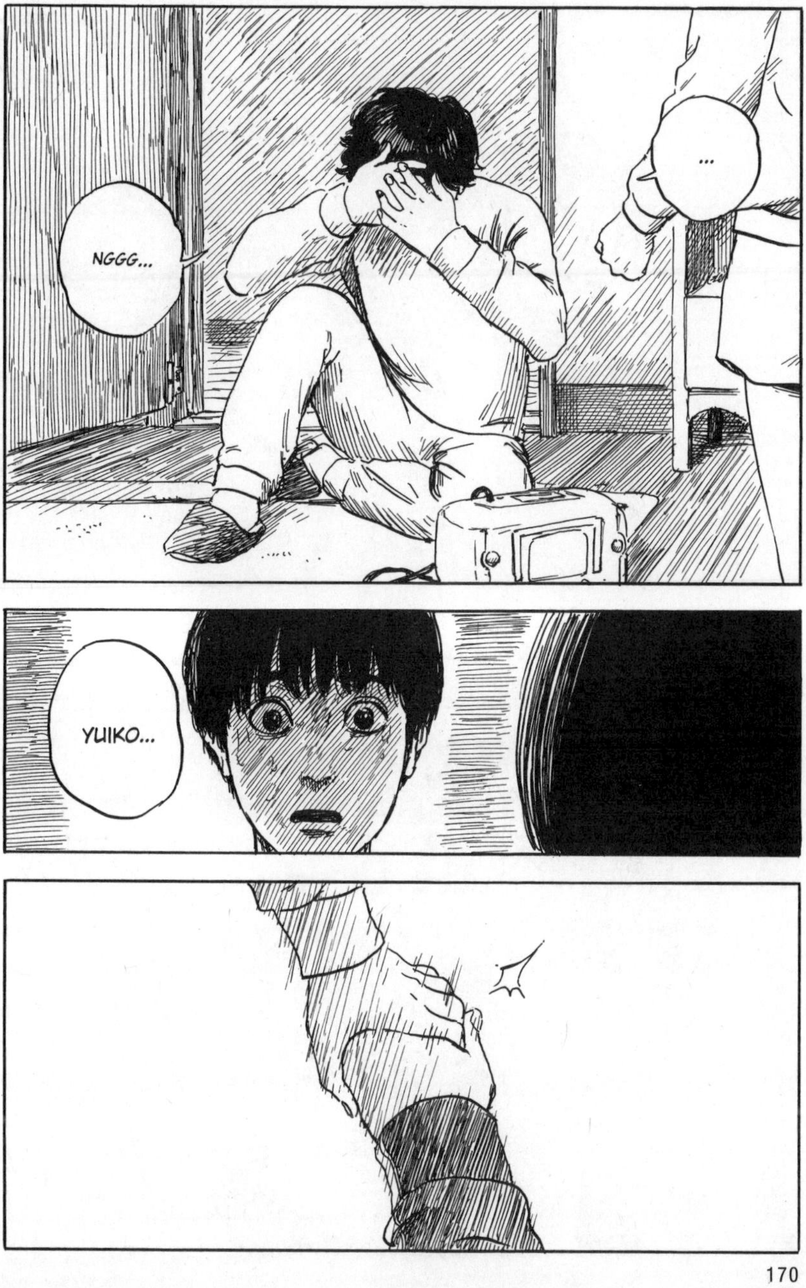
...
NGGG...
YUIKO...

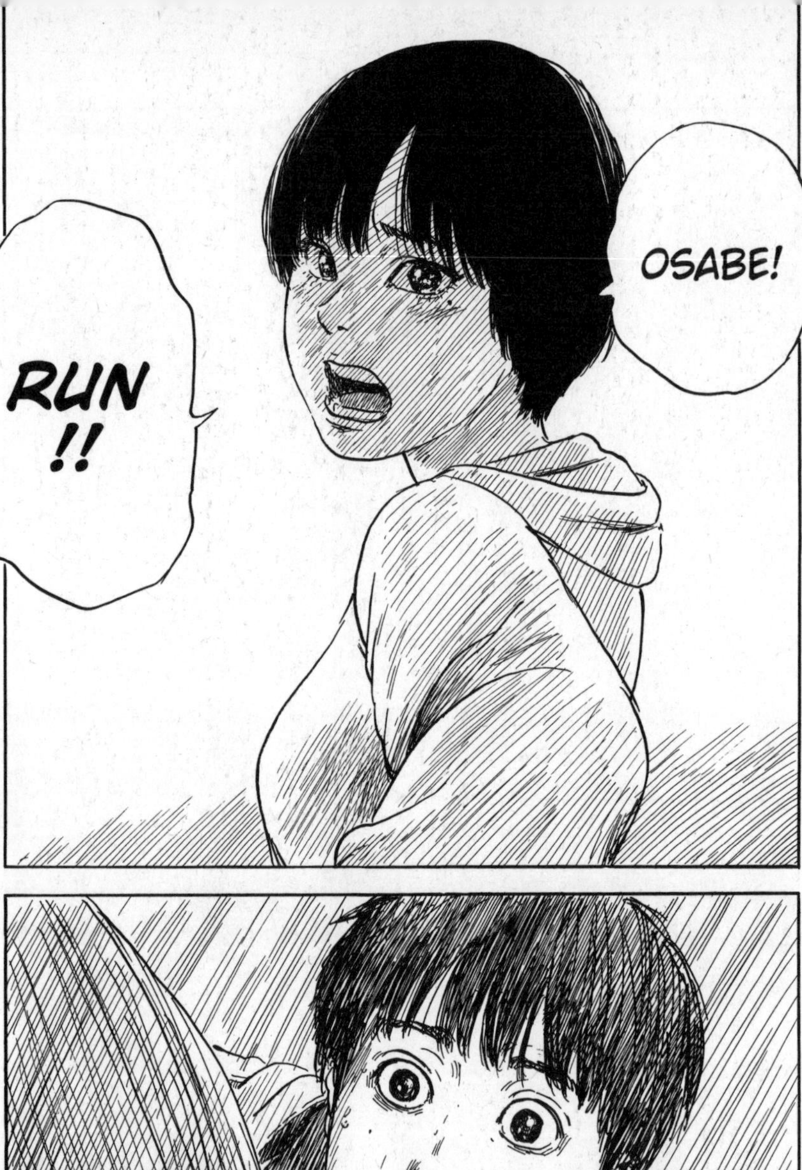
OSABE!
RUN!!

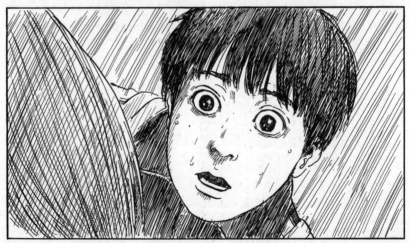

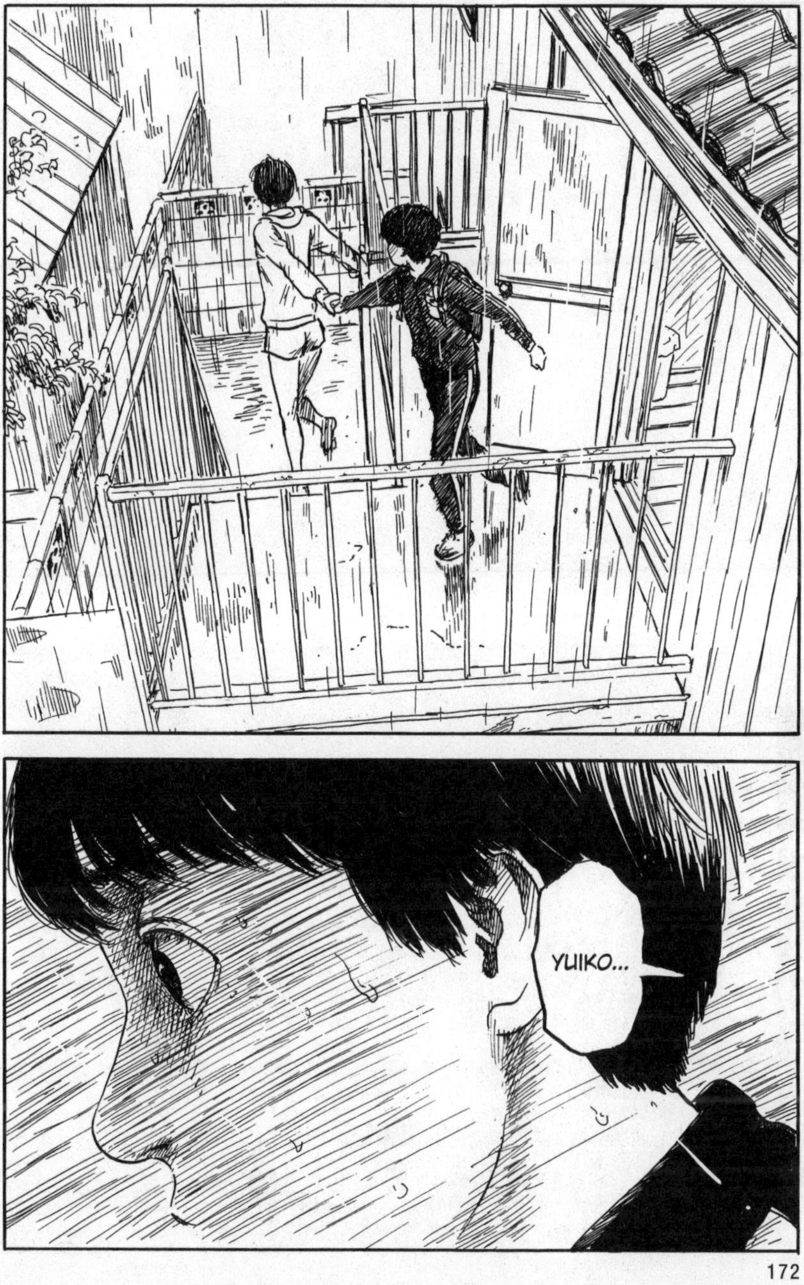
YUIKO...

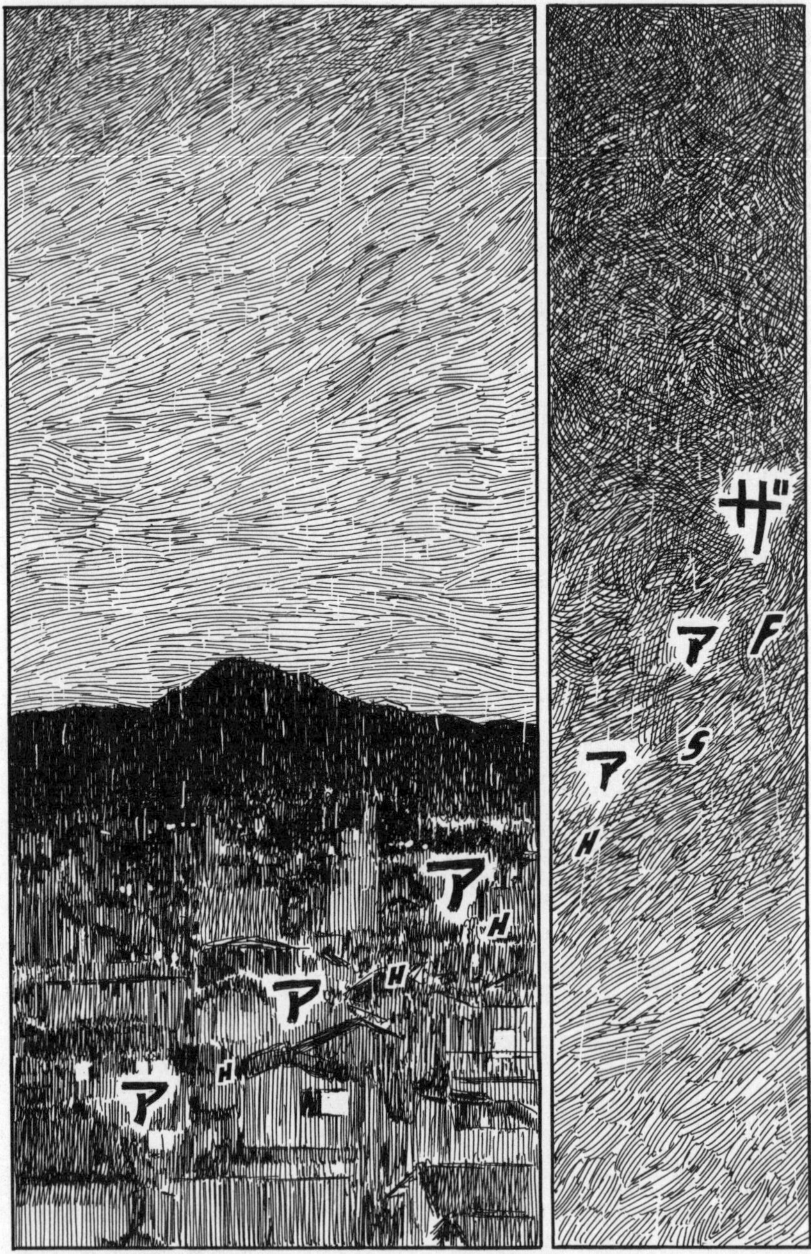
ザアア
FSH
アアア
HHH

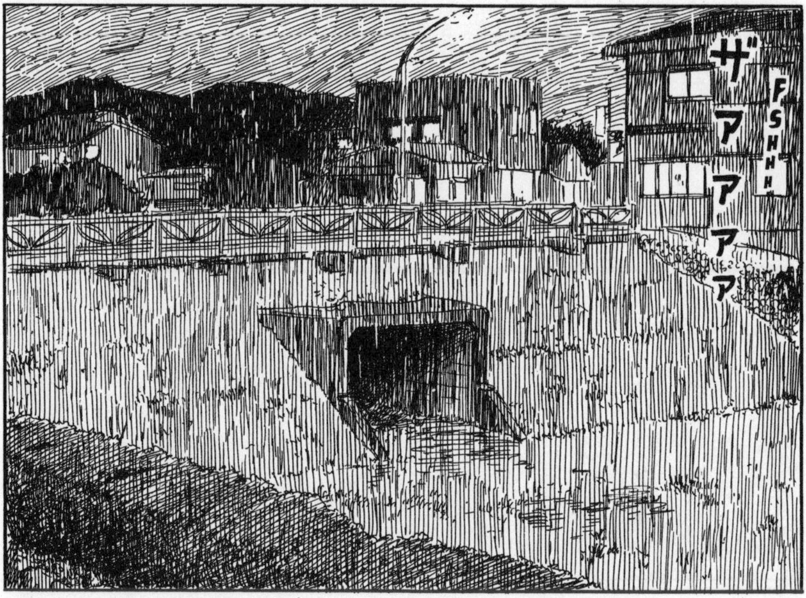
ザァァァァ
FSHHH
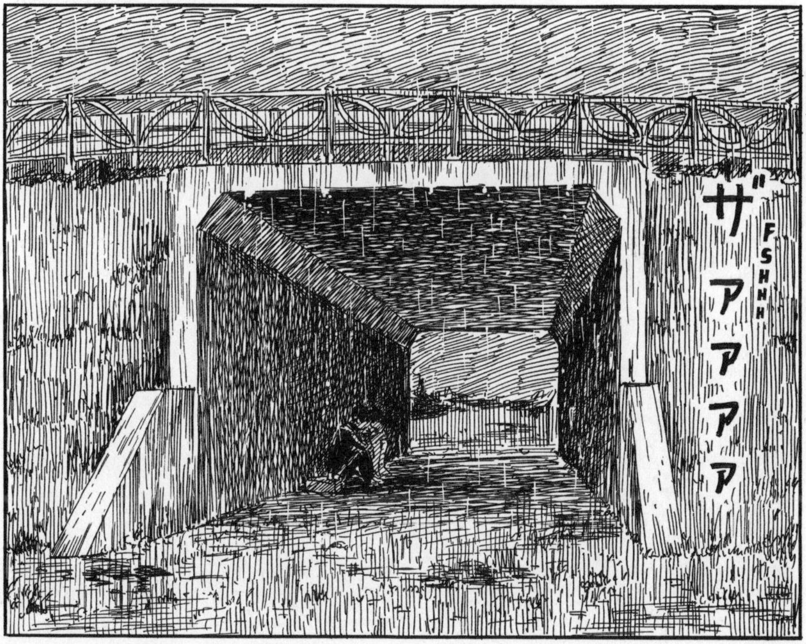
ザァァァァ
FSHHH

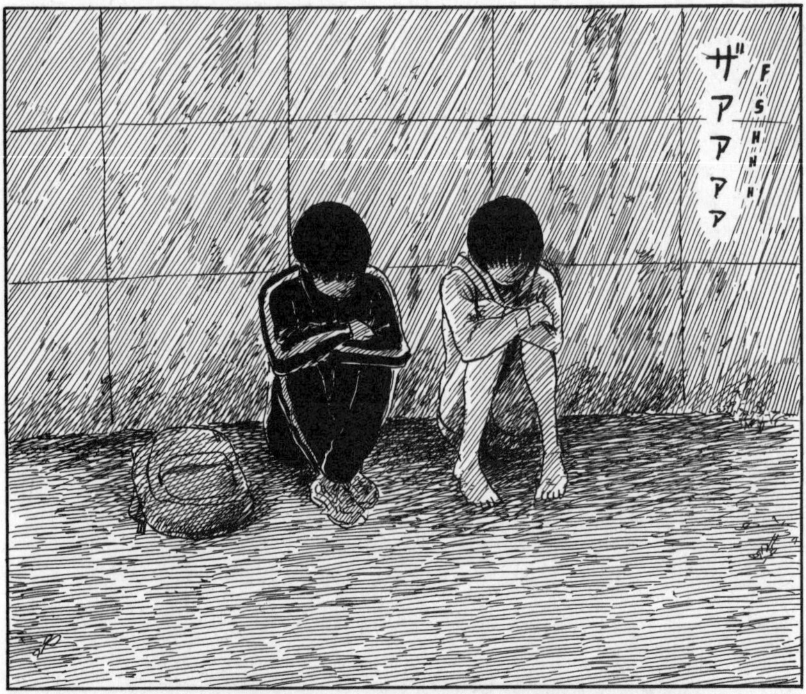
ザァァァァ
FSHHH
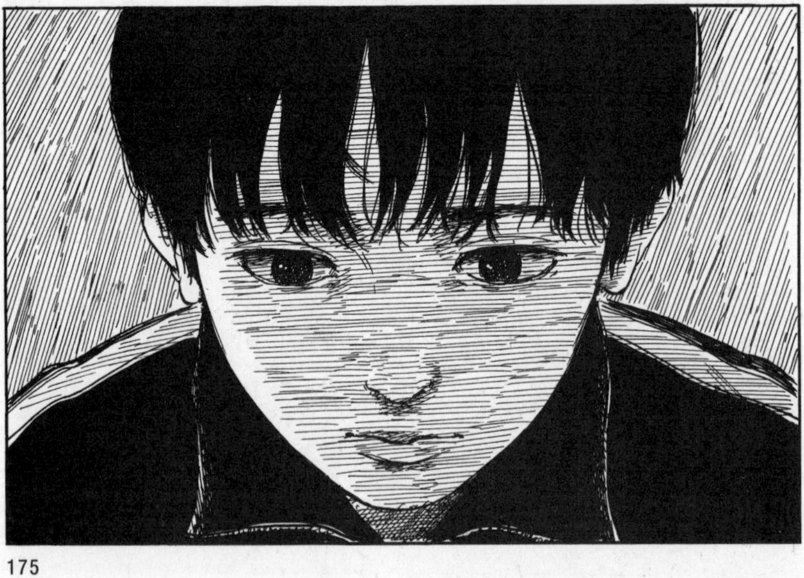

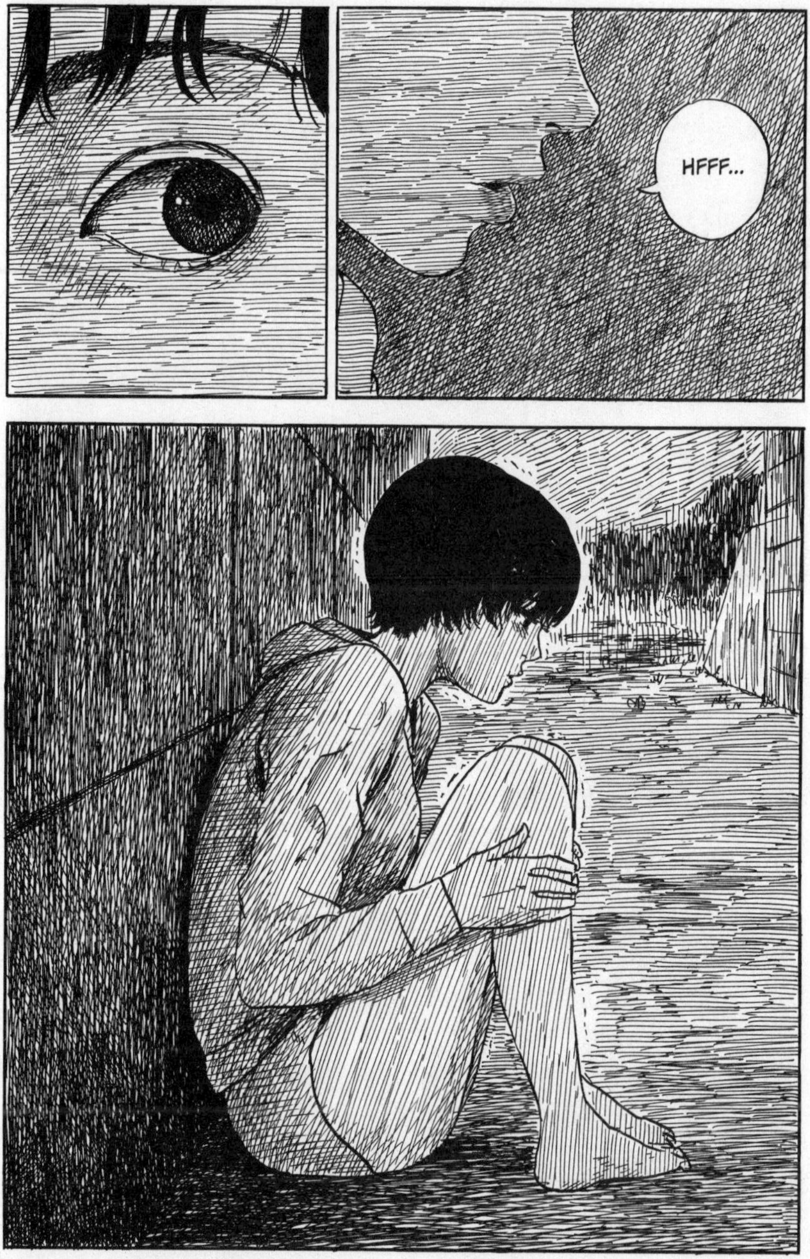
HFFF...

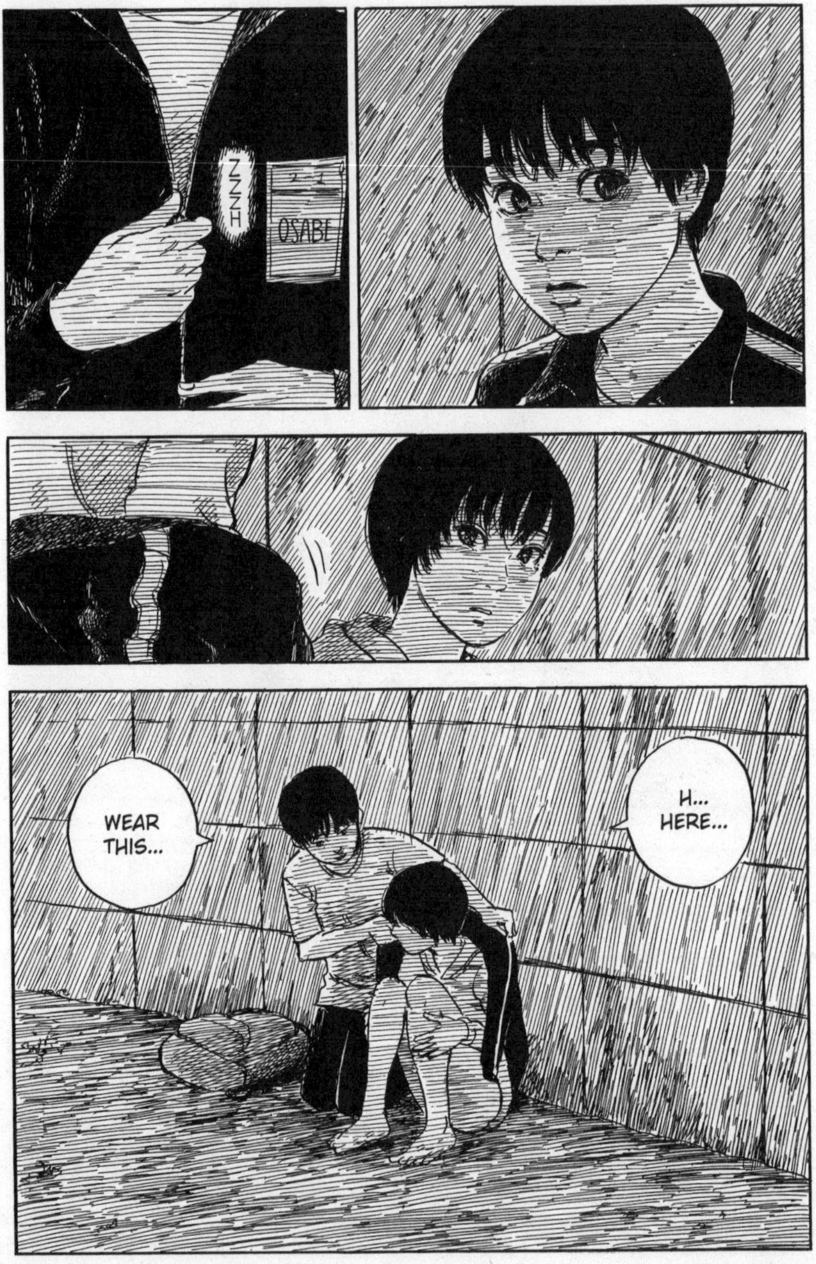
ZZZH
OSABE
H... HERE...
WEAR THIS...

IT'S OKAY...
WON'T YOU BE COLD?
I'M...
I'M FINE...
ALL RIGHT.
THEN, HOW 'BOUT THIS?

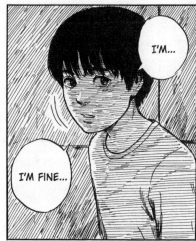

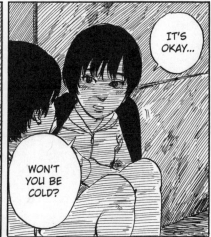

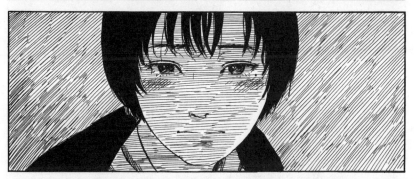

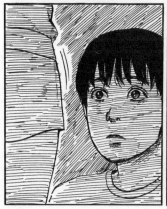

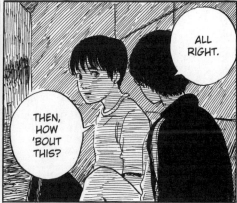

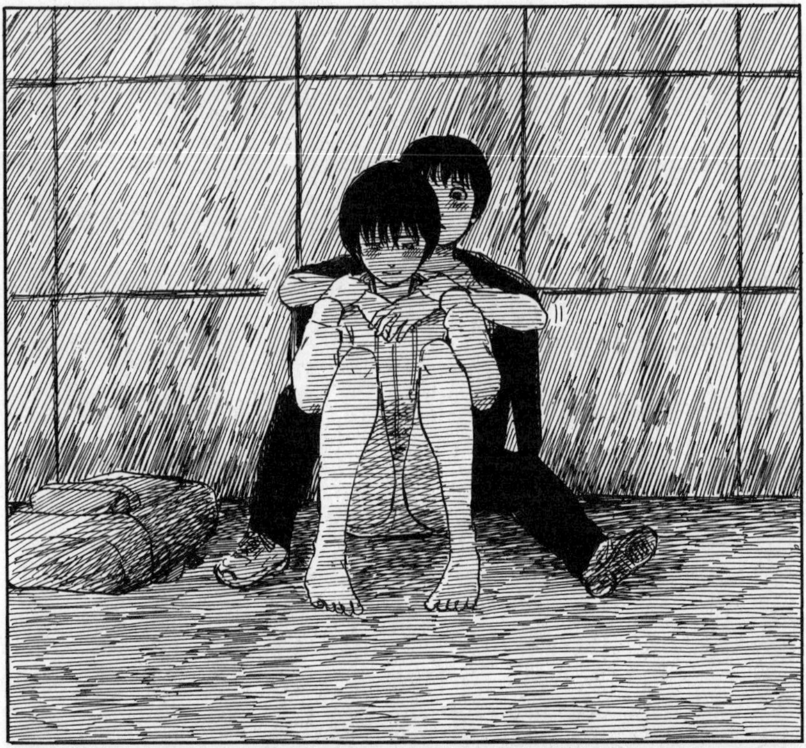

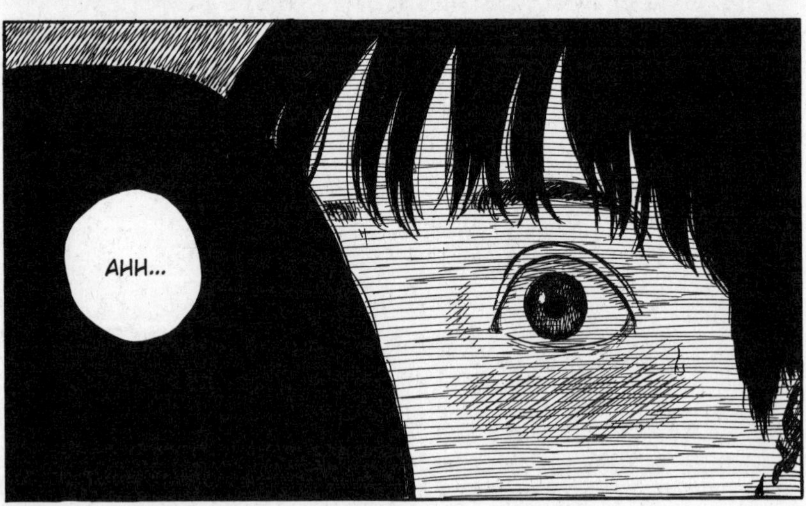
AHH...

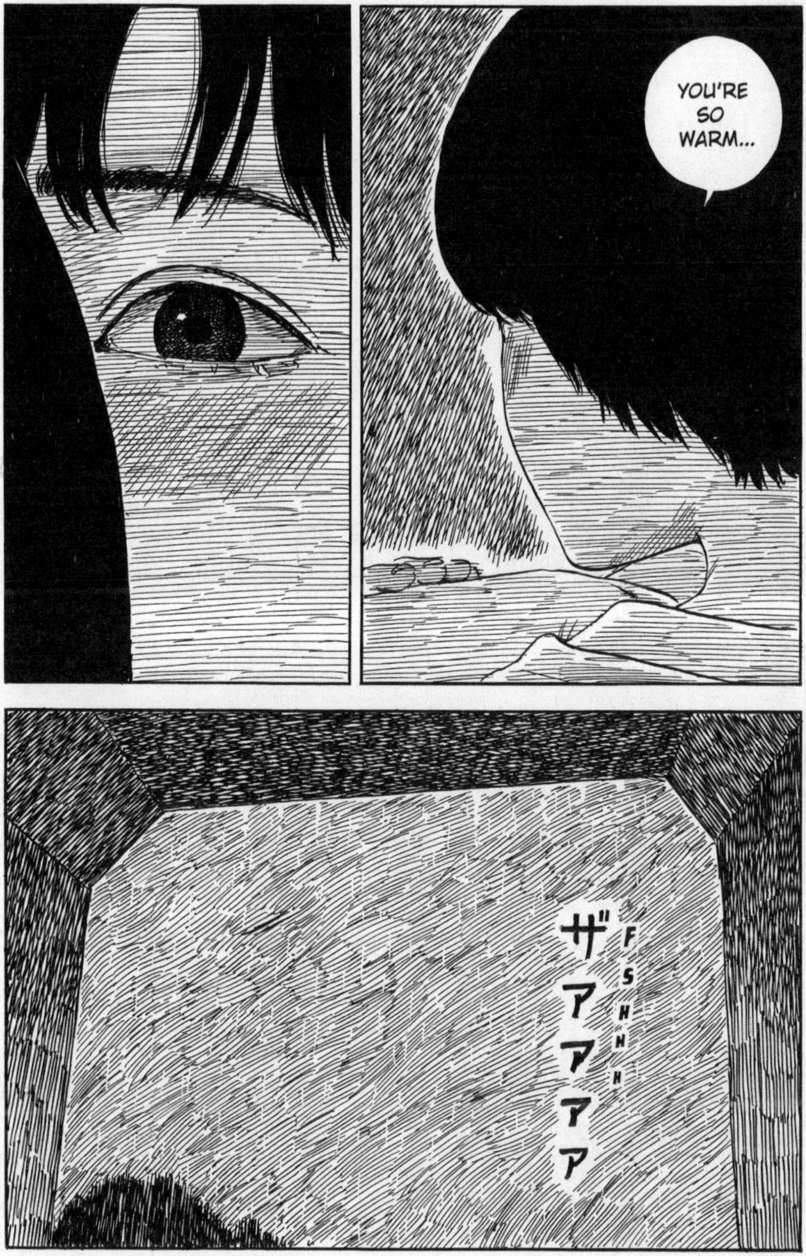
YOU'RE SO WARM...
ザアアアア
FSHHH

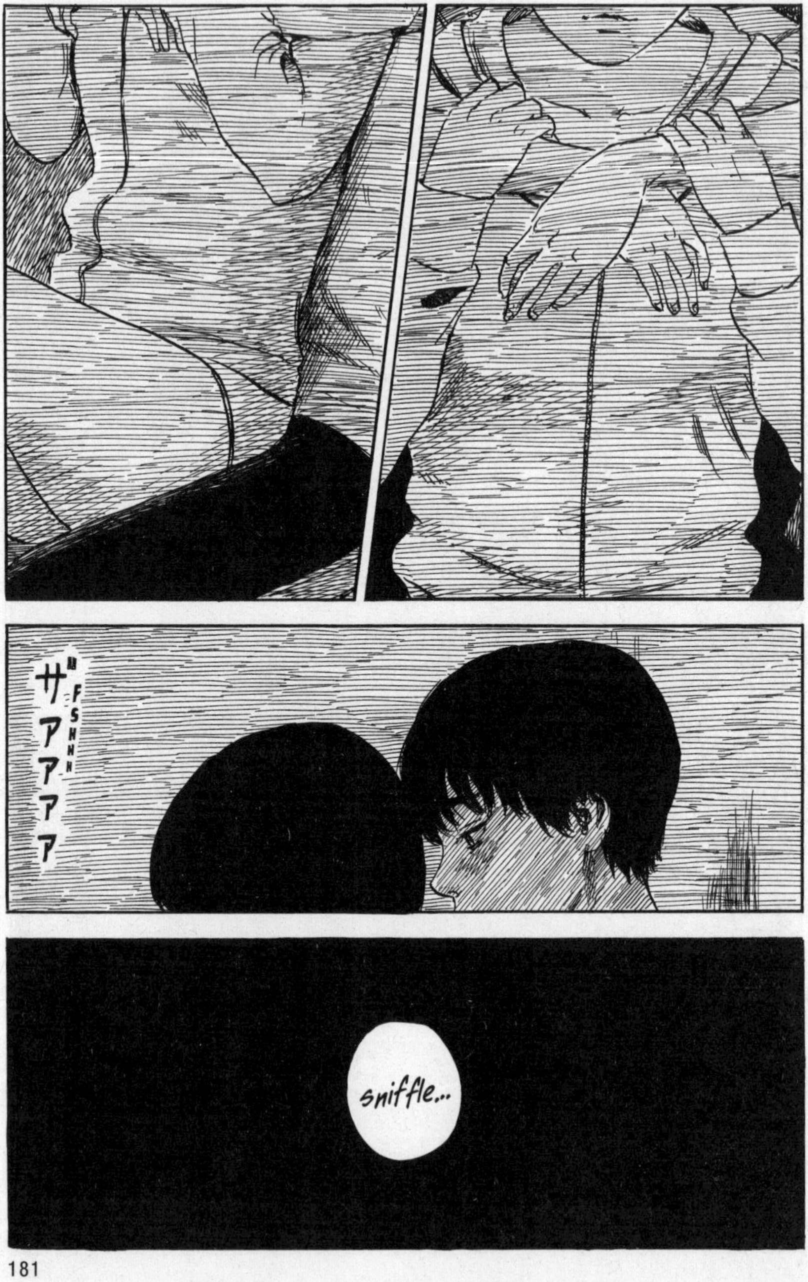
サァァァァ
FSHHH
sniffle...

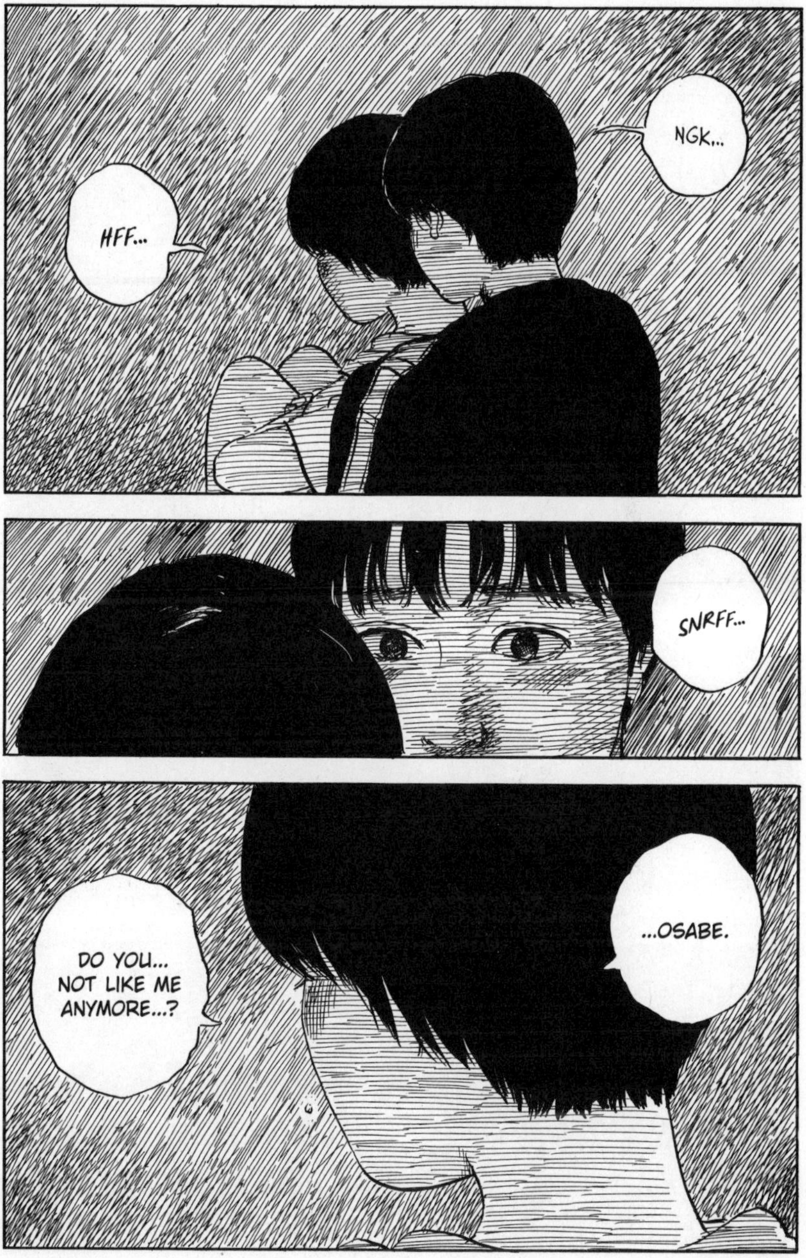
NGK...
HFF...
SNRFF...
...OSABE.
DO YOU... NOT LIKE ME ANYMORE...?

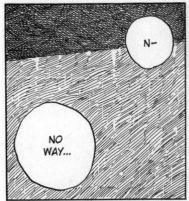

N-

NO
WAY...

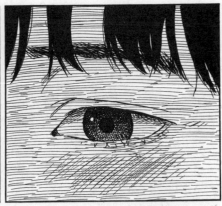

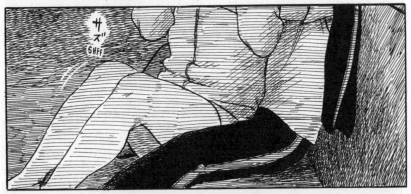

サズ
SHFF

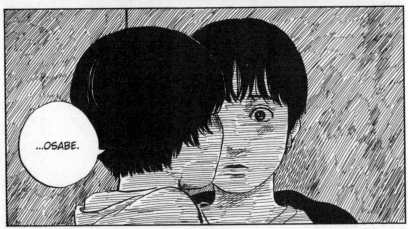

...OSABE.

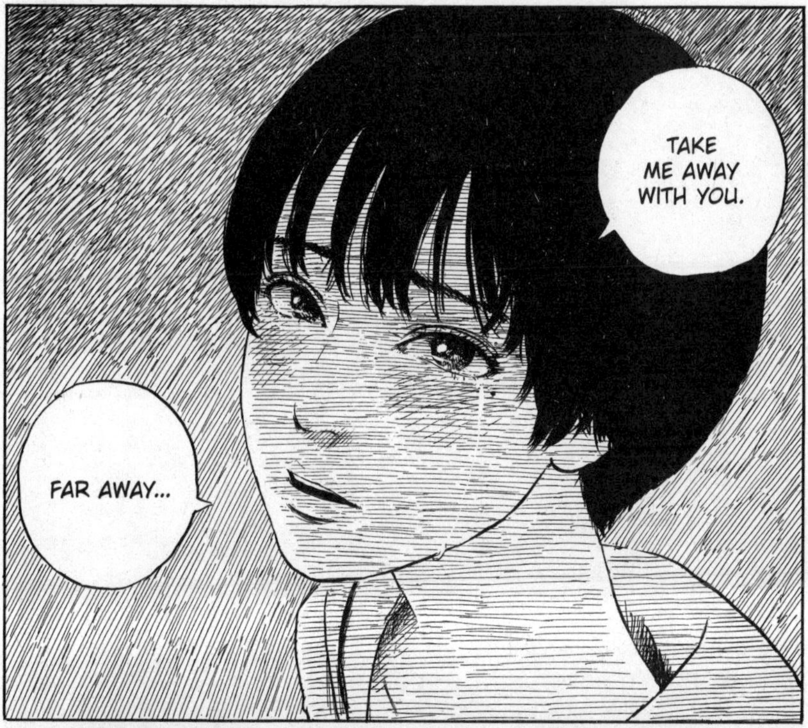
TAKE ME AWAY WITH YOU.
FAR AWAY...

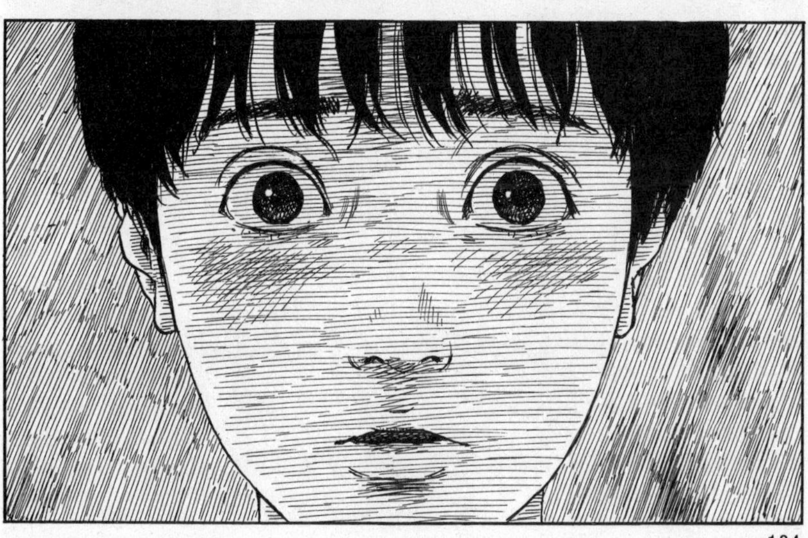

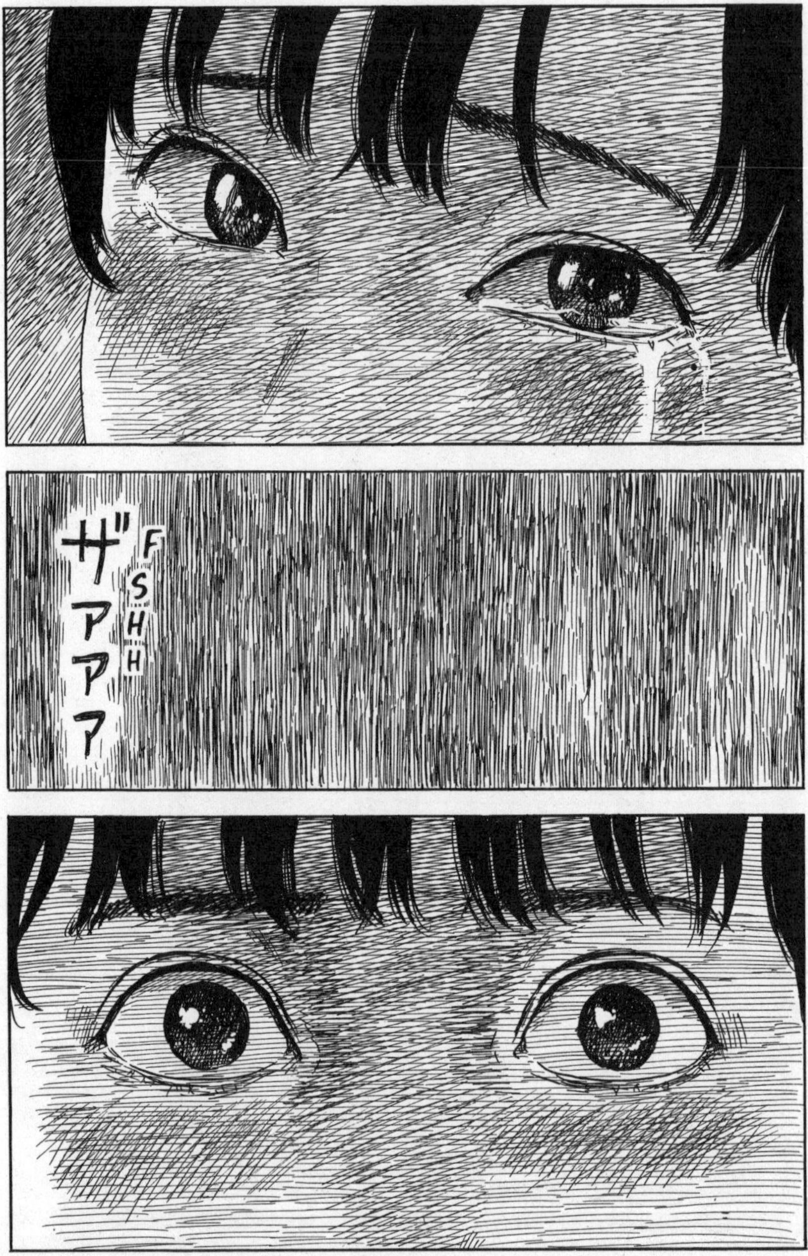
ザァァァ
FSHH

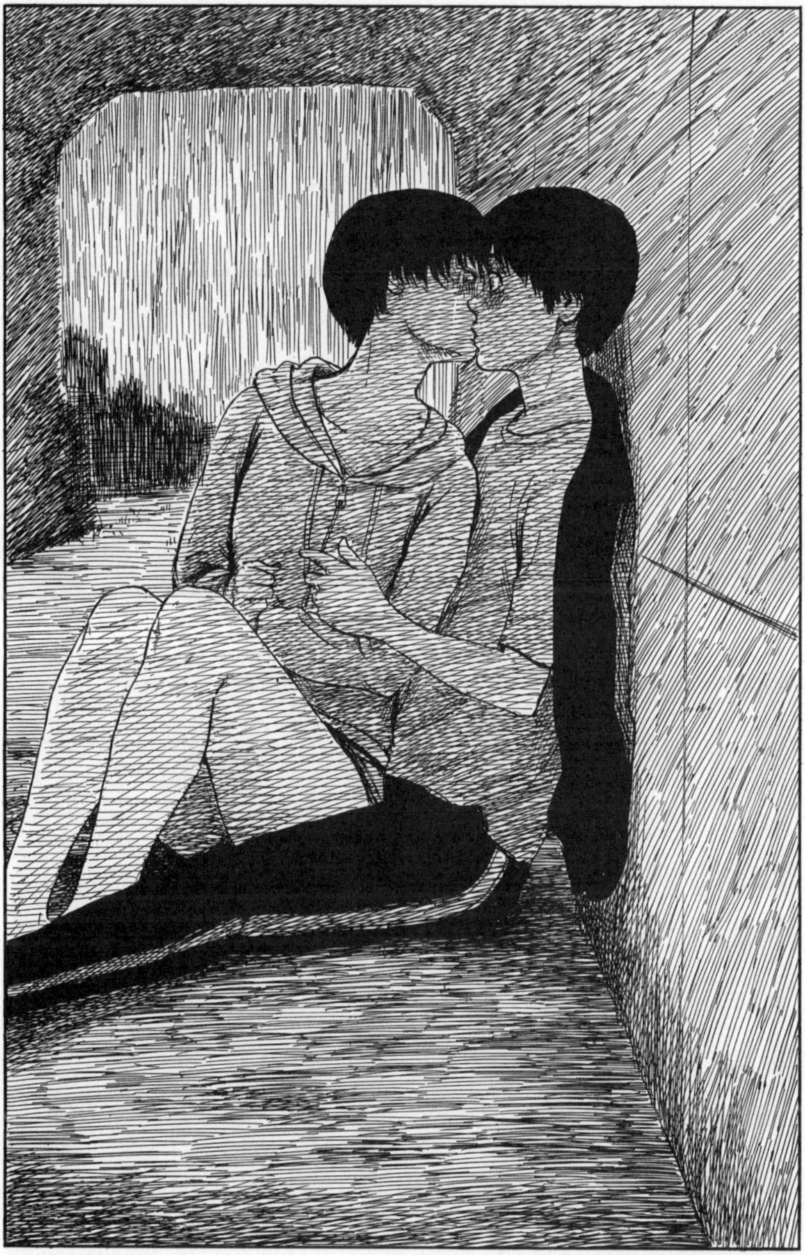

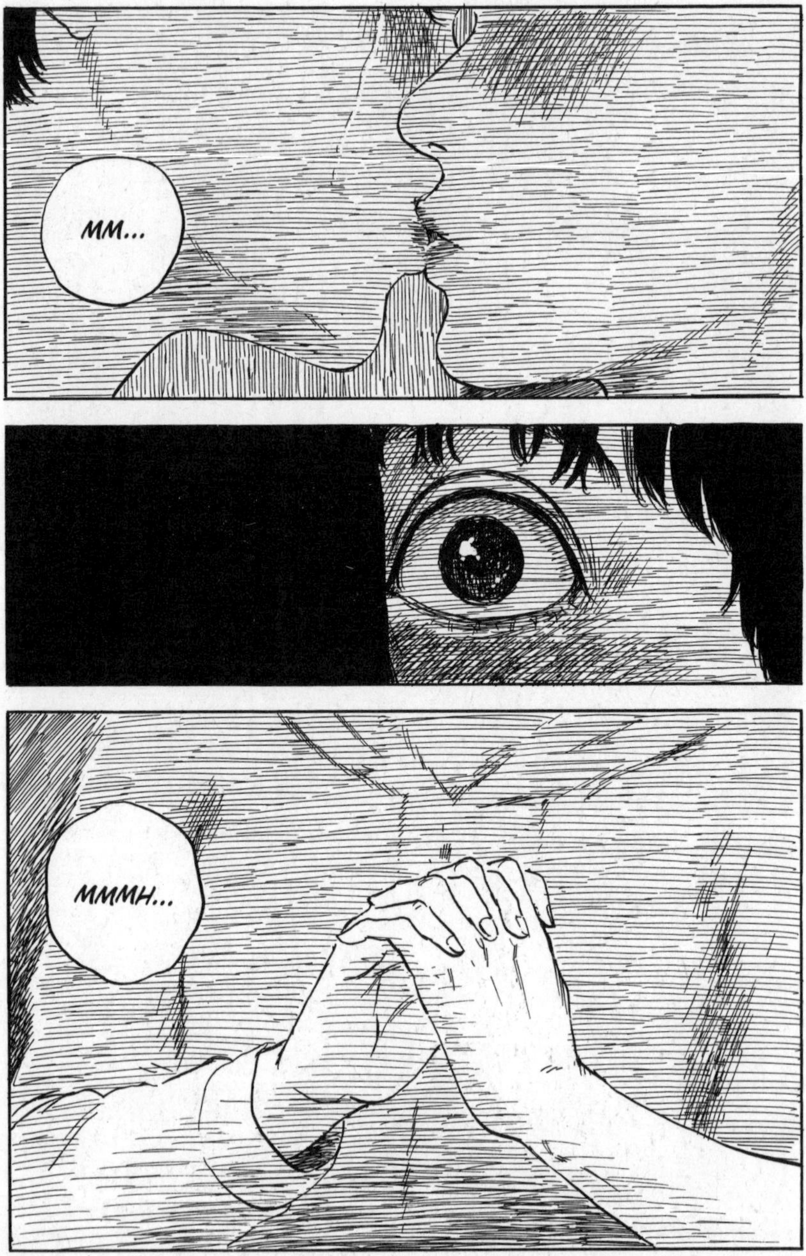
MM...
MMMH...

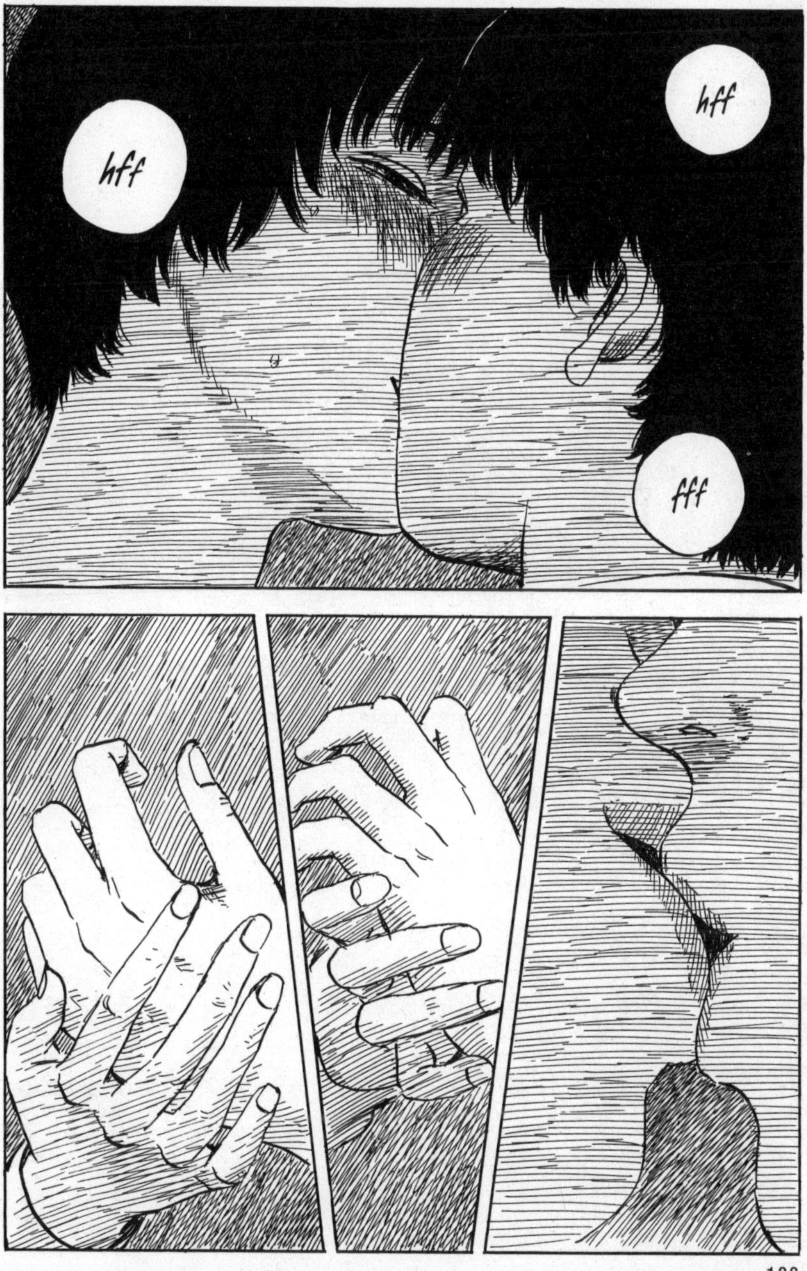
hff
hff
fff

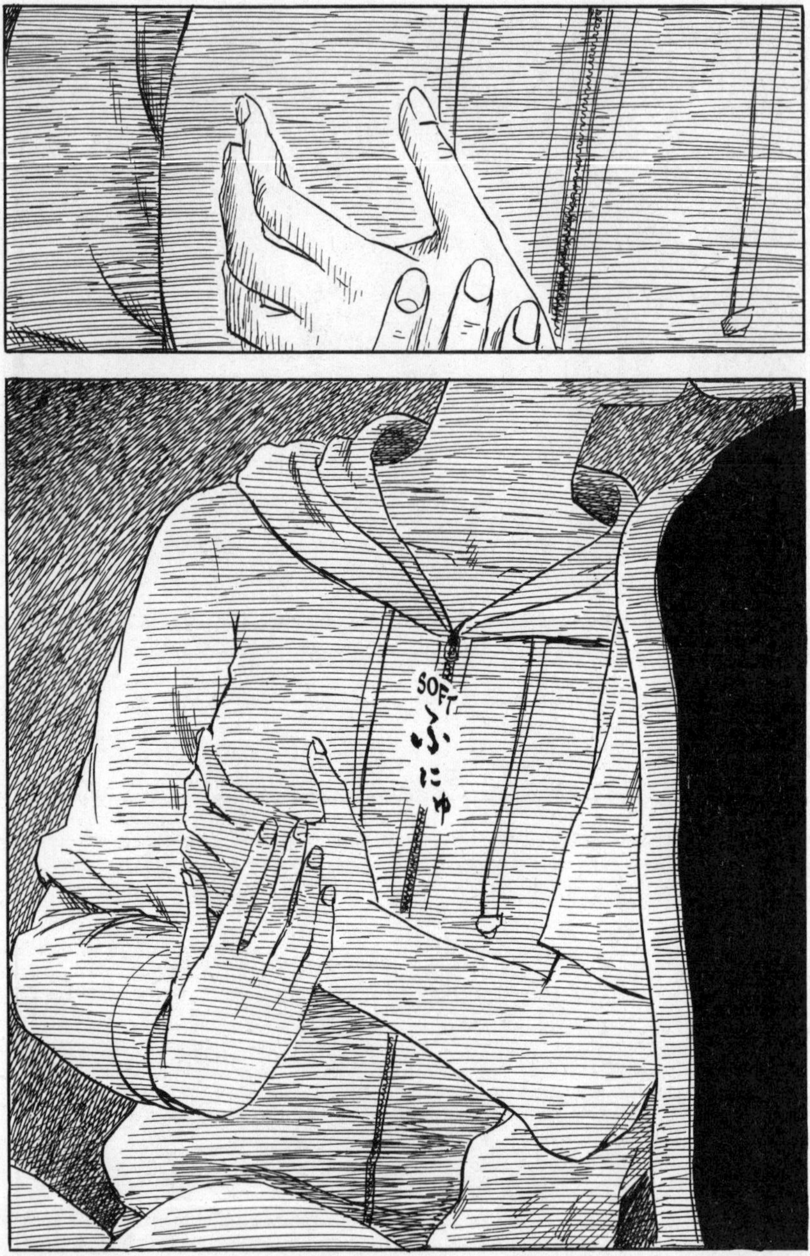
SOFT
ふにゅ

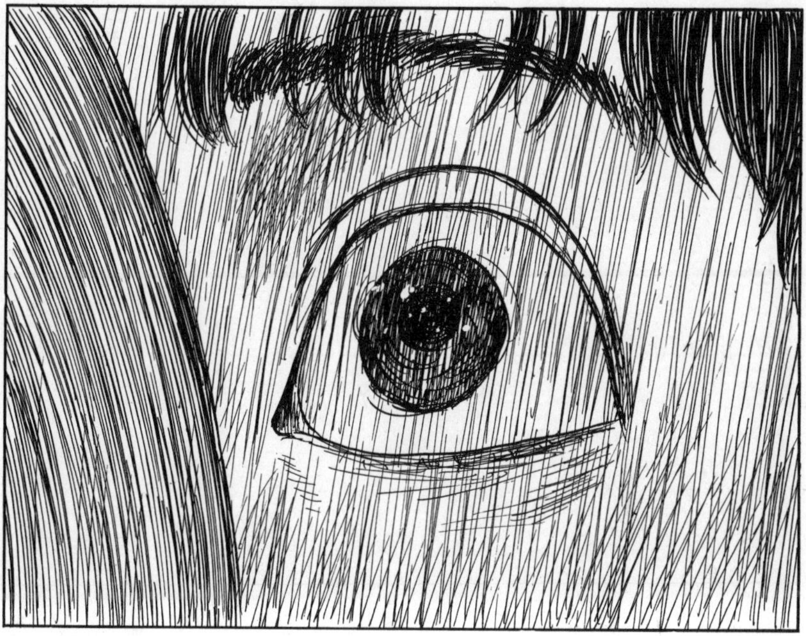

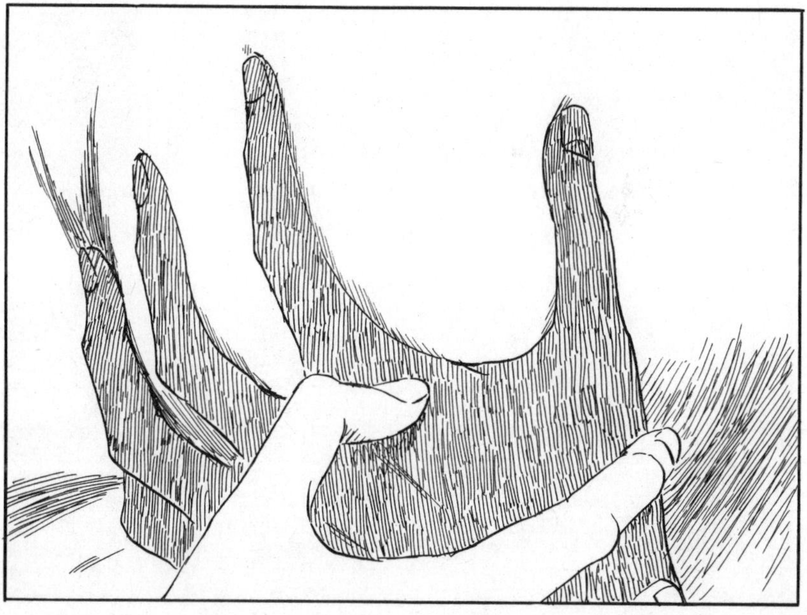

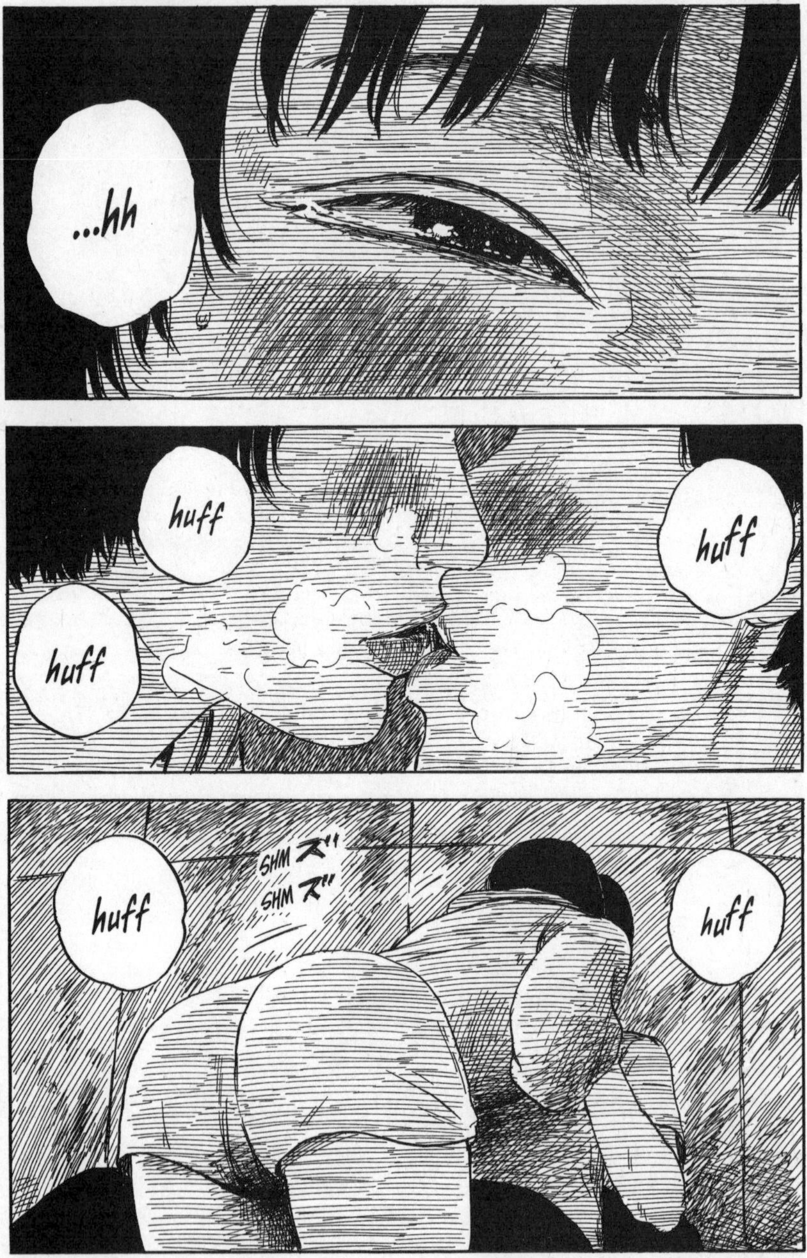
...hh
huff
huff
huff
huff
SHM ズ
SHM ズ
huff

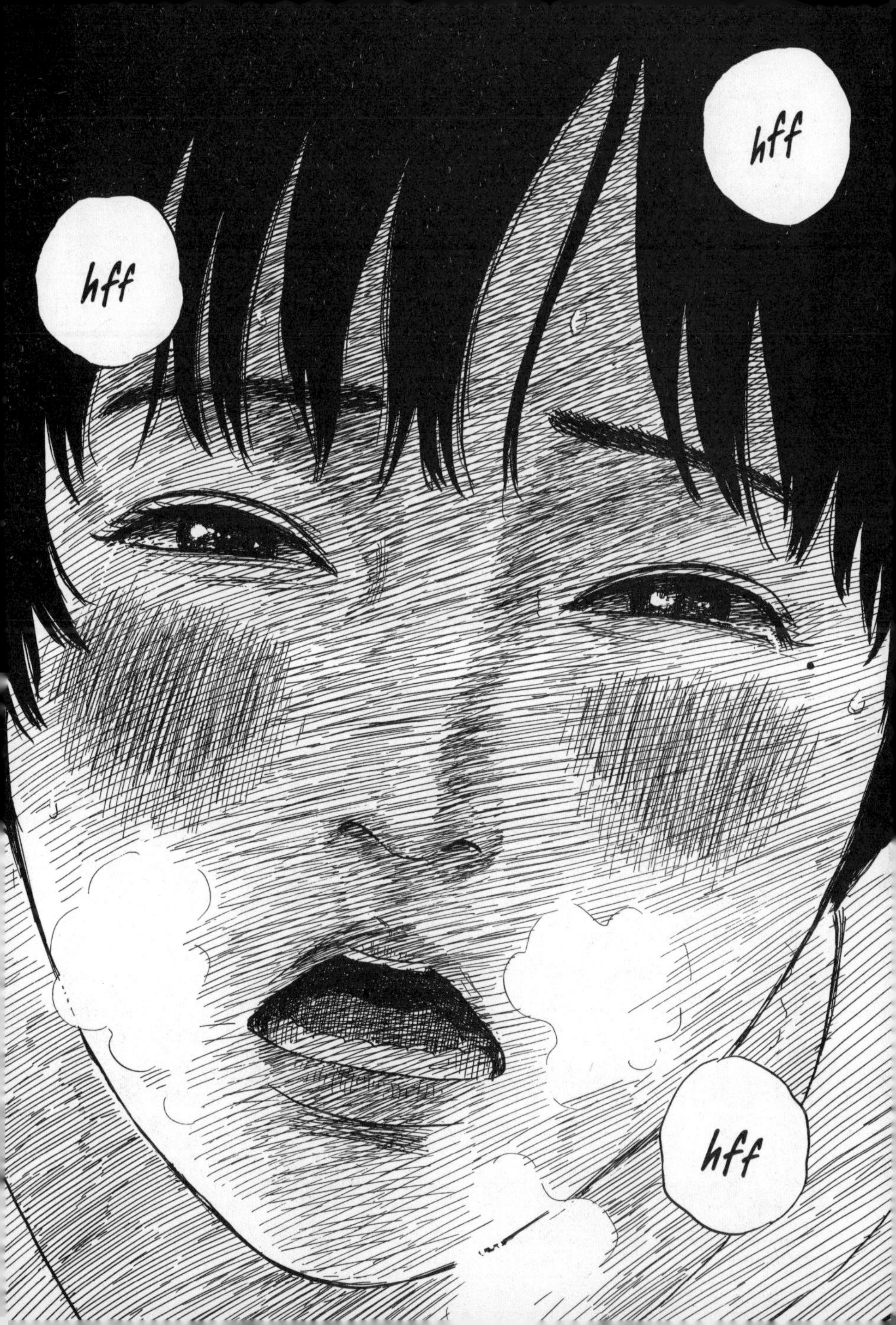
hff
hff
hff

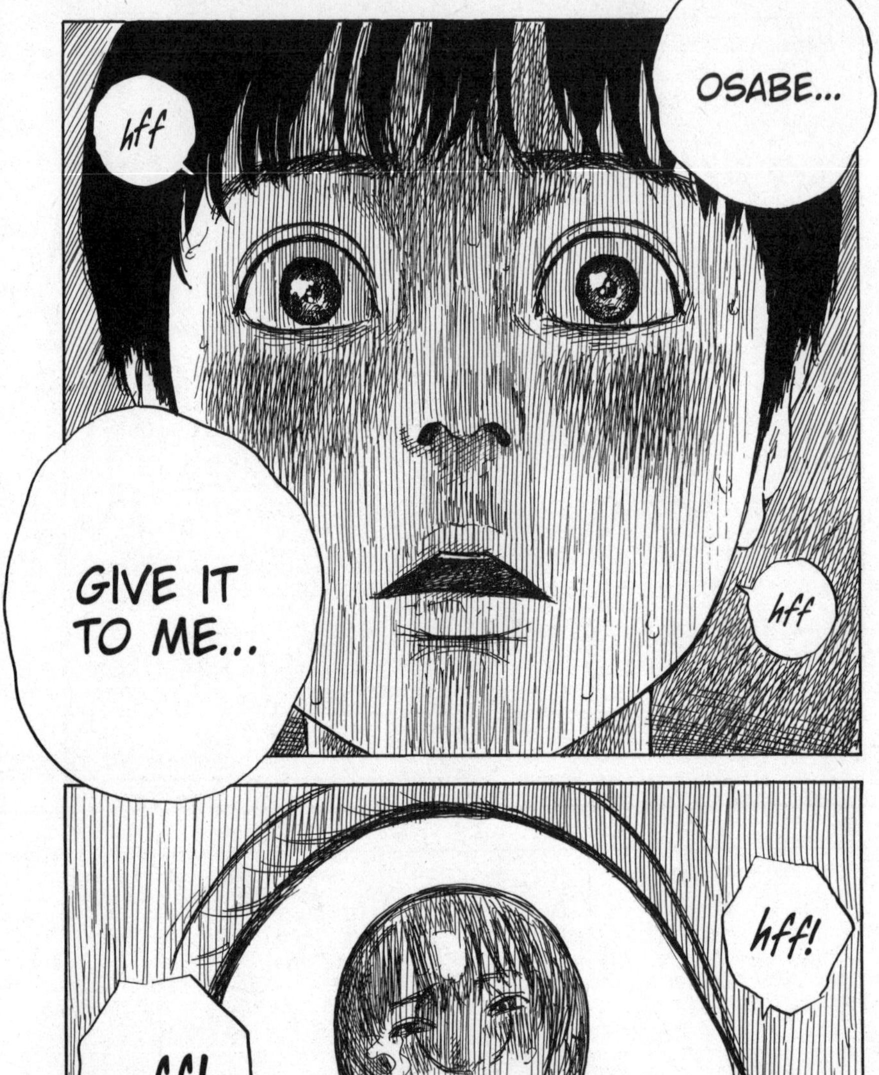
OSABE...
hff
hff
GIVE IT TO ME...
hff!
hff!

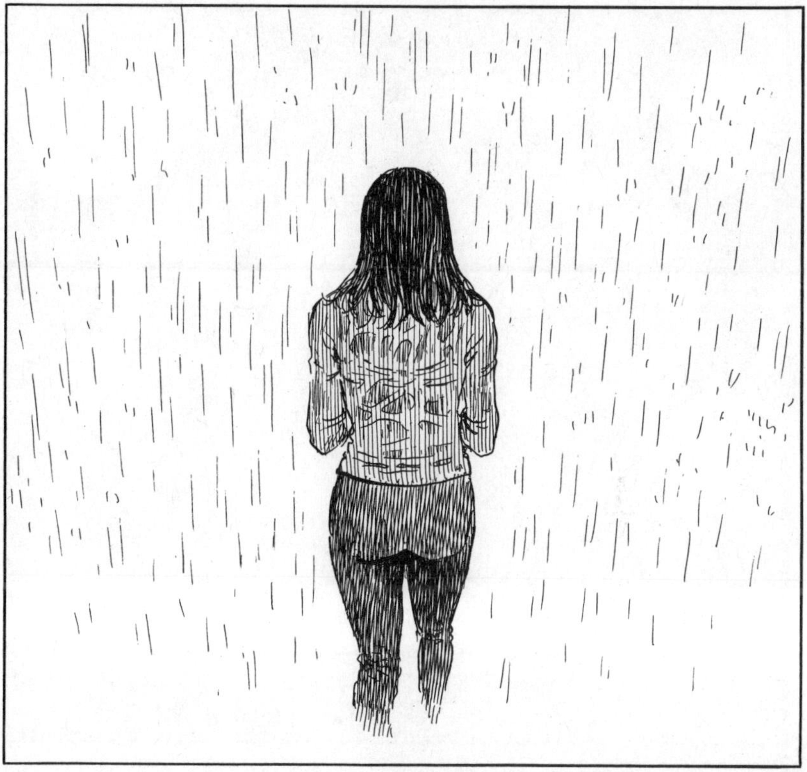

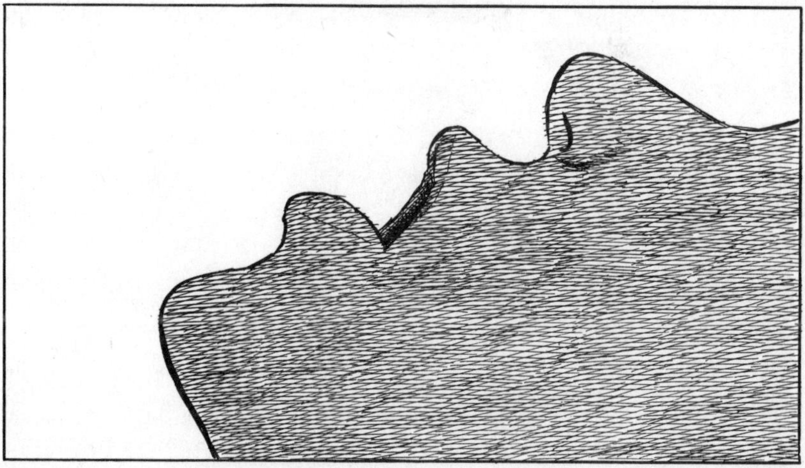

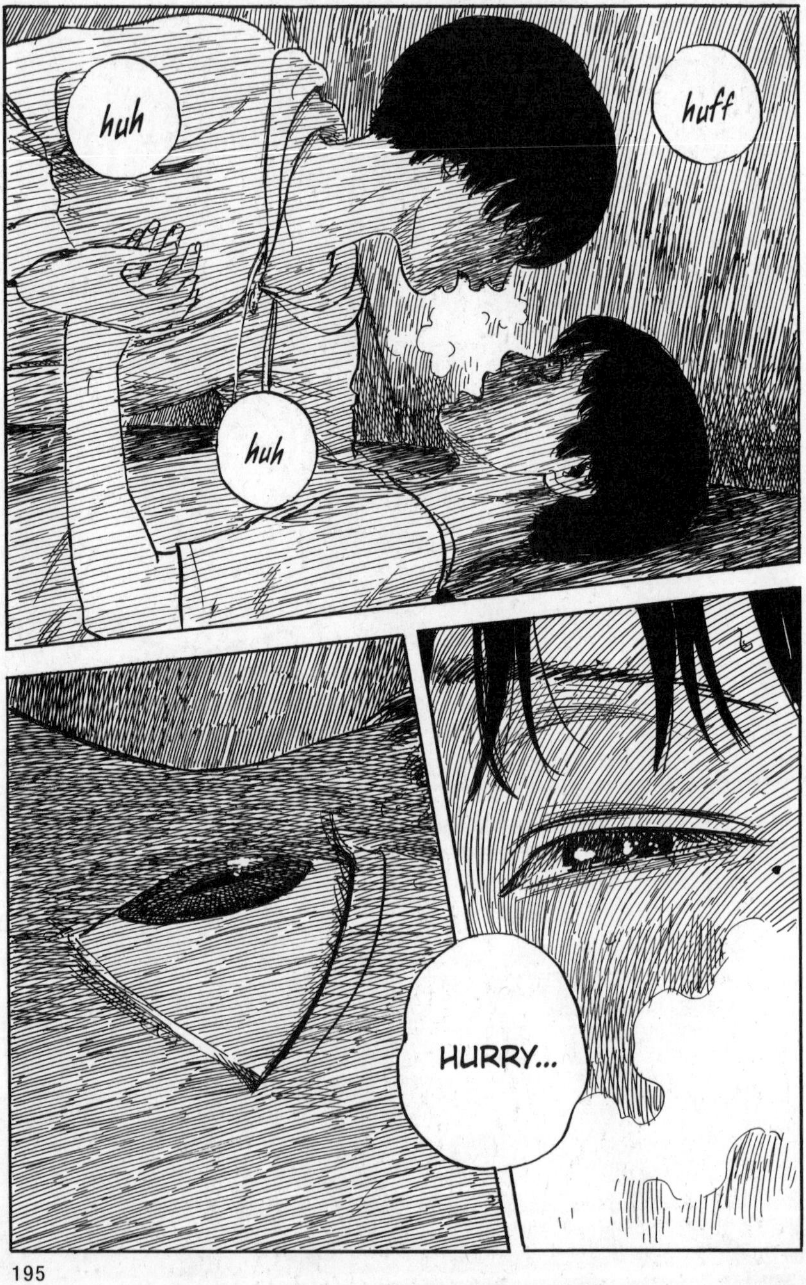
huff
huh
huh
HURRY...

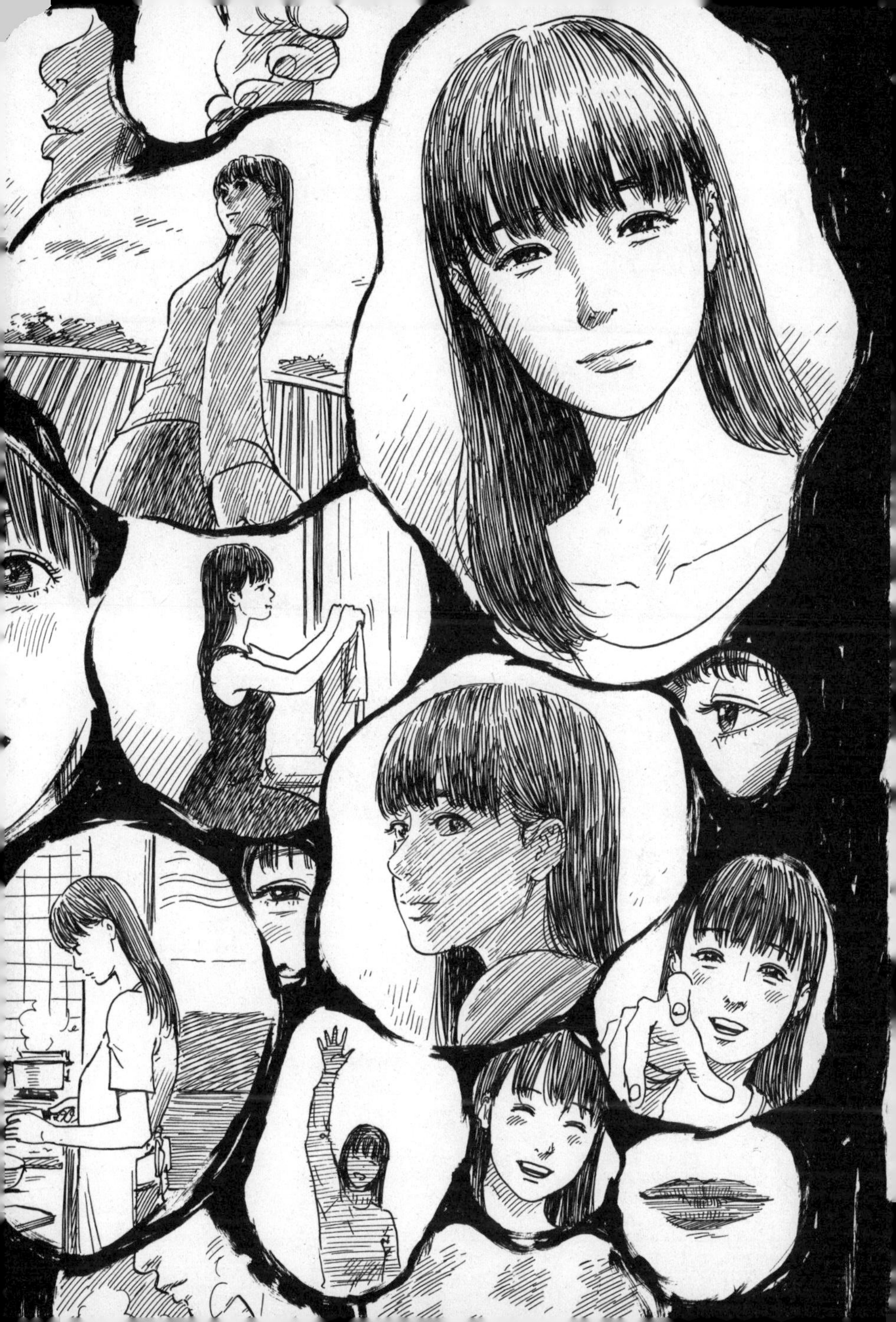

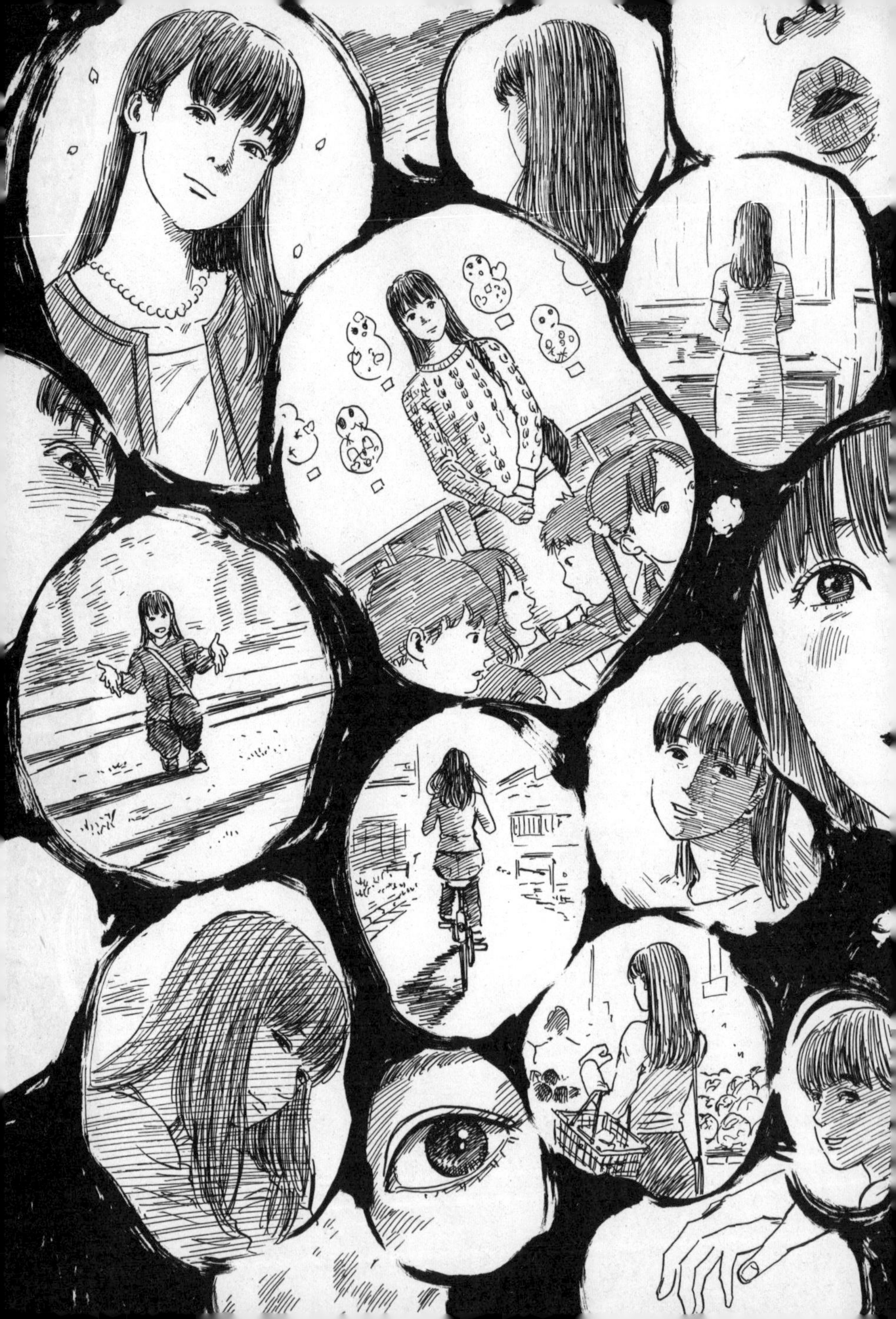

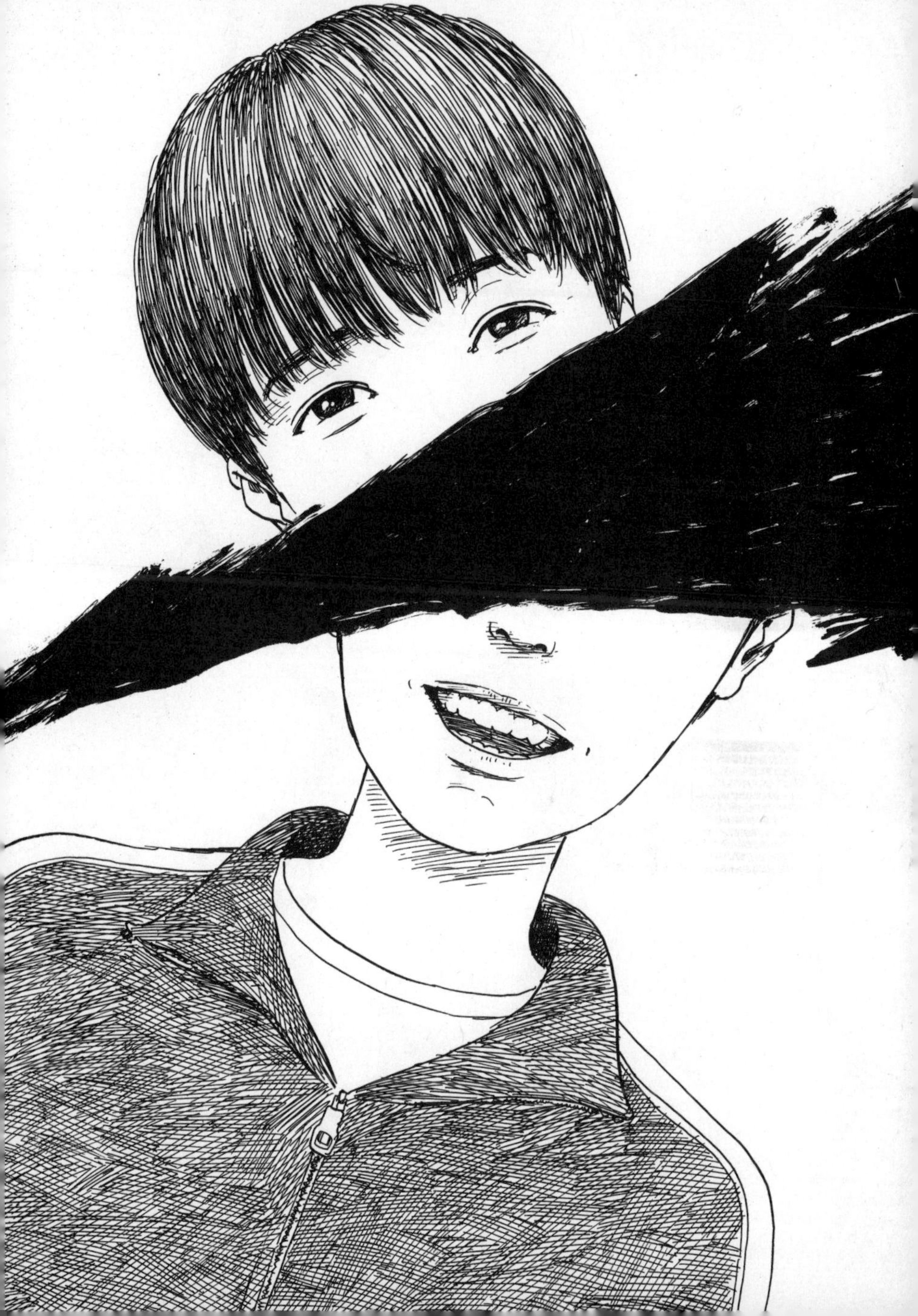

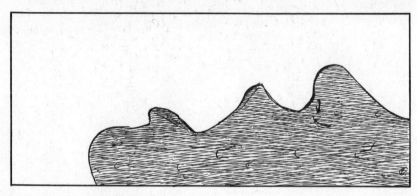

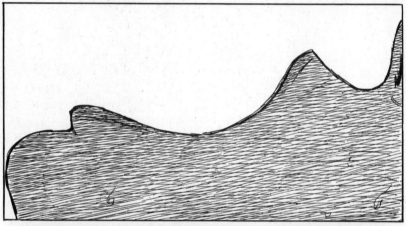

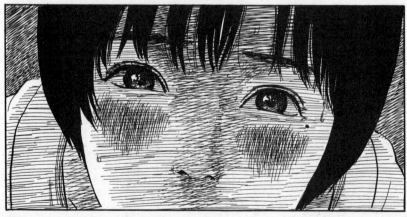

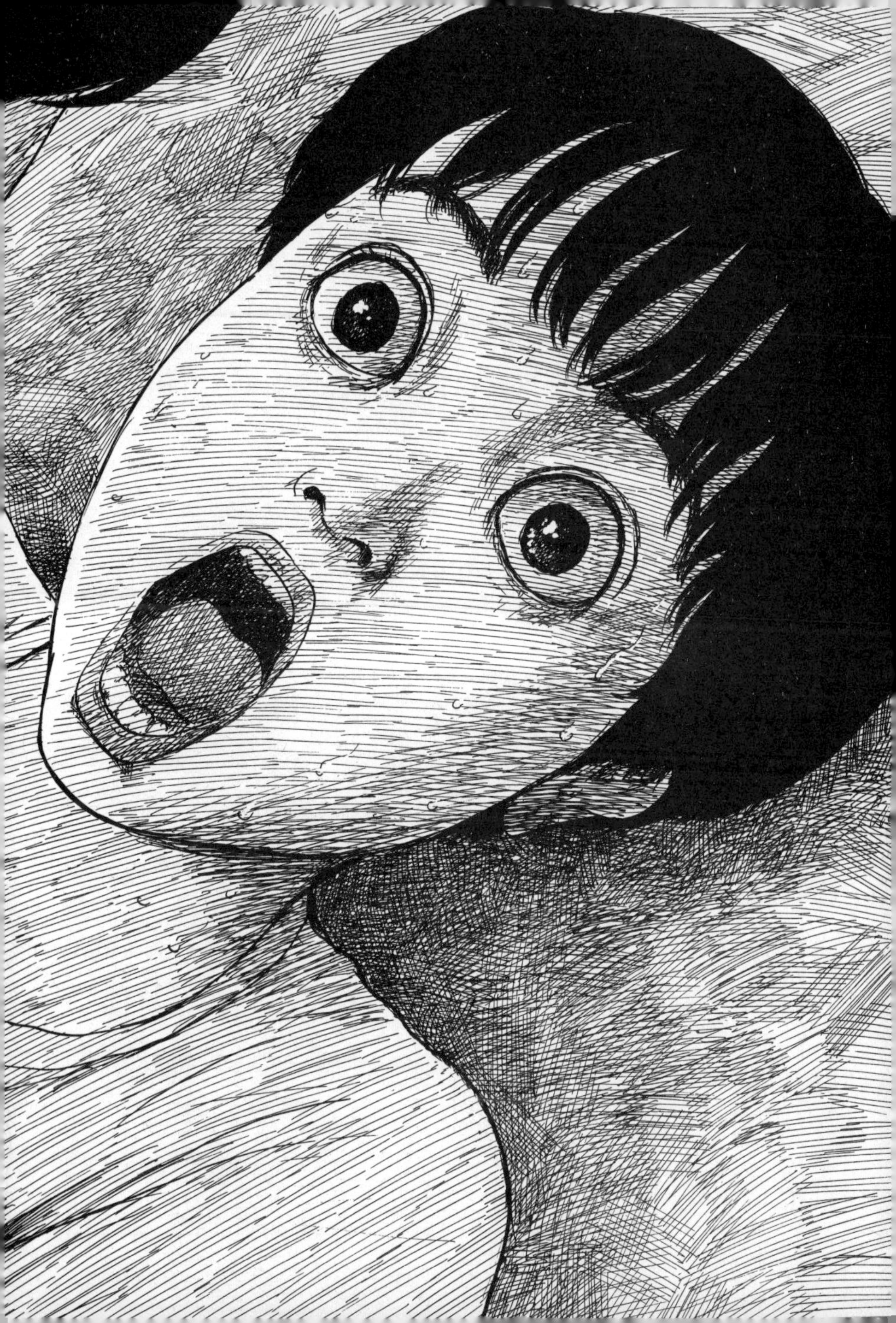

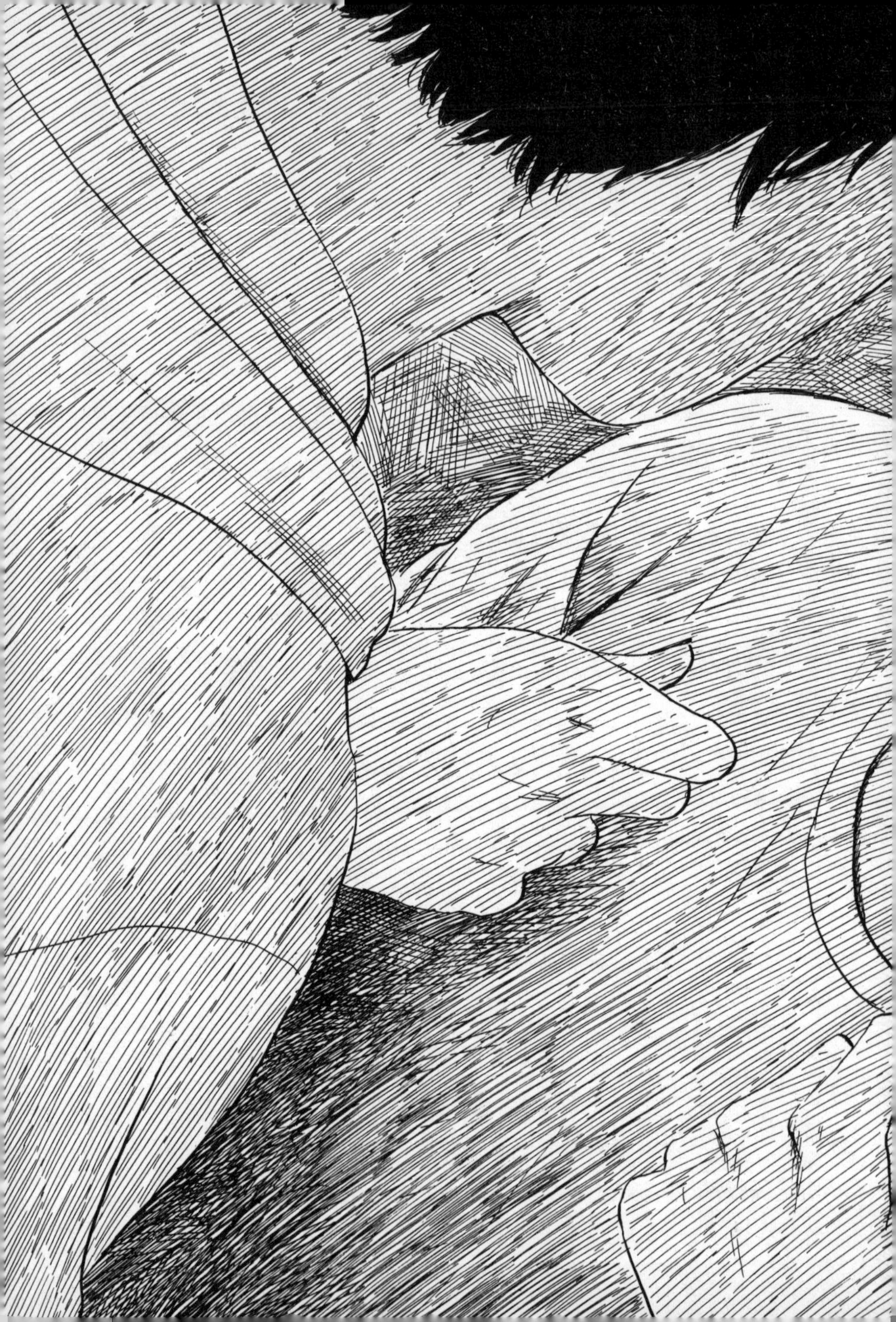

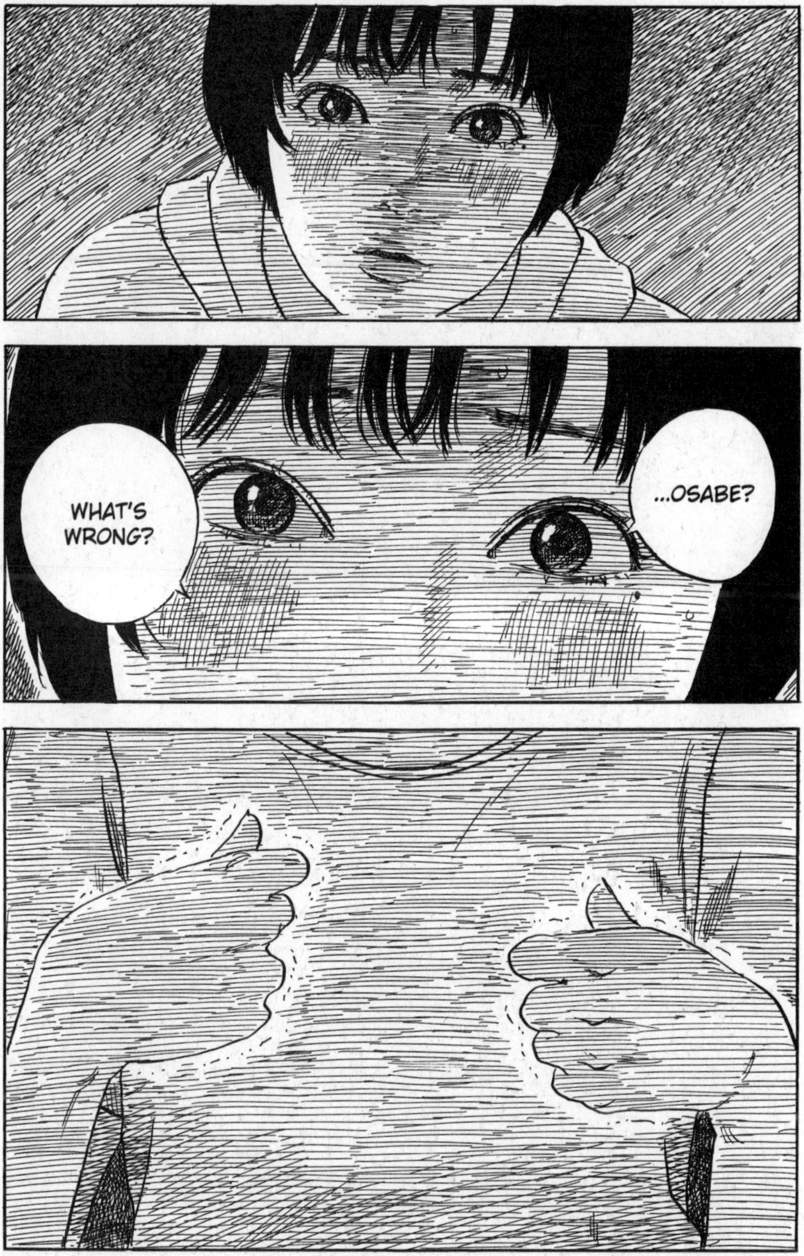
...OSABE?
WHAT'S WRONG?

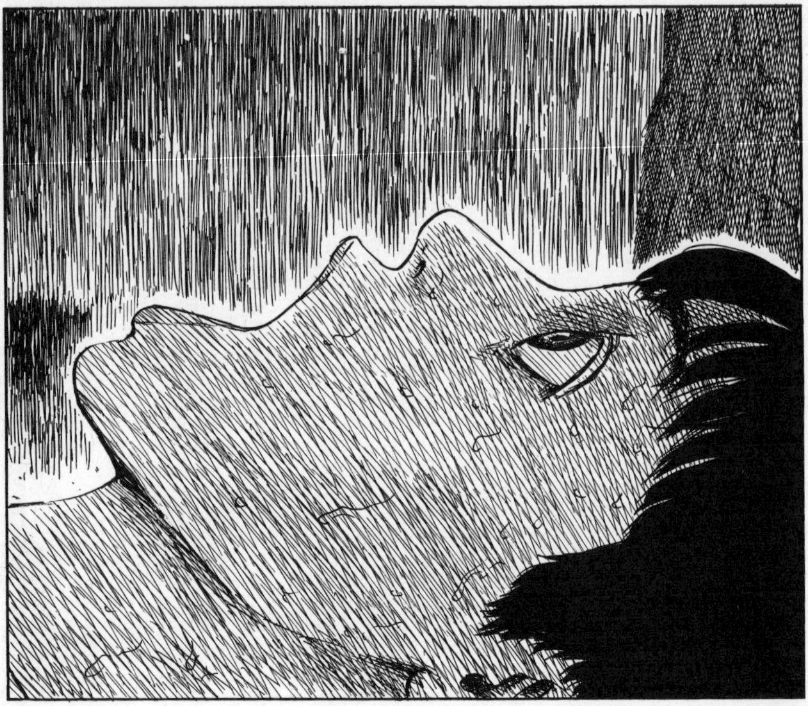
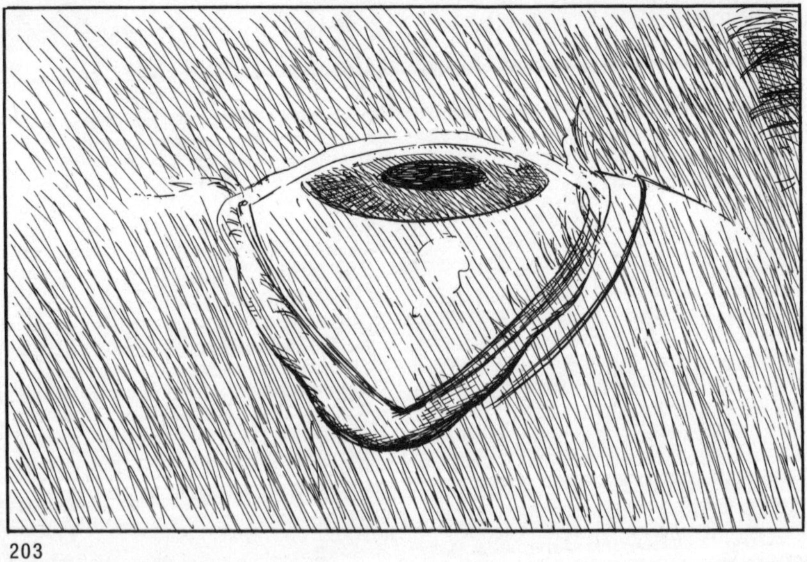

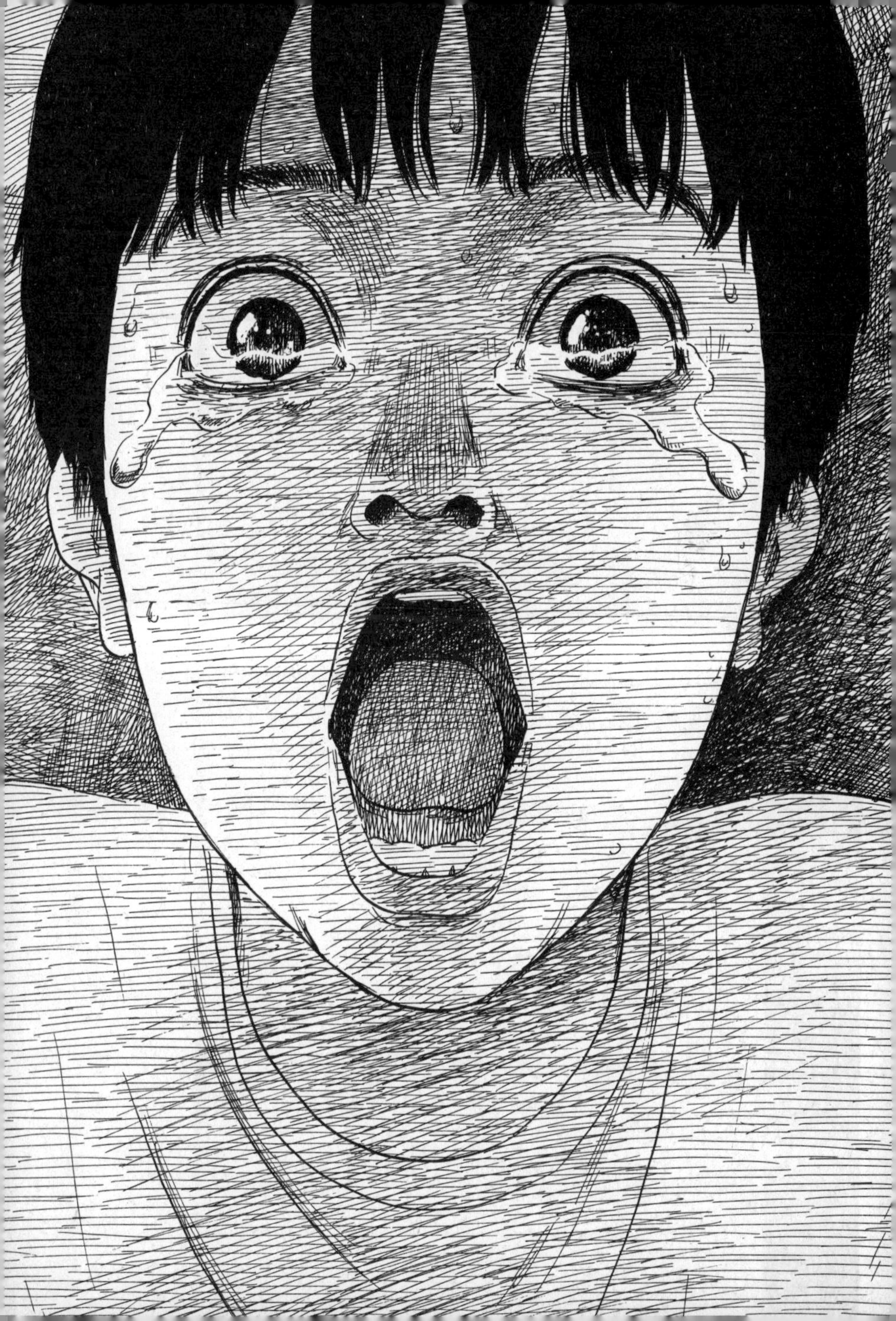

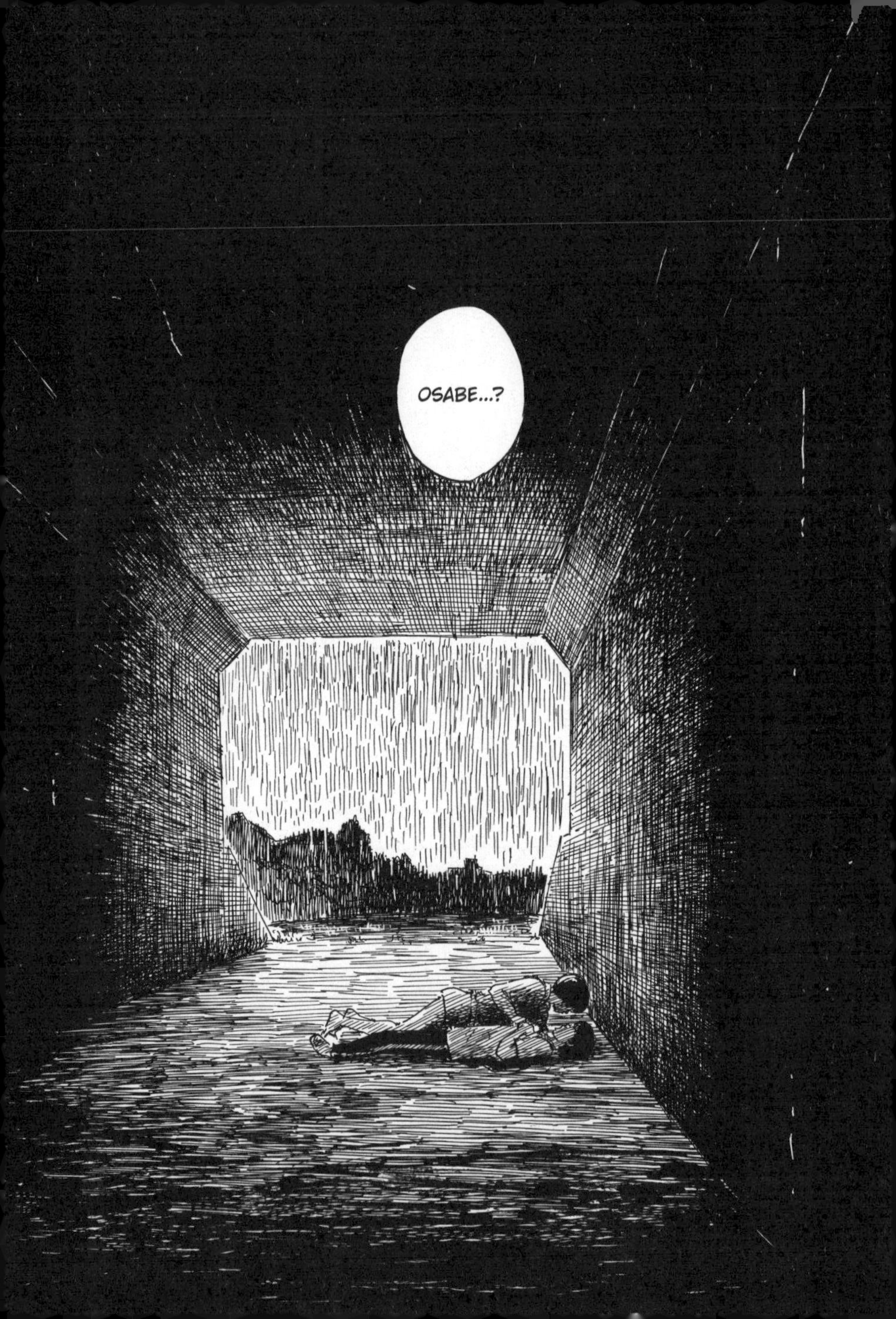
OSABE...?

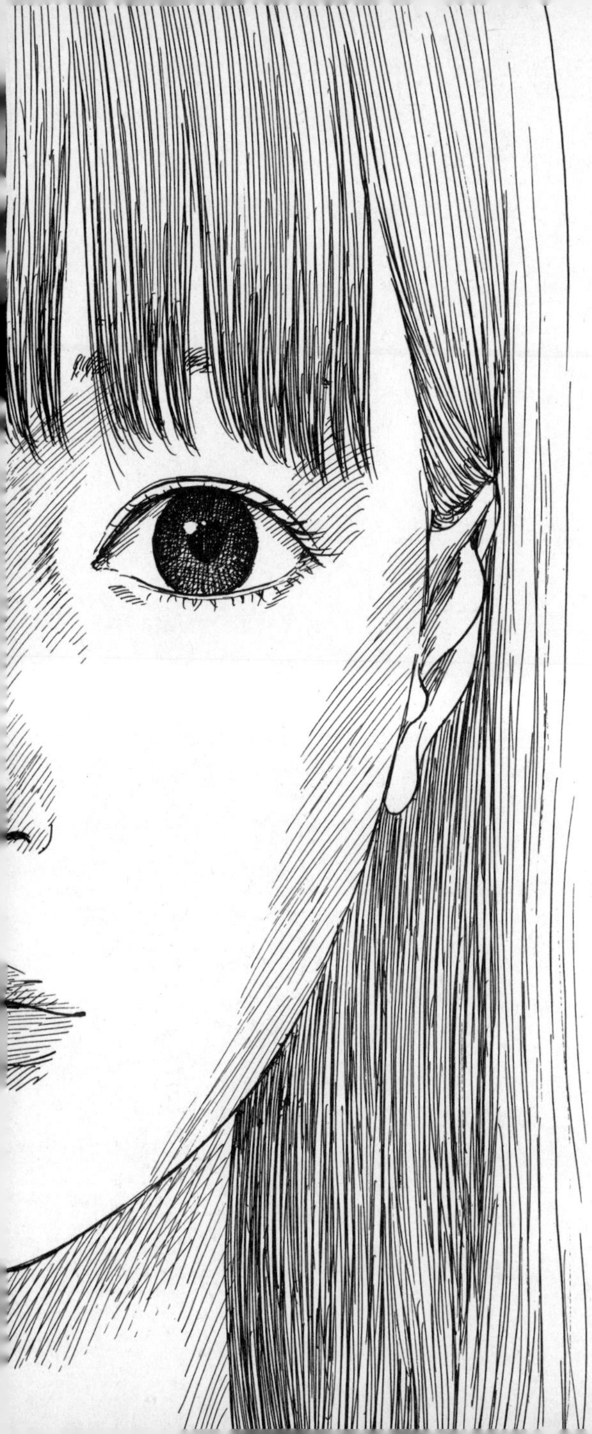

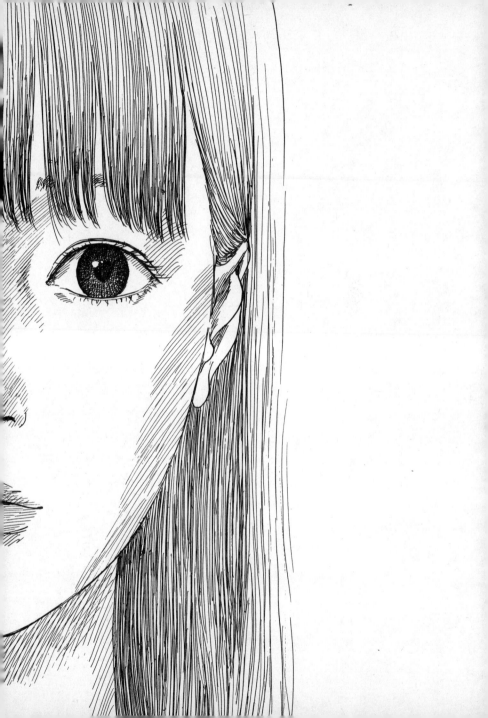

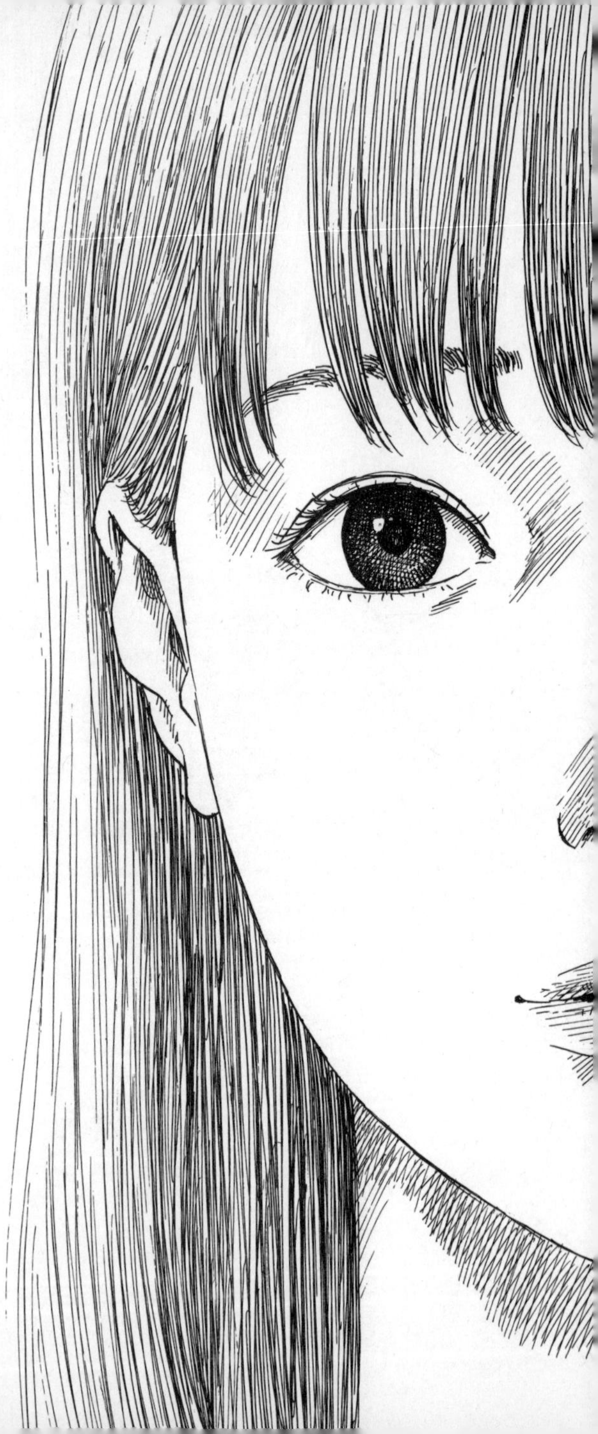

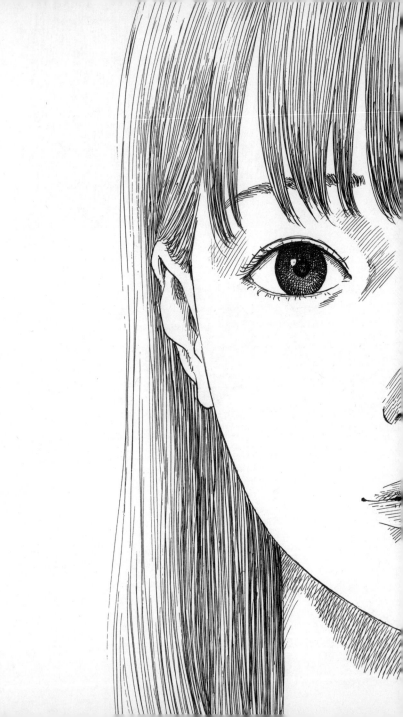

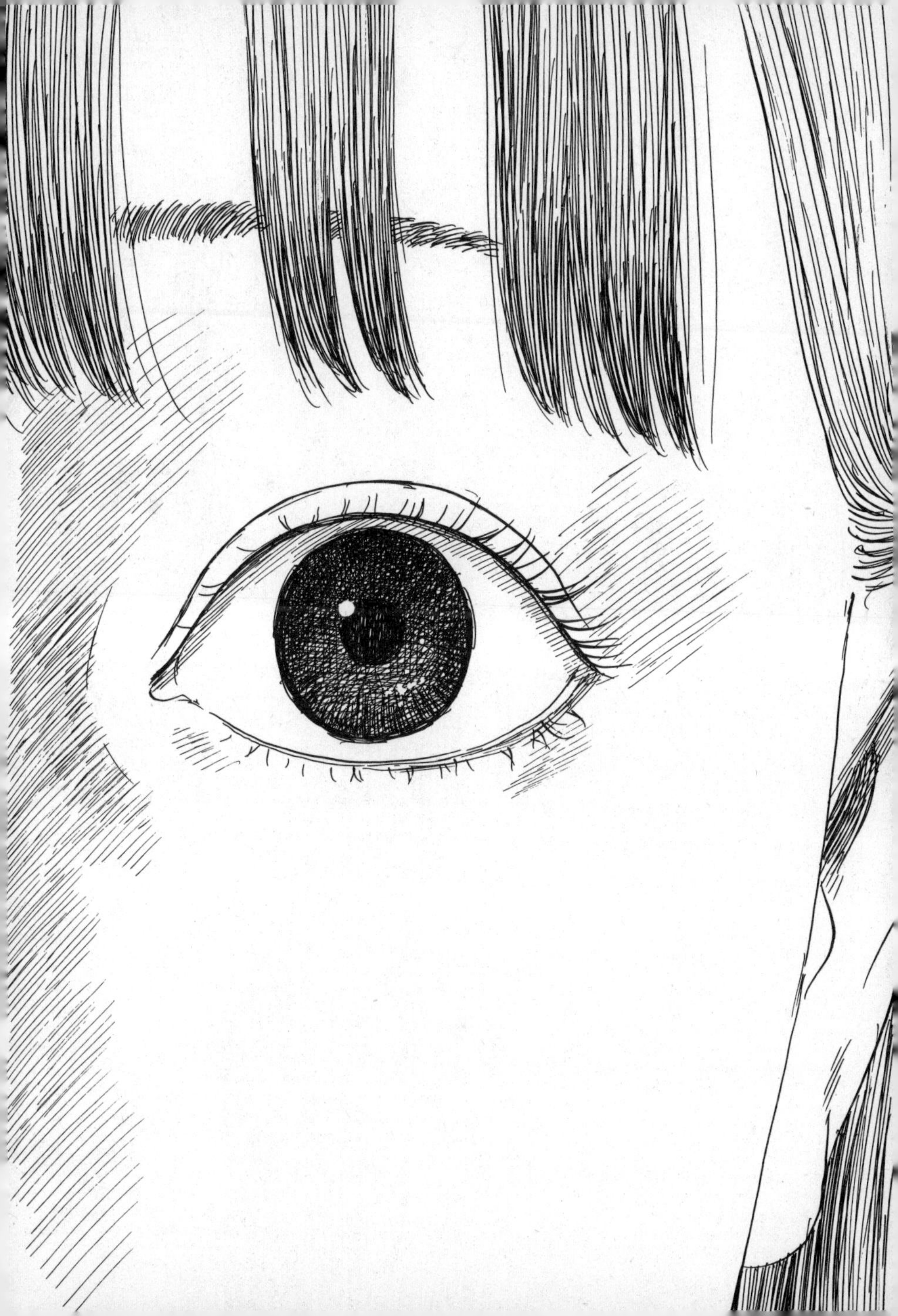

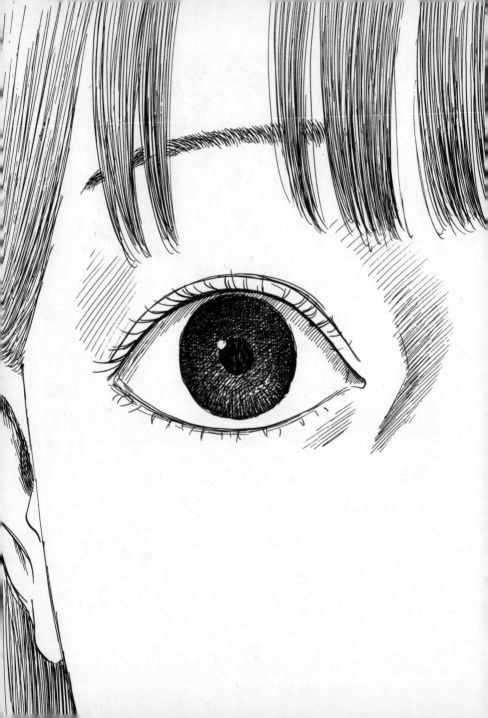

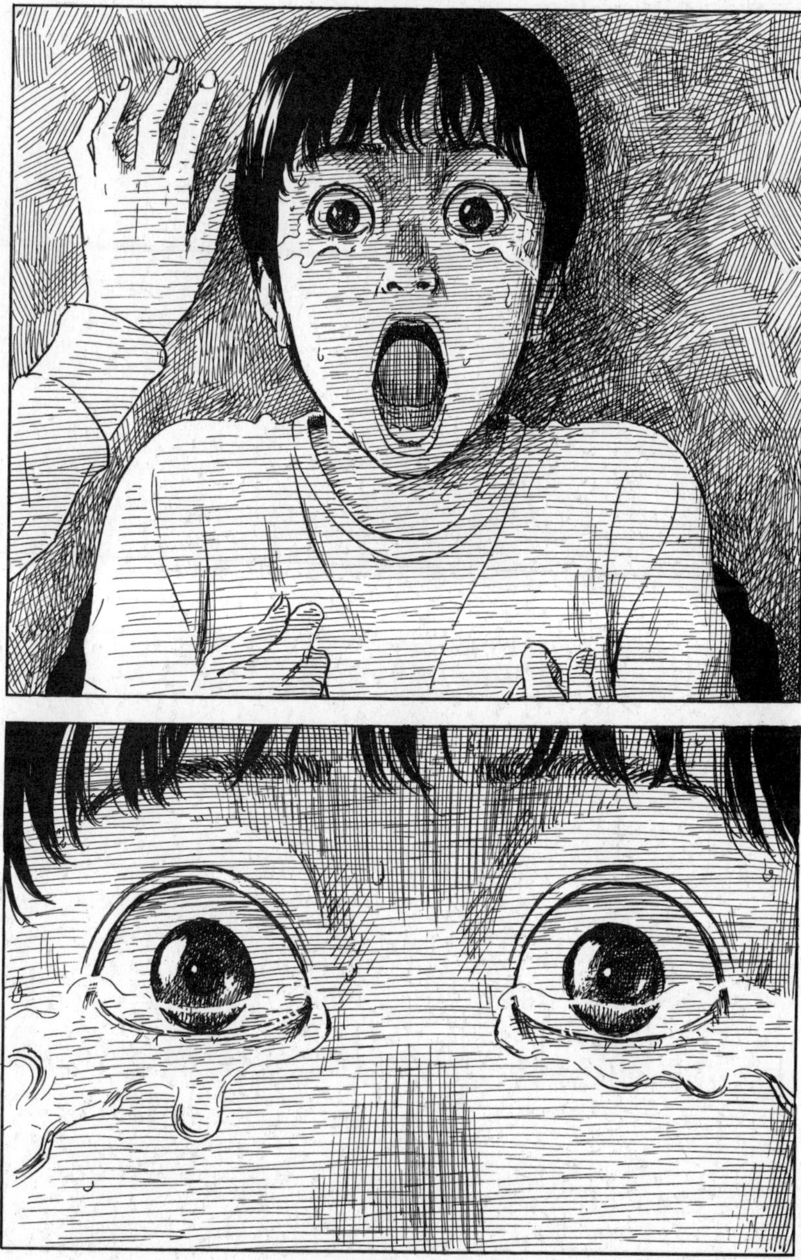

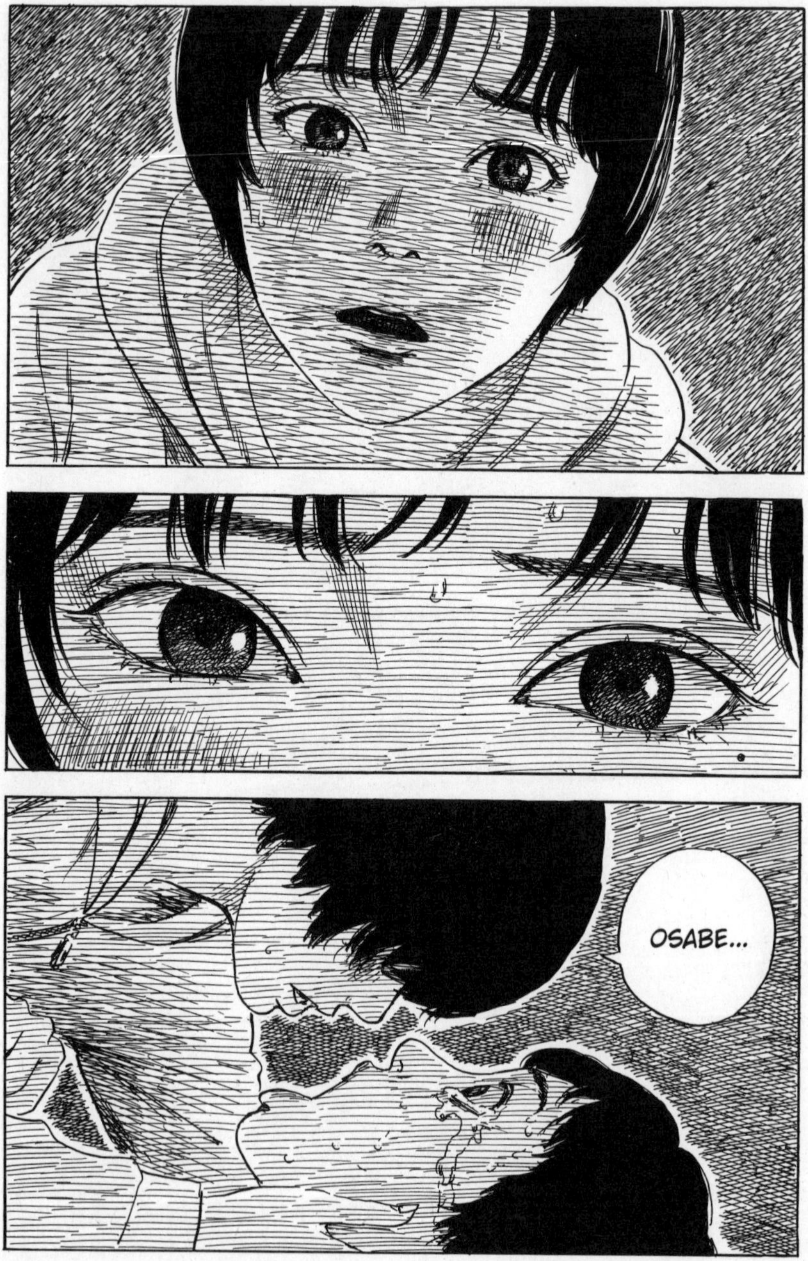
OSABE...

IT'S OKAY...
IT'S OKAY...
OSABE...

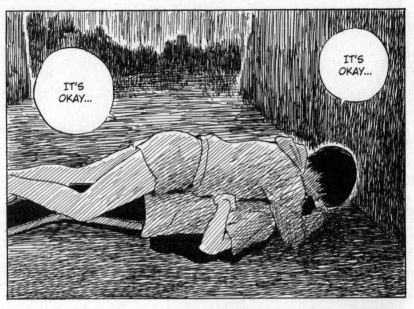

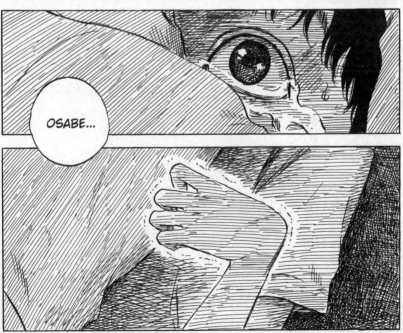

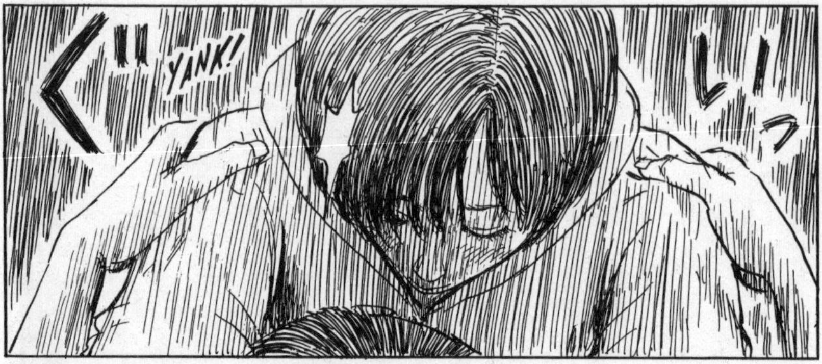
ぐ
YANK!
いっ
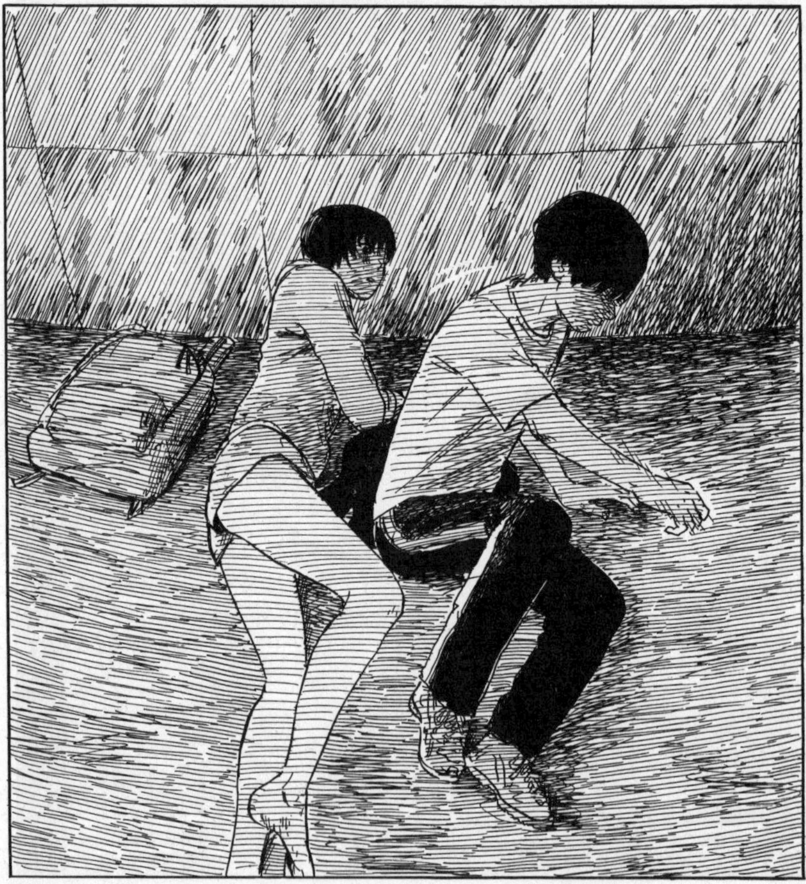

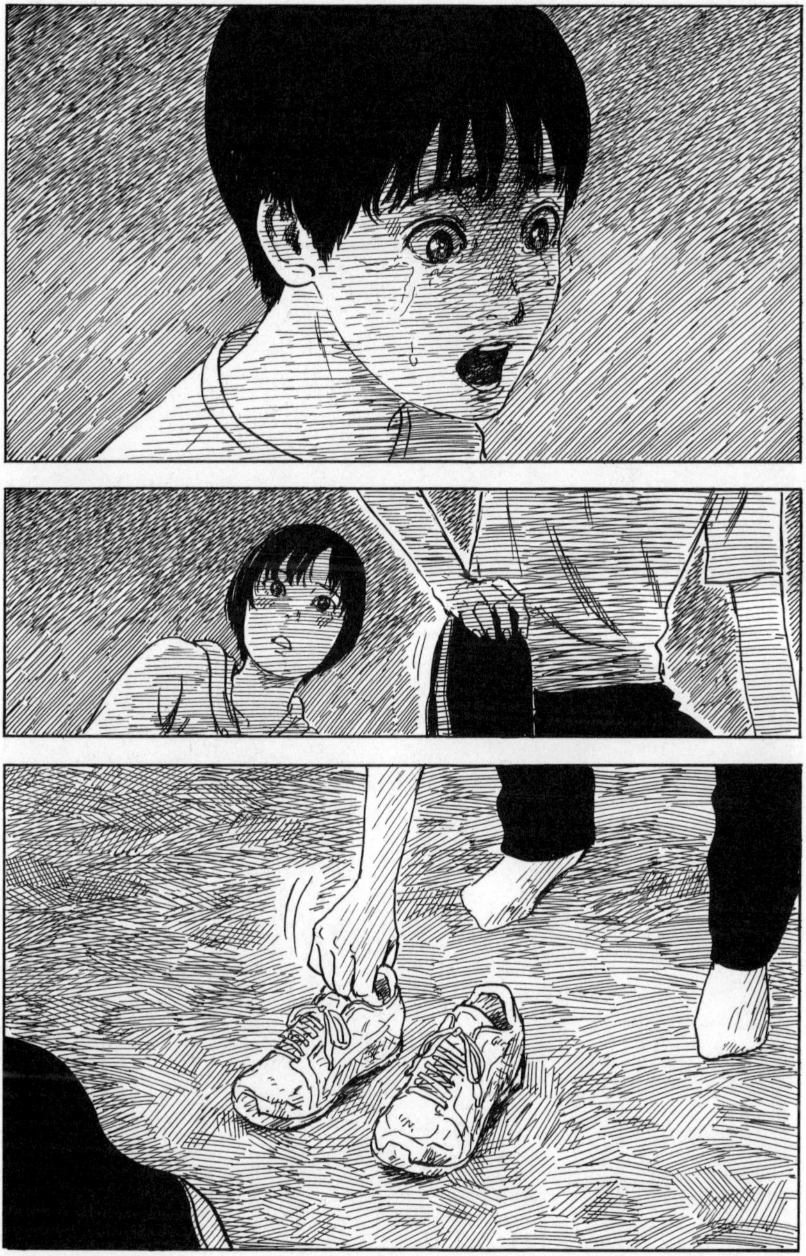

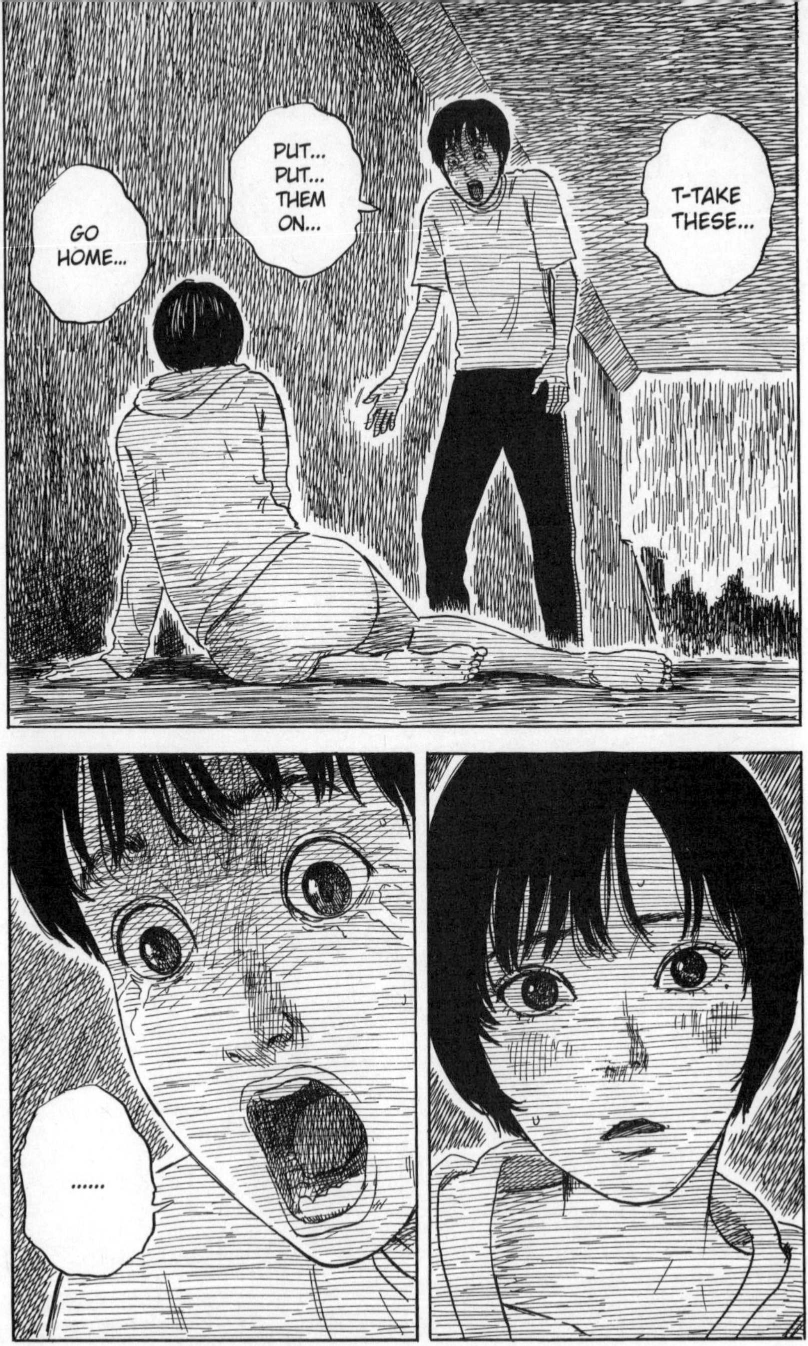
T-TAKE THESE...
PUT... PUT... THEM ON...
GO HOME...
......

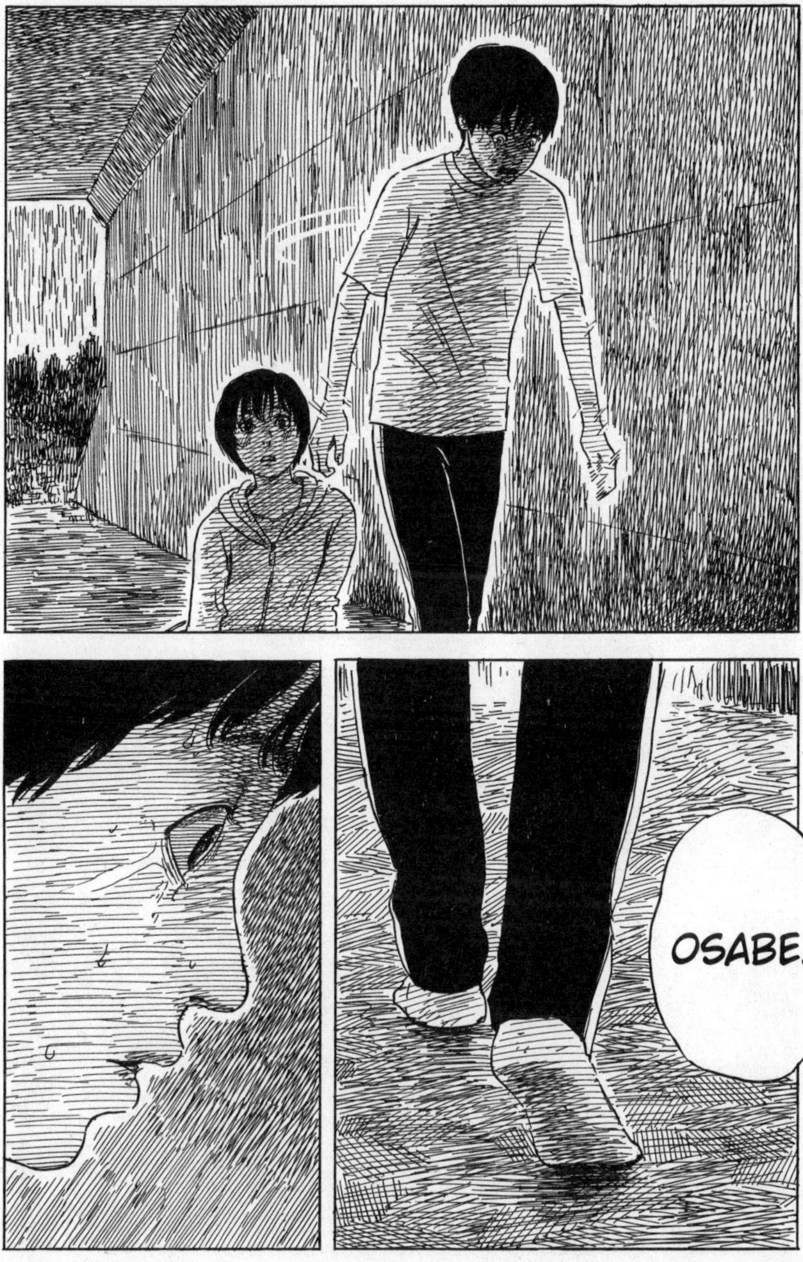
OSABE!

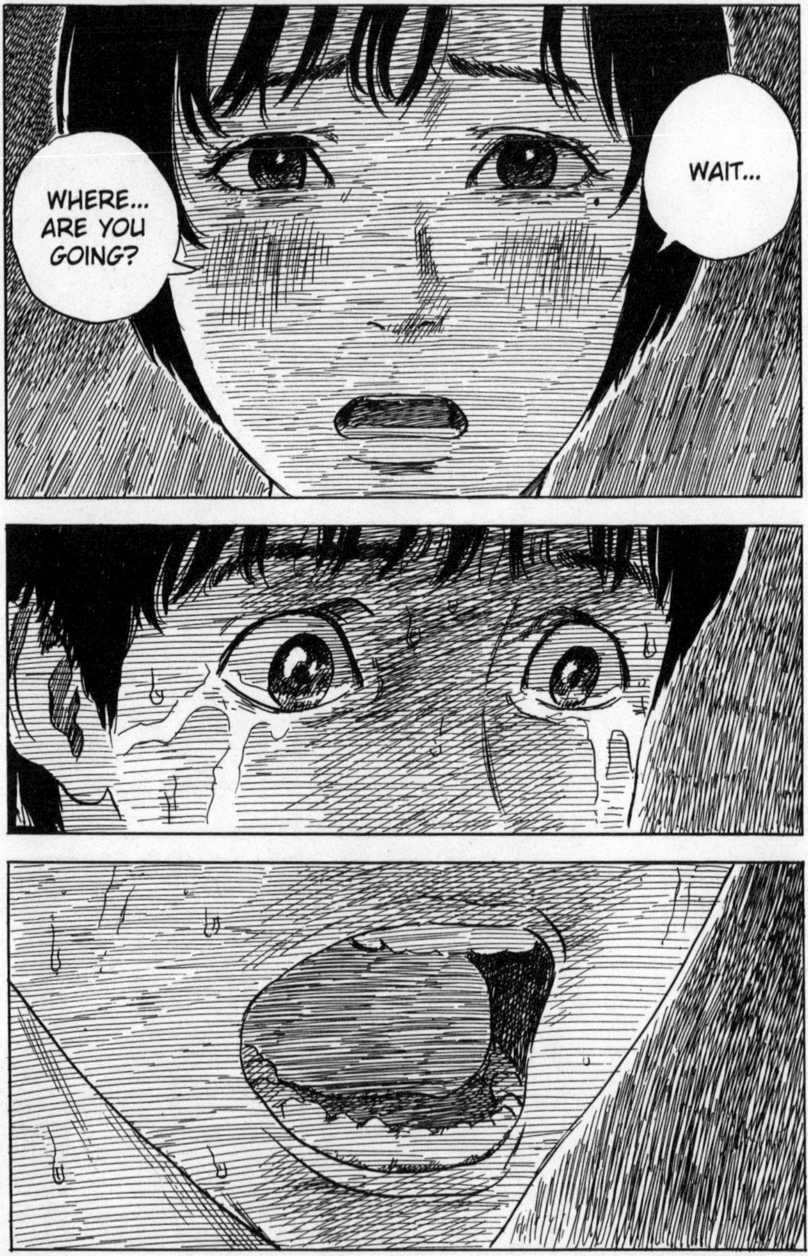
WAIT...
WHERE... ARE YOU GOING?

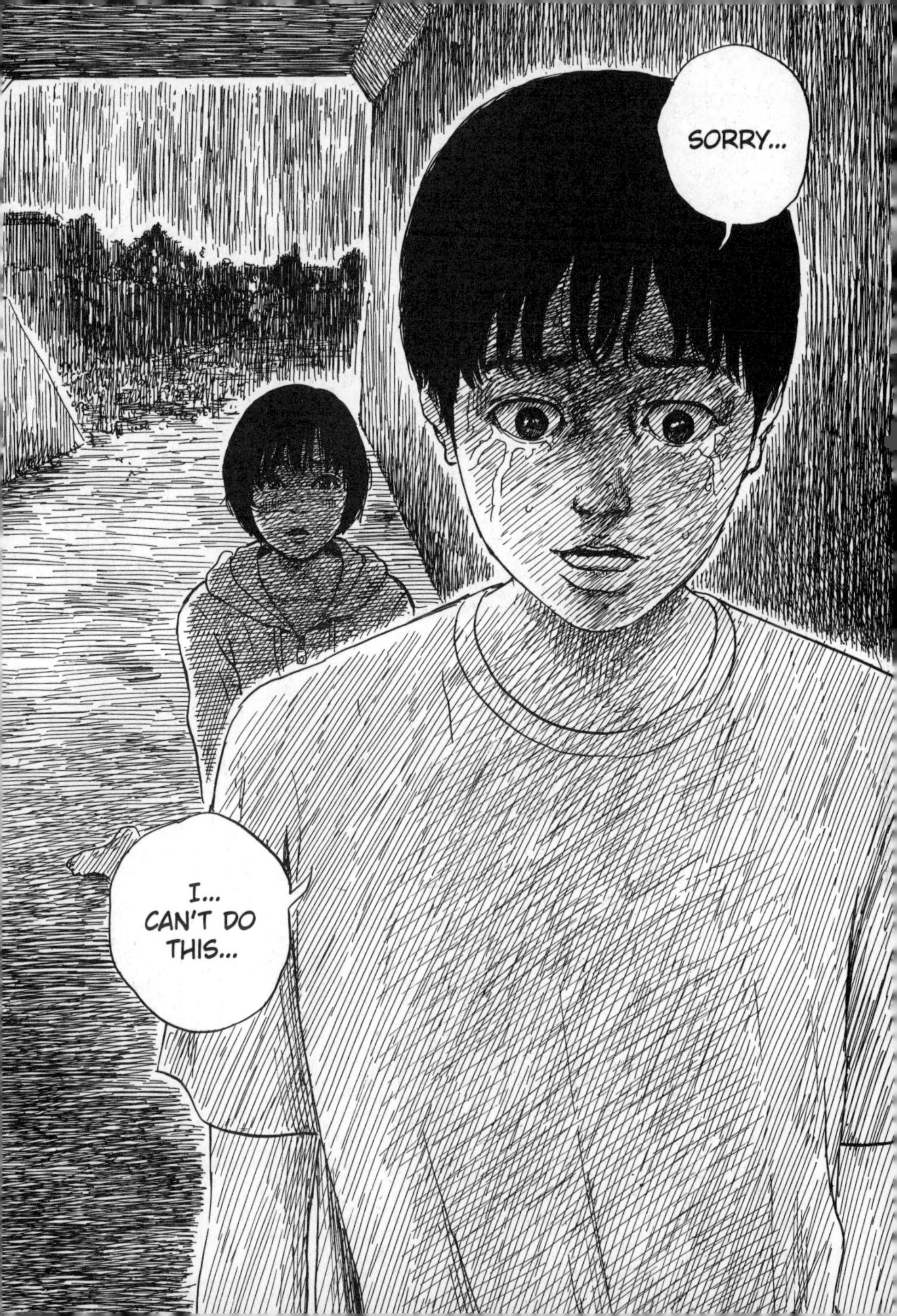
SORRY...
I... CAN'T DO THIS...

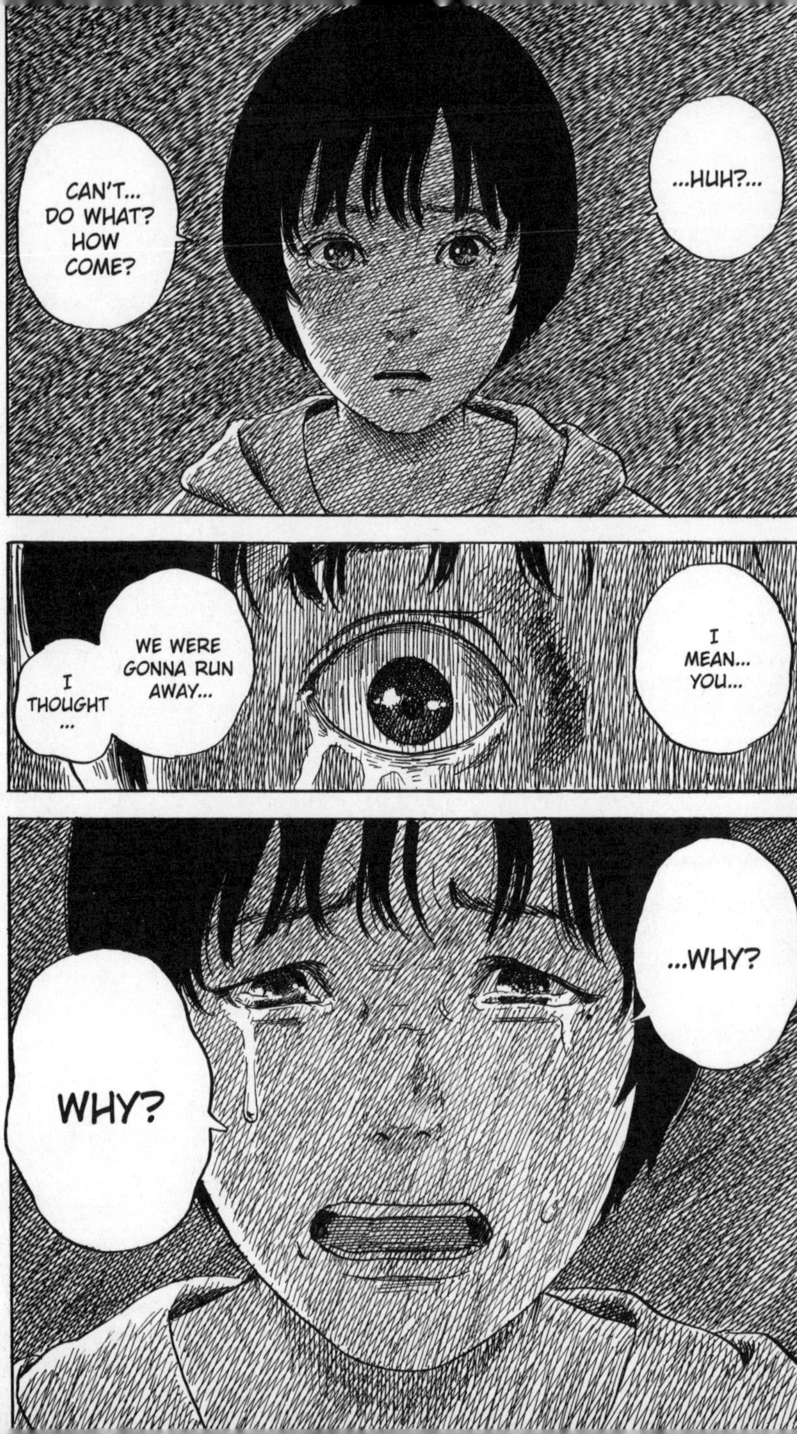
...HUH?...
CAN'T... DO WHAT? HOW COME?
I MEAN... YOU...
I THOUGHT ... WE WERE GONNA RUN AWAY...
...WHY?
WHY?

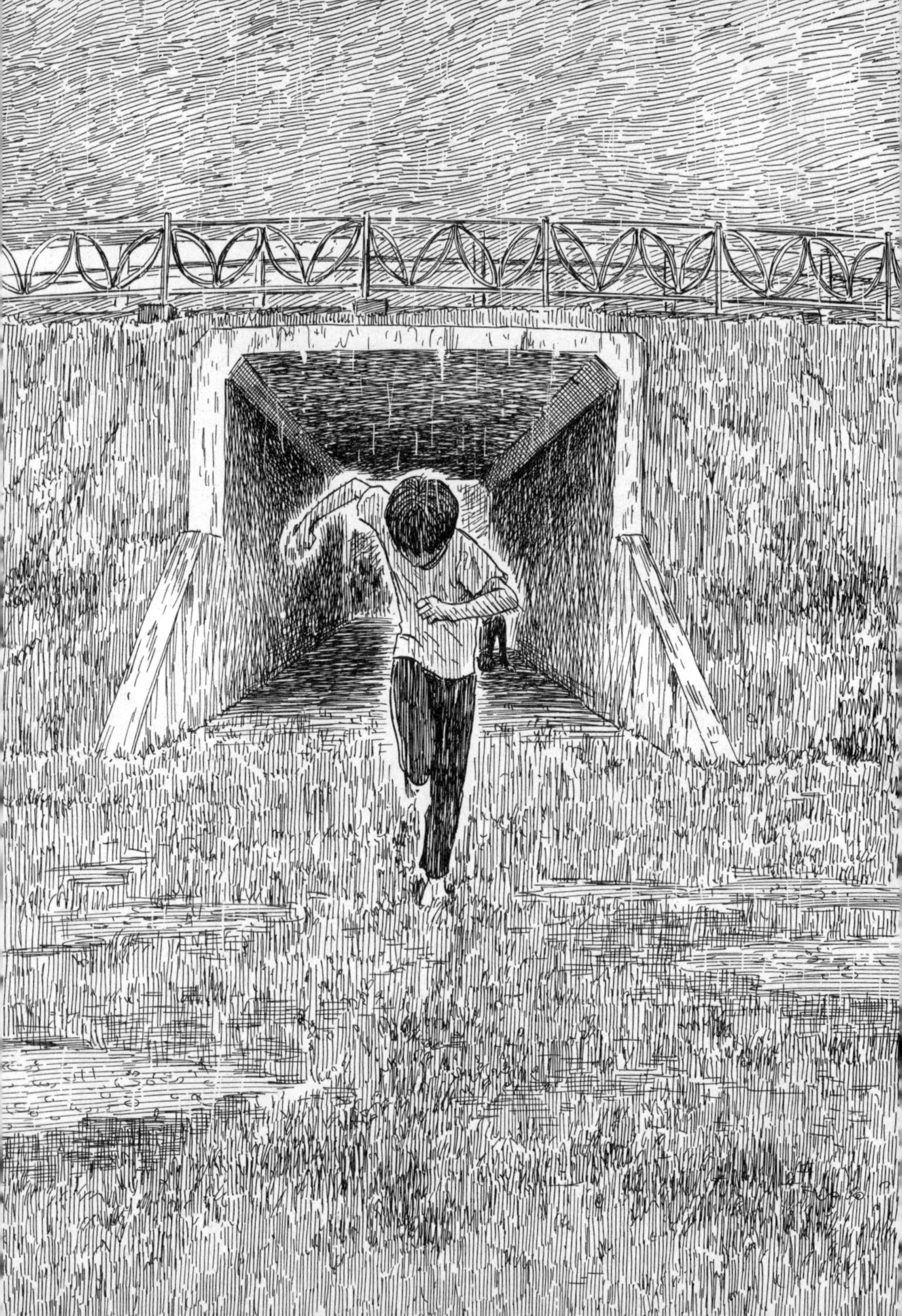

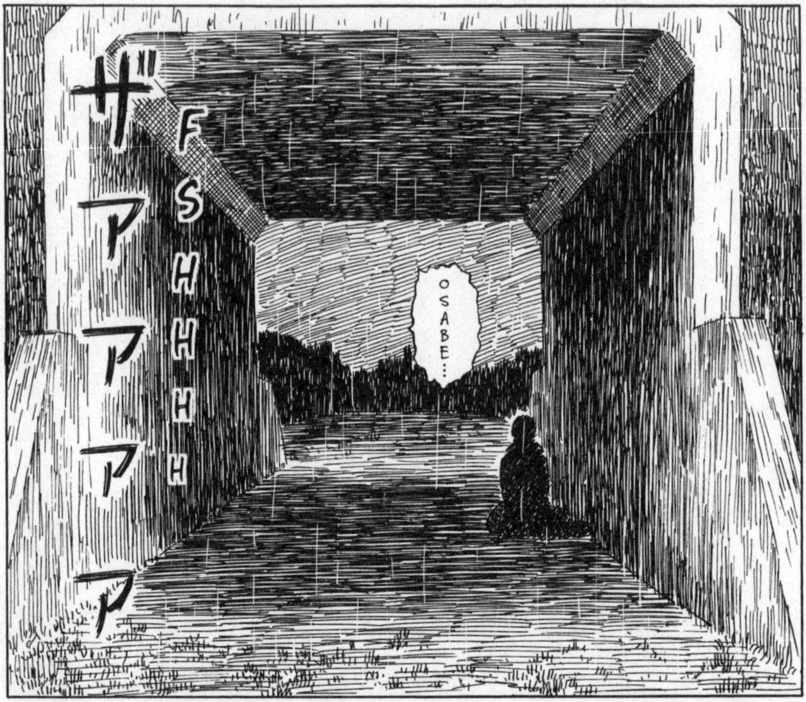
ザァァァァ
FSHHHH
OSABE...

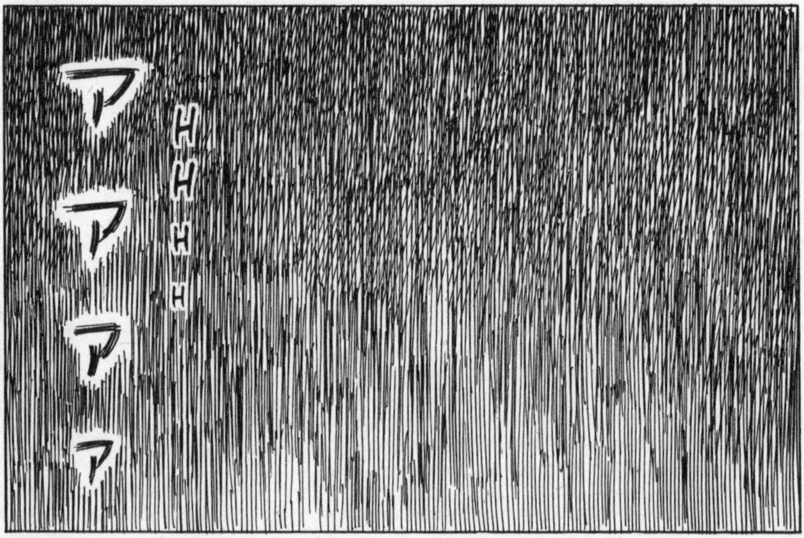
アァァァ
HHHH

Blood on the Tracks VOLUME 5 • END

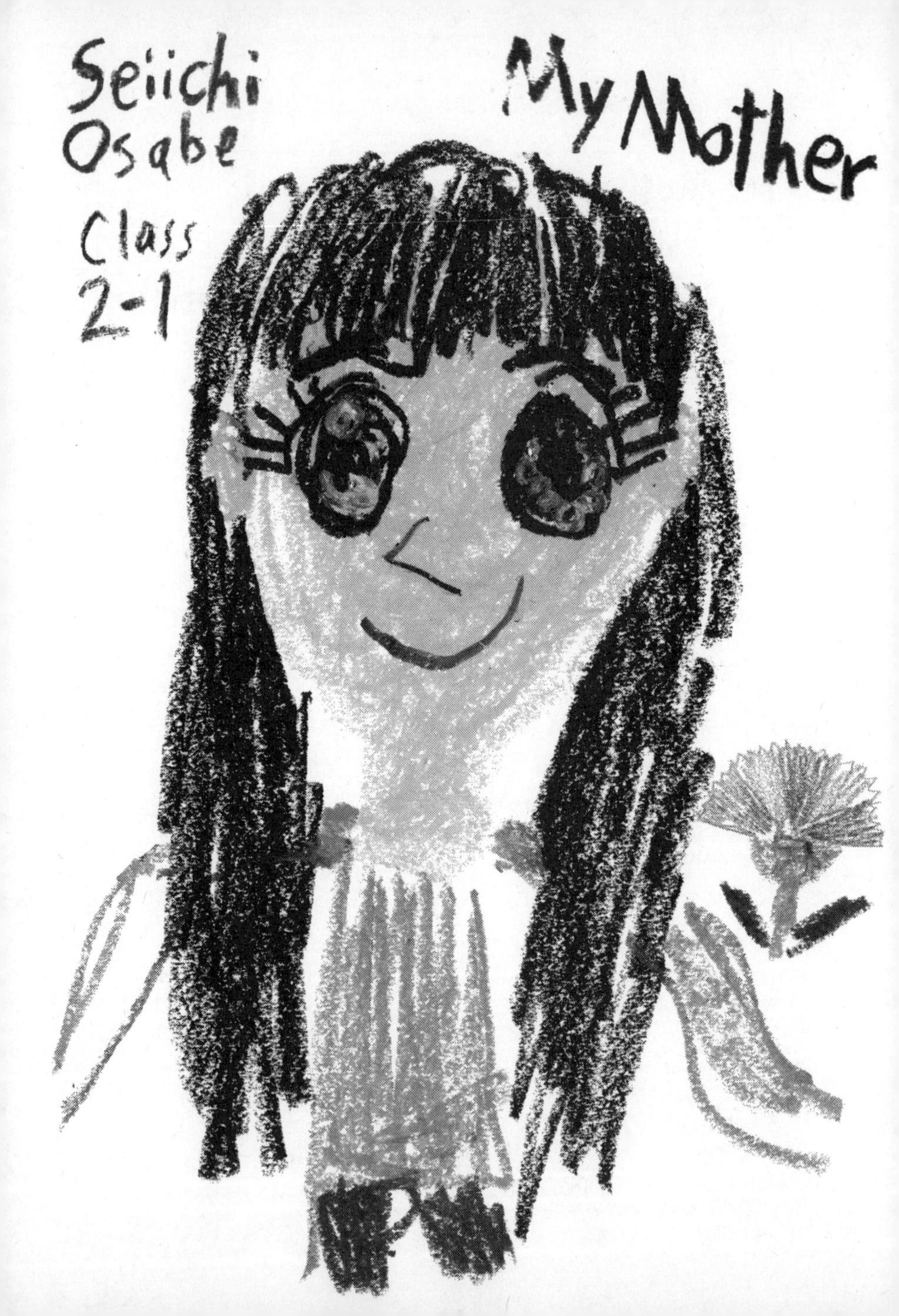
Seiichi Osabe
Class 2-1
My Mother

My mother touches me a lot.

When I yawn, she sticks her finger sideways into my mouth. When I close my mouth on it without realizing, she laughs,

Tee hee hee.

Mother, thank you for everything.

Please keep thinking about me forever.

Excellent!
Sounds like your mom really loves you, Seiichi.

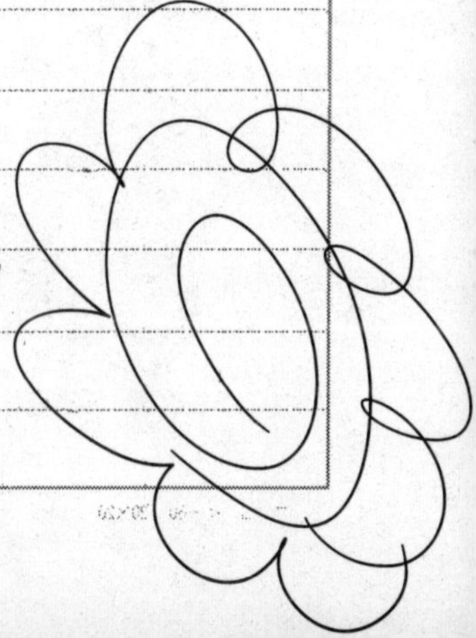

Seiichi Osabe,
Class 2 -1

My Mother

My mother's name is Seiko.

The "Sei" in her name is the same as in mine.

My mother is always thinking about me.

When I have a fight with my friends or when I feel sad, my mother always notices and asks me, "What's wrong." And she always understands how I feel.

from your daddy Ichiro's.

Please let me keep watching over
you forever.

Love, Mommy

Dear Sei,

When you were born, I thought hard about your name. Choosing a name is very important. Your name may even decide your whole life. The "Sei" in our names means "quiet." Ever since I was a child, I felt that I had to be quiet because my name was Seiko. I was jealous of the lively girls who could just say whatever they wanted. But I like where I am very much, quietly looking all around. I want to quietly give you all of my love. That's why I gave you the "Sei" from my name along with the "Ichi"

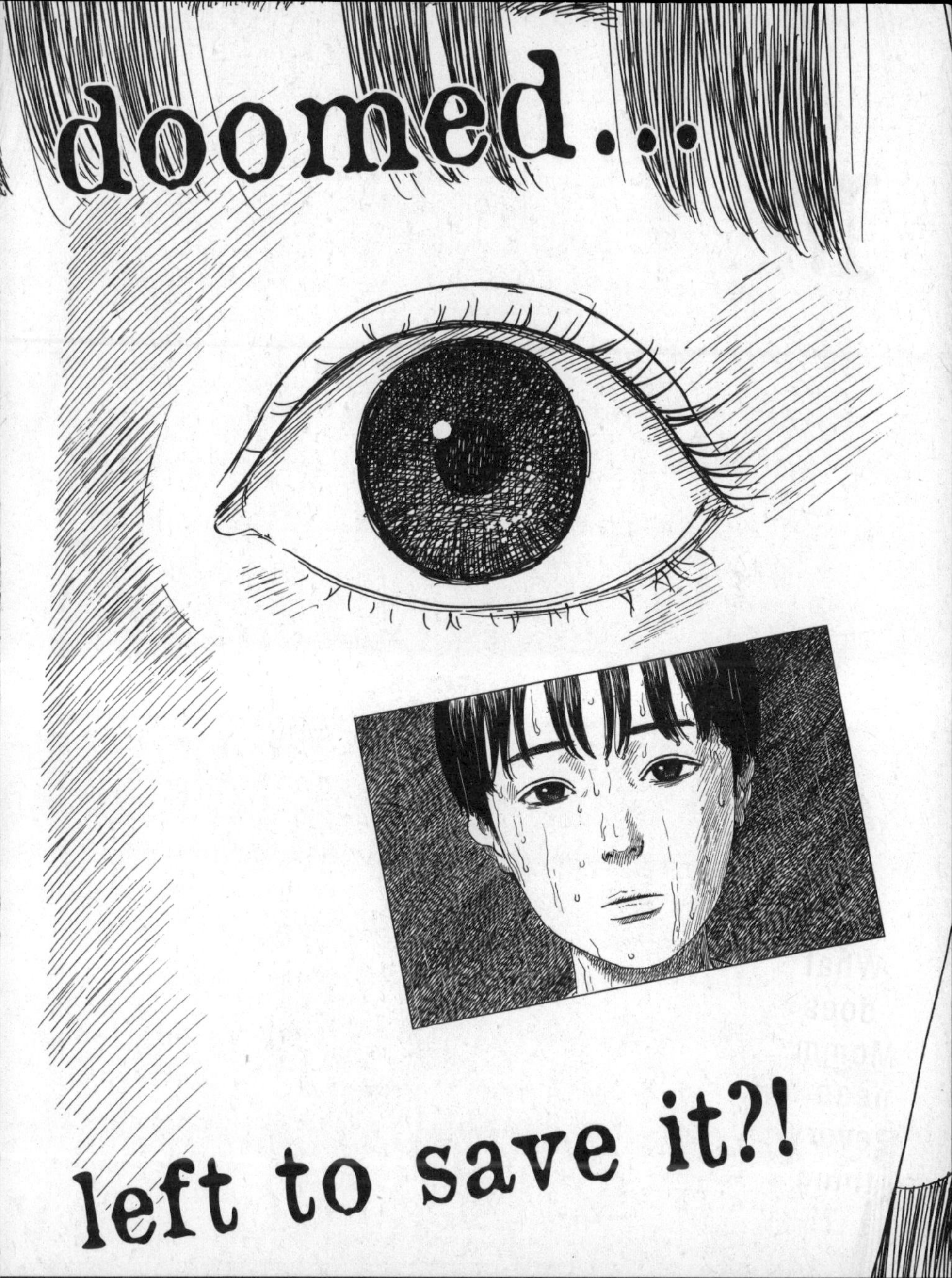
doomed...
left to save it?!

Volume 6 available now!!

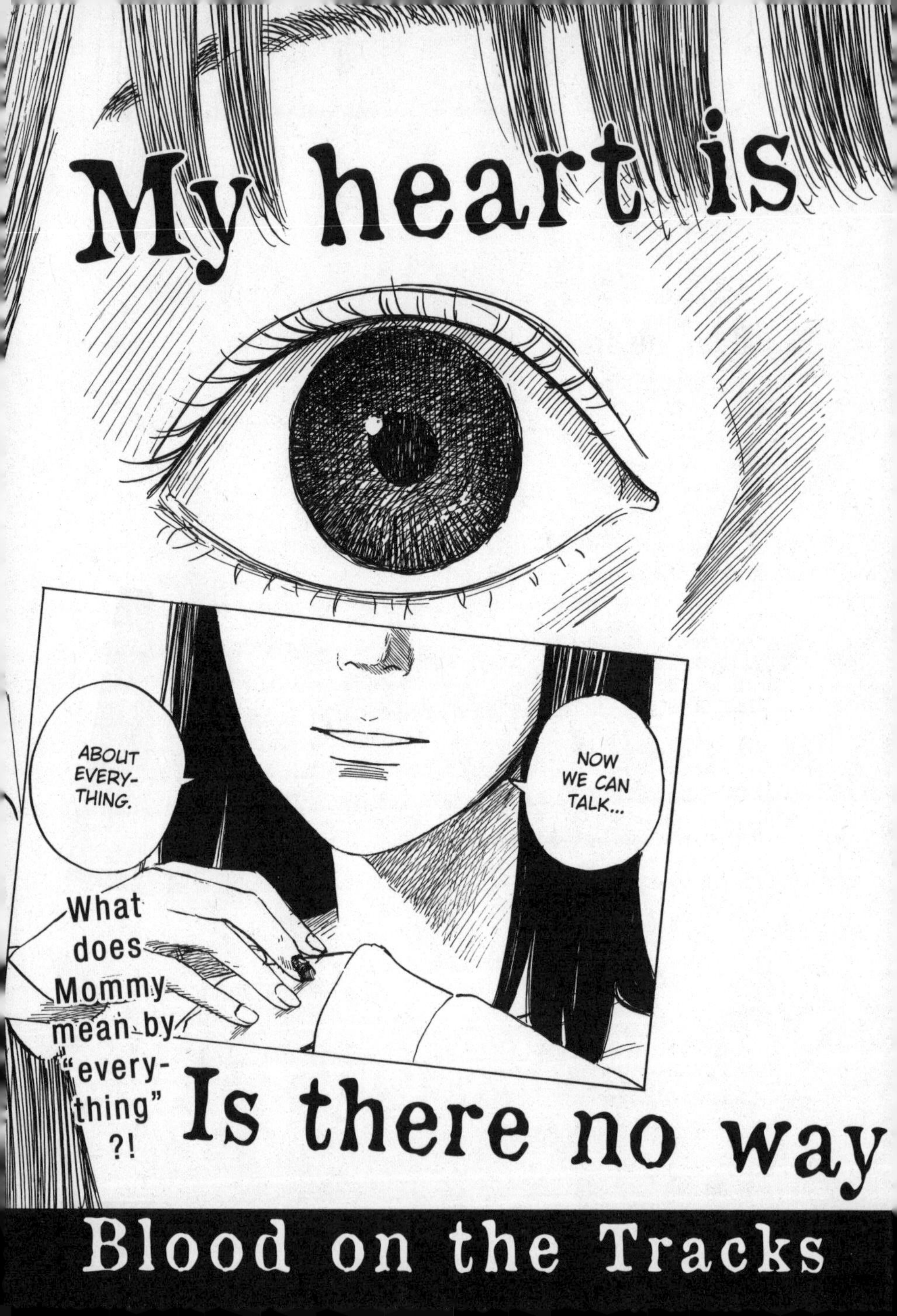
My heart is
NOW WE CAN TALK...
ABOUT EVERY-THING.
What does Mommy mean by "every-thing"?!
Is there no way
Blood on the Tracks

Blood on the Tracks 5
A Vertical Comics Edition

Editor: Daniel Joseph
Translation: Daniel Komen
Production: Risa Cho
              Evan Hayden

CHI NO WADACHI 5
by Shuzo OSHIMI

Translation provided by Vertical Comics, 2021
Published by Vertical Comics, an imprint of Kodansha USA Publishing, LLC, New York

Originally published in Japanese as *Chi no Wadachi 5* by Shogakukan, 2019
Chi no Wadachi serialized in *Big Comic Superior*, Shogakukan, 2017-

This is a work of fiction.

ISBN: 978-1-64729-000-9

Manufactured in the United States of America

First Edition

Second Printing

Kodansha USA Publishing, LLC
451 Park Avenue South
7th Floor
New York, NY 10016
www.kodansha.us

Vertical books are distributed through Penguin-Random House Publisher Services.